Iistorians consider the Battle of Rzhev "one of the bloodiest in the history of the Great Patriotic Var" and "Zhukov's greatest defeat". Veterans called this colossal battle, which continued for a otal of 15 months, "the Rzhev slaughterhouse" or "the Massacre", while the German generals amed this city "the cornerstone of the Eastern Front" and "the gateway to Berlin". By their terri-orial scale, number of participating troops, length and casualties, the military operations in the rea of the Rzhev - Viaz'ma salient are not only comparable to the Stalingrad battle, but to a great xtent surpass it. The total losses of the Red Army around Rzhev amounted to 2,000,000 men; the *Vehrmacht's* total losses are still unknown precisely to the present day.

Why was one of the greatest battles of the Second World War consigned to oblivion in the Soviet Jnion? Why were the forces of the German Army Group Center in the Rzhev - Viaz'ma salient ot encircled and destroyed? Whose fault is it that the German forces were able to withdraw from pocket that was never fully sealed? Indeed, are there justifications for blaming this "lost victory" n G.K. Zhukov?

In this book, which has been recognized in Russia as one of the best domestic studies of the zhev battle, answers to all these questions have been given. The author, Svetlana Gerasimova, as lived and worked amidst the still extant signs of this colossal battle, the tens of thousands of nmarked graves and the now silent bunkers and pillboxes, and has dedicated herself to the study f its history.

Svetlana Aleksandrovna Gerasimova is a historian and museum official. After graduating fro Leningrad State University with a history degree, she worked in the Urals as a middle school histo teacher, before moving to Tver, where she taught a number of courses in history and local histor and about museum work and leading excursions in the Tver' School of Culture. She earned h Ph.D. in history from Tver State University in 2002. For more than 20 years, S.A. Gerasimov has been working in the Tver' State Consolidated Museum, and is the creator and co-creator a many displays and exhibits in the branches of the Museum, and in municipal and institution museums of the Tver' Oblast. Recent museum exhibits that she has created include "The Battle Rzhev 1942-1943" and "The Fatal Forties … Toropets District in the Years of the Great Patriot War." She has led approximately 20 historical and folklore-ethnographic expeditions in the ar of Tver' Oblast and is the author of numerous articles in such journals as *Voprosy istorii* [Questio of History], *Voenno-istoricheskii arkhiv* [Military History Archive], *Voenno-istoricheskii zhurn* [Journal of Military History] and *Zhivaia starina* [The Living Past], and other publications. 2009, she served as a featured consultant to a Russian NTV television documentary about the Batt of Rzhev, which quickly became controversial for its very frank discussion of the campaign. 2002, S. A. Gerasimova defended her doctoral dissertation "*Voennye deistviia v raione rzhevsko-v azemskogo vystupa v ianvare 1942 – marte 1943*" ["Combat operations in the area of the Rzhe Viaz'ma salient in January 1942 – March 1943"], thereby earning her doctorate in National Histo from Tver' State University. Her dissertation serves as the basis for the present book.

Stuart Britton was a freelance translator and editor residing in Cedar Rapids, Iowa. He w responsible for making a large number of Russian titles available to readers of the English languag consisting primarily of memoirs by Red Army veterans and recent historical research concerning t Eastern Front of the Second World War and Soviet air operations in the Korean War. Notable titl included Valeriy Zamulin's award-winning *Demolishing the Myth: The Tank Battle at Prokhorovk Kursk, July 1943: An Operational Narrative* (Helion, 2011), Boris Gorbachevsky's *Through t Maelstrom: A Red Army Soldier's War on the Eastern Front 1942-45* (University Press of Kansa 2008) and Yuri Sutiagin's and Igor Seidov's *MiG Menace Over Korea: The Story of Soviet Fighter A Nikolai Sutiagin* (Pen & Sword Aviation, 2009). Stuart passed away in 2024.

THE RZHEV SLAUGHTERHOUSE

THE RED ARMY'S FORGOTTEN 15-MONTH CAMPAIGN AGAINST ARMY GROUP CENTER 1942-1943

Svetlana Gerasimova

Translated and edited by Stuart Britton

Helion & Company

Helion & Company Limited
Unit 8 Amherst Business Centre
Budbrooke Road
Warwick
CV34 5WE
England
Tel. 01926 499619
Email: info@helion.co.uk
Website: www.helion.co.uk
X (formerly Twitter): @Helionbooks
Facebook: @HelionBooks
Visit our blog at https://helionbooks.wordpress.com/

Published by Helion & Company 2013. This new edition published in paperback 2025
Designed and typeset by Farr out Publications, Wokingham, Berkshire
Cover designed by Paul Hewitt, Battlefield Design (www.battlefield-design.co.uk)

Originally published as *1941: Viazemskaia katastrofa* (Moscow: Yauza, Eksmo, 2008).

ISBN 978-1-804517-83-3

British Library Cataloguing-in-Publication Data.
A catalogue record for this book is available from the British Library.

For details of other military history titles published by Helion & Company Limited, contact the above address, or visit our website: http://www.helion.co.uk

We always welcome receiving book proposals from prospective authors.

Contents

List of photographs

List of maps

In colour section

List of map abbreviations

A	Army
AA	Air Army (Soviet)
AC	Army Corps (German)
Abn	Airborne (Soviet)
CC	Cavalry Corps (Soviet)
CR	Cavalry Regiment (Soviet)
GCC	Guards Cavalry Corps (Soviet)
GRC	Guards Rifle Corps (Soviet)
ID	Infantry Division (German)
IR	Infantry Regiment (German)
MC	Mechanized Corps (Soviet)
MG	Mobile Group (Soviet)
PzA	Panzer Army (German)
PzC	Panzer Corps (German)
PzD	Panzer Division (German)
RD	Rifle Division (Soviet)
RR	Das Reich Regiment (German)
ShA	Shock Army (Soviet)
TC	Tank Corps (Soviet)

List of tables

Introduction

That there are still blank spots in the history of the Great Patriotic War [the Russian name for the Eastern Front of the Second World War] is indisputable even 65 years after its conclusion. To be sure, in the last 20 years much has been done to reduce their number. New documents have been published, previously unknown facts have been introduced into scholarly circulation, and books, articles and papers on individual wartime events and episodes have appeared that contain alternative assessments to the official ones.

This, in particular relates to the history of combat operations in the region of the Rzhev – Viaz'ma salient in 1942 and early 1943. In the Soviet era, they never became a subject of serious scholarly research by military historians. For ideological reasons, an objective study of them was taboo. The volume of information about what took place on this sector of the front increased only gradually, as the Soviet government strictly controlled the release of factual material about the battles to the public.

By the start of the political changes in Soviet society in the middle of the 1980s, textbook, research and memoir literature recognized three major Soviet offensives on the Moscow axis in the period of the Great Patriotic War that we are examining here: the Rzhev – Viaz'ma strategic offensive of 1942, the Rzhev – Sychevka offensive in July-August 1942, and the Rzhev – Viaz'ma offensive of 1943. The operations were always described in positive terms, while downplaying or concealing blunders and failures. One more offensive operation at the end of 1942 was very rarely mentioned, sometimes even without a name, which is today known as Operation Mars. There was no attempt to link these operations, even though they involved the very same *fronts* virtually on the same territory and had essentially a common aim – the destruction of the German Army Group Center.[1]

The official assessment of the fighting in the area of the Rzhev – Viaz'ma salient in the Soviet era was unequivocal. In response to a query from the Rzhev Regional Museum, the USSR Ministry of Defense's Institute of Military History said, "The fighting in the area of Rzhev was part of the overall battle for Moscow."[2] This official response created a paradoxical situation: if according to the official determination of those times the Battle of Moscow concluded on 20 April 1942, while its main results before this date were determined by the end of December 1941, then where do the operations of the Red Army on this sector of the front in the summer and winter of 1942 and the spring of 1943 belong? If they should be considered "part of the overall battle for Moscow", then according to this logic the Battle of Moscow ended with the liquidation of the German Rzhev bridgehead at the gates of the capital in March 1943. That is to say, the official point of view created more ambiguities than answers in the assessment of combat operations on the Moscow axis.

In the 1990s and the first years after the year 2000, interesting publications appeared, in particular regarding the Soviet casualties in the operations of the Great Patriotic War, including in the Rzhev – Viaz'ma area. Although these estimates were plainly conservative, the data immediately placed the combat operations in the Rzhev – Gzhatsk – Viaz'ma area on par with the Battle of Stalingrad in terms of the casualties they generated. The study of Operation Mars written by the American historian David Glantz, and then its official Russian version as well filled one blank spot in the historiography of the Red Army's operations to eliminate the dangerous German bridgehead on the approaches to the capital city of the Soviet state.[3]

These materials, as well as the wartime archival records, to which access for a certain time was expanded, allowed individual regional scholars and local historians to take a fresh look at the Red Army's operations directed at eliminating the dangerous German salient in the center of the Soviet-German front. While relying on the existing conceptual framework in military-historical studies, they smashed the accepted understanding and declared that between January 1942 and March 1943 there occurred on this sector of the front one of the bloodiest battles of the Great Patriotic War – the Battle of Rzhev. In this case, the city of Rzhev stands as a symbol, giving its name to a battle that unfolded in the expansive Belyi – Rzhev – Zubtsov – Sychevka – Gzhatsk – Viaz'ma area, just as Moscow lent its name to a battle that sprawled over the territory of several oblasts.[4]

This point of view about a separate battle on the Moscow axis has not been accepted by official military science. There are disputes as well over the enormous casualty figures from the fighting over the Rzhev – Viaz'ma salient. As a result, a strange situation has arisen. On the one hand, the presence of a great number of facts and documents upon which contemporary military historical theory rests permit one to view the combat operations of the Soviet and German forces in the area of the Rzhev – Viaz'ma salient as a battle distinct from the Battle of Moscow. On the other hand, the military-historical literature produced by government research institutes still clings to traditional assessments. Leading Soviet military historians, not wishing to see the obvious, took things even further: they accused the revisionists of distorting and besmirching the history of the war. One must agree with the opinion of the historian Iu.N. Afanas'ev, who asserts that too many personal fates, remembrances of youth and the pain of losses have been mixed into the existing historical boilerplate text:

> The immutable, sacred text genuinely rests on so much: the millions who stood to the death for their ancestral home, [for] their families, for the Motherland ... Any negative interpretations connected with these events – even fully reasoned ones – can wound and do wound the deeply personal, the individual and the historical memory. However we cannot, we must not, and simply do not have the right to remain prisoner to a unified perception, which is not interested in the search for historical truth.[5]

The well-known Russian author M. A. Bulgakov, author of *The Master and Margarita*, said through the lips of his hero: "A fact is the most stubborn thing in the world." Even if a fact isn't noticed, it still doesn't disappear. On the basis of facts, even a non-professional can draw conclusions. The English historian T. B. Macauley maintained that the beginning of wisdom was the recognition of facts.

The aim of this book is to lay out the history of combat operations in 1942 and early 1943 on the central – the Moscow – axis of the Soviet-German front, taking into account the facts and documents known to the author at the current time, so that the readers themselves can determine the truth of one viewpoint or another. At the same time, we don't pretend to exhaust all the possible research on the subject. Given the many years of official silence over the events, it is difficult to research and illuminate such a major subject, especially over a short period of time and with limited access to archival documents. This book aims only to create a "skeleton", the outline of an unrecognized battle, which subsequently we dare hope will be fleshed out with more details, facts, documents and personalities. At the same time we acknowledge that the appearance of new documents, which at the time of writing still remained closed to scrutiny (the authors was unable to gain access to the documents of the *Stavka* of the Supreme High Command, the General Staff, the Western Direction and many others[6]) might refute individual suppositions and conclusions of the book's author. Those who keep the sources classified are in large measure responsible for the appearance of mistaken assertions and conjectures about the war.

While studying the subject, the author used a wide circle of various sources. This first of all concerned archival materials, both published by and preserved in the Central Archive of the Russian Federation's Ministry of Defense [TsAMO] in the city of Podol'sk. This also includes wartime press materials and the political-military journalism of both the Soviet Union and Germany. The memoirs and diaries of veterans of the battle on both sides, from the generals down to the privates, were actively used. Certainly, the author studied the foreign and domestic scholarly works concerning the combat operations on the central sector of the Soviet-German front.

A special note on the photographs in the book: the book uses photographs of both professionals – military photojournalists – and of hobbyists, soldiers who fought in the Rzhev – Viaz'ma salient on both sides. The German photographs are mostly from German sources including veterans' studies. The Soviet photographs, taken between 1941 and 1943, have been published in part in the photo albums of the *Velikaia Otechestvennaia voina v fotografiiakh i kinodokumentakh* [*The Great Patriotic War in Photographs and Documentary Film*], which came out in 1985. The photographers B. E. Vdovenko, who was a photo journalist in Kalinin Front's Political Department at that time during the war, and N. N. Novak, a photographer for the newspaper of Kalinin Front's 31st Army who focused on capturing images of frontline life, are responsible for most of the Soviet photographs. Negatives of their photographs, as well as a considerable amount of other photographic materials presented in this book, are today kept in the files of the Tver' State Consolidated Museum and its branches. In some cases, the photos are from the author's personal collection and will be noted as such.

It is hoped that the subject of the book will interest historians and scholars, and that they will continue to study the Battle of Rzhev. Individual scholars might elaborate various aspects of the contemplated problem and in the process fill in more of the blank areas in the total canvas of the battle's history. In doing so it isn't necessary to start with the refutation of the already written history, but with new research into the entire realm of wartime documents, primarily archival. As practice has shown, the history of the war written in the Soviet era contains errors even with respect to dates. An example is the date of A. Matrosov's exploit, which is known to many history lovers.[7] There are also similar examples in the history of the Rzhev battle. Only research into the entire complex of documents from the *Stavka* VGK, the Red Army's General Staff, the directions and *fronts*, the armies, and also of the *Wehrmacht* (primarily Army Group Center), and the divisions and units of both warring sides will permit the creation of a complete history of the battle on the Moscow axis in 1942 and early 1943.

So, the Battle of Rzhev – is it a myth or a reality?

1

The Enemy Staging Area on the Approaches to the Capital

By definition, a *platsdarm* is a territory used by any state for assembling and deploying its armed forces.[1] In the military-historical literature, one also often comes across synonymous terms, such as "The Rzhev – Viaz'ma bridgehead, a salient that was formed ...."[2]

In the course of the Soviet December 1941 counteroffensive at Moscow, the German forces were hurled back by 100-350 kilometers. In the historiography of the Great Patriotic War, one encounters such expressions as "the rout of the German-fascist forces at Moscow." However, "seditious" thoughts, and not only those of authors, forces one to ask about who then put up such bitter resistance to the Red Army's attacking formations in January 1942, and put a stop to the offensive at a distance of 150-220 kilometers from the capital? In reality, in December 1941-January 1942, the enemy was thrown back from Moscow, but not as far as desired or as far as official propaganda would have led us to believe. In actuality, one of the largest enemy force groupings – Army Group Center – continued to hold a threatening salient on the approaches to the capital once the Soviet winter counteroffensive ran out of steam. We'll add that back in 1989 at an academic meeting of the Institute of Military Historiography to examine the idea of bringing the Battle of Moscow to light, the need to reject the former view of the "rout" of enemy forces was emphasized: "How is possible to speak about any rout, if Soviet losses in the battle were 3.7 times greater than enemy losses?"[3]

By the end of January 1942, as a result of the Soviet counteroffensive the front lines in the central sector of the Soviet-German front were very convoluted, creating bulges in both the German and the Soviet lines. For example, forces of the Soviet 3rd and 4th Shock Armies had advanced as far as Kholm, Demidov and Velizh, while the German Army Group Center still held a deep wedge in the Soviet lines in the Belyi and Rzhev areas. The front lines here ran west of Belyi, north of Olenino, north and east of Rzhev, east of Zubtsov and Gzhatsk, and until March 1942, east of Iukhnov, before Soviet forces pushed the Germans out of that town.

The Germans were holding this salient, which formed a rough quadrilateral protecting the Smolensk – Viaz'ma – Sychevka – Rzhev – Olenino railroads, plus the rail line running to Velikie Liuki. These railroads were the primary lines of supply and communications within Army Group Center's salient. Further, railroads ran from Viaz'ma and Smolensk toward Briansk, Orel and points further south. The importance of this sector of the front is also explained by the fact that Army Group Center's vital rear services and most important airbases were located here. The headquarters of Army Group Center was located in Smolensk. Rzhev, Viaz'ma, Sychevka, Zubtsov, Belyi and Gzhatsk became the major German strongpoints in this salient. The most savage fighting had developed just for these towns and cities, especially for Rzhev and Viaz'ma, which being linked by a railroad, designated the conventional end points on the eastern side of the salient. Therefore this portion of the Eastern Front has also been called the Viaz'ma – Rzhev salient in Soviet historical literature. In its outlines, the salient suggested a reversed Russian letter "Г". The well-known English historian of the Second World War, B. Liddell Hart wrote: "After the winter campaign of 1941-2, the German front facing Moscow had the shape of a clenched fist, with the Russians lapping round the wrist – where Smolensk lay."[4]

Between February and July 1942, there was a smaller salient within the salient, protruding into the German defenses east of Belyi and west of Sychevka. It was centered on the town of Kholm-Zhirkovskii and became known as the "Belyi salient".

In German historical literature, there are also such word combinations as "Rzhev salient", "Rzhev bulge", and "Rzhev bridgehead". In the recollections of many German veterans of the war, they were defending Olenino, Rzhev, Zubtsov, Sychevka and Viaz'ma in the "*Grossraum Rshew*" [Greater Rzhev area].

According to data in the Soviet Military Encyclopedia, the dimensions of the Rzhev – Viaz'ma salient approached 160 kilometers in depth (at its base) and up to 200 kilometers in width. Moscow lay 150 kilometers on a direct line from the salient at Gzhatsk, and 220 kilometers from Rzhev. If one measured the entire length of the front lines around the perimeter of the salient, with all its convolutions, then together with the 280-kilometer front around the Belyi salient it exceeded 700 kilometers. The former commander of the Sixteenth Army's 30th Infantry Division and later historian, K. von Tippelskirch, describing the position which the German Ninth and Fourth Panzer Armies held in February 1942, wrote: "The capriciously convoluted line, which faced to the north, east, south and west on the front of both German armies, ultimately comprised a total length of 600 kilometers."[5] If one considers the territory southwest of Viaz'ma, where the Soviet Group Boldin was operating, then this figure would be even longer.

Over the course of 1942, the length of the front lines here shrank as the result of combat operations. That is what happened in July 1942, when the *Wehrmacht* managed to liquidate the Belyi salient. The front lines also became somewhat shorter as a result of the Soviet offensive operations in the second half of 1942. By March 1943, when the Germans finally withdrew from the Rzhev – Viaz'ma salient, the line of contact between the two sides in this area totaled around 550 kilometers in length.[6] Of course, such matters as dating the salient's formation and the length of its perimeter are open to discussion.

The *Wehrmacht* command assigned particular significance to holding this salient, which was favorable in a strategic sense, and especially to keeping possession of the roads within it. In his directive from 15 January 1942, in which he gave authorization for troop withdrawals, Hitler stressed that "the commanders are obliged to keep the roads Iukhnov – Gzhatsk – Zubtsov – Rzhev free as a line of traverse behind the front of our forces ...." The troops of Army Group Center were ordered to hold the Smolensk – Rzhev – Viaz'ma triangle, the lateral Rzev – Viaz'ma – Briansk railroad and the vital Gzhatsk – Smolensk supply line at all costs. The Smolensk – Viaz'ma – Rzhev – Olenino railroad had particular significance to keeping the German Ninth and Fourth Panzer Armies supplied. As von Tippelskirch wrote about the events of January 1942, "If the railroad between Smolensk and Viaz'ma had been cut, then the fate of both armies would have been decided."[7]

As long as the roads and railroads were in the hands of the German army, the *Wehrmacht* command could use the salient as a staging area for preparing a new offensive on the central strategic axis of the Eastern Front. It was precisely because of this that in all the operations against the Rzhev – Viaz'ma salient, Soviet forces were attempting to disrupt the supply of Army Group Center by seizing these roads and railroads. Even in the summer of 1942, when the *Wehrmacht's* main offensive operations were unfolding in the south, the *Wehrmacht* command still gave great significance to "preserving the situation on the central sector", and to maintaining possession of the existing airfields here, close to Moscow.

In order to hold the staging area within the salient, the *Wehrmacht* constructed a strong, deeply-echeloned defense. Work on it had already begun in the course of the German retreat from Moscow. On 28 December 1941, the OKW [*Oberkommando der Wehrmacht* – the Supreme Command of Armed Forces] issued an order about organizing a defense, to include "fortifying all populated points and villages as strongpoints, as well as the maximum echeloning of forces in depth ... On the central sector Eastern Front set about fortifying the rear position ...."[8]

Initially, there was no continuous line of German defenses around the salient. At the beginning of 1942, Gzhatsk, Sychevka, Rzhev and Viaz'ma were converted into major bulwarks of the German defenses. Liddell Hart called them "bastion-cities".[9] However, gradually a powerful line of fortifications emerged. Throughout the entire time that German troops occupied the salient, the building of defensive fortifications was an on-going process. By the time of the Soviet Rzhev – Sychevka offensive in the summer of 1942, a belt of extensive defenses confronted the Soviet attackers. As an example, a description of the German defenses facing Western Front's 24th Army can be cited:

> The main belt of defenses here had a depth of 5-8 kilometers and consisted of a first line, which included strongpoints linked by a single continuous and one to two intermittent trenches, and a second band in the form of a line of separate strongpoints, prepared for an all-round defense and tied together by closely-knit fire support between the strongpoints. The forward edge of the defense passed along the eastern outskirts of settlements and along the roads between them, along the eastern edges of forests and patches of woods, and along the western banks of rivers. As a rule, all stone and wooden buildings were converted into earth and timber emplacements, covered by three to six layers of logs, which protected them against a direct hit by 76mm shells. In Pogoreloe Gorodishche, for example, all the stone buildings and basements were converted into pillboxes with two or three embrasures. The continuous trench of the forward edge contained a large portion of the weapons of the front-line troops, which were set up in separate emplacements, linked with squad-sized living quarters, bunkers and dugouts by communication trenches. In order to conceal troop movements, these communication trenches had several exits hidden behind reverse slopes. Certain buildings and structures, situated on elevations, were used as observation posts. About 20 to 100 meters in front of the front line, a continuous wire barrier had been erected in several rows, consisting of alternating stretches of hedgehog obstacles and barbed wire entanglements. The most vulnerable sectors had coils of concertina wire fronting the trenches. The wire obstacles were made more effective by anti-tank and anti-personnel minefields, laid in checkerboard fashion or randomly. Each strongpoint was equipped with several emplacements for anti-tank guns, and company and battalion mortars. Communication trenches linked the positions to allow for rapid maneuver.
>
> Artillery batteries, as a rule, were positioned 2 to 5 kilometers behind the front

> line. The artillery's firing emplacements were carefully positioned and well dug-in. The positions were equipped with special gun pits equipped with drains and catchment basins for water run-off and recessed shelters for the crews. Wire obstacles protected the emplacements from the front, while trenches flanked the position for anti-tank defense. The shells were stored in cases in separate bunkers.
>
> Regiment and battalion headquarters were situated in villages. The command staff was accommodated in well-furnished bunkers, dugouts and residences, usually on one of the main streets; travel on these streets was prohibited to the local population. Officers' quarters had telephones, electric lighting, and were equipped with radios. Further, in the depth along the Vazuza and Gzhatsk Rivers, in the most important sectors the Germans had prepared a second defensive belt.[10]

In front of Western Front's 31st Army in the summer of 1942, the German defensive line was a continuous trench with a dense network of well-built communication trenches, protected by two to three rows of barbed wire entanglements. Anti-tank and fougasse mines were laid to a depth of 10 kilometers on the tank-vulnerable directions, scarps and anti-tank ditches were dug, and log obstacles were constructed. Bunkers for each squad were covered with three to six layers of logs that had diameters of up to 20 cm each. In the villages, all the stone buildings and part of the wooden structures, plus their cellars, were converted into firing positions with two or three embrasures. The depth of the main belt of defenses extended to 5 kilometers.[11]

In Sychevka, in the city itself and at the railroad station, strong fortifications were erected, and the banks of the Kasnia and Vazuza Rivers were well-fortified. Numerous log and earthen bunkers were linked by a dense network of communication trenches.

Several lines of defenses were constructed in the Gzhatsk area. The first line ran along the fortified heights in front of the city, the second – along the Aleshnia River, and the third ran through the city itself with its stone buildings, and was split by the Gzhatsk River into two parts.[12]

Rzhev was thoroughly fortified. For example, in front of Kalinin Front's 30th Army alone, in the course of May – June 1942 German troops built 559 log pillboxes and bunkers, dug 280 trenches and 7 kilometers of anti-tank ditches, and created 23.5 kilometers of abatis from felled trees. Also in May – June, the so-called "Königsberg Line" was constructed north and east of Rzhev along the entire front of the Ninth Army. In places, bunker complexes the size of villages arose, for example, on the front of the 6th Infantry Division's 18th Infantry Regiment, where the bunkers were even named after German cities.

As the Germans gradually withdrew under the hammer blows of the Red Army, new defensive lines were built. For example, anticipating the possible withdrawal from the Königsberg Line during the Soviet Rzhev – Sychevka summer offensive, a new, so-called "Neu Kolberg Line" was constructed in the latter half of August 1942 in the northern part of Rzhev. Not only sappers participated in building it, but also soldiers returning from leave, supply units and even local residents. Veterans of the 30th Army who participated in its September 1942 offensive later recalled that the German defenses on the northeastern outskirts of Rzhev consisted of minefields, several rows of barbed wire, then two finished trenches with pillboxes and bunkers located every 500 meters or so from each other. All the buildings were linked by covered communication trenches, and the basement of each building had been converted into a concrete pillbox adapted for an all-round defense.

Construction of a bunker in the sector of the 6th Infantry Division's 18th Infantry Regiment, north of Rzhev, summer of 1942.

Entrance to a German bunker in the sector of the 18th Infantry Regiment, north of Rzhev, summer of 1942.

Tanks had been dug-in on street corners.[13]

According to recollections of veterans of the fighting, the Germans often set up nasty surprises in the obstacles. For example, near the village of Kosmarikhi in the Rzhev area, the Germans connected anti-tank and anti-personnel mines to the wire obstacles; any contact with the wire would trigger the mines.[14]

As a result of almost year-long work, the Rzhev – Viaz'ma salient was fortified along almost its entire front and to a depth of many kilometers. Soviet literature of the beginning of the 1950s said that this sector "was fortified with the use of modern engineering equipment." More contemporary works speak about a defense echeloned in depth up to 80-100 kilometers. After the Germans withdrew from the salient, Red Army command staff used the positions east of Gzhatsk to analyze German defensive works. They were said to be characteristic of the entire *Wehrmacht* and study of them would benefit the Red Army. In fact, a group of instructors from the prestigious Frunze Military Academy were authorized to visit the Gzhatsk and Rzhev areas in order to examine the German defensive positions.[15]

The German troops also made use of the fortifications of the former Soviet Rzhev – Viaz'ma defensive line that ran through the territory of the salient, which had been under construction in the summer and autumn of 1941, and was 40-50 percent complete by October 1941.

The complex of defensive fortifications in the Sychevka area was known as the Stalin Line. The line's fortifications had not been used by Soviet troops during the retreat prompted by the German Operation Typhoon, and on the territory of the Tver' Oblast, for example, in places the pillboxes continue to stand intact and well-preserved. Their use by the Germans was sometimes completely unexpected to the command of the Soviet forces that fought here. Thus, for example, according to the report of combat operations from Kalinin Front's 39th Army in January 1942, when the army was advancing toward Sychevka through the German rear, it came as a complete shock: "The adversary was using the fortified belt, which had been prepared and built by our units during the autumn retreat, and about the presence of which the army was completely unaware. This fortified belt had pillboxes and bunkers. The enemy, relying on these defensive fortifications, significantly increased their resistance …"[16]

The same thing occurred in 1943 as well, during the retreat of the *Wehrmacht* from the Rzhev – Viaz'ma bridgehead. Out of fairness it should be noted that units of our 29th and 39th Armies also used these fortifications in 1942.

Thus in the first half of 1942, a fortified staging area for German forces had been created not far from Moscow, which the *Wehrmacht* command, planning to use it for an offensive on the Eastern Front's central strategic axis, constantly strengthened and stubbornly held through all of 1942. In order to hold the salient against the heavy pressure of the Western and Kalinin Fronts in 1942, the *Wehrmacht* command concentrated up to two-thirds of its entire strength on the Eastern Front here on the central axis, including in the area of the salient.

At various times, from half to two-thirds of Army Group Center, which was concentrated in the central sector, were located in the Rzhev – Viaz'ma salient. General H. Grossmann, the former commander of the 6th Infantry Division, which fought in the area of Rzhev, when listing the forces of the Ninth and 3rd Panzer Army that were operating in the salient, named 42 infantry, panzer, SS and *Luftwaffe* Field divisions. The contemporary German historian K. Zatler, who includes the divisions of the Fourth and Fourth Panzer

A pillbox on Novaia Street in the village of Selizharovo, Tver' Oblast; a 1968 photograph, author's collection.

A pillbox on the Kirov Embankment in the village of Selizharovo, Tver' Oblast; a 2004 photograph, author's collection.

Views of two more pillboxes in the Olenino District of Tver' Oblast, 1980s photographs, author's collection.

Armies in his count, determined that 57 infantry, motorized, panzer, SS and *Luftwaffe* Field divisions operated in the *Rshew Brückenkopf* [Rzhev bridgehead] between January 1942 and March 1943 (see Table 1).

Table 1: Concentration of German Troops and Divisions on the Central (Moscow) Axis (according to Soviet Sources)

		Men (thousands)	Guns and Mortars	Tanks
1 January 1942	Soviet-German Front	3,909	35,000	1,500
	Central Axis	1,569	13,000 (approx.)	1,100
Spring of 1942	Soviet-German Front As of 4/1/1942	176 divisions		
	Moscow Axis	More than 70 divisions		
By November 1942	Army Group Center	79 German divisions, 41% of all German divisions on Eastern Front		
By beginning of February 1943	Army Group Center	77 divisions and brigades – almost 30% of all such German formations on the Eastern Front		
	Rzhev-Viaz'ma salient	More than half of Army Group Center's strength		

Source: *Istoriia vtoroi mirovoi voiny*, Vol. 4, p. 305, 307; Vol. 5, p. 25, 113; Vol. 6, p. 142

These figures plainly demonstrate the great significance which the German military command gave to the central axis and to holding the Rzhev bridgehead, even at a time when the main military operations were unfolding on the southern sector of the front.

Soviet wartime periodical literature reproduced the words of German generals from German newspapers and leaflets. They called the Rzhev – Viaz'ma salient "a trampoline for a leap toward Moscow", a "pistol" aimed at Moscow, the heart of Russia. At the beginning of August 1942, F. Halder, the chief of staff of the OKH [*Oberkommando des Heeres* – High Command of the Army] writing in his diary called Rzhev and Sychevka the "main supports of our offensive to the east." However, already in the middle of August the assessment of the bridgehead's significance was changing. In a frontline newspaper, which came out on the Eastern Front and was printed in Rzhev, the city was called "the cornerstone of the German line of resistance", a "deadbolt". At the end of 1942, in radio addresses to the German troops it was said that Rzhev was "the Führer's impregnable line" and "the loss of Rzhev is equivalent to the loss of half of Berlin"; Rzhev was now even called "the Russians' trampoline toward Berlin". During the German withdrawal from the city in March 1943, Adolf Hitler wanted to hear the explosion of the bridge across the Volga in Rzhev personally. An impartial indicator of the enormous attention that the German higher command paid toward the events in the Rzhev – Viaz'ma salient is the "Index of Geographic Names" for the book of F. Halder's wartime diaries [found in the Russian edition], in which he discusses the combat operations in the Soviet Union and elsewhere. It indicates that in addition to Moscow, Leningrad, Sevastopol, the Caucasus, Africa and other places, the cities of Rzhev and Viaz'ma are mentioned throughout the entire book. It should be noted that in addition to the words from Hitler's directives, cited above, and Halder's daily notes, all the remaining statements are models of German propaganda.[17]

The Soviet leadership and the command of the Red Army unquestionably viewed the December 1941 counteroffensive as incomplete and recognized the enormous danger of the major enemy grouping close to Moscow. More than one-third of all the Red Army's strength and assets was concentrated here through all of 1942, struggling against the German troops of Army Group Center (see Table 2).

Table 2: Soviet concentration of strength and means on the central (Moscow) axis, expressed as a percentage of their total quantity on the Soviet-German front

	Rifle Divisions	Cavalry Divisions	Tank Brigades	Artillery Regiments	Anti-aircraft Battalions	Guards Mortar (*Katiusha*)	
1 Jan 1942[a]	33.0	54.0	49.0	39.0	25.0	74.0	
1 Apr 1942	39.0	41.0	50.0	40.0	30.0	64.0	
1 July 1942[b]	Armies[d]	Air Armies	Divisions	Manpower	Guns and mortars	Tanks	Combat aircraft
	32.7	28.6	31.3	33.2	31.6	40.3	32.7
For 19 Nov 1942[c]	Men	Guns and mortars		Tanks		Aircraft	
	31.4	32.0		45.9		38.6	

Notes:

[a] The figure for 1 January 1942 does not include the Stavka reserves, including the people's militia divisions.

[b] Kalinin and Western Fronts

[c] Kalinin and Western Fronts, plus Moscow Zone of Defense

[d] Combined-arms armies only.

Sources: D. Muriev, "Nekotorye voprosy sovetskoi voennoi strategii v Moskovskoi bitve" ["Certain questions of Soviet military strategy in the Battle of Moscow"] *VIZh*, No. 12 (December 1971), p. 12; *Istoriia vtoroi mirovoi voiny*, Vol. 5, p. 142 and Vol. 6, pp. 34-34.

These powerful forces throughout all of 1942 and right up to March 1943 tried repeatedly to destroy the major enemy grouping standing on the approaches to the capital.

2

The First Attempt at Encirclement – the First Rzhev-Viaz'ma Offensive 8 January–20 April 1942

The presence of a major enemy grouping and its powerful bridgehead on the approaches to the capital of the Soviet government compelled the Soviet leadership and the Red Army command to conduct offensive after offensive for 15 months, in order to eliminate the danger threatening Moscow. The Nazi government and the OKW, in turn, didn't want to lose this very advantageous staging area in the center of the Eastern Front, and invested heavy manpower and assets to keep possession of it. Forces of the Western and Kalinin Fronts on the Soviet side, and sometimes neighboring *fronts* as well, and of Army Group Center on the other side, came together in savage combat over the Viaz'ma – Gzhatsk – Rzhev – Belyi territory. Here in the area of the Rzhev – Viaz'ma salient, men, equipment, and the theory and praxis of military science collided and competed.

Even as the Rzhev – Viaz'ma salient was forming during the Soviet Rzhev – Viaz'ma strategic offensive operation at the start of 1942, the Soviet command already undertook an effort to destroy the German grouping on the central strategic axis. This was one of the largest operations of the Great Patriotic War, and it would seem already quite a lot has been written about it. Nevertheless, up to the present date this offensive still hasn't received full and objective coverage. Its history deserves a separate book. As far as possible, here we will examine its basic stages and its most significant battles. In so doing, primarily well-known and published Soviet materials will be used, and thus there is the concern that they don't always depict events as they really happened.

The main objective of the Rzhev – Viaz'ma offensive operation was to complete the destruction of Army Group Center. A *Stavka* directive issued on 7 January 1942 planned "to encircle, and then capture or destroy the enemy's entire Mozhaisk – Gzhatsk – Viaz'ma grouping" through enveloping, converging attacks: the Kalinin Front's right wing from an area northwest of Rzhev toward Sychevka and Viaz'ma, and the Western Front's left wing toward Iukhnov and Viaz'ma, simultaneously with an attack by other elements of both *fronts* toward Rzhev, Sychevka and Gzhatsk. An airborne landing west of Viaz'ma was planned to assist with the encircling of the city. Judging from the published map of the *Stavka*'s plan, an all but double encirclement was envisioned, since the forces of the Northwestern Front's 3rd and 4th Shock Armies were supposed to advance as far as Rudnia (60 kilometers west of Smolensk) and to cut the Smolensk – Polotsk railroad. This was the first attempt at a large-scale operation by the Red Army aimed at encircling the enemy grouping on the Moscow axis. *Front* operations were an integral part of this strategic operation. Reference literature from the Soviet period refer to the Sychevka – Viaz'ma (8 January – 20 April 1942), the Toropets – Kholm (9 January – 6 February 1942) and the Viaz'ma airborne (18 January – 28 February 1942) operations, also known as the Rzhev and Bolkhov offensive operations. In

A Soviet infantry attack, beginning of 1942.

1998, the *Voenno-istoricheskii zhurnal* [Military History Journal] modified and expanded the list of *front* operations: the Sychevka – Viaz'ma offensive of 8 January – 28 February 1942, the Rzhev offensive of 3 March – 20 April 1942 by forces of the Kalinin Front, and an additionally named Mozhaisk – Viaz'ma offensive of 10 January – 28 February 1942 by the Western Front.[1] The last date isn't very comprehensible: did the forces of the Western Front really not conduct any offensive actions on the Viaz'ma axis after 28 February, simply because they didn't take place within the framework of an offensive operation?

The *Wehrmacht's* plan on the Moscow axis in the winter of 1941-1942 was determined by an OKH directive regarding the army in the east from 8 December 1941:

> Army Group Center after completing operations in the Moscow area should echelon its forces in such a way so as to be in a condition to repulse Russian attacks against the sector of the front that extends in the direction of Moscow, and against its left flank. For the defense of the extended flank, the Group should anticipate bringing reserves into combat readiness in the area south of Ostashkovo.[2]

The Red Army's January offensive was conducted with General of the Army G. K. Zhukov's Western Front and Colonel General I. S. Konev's Kalinin Front, in conjunction with forces of the Northwestern and Briansk Fronts. Initially, a combined 14 armies of the two *fronts* took part in the operation (Kalinin Front's 22nd, 29th, 30th, 31st and 39th Armies; Western Front's 1st Shock, 5th, 10th, 16th, 20th, 33rd, 43rd, 49th and 50th Armies), with three cavalry corps and the reinforced *front* air forces. If the 4th Airborne Corps, the 3rd and 4th Shock Armies and the 61st Army are added, which were committed in the course of the operation to replace the 1st Shock Army after it was transferred to a different sector of the front, the forces activated for this operation were impressive. Field

Red Army soldiers on the attack, beginning of 1942.

Marshal H. von Kluge's Army Group Center, which was opposing them, had at that time the Fourth and Ninth Armies, and the 3rd and 4th Panzer Armies.[3]

With respect to the numbers involved, according to the latest edition of the *Voennaia entsiklopediia* [Military Encyclopedia], Soviet forces numbered more than 688,000 men, with 10,900 guns and mortars and 474 tanks. The opposing *Wehrmacht* forces had approximately 625,000 men, with around 11,000 guns and mortars and 354 tanks.[4]

The first stage of the offensive, from 8 January 1942 until the end of the month, was rather successful for the Soviet forces, despite a certain delay in the middle of the month. Troops of the Kalinin Front were first to go on the attack on 8 January. The Front's shock grouping, consisting of the divisions of Lieutenant General I. I. Maslennikov's 39th Army and Major General V. I. Shvetsov's 29th Army, plus Colonel N. V. Gorin's (until 17 January, when Colonel S. V Sokolov assumed command) 11th Cavalry Corps were supposed to envelop the enemy from the west. Having breached the German defenses west of Rzhev, the divisions of the 39th Army drove southward through the German rear areas. By the third week of January, having penetrated 80 kilometers into enemy territory, they were involved in savage fighting for Sychevka and to the west of it. The enemy lost possession of the Sychevka railroad station. Yet even though the headquarters of Colonel General Adolf Strauss's Ninth Army had been withdrawn from Sychevka to Viaz'ma back on 12 January, the Germans stubbornly continued to defend the town, because the Ninth Army's supply line passed through it.

On 12 January 1942, the 11th Cavalry Corps and the 29th Army were introduced into the breach that had been created by the 39th Army. No matter how venturesome the plan was to send the mobile mounted group deeply into the German rear through the snow-covered forests and swamps, despite a certain hold-up in the middle of the month, it was successful: the 11th Cavalry Corps, consisting of 5,800 men, 5,000 horses, 2 122mm howitzers, 47 37mm and 45mm guns, and 35 82mm and 120mm mortars, advanced 110 kilometers and on 26 January reached and cut the highway west of Viaz'ma, thereby completing its assignment.[5]

The divisions of the 29th Army began to envelop Rzhev from the west. The first days

Fighting for a village, January 1942.

Soviet infantry manning positions, January 1942.

of the offensive gave hope of a quick liberation of the city. At the time, there were only German supply and rear units in Rzhev, and Soviet forces were only 8 kilometers to the west of it.[6] A *Stavka* directive from 11 January 1942 ordered the commander of the Kalinin Front:

> Seize control of Rzhev on 11 January or in no case later than 12 January ... The *Stavka* recommends for this purpose the use of all available artillery, mortar and aviation in the area to hammer the city of Rzhev, not stopping short of serious devastation of the city.[7]

Despite the fact that three divisions from the 39th Army were transferred to the 29th Army and deployed to the north and northeast of Rzhev as well, neither on this nor on subsequent days was the city taken, despite bitter fighting for it.

P. O. Bystrov, a former company commander in the 183rd Rifle Division, recalled the fighting for the village of Pekhurovo, which lay 9 kilometers west of Rzhev. After the first attack faltered, Bystrov's company had only six men left:

> In the morning we were given support from a battalion of ski troops, which had 15 machine guns. Yet once again our attack was repulsed. I remained with four Red Army men, but the order had to be fulfilled. I searched out the ski troop commander and suggested moving around the village that night and breaking into it from the rear. Leaving behind a covering force, that night we skirted around the village and stealthily approached some outlying buildings on the other side. There a German patrol spotted us and opened fire, but it was too late. We rushed onto the street and employed our bayonets. Everything became jumbled. There was the thrust of bayonets, pistols fired, and exploding grenades ... By dawn the company had taken a defense beyond the village. The Germans threw tanks against Pekhurovo. Our guys retreated, but that same night we drove the Germans back out of village, though now there was nothing left of it but ashes.[8]

On 15 January, Major General V. I. Vostrukhov's 22nd Army began its offensive. Despite the later start, which did not contribute to the advance of the 39th Army, Vostrukhov's army drove 120 kilometers to the south and southeast, deeply enveloping the enemy's Olenino grouping. As a result of the actions of the three armies, seven German divisions were encircled in the Olenino area. The command of the Ninth Army was compelled to resupply them with the help of transport aircraft. A portion of the 22nd Army's divisions advanced toward Belyi. Together with forces of the 39th Army, they "compressed" the German Belyi grouping along the Belyi – Dukhovshchina road, where the enemy set up an impregnable line.

On the left of the 29th Army, Major General V. A. Iushkevich's 31st Army with its attack secured the advance of the main grouping and prevented the enemy from shifting units to Rzhev. Major General D. D. Leliushenko's 30th Army together with the right-flank army of the Western Front was to destroy the enemy's Lotoshino grouping and attacked actively in the direction of Pogoreloe Gorodishche.

On 9 January, the Northwestern Front's 3rd and 4th Shock Armies went on the offensive as part of the Toropets – Kholm operation; on 22 January they transferred to

Commander of the 39th Army, Lieutenant General I. I. Maslennikov; a post-war photograph.

Commander of the 29th Army, Major General V. I. Shvetsov; a late 1940s photograph.

Medics of Kalinin Front's 31st Army evacuate wounded from the battlefield, early 1942. Photo by B. Vdovenko.

the command of the Kalinin Front. Initially, their troops enjoyed considerable success: over 25 days of fighting, they advanced almost 250 kilometers; liberated the village of Peno and the cities of Andreapol', Toropets, and Western Dvina; cut the Rzhev – Velikie Liuki railroad; outflanked the enemy Demiansk grouping from the south; and in sum, drove deeply into the rear of Army Group Center while disrupting its operational cooperation with Army Group North. The American AP war correspondent in Moscow Henry Cassidy wrote, "... the Russians held a deep salient from the Kalinin front through Toropets. That proved a sharp thorn in the German side throughout the next year."[9] The divisions of these armies reached the cities of Kholm, Velizh and Demidov; in each case, the Germans were determined to hold the city and heavy street fighting erupted.

The Western Front joined the operation on 9-10 January. The main attack, pursuant to the *Stavka* directive, was delivered on the Viaz'ma axis by the armies of the Front's left wing. Units of Lieutenant General I.V. Boldin's 50th Army and Major General P.A. Belov's 1st Guards Cavalry Corps outflanked Iukhnov from the south and southeast, while Major General K.D. Golubev's 43rd Army and Lieutenant General I.G. Zakharin's 49th Army outflanked it from the north and northeast. With bitter fighting, the enemy's Iukhnov grouping was enveloped on three sides.

According to the Front's directive, signed back at the beginning of January, Group Belov was the shock force and was together with the Rzhev grouping to play "the main role" in the encirclement of the German Fourth and Ninth Armies. By the middle of January, Group Belov was battling German defenses along the Warsaw highway; on 27-28 January five of its cavalry divisions slipped through a gap in the German lines and, in the words of P.A. Belov, "began a raid toward Viaz'ma." According to Belov's information, 7,000 cavalrymen crossed the Warsaw highway, though without the Group's rifle divisions, artillery, anti-aircraft means and the cavalry corps' rear services, which were kept in check on the other side of the highway by the German defenders. Already in the first days of February, Belov's corps was fighting for the city.

A Soviet cavalry unit on the march, winter 1941/1942.

Lieutenant General M.G. Efremov, commander of the 33rd Army.

Lieutenant General P.A. Belov, commander of the 1st Guards Cavalry Corps.

Airborne operations in the difficult winter conditions were another feature of the offensive. Between 18 and 22 January, paratroopers of the 5th Airborne Corps' 201st Airborne Brigade and troops of the 250th Separate Rifle Regiment were inserted south of Viaz'ma and rendered definite assistance to Belov's divisions. On 27 January, the 4th Airborne Corps' 8th Airborne Brigade began an airborne assault, but it didn't go well: of the 2,300 men who dropped in the Ozerechni area, only 1,300 were able to assemble on the ground. Approximately one-quarter of the transport aircraft returned to base without fulfilling their mission. In the first two or three days after the landing they were only able to gather approximately 30 to 50 percent of the equipment and supply bundles dropped with them. Given all this, as well as the fact that the command of the 4th Airborne Corps hadn't received directions from the Front command regarding the arrangement of logistics support for the paratroopers, because it hadn't reckoned with prolonged operations of the airdropped troops in the enemy rear, the 4th Airborne Corps' operation was halted.[10] The paratroopers that had already dropped attempted to carry out the corps' assignment to seize a section of the highway and railroad west of Viaz'ma, but they wound up encircled and units of the 1st Guards Cavalry Corps had to come to their rescue. Later, they passed to Major-General Belov's operational control.

On 19 January, attacking units of the 33rd Army took possession of the town of Verei after breaking through the enemy's defenses. On 30 January, the Western Front commander ordered the 33rd Army's shock group to push ahead vigorously to cover a distance of 25 kilometers to 90 kilometers in less than two days, and "in the future cooperate with Group Belov to seize Viaz'ma." The order was fulfilled and on 1 February, divisions of the 33rd

Army entered the fighting for the city 7 to 8 kilometers south and southeast of Viaz'ma. According to various data, the four divisions and other units of the 33rd Army that broke through numbered between 10,000 and 16,000 men.[11]

Here again one can express surprise over the lack of simple good judgment and the decisions to send divisions, particularly the cavalry divisions, which had been weakened and worn out after long days of combat, deep behind enemy lines. However, the *front* commands were acting in accordance with an 8 December 1941 order from the Chief of the General Staff B.M. Shaposhnikov: "Upon encountering enemy strongpoints, leave small screening detachments to contain them, and resolutely develop the offensive in force against flank boundaries and gaps in the enemy line …." These strongpoints were to be destroyed by "the operations of second and following echelons", which often simply did not exist.[12]

The right wing of the Western Front back on 6 January 1942 was ordered by G.K. Zhukov to break through the German defenses on the Lama River. Its shock grouping, which had been strengthened at the expense of the neighboring 20th Army commanded by Lieutenant General A.A. Vlasov, began its offensive on 10 January and despite difficulties as the Germans slowly withdrew, liberated Lotoshino on 16 January, Shakhovskaia on 17 January, and Mozhaisk on 20 January, while also cutting the Moscow – Rzhev railroad. However, at the height of the offensive, the *Stavka* decided to withdraw the 1st Shock Army into its reserve, while the 16th Army headquarters and the troops directly subordinate to it were shifted to the vicinity of Sukhinichi at the order of G.K. Zhukov. These decisions weakened the offensive capabilities of the armies of Western Front's right wing, and on 25 January they were brought to a halt on the enemy's prepared Gzhatsk defensive line. The final success achieved by Western Front at this stage of the offensive was the liberation of Sukhinichi after heavy fighting by Lieutenant General K.K. Rokossovsky's 16th Army.

The Briansk Front's offensive toward Bolkhov ground to a halt already by 14 January 1942. The *Stavka* ordered it to go on the defensive on all sectors and to cover Western Front's left flank.

At the start of the Soviet counteroffensive, the situation of Army Group Center was very grave. Already on 4 January 1942, in his diary F. Halder noted the sharpening of the situation, while his entry on 13 January was almost completely devoted to the situation in the Rzhev – Viaz'ma sector. Noted at the outset as "A particularly difficult day", the entry has this to say about Army Group Center: "Several desperate phone calls from commander of army group …", then offers the following comments on the situation: "Consequences for continued supply of Fourth Army cannot yet be predicted"; "The gap north of Medyn is as perturbing as ever"; "To clean up Rzhev, the army group … can expect no success". Repeatedly, Halder notes orders or proposals to close gaps in the German line.[13] K. von Tippelskirch later wrote that it seemed that the Fourth Panzer, Ninth Army, and the 3rd Panzer Army situated between them:

> … were facing a catastrophe. Russian forces broke through at the boundary between the Ninth and Sixteenth Armies to Belyi. There they were deep in the rear of the Ninth and Fourth Panzer Armies. The forward detachments of the enemy's developing envelopment reached an area northwest of Viaz'ma. The Ninth and Fourth Panzer Armies were nearly encircled. If … the railroad between Smolensk and Viaz'ma had been cut, the fate of both armies would have been decided.[14]

Wehrmacht soldiers, early 1942.

A German infantry column, early 1942.

German infantry on the march, early 1942.

On 15 January, Hitler authorized a German withdrawal. His directive says:

> After the failure to close the gaps that arose north of Medyn and west of Rzhev, I issued an order to the commander of Army Group Center in response to his petition: to withdraw the front of the Fourth Army and Third and Fourth Panzer Armies to a line east of Iukhnov – east of Gzhatsk – east of Zubtsov – north of Rzhev. The commanders have a requirement to keep the Iukhnov – Gzhatsk – Zubtsov – Rzhev roads free as a lateral link behind the front of our forces ... The line must be held.[15]

Hitler acknowledged, "For the first time in this war, I've had to order the withdrawal of a large sector of the front."[16] The line, to which the Germans withdrew, had already been fortified.

As early as the first ten days of January 1942, with Army Group Center's divisions and regiments hard hit by casualties (according to Grossmann, on 10 January the XXIII Army Corps' 206th Infantry Division numbered 2,283 men; its 102nd Infantry Division had 2,414 men while its 253rd Infantry Division had 2,380[17]), the Germans began to commit auxiliary units into the battle. For example, west and southwest of Rzhev, a group formed from supply and construction units, march battalions and *Luftwaffe* personnel was thrown into the fighting. However, already in January, new divisions from Western Europe were transferred here to the central sector of the Soviet-German front. The commander of the Ninth Army, Colonel General Strauss, was replaced on 16 January by the more resolute and tough Colonel General of Panzer Forces W. Model, who immediately undertook some decisive steps.[18]

On 21-22 January, the German forces southwest and west of Viaz'ma went on the attack. The immediate aim was to free the German troops encircled in the Olenino area and to close the gap, through which supplies were flowing to the Soviet 29th and 39th Armies and the 11th Cavarly Corps. In the process, it was hoped to trap the divisions of the 29th Army. On 23 January, they succeeded in closing the throat of the Soviet breakthrough with the assistance of meeting attacks from Rzhev and the Olenino area. The troops of Maslennikov's and Shvetsov's armies wound up nearly encircled; contact with the Kalinin Front was maintained only through a narrow corridor between the cities of Nelidovo and Belyi.

The commander of the Kalinin Front saw the dangerous development of the situation. On 21 January he ordered General Leliushenko to move the 30th Army (with all its rear services) from the Front's left flank to its right flank by the end of 23 January. The 30th Army commander appealed to the People's Commissar of Defense about the senselessness of such a decision, pointing to the impossible deadline, the need to travel across the lines of supply of three armies, and the numerically weak strength of the three divisions remaining in the 30th Army (after the recent savage fighting, most of the regiments numbered only 80-120 troops). His message stated that his army "could not yield the effect desired by Comrade Konev." However, the *Stavka* backed the Front commander, and the 30th Army was shifted to an area west of Rzhev. Together with two attached divisions from the 29th Army, the 30th Army entered the fighting with its front facing the south, while the 29th Army's remaining divisions primarily faced to the north.[19]

One can say that by the end of January 1942, the relatively successful stage of the Soviet winter offensive had come to an end. The armies' situations began to deteriorate significantly; exhausted by the prolonged offensive in difficult wintry conditions, the

German supply wagons, winter of 1941-1942.

Major General (from January 1942) Lieutenant General D.D. Leliushenko, commander of the 30th Army; a late 1941 photograph.

depleted forces had largely expended their offensive capabilities given the tangible shortage of supplies.

For example, the total losses of the Kalinin Front alone (minus the 3rd and 4th Shock Armies) approached 80,000 men.[20] At the same time the enemy, despite heavy losses of their own, had managed to weather the Red Army's onslaught and to endure in a very serious situation. According to K. Reinhardt, the Germans had managed to stabilize the front again: "At the end of January, as a consequence of insufficient strength, the Russian counteroffensive had also sputtered to a stop, just like the German offensive did on 5 December 1941."[21]

However, the *Stavka* demanded that the offensive continue. In view of the Kalinin Front's and Western Front's largely shared objective of Viaz'ma, with the aim of obtaining closer cooperation between them the main command of the Western Direction was re-established on 1 February 1942 under the leadership of G.K. Zhukov. In the directive that restored overall direction of the two Fronts to the Western Direction command, the operation's initial objective was confirmed: "The Western Direction's task of the nearest days, together with the capture of Viaz'ma, is the encirclement and capture of the enemy's Rzhev – Viaz'ma grouping … ."[22] However, the conditions for carrying out this assignment were no longer as propitious as they'd been at the start of the operation.

The second phase of the Rzhev – Viaz'ma operation began at the beginning of February 1942, when German forces launched counterstrokes on all the main directions of the Soviet armies' operations. The situation of those units, which had broken through into the

German rear, particularly deteriorated. The command of Army Group Center, fearing the loss of Viaz'ma, which was a key rail center on the main supply artery feeding the German forces on the central sector of the Eastern Front, already by the beginning of February had concentrated up to six divisions at Viaz'ma. The attacks of the weakened Soviet forces, which had virtually run out of ammunition, food and fodder, were met by an organized system of fire and infantry counterattacks, supported by panzers and the *Luftwaffe*. On 2 February 1942, F. Halder gave a description of this fighting in his war journal: "The 5th Panzer Division is destroying the enemy group that had infiltrated into our rear. The fighting behind the front lines is of a comically misshapen character and demonstrates that a war like that begins to degenerate into a tussle, far from all previously known forms of warfare."[23]

The Soviet forces were simply unable to take Viaz'ma. Units of the 11th Cavalry Corps were thrown back from the highway, reopening the German supply lines west of the city. On 2-3 February the Nazi forces were also successful in liquidating the Red Army's penetrations north and south of Iukhnov. Units of the Western Front's 33rd Army, the 1st Guards Cavalry Corps, and the 8th Airborne Brigade wound up encircled as well. On the Kalinin Front, on 5 February divisions of the 29th Army were cut-off from units of the 39th Army and were forced to struggle in complete encirclement.

As a result of the operation, major Soviet force groupings wound up encircled or semi-encircled north and south of Viaz'ma. However, from the beginning of February 1942, in the words of K. Reinhardt, "the Soviet forces that had broken through into the German rear areas no longer represented any operational threat."[24]

North and south of the Rzhev – Viaz'ma salient that had formed, fighting to free the encircled units developed. West of Rzhev, divisions of the 30th Army made repeated attempts to break through the German defenses in the areas of the villages of Nozhkino and Kokoshkino to link-up with the encircled units of the 29th Army. After the war, veterans of both sides recalled these battles with horror. Sometimes only 3-4 kilometers remained to reach the encircled units, which were striving to break out to the north. By the middle of February according to the opinion of the Western Direction's commander-in-chief, "the enemy had brought up sufficient strength and means to block the path of Leliushenko's army to the south", and therefore he ordered a regrouping of forces into the sector of the neighboring 22nd Army, where the enemy was weaker, while continuing the fighting on the previous sector. From there, he hoped to resume the offensive to the south.

However, the commander of the Kalinin Front I.S. Konev had already ordered the encircled 29th Army "to withdraw in the general direction of Stupino", that is, to the southwest toward units of the 39th Army. General Shvetsov was ordered "to bring out the troops in an organized fashion; if it is impossible to bring out the artillery, heavy machine guns and mortars, to bury such equipment in the woods."[25] In order to assist the withdrawing units, on the night of 16 February a small group of paratroopers (according to various sources, 300 to 400 men) were dropped within the pocket, but it "had no real influence". A tank group consisting of 10 tanks and 100 submachine gunners and sappers from the 81st Tank Brigade was also sent to the relief of the encircled divisions. Passing through the enemy rear, this combined force failed to make contact with the encircled forces in the indicated area. Two tanks and eight paratroopers, having collected a group of 120 mostly wounded men, returned to the north to friendly lines.[26]

The formations of Shvetsov's army began to trickle out of encirclement to link up with

Red Army troops who have emerged from encirclement in the Frolovo area, February 1942. Photo by B. Vdovenko.

the 39th Army on the night of 17 February and continued for the next several days. Those who managed to get out were sent to various medical sanitation battalions for treatment. According to a former nurse of the 449th Medical Sanitation Battalion A.N. Zakharova, the majority of the men arrived with frostbitten limbs and wounds – "there was not a single healthy one among them."

Separate groups also emerged from encirclement in the sector of the 30th Army. The deputy political director of a separate mortar company in the 1211th Rifle Regiment, A.Ia. Shiriaev, recalled that before escaping from the pocket, he and several comrades, having exhausted all their ammunition, hid in some woods. They didn't light any fires in order to avoid detection and fed upon the frozen meat of dead horses and the bark and roots of trees. On 24 February he was wounded:

> Local partisans stumbled upon us and led us back to friendly lines. A rather large group had gathered, not less than 100 men. We resolved to launch desperate attacks against the enemy blocking forces. At dawn we bumped into machine-gun positions. We rushed through the raking fire with desperate cries of "Ura!" ... We managed to hide from our pursuers in some woods and waited until nightfall. Finally we crossed the front lines. Turning over our documents for checking, I discovered that my Party card was so saturated with blood that you could barely make out the number.

Of the 6,000 men who fell into encirclement, on 28 February 5,200 came out of the pocket, 800 of which were wounded. The losses of the 29th Army between 16 January and

A Pe-2 taxis to a stop at a forest airstrip, Kalinin Front, early 1942. Photo by B. Vdovenko.

28 February amounted to 14,000 men.[27]

The Western Front command also tried to help its cut-off forces. The Front commander at first demanded that the 43rd Army commander restore the situation at Iukhnov. Then troops of the 49th and 50th Army's became involved. The encircled divisions fought actively. The Front commander promised Efremov and Belov: "Three or four days from now, Golubev's and Boldin's units will be arriving." He ordered that those guilty for the 33rd Army's failure to hold the flanks of the breakthrough "be arrested, tried and shot on the spot, no matter the number." However, the command of Army Group Center reinforced the troops defending Iukhnov, and all attempts to break through to the encircled troops from outside the pocket failed. General Belov's units were unable to link up with the Kalinin Front's 11th Cavalry Corps in the middle of February, even though only 6 kilometers separated them. Also in the middle of February, according to P. A. Belov's recollections, when they wanted to form a common front with M.G. Efremov's 33rd Army, the headquarters of the Western Front sent him a strange telegram: "You don't need an elbow to elbow connection with the infantry [the 33rd Army]." Possibly, later this would be one of the causes for the destruction of units of the 33rd Army.[28]

The situation of the encircled forces with food and ammunition was becoming catastrophic, moreover because G.K. Zhukov issued an instruction "Search for food locally; we will not be supplying it, because we don't have the airplanes; search for shells also in place." The encircled units had to rely on self-supply and cooperation with partisans. On 9 February 1942, I.V. Stalin signed an order for the armies' military councils to mobilize anyone between the ages of 17 and 45 on the territory liberated from German occupation. This enabled the encircled units to increase their strength.[29] They began to operate actively against enemy communication lines, seizing stockpiles of food and weapons, while partisans

The crew of a Pe-2 receives an assignment, Kalinin Front, early 1942. Photo by B. Vdovenko.

assisted the regular units. On 15-16 February, partisan detachments operating south and southwest of Viaz'ma liberated Dorogobuzh.

Partisans and General Belov's units were holding several railroad stations on the Zanoznaia – Viaz'ma line, thereby totally disrupting traffic along it for four months. As a result, an area was created in the rear of Army Group Center where units of the 1st Guards Cavalry Corps, paratroopers of the 4th Airborne Corps and partisan detachments successfully operated. At the end of February, all of these units and partisan detachments, apart from units of the 33rd Army, were subordinated to General Belov. The German General Otto Beutler wrote: "Enemy troops, located in the area of Dorogobuzh for several months, created a genuine threat to the rear communications of the Fourth Panzer and Ninth Armies, and at times even cut them. They tied up major German forces, which were hastily withdrawn from the front and sent to this place."[30]

On 16 February 1942 the *Stavka* of the Supreme High Command issued a new directive, which reiterated the task for the troops of the Western Direction "to smash and destroy the enemy's Rzhev – Viaz'ma – Iukhnov grouping and by 5 March reach and dig-in on our old defensive line with prepared anti-tank ditches"[31], that is the line Olenino, Dnepr River, El'nia and further along the Desna River to Briansk. In those conditions, that was plainly unrealistic. This directive is surprising and raises doubts that the *Stavka* knew the real situation.

From the date of this 16 February directive, it is possible to distinguish three stages of the operation: the resumption of active Soviet offensive operations; their gradual fading away; and the conclusion of the operation on 20 April. In February the *Stavka* allocated supplementary forces from its reserve: Kalinin Front received a Guards rifle corps, seven rifle divisions and four aviation regiments, while Western Front received a Guards rifle corps, three rifle divisions, two airborne brigades, 200 tanks, 40 aircraft, and 60,000 additional replacements. A note in Halder's diary indicates that German intelligence detected the transfer of these reserves.[32]

On the Kalinin Front, after the emergence of the 29th Army's units from encirclement, the center of gravity shifted to the destruction of the enemy's Olenino grouping through the joint effort of three armies. In an order of the Front commander on 19 February, the reinforced 22nd Army was instructed to seize Belyi on 22 February and already by the end of 23 February to take possession of the Olenino area. The 30th Army was to reach the Chertolino area already by 22 February, while the 39th Army was to link-up with the 30th Army on 23 February. The 31st Army was given the order to seize the Zubtsov area by the end of 23 February.[33]

Only the 31st Army was able to get underway on the offensive's designated start date of 20 February; the others started on various days thereafter. For example, the 39th Army launched its offensive only on 25 February. On its sector, Shvetsov's group, consisting of those units of the 29th Army that had escaped encirclement, also participated in the offensive. Daily grinding attacks by Soviet troops began, including in the streets of Belyi, none of which brought any real results. However, the *Wehrmacht* divisions were standing to the death. At the beginning of March, Leliushenko's 30th Army was reinforced, but even this didn't generate much success.

Troops of the Western Front also began offensive operations. Between 17 and 23 February, there were additional airdrops of units of the 4th Airborne Corps. West of Iukhnov more than 7,000 paratroopers of the 9th and 214th Airborne Brigades were dropped, as well as ammunition, weapons, rations and equipment. The Corps' command and staff also flew into the enemy rear. During an attack by a German fighter, corps commander General A.F. Levashov was killed and several more officers were wounded. Chief of staff Colonel A. F. Kazankin assumed command of the 4th Airborne Corps. The paratroopers were supposed to link up with the 50th Army, which was attacking toward

Dead Red Army troops in front of the positions of the 129th Infantry Division, February 1942.

After an attack against German positions in the Rzhev area, early 1942.

them in the direction of Viaz'ma, but the airdrop went unsuccessfully.

Because of delays in receiving replacements, the Western Front's armies also went on the offensive in an uncoordinated fashion over the course of ten days. On not a single one of the designated breakthrough sectors were they able to create the necessary superiority over the enemy.[34]

At the beginning of March, an attempt was undertaken to breach the ring of encirclement by encircled units of the 33rd Army from within and a shock group of the 43rd Army from without. The German command brought up additional forces. The gap between the two attacking Soviet groups narrowed to just 2 kilometers, but they were unable to overcome the remaining distance. At this time, the situation of the encircled grouping of the 33rd Army began to worsen with each passing day. On 11 March, the encircled divisions and units of the 33rd Army numbered 12,780 men, while at the end of March Belov's group had up to 17,000 men. A special communication from the Western Front's chief of the NKVD Special Department on 8 April 1942 spoke of a critical situation with the supply of ammunition and food in the 33rd Army's shock group:

> ... a significant amount of the artillery has been idled by a lack of fuel and ammunition. Casualties from 1 February to 13 March 1942 amount to 1,290 killed and 2,351 wounded. We are not receiving replacements ... Sustenance ... consists of a small quantity of boiled rye and horse meat. There is no salt, fats or sugar at all. Due to the starvation diet, cases of illness among the troops are becoming more frequent. ... on the night of 14 March, two soldiers died from emaciation.

The document contains a resolution: "That which has been set forth here has been reported to the Western Front's Military Council for taking measures." However, even in this situation, the encircled units of the 33rd Army continued to draw away significant enemy strength.[35]

The only real success of the Front's forces in this stage was the liberation of Iukhnov on 5 March 1942. The operations of the 4th Airborne Corps' paratroopers, though the drops were scattered, still diverted a significant amount of strength from the enemy's Iukhnov grouping. At the same time, in the sectors of attack of all 12 armies of the two *fronts*, despite the almost month-long bloody fighting, progress was minimal. Attempts to link-up with the encircled forces once again were not crowned by success. In the opinion of the commander of the Sixteenth Army's 30th Infantry Division K. von Tippelskirch, "the attacking force of the Russians was spent" already on 21 February.[36]

Nevertheless, on 20 March 1942 the *Stavka* again demanded that the *fronts* continue to execute the previously assigned orders more energetically, declaring that "the liquidation of the enemy's Rzhev – Gzhatsk – Viaz'ma grouping has been impermissibly delayed." The Kalinin Front's reinforced 30th Army was ordered in cooperation with the 22nd and 39th Armies to destroy the enemy's Olenino grouping. In addition, the bulk of the army was to pivot to the east and together with the newly refitted 29th Army and the 31st Army to seize Rzhev by 5 April. Simultaneously, a shock group comprised of divisions of the 22nd Army and the reserve of the Fourth Shock Army was ordered to take Belyi by 3 April. The Western Front's 43rd, 49th and reinforced 50th Armies by 27 March were to link-up with the encircled forces of the 33rd Army and Group Belov. In addition, the 5th Army was to capture Gzhatsk on 1 April. At the same time, the 16th and 61st Armies were ordered to attack in the Briansk direction and destroy the enemy Zhizdra – Bolkhov grouping.[37]

Apparent is the dispersal of forces on both fronts. When reading this directive and the orders of the *front* commanders and given the knowledge of the genuine situation, again doubts arise about the information the *Stavka* and the General Staff had available regarding the condition of the troops, their understanding of the situation confronting them, and the soundness of the decisions of the high-ranking military and state leaders.

It might have been possible to distinguish another stage of the operation to destroy the German Rzhev – Gzhatsk – Viaz'ma grouping starting 20 March, but here only attempts by the Soviet forces to launch offensive operations are evident. The armies, having started the offensive at the end of March and beginning of April, had no success on any of the attack directions. This can be explained by the general exhaustion of the troops after the prolonged offensive. Thus, for example, the 22nd Army since the start of the winter offensive in January had lost its entire complement twice over. Replacements for the *fronts* on the Western Direction in the period between January and April 1942, though 5.6 times greater in number than in December 1941, were untrained and immediately consumed in the fighting. The artillery of several of the attacking divisions in March-April was down to one-tenth to one-third of a standard allotment of shells and only 10 mortar rounds. It was unable to inflict any perceptible damage to the enemy's defenses. In addition, the muddy season began in April.[38]

The enemy was also operating more actively. E. P. Tarasov, a veteran of the 234th Rifle Division, who was fighting from the end of March in the Belyi area, recalled:

> The enemy attacked incessantly. Enemy aviation literally didn't allow us to raise our heads. At the beginning of April, there were days when hundreds of individual combat sorties were conducted against our positions. They especially savagely bombed

Kalinin Front, spring 1942.

The command of the 31st Army on the Zubtsov axis, spring 1942.

Kalinin Front commander I. S. Konev's visit to the 31st Army on the Zubtsov axis, spring 1942.

> us between 3 and 5 April. When you try to picture the end of March – beginning of April 1942 in your mind, the many days merge into one, and this entire endless day drags on with exceedingly hard combat. Almost every day, there was a carousel of German dive bombers overhead. Having formed into a circle, they in turn would go into a dive, turn on their sirens, and bomb and strafe us. It is impossible to forget the dense mortar fire that the enemy mortar crews rained down upon us, not forgetting the shells, and the heavy, unceasing fatigue from the constant lack of sleep and nervous stress.[39]

The death of the encircled units of the 33rd Army became the final note of this operation. The German command, having strengthened its positions in the center of the Eastern Front, started to focus its attention on the liquidation of the Soviet units in its rear. For example, two German divisions were committed against the 11th Cavalry Corps at the end of March. Units of the Corps and the 39th Army had to conduct heavy fighting in semi-encirclement, but a satisfactory staging area for the Soviet forces between Sychevka and Belyi in this period was retained. Its elimination, in the words of K. von Tippelskirch, was left for the forthcoming summer campaign.[40]

The command of Army Group Center concentrated units of seven divisions against General Efremov's divisions. The pocket shrank to an area of 10x25 kilometers. In April, authorization to Generals Efremov and Belov to escape the encirclement was finally given. General Efremov was directed to withdraw through forests under partisan control in the direction toward Kirov, where a breach in the enemy's defenses would be created by the 10th Army. However, the famished men, among which were many sick and wounded, in the conditions of the spring muddy season were hardly able to overcome the distance of 150-

180 kilometers expected of them. General Efremov selected the shortest path to breakout to reach the Front's main forces. This attempt in the middle of April had no success: the main portion of those moving to break out with General Efremov – approximately 2,000 men – were killed. The commander of the 33rd Army Lieutenant-General Efremov refused to fly out in an airplane, was wounded during the breakout attempt and shot himself. The encircled grouping of 33rd Army, numbering around 10,000 men, ceased to exist. The irrevocable losses of the 33rd Army over the two and a half months amounted to more than 8,000 men, including approximately 6,000 soldiers and officers during the breakout attempt.[41]

Troops of the 43rd and 49th Armies tried to assist General Efremov's units that were attempting to break out, but unsuccessfully. The 50th Army on 14 April attempted an attack to meet the units of Belov's group that were trying to break out. There was a moment when only 2 kilometers remained to a successful link-up, but on 15 April the Germans hurled back the units of the 50th Army and the attack was halted.[42]

It is considered that 20 April 1942 is the final day of the Rzhev – Viaz'ma offensive, when the *Stavka* ordered the forces of the *fronts* to go over to a defense on their present lines. This was the largest Soviet offensive of the 1941/1942 winter campaign and of the entire first period of the war. The destruction of the enemy grouping on the Moscow – Smolensk axis occupied the central place in the *Stavka*'s plans. During the operation, Soviet troops fully liberated the oblasts of Moscow and Tula and part of Kalinin Oblast, but its main goal – the destruction of Army Group Center – was not achieved. A powerful German grouping continued to stand at a distance of 150-300 kilometers from Moscow, though it is true that it had lost more than 333,000 men between 1 January and 30 March 1942. Its divisions were worn out and bled white: according to F. Halder's data for Army Group Center, on 1 May 1942 the infantry divisions were 35 percent below their initial infantry combat strength, and all the formations lacked sufficient mobility for extensive operations. Part of Army Group Center was occupying an extremely unfavorable operational position, the Rzhev – Viaz'ma salient which projected like a thumb into Soviet-held territory and had been enveloped on the west, north and east by Soviet armies. It was only able to avoid complete destruction by the hasty transfer of 12 divisions and two security brigades from Western Europe.[43]

Casualties of the Soviet forces were extremely heavy. Today, the Rzhev – Viaz'ma operation of 1942 is considered one of the bloodiest operations of the Great Patriotic War. Officially, the Western and Kalinin Fronts lost 776,889 men in the operation, though military historian S. N. Mikhalev places the losses at 948,000 men.[44]

In the historical literature, many reasons have been offered for the failure of the Rzhev – Viaz'ma operation. In the Soviet era they were divided into objective and subjective causes. Initially greater attention was given to the objective causes, but in the 1980s and 1990s, attention shifted to the subjective reasons. I will only list the main explanations here: the enormity of the plans and their lack of grounding in reality; the exaggerated notion of the potential of our forces and an underestimation of the enemy; the launching of the operation without any pause after the Moscow counteroffensive; the absence of a general numerical superiority over the enemy and the disadvantages in the technical equipping of the troops; the dispersal of force by attempting to attack in so many directions simultaneously; the great delays in the arrival of reserves and replacements, and their introduction into combat often from the march and in a piecemeal fashion, without adequate preparation; the

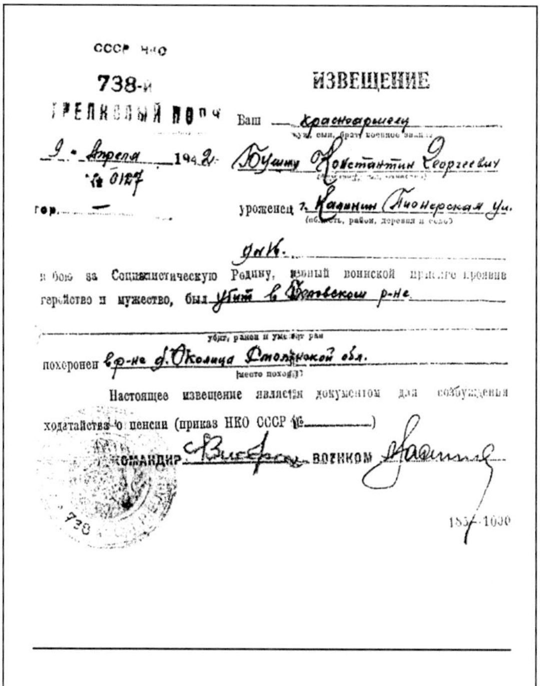
СССР НКО
738-й стрелковый полк
9 апреля 1942
№ 0127
гор.

ИЗВЕЩЕНИЕ

Ваш красноармеец Бушма Константин Георгиевич
уроженец г. Калинин (Пионерская ул.)
в бою за Социалистическую Родину, верный воинской присяге проявив геройство и мужество, был убит в Бельском р-не
похоронен в р-не д. Околица Смоленской обл.
Настоящее извещение является документом для возбуждения ходатайства о пенсии (приказ НКО СССР №)
Командир Военком

"Похоронка"

An official condolence letter, notifying a family of the death of a Red Army man in the Rzhev region.

constant and acute lack of equipment, especially ammunition (often Zhukov's own words from his memoirs are cited: "Believe it or not, the normal rate of ammunition expenditure we had to establish was one or two rounds per artillery piece a day. And that, you will note, during an offensive campaign!"); the loss of operational aerial superiority; the command staff's lack of experience in organizing and conducting major offensive operations and large-scale encirclement operations; the inadequate flexibility in handling the troops; the insufficiently detailed elaboration of *front* operations; the exhaustion of the troops rising from the constant offensive; and the growing enemy resistance due to the shrinking front as the German divisions fell back to previously prepared lines, strengthened with reserves.[45]

Several points of view exist when determining personal responsibility for the failures and the heavy casualties in the operation. The first assertion, one of the sources of which is G.K. Zhukov, is that the Supreme Commander I.V. Stalin is exclusively guilty for the failures of the Rzhev – Viaz'ma operation. It was he who dispersed the forces, having launched in January 1942 a grand offensive on all the fronts, rather than concentrating the available strength on the fronts of the Western direction and conducting a more powerful offensive there, as proposed by the author of this point of view. Zhukov expressed it thusly: "The entire conception of going over to a grand offensive on all the directions – this of course was not the idea of the General Staff and not the idea of Shaposhnikov ... this was exclusively the idea of Stalin himself." Many Soviet historians have supported this point of view. For example, the well-known historian N.G. Pavlenko wrote: "The most convincing indicator of the inadequacy of Stalin's decisions was that on the primary axis of the campaign, that is the Western direction, we had no results whatsoever."[46]

The second point of view has been expressed very actively in the last 15 years, primarily by authors who have some personal connection with the fate of the Western Front's 33rd Army, as well as by authors who oppose Zhukov's apologists. In their opinion, the main guilty party in the death of the encircled units of the 33rd Army and of General M. G. Efremov was the commander-in-chief of the Western Direction himself, G.K. Zhukov. Using as evidence of this the analysis of operations of the 33rd and 43rd Armies later conducted by a group of officers in the Red Army General Staff's Operations Department under the leadership of K.F. Vasil'chenko, they also accuse G.K. Zhukov for the mistakes of the entire operation: "In our understanding the Rzhev – Viaz'ma ... operation is one of the unsuccessful pages in the combat biography of Marshal Zhukov. Even though he initially spoke up against the planned operation, he later took responsibility for implementing it, and thereby took responsibility for the way it was handled." These authors sometimes use very sharp, emotional expressions: "In an operational respect, the Rzhev – Viaz'ma operation was conducted with crude blunders"; "... the authoritative hand of G. K. Zhukov hurled Efremov's 33rd Army to its death at Viaz'ma ... an imitation of an operation with the grand name of the 'Rzhev – Viaz'ma offensive' was going on, but there was no operation as such. A game was going on, a grand fraud."[47]

It is asserted that Zhukov deliberately set up Efremov as a sacrifice, fearing his rivalry. Incidentally, G.K. Zhukov himself once gave a basis for such an assertion. Speaking about the operations of Efremov's and Belov's units, at a meeting with historians of the *Voenno-istoricheskii zhurnal* in August 1966, he declared: "Speaking personally, there wasn't even any sort of operation. They broke through ... and they were cut-off. They started against Viaz'ma and stopped ... Thus there cannot even be any talk about the faltering of an operation here; they simply didn't have the capability to conduct one." This is a strange assertion, if the orders of the commander-in-chief of the Western Direction to these forces are recalled, and if you remember that these encircled divisions were under the command of his own *front*. The former commander is absolving himself of any responsibility for the disaster.[48]

However, all of these authors, including G.K. Zhukov, are speaking only about the operations of the 33rd Army and are not considering the operations of all the armies of the Kalinin and Western Fronts, which took part in the Rzhev – Viaz'ma offensive operation. Incidentally, G.K. Zhukov himself laid the blame for the perishing of the 33rd Army's units on M.G. Efremov, their commander.[49]

The authors of the compiled work *Strategicheskie resheniia i Voennye Sily* [Strategic Decisions and the Armed Forces] (Moscow, 1995) also cite "the underestimation by the commander-in-chief of the Western Direction and his staff of the strength of the enemy's possible resistance and his capability to maneuver reserves rapidly." However, in this case they split the blame of the Western Direction commander-in-chief with the higher military leadership, noting among the causes of the failure to reach the operation's goals "the assignment of tasks to the troops of the Western Direction beyond their capabilities." It is impossible not to agree with this assessment, since in addition to the 1st Guards and 11th Cavalry Corps, Kalinin Front's 29th and 39th Armies were sent into the enemy's deep rear. One needn't be a major military specialist to understand that without follow-up echelons, this might easily lead to the encirclement of the breakthrough forces, which is indeed what happened. The English historian B. Liddell Hart also wrote about this:

> As the Red Army failed to undercut these bastions to cause their collapse, the deep advances it made in the intervening spaces tended to turn out to its own disadvantage later. For the bulges it made were naturally less defensible than bastion-towns, and thus absorbed an excessive quantity of troops in holding them, while they could more easily be cut-off by flanking strokes from the German-held bastions, used as offensive springboards.

Given the knowledge that these units and formations, which were knowingly sent into the enemy's deep rear without sufficient strength and resources and without sufficient support, were given assignments beyond their capabilities, even a dilettante can see the venturesome nature of the operation's plan to take Viaz'ma and encircle the main forces of Army Group Center in January 1942. If at first the troops actually did almost reach Viaz'ma, then already by the end of January the operation had in all effects turned into a survival test for the encircled and semi-encircled forces and their ability to make contact again with friendly main forces.[50] The Russian authors of the other major work – the military historical essays on the history of the Great Patriotic War, which came out in 1998 – also highlight an entire number of errors during the conducting of the offensive.[51]

It is possibly not excessive to mention as well the mutual relations among the commanders at various levels, including at the higher echelon, which were customary in the Red Army. Lower-ranking commanders were more often subjected to threats and verbal abuse than support with reserves or at least moral support. For example, on a report from General P.A. Belov about the operations of his troops in the enemy rear and the failure to take Viaz'ma, G.K. Zhukov wrote "Here's an example of a lack of giftedness." In Colonel K.F. Vasil'chenko account about the operations of the 33rd Army, he wrote, "The Front is only concerned with hastening the army toward a sweeping, not at all secured advance." It was the same thing on the Kalinin Front. The reason for the 29th and 39th Armies' failure was considered to be the confusion of their commanders. I.S. Konev in a conversation with a member of the Front's Military Council D. S. Leonov on 13 October demanded:

> Warn Shvetsov that he will be put on trial for failing to carry out the task to seize Rzhev ... Give Maslennikov a menacing warning that for the indecision in his actions, overestimation of the enemy, and susceptibility to all sorts of rumors, he will be removed from his post as army commander regardless of anything else ..."

Such moral "support" hardly helped in the cruel struggle with the enemy.[52]

★★★

Continuing the tradition of Soviet historiography of the war, Russian historiography considers the Rzhev – Viaz'ma offensive part of the battle for the capital and asserts that it "closed the books" on the Moscow battle. On one hand, this is logical; after all, there was no operational pause between Red Army's December 1941 offensive and the Rzhev – Viaz'ma offensive. The January 1942 offensive was a "continuation of an unceasing counteroffensive." On the other hand, is it possible to consider the battle for Moscow over, if Soviet troops on the Moscow axis still remained standing in front of the enemy's Gzhatsk defensive line 150 kilometers from the capital, where they were stopped at the end of January?[53]

We'll remind you that in the military-historical literature of the 1960s, the conclusion of the battle for the capital is dated as the end of January 1942.[54] This is completely understandable; after all, the subsequent combat operations on the Moscow axis up to April 1942 brought no results. The operation's ultimate goal was not attained, thus it is called "unfinished" – a very slick treatment of an unsuccessful operation.[55] When summing up the results of the Moscow battle, historians strive to put some distance between it and the failures from the beginning of 1942. They speak primarily about the success of the Red Army's December counteroffensive, ignoring the failures of the first four months of 1942. As a result, the Rzhev – Viaz'ma operation is left hanging in the air. In December 2006, the authors of a new work about the regions' contribution to the victory over fascism once again proposed the former dates for the Rzhev – Viaz'ma operation – 8-25 January 1942.[56] In this case, however, where should all the Soviet offensive operations between February and April be placed?

However, it is also possible to view the place of the 1942 Rzhev – Viaz'ma offensive in the history of the war in non-traditional manner. If we take as the basis the assertion that the Battle of Moscow concluded in the first days of January 1942 following the successful December offensive, then the Rzhev – Viaz'ma operation of 1942 began an entire series of offensives in the area of the Rzhev – Viaz'ma salient, similar to each other in objectives, course, participants, names and outcomes. As is known, the goal of the operation, as determined by the *Stavka* directive of 7 January 1942, was the encirclement and destruction of the enemy forces in the Rzhev – Viaz'ma – Gzhatsk area and the liberation of these cities. In the course of the year 1942, the Red Army conducted several offensives on this sector of the front, designed to destroy the enemy in the areas of Rzhev, Sychevka, Gzhatsk and Viaz'ma. These tasks, which were assigned to the Soviet forces in January 1942, were partially achieved only in March 1943.

Immediately after the conclusion of the 1942 Rzhev – Viaz'ma winter offensive, preparations for a new offensive on this sector of the front began. The bloody fighting for the Rzhev – Viaz'ma salient had only begun.

3

The *Wehrmacht* Mops up the Rear of Army Group Center – Combat Operations in May-July 1942

In the spring of 1942, the high commands of both sides debated plans for the summer campaign. The Soviet Supreme Commander I.V. Stalin, according to Zhukov, was most of all concerned about the Moscow axis, where the Germans might fully unleash offensive operations, because they had more than 70 divisions here. According to S.M. Shtemenko:

> When assessing the significance of [different] sectors of the strategic front, the Rzhev – Viaz'ma salient stood out first of all. It was close to Moscow and was occupied by troops of the enemy's most powerful grouping, Army Group Center ... Stalin was convinced that sooner or later, the adversary would again launch a strike toward Moscow ... It was decided that the fate of the 1942 summer campaign would be decided at Moscow.

In A. Vasilevsky's opinion, this "biased, mistaken judgment ... weighed upon the Supreme Commander right up until July."[1]

Other members of the *Stavka*, the General Staff and the majority of *front* commanders shared the belief that Moscow was the *Wehrmacht's* goal and that this axis would be the critical one. Work resumed in the spring to construct lines of defensive fortifications on the approaches to the capital. A doctor working for Moscow's Emergency Aid service noted in her diary on 24 April 1942, "They're erecting street barricades in Moscow again."[2] The most powerful Soviet force grouping continued to remain on the central sector of the Soviet-German front. Thus, in May 1942 rations were allocated to the Kalinin Front for 601,894 officers and men, and to the Western Front for 823,101 officers and men. Even if you consider the misrepresentation of figures, more than a million individuals were serving in the two *fronts*.[3]

It is known that at this time I.V. Stalin was advocating an active strategic defense and the simultaneous staging of major offensive operations on multiple sectors of the Soviet-German front. B.M. Shaposhnikov was only arguing for an active strategic defense and wanted to postpone large-scale offensive operations until the summer. G.K. Zhukov, fully supporting Shaposhnikov, believed that at the beginning of summer it would be necessary first to launch powerful blows on the western strategic axis with the aim of eliminating the Rzhev salient.

It was ultimately decided to seek the destruction of the Germans' entire Rzhev – Viaz'ma – Gzhatsk grouping in the first half of May. Again, the main attacks would be launched by the Western and Kalinin Fronts, with supporting attacks by neighboring *fronts*. The troops of the two *fronts* that were still encircled or semi-encircled in the enemy rear were

A Lenin kiosk. Kalinin Front, summer 1942.

Red Army troops waiting to be served at a field kitchen, summer 1942.

instructed to hold out. According to the memoirs of P.A. Belov, on 4 May 1942 the Western Front headquarters gave him the following order: "You with the 4th Airborne Corps and the partisan detachments are to hold the ground you currently occupy at whatever the cost." Units of the 39th Army and the 11th Cavalry Corps were also instructed to strengthen their current positions and build defensive fortifications, which were inspected by a special commission in the period between 15 May and 15 June.[4]

The Western Front command developed a plan for an offensive with the aim of breaking through to Belov's group with major forces and to hold it as a staging area for further operations. P.A. Belov was informed of the operations, which was planned to begin no later than 5 June, back on 9 May by the Front's chief of operations Major General S.V. Golushkevich, who had flown into the pocket to meet with him. The operation's plan was confirmed by a *Stavka* directive on 18 May.

Before the start of the offensive, the Western Front was bolstered from the *Stavka* Reserve with seven rifle divisions, two long-range artillery regiments, four to five regular artillery regiments, and two anti-tank artillery regiments. The allocation of tank brigades and an aviation regiment was also intended. On 20 May 1942 by Front order, the "Special Group of General Belov" was created and included the 1st Guards Cavalry Corps, the 329th Rifle Division, units of the 4th Airborne Corps, the 1st and 2nd Partisan Divisions and the 1st Separate Partisan Detachment, which were all operating in the area southwest of Viaz'ma. Between 10 and 25 May, an airlift operation was conducted to reinforce Group Belov. It was intended to bring in 9,000 soldiers and officers by air, as well as arms and ammunition, fuel and rations.[5]

Subsequently, judging from a map of the plans for the 20th and 43rd Armies for taking Viaz'ma dated 17 June 1942, it was proposed for these armies to strike first at Gzhatsk, with a subsequent attack toward Viaz'ma. Twelve rifle divisions, three rifle brigades, the 41st Tank Brigade, ten artillery regiments and thirteen Guards mortar battalions of *Katiusha* rocket-launchers were to be part of the attack's first echelon. Guards rifle corps, and a cavalry and tank corps, were in the Front's reserve, prepared to exploit the anticipated breach in the enemy lines.[6]

The Western Front's offensive was to be supported by the Kalinin Front. The combat order from the Kalinin Front commander dated 24 May 1942 stated: "Forces of the KF [Kalinin Front's] left wing, the 30th, 29th and 31st Armies [working] in close cooperation have the immediate task to seize the Rzhev, Zubtsov region. Subsequently in conjunction with the 22nd and 39th Armies it is to destroy the enemy's Rzhev – Olenino grouping." Divisions of the 1st and 3rd Air Armies and long-range aviation were committed to the operation. In his war diary on 24 and 26 May, F. Halder noted the concentration of Russian forces in the Belyi area and the possible preparation for an offensive.[7]

So a large-scale offensive operation involving the troops of two *fronts* was being prepared. The goals of this planned offensive were essentially the same as that of the preceding "incomplete", four-month Rzhev – Viaz'ma operation. However, the May-June 1942 operation for a number of reasons was never implemented, in particular because the Germans preempted it with an offensive of their own. However, a Western Front order from 21 May noted the poor organization of the airlift operation designed to support Group Belov. For example, between 10 May and 31 May, only 1,663 men, 21 of the planned 200 82mm mortars, 33 of the planned 200 50mm mortars, and 162 of the planned 600 anti-tank rifles had been delivered to Group Belov.[8]

It is known that the Soviet command committed a miscalculation when planning the 1942 summer campaign: the German high command decided to launch its main attack with Army Group South, toward the Caucasus oil fields. The *Wehrmacht* plans for the summer were determined by OKW Directive No. 41 from 5 April 1942. Although the German command had no concrete plans for a new offensive against Moscow, when working out its 1942 summer campaign it was counting upon the creation of favorable conditions for a finishing strike against the central grouping of Soviet forces. It was assumed that the seizure of Stalingrad would cut the center of the country off from the south, and having seized the Murmansk railroad in the north, Moscow would become isolated from the delivery of critical supplies and resources. Maintaining the bridgehead in the center of the Soviet-German front for further operations was given very great significance: "The rapid restaging of aviation to the central and northern sectors of the front must be considered; for this, existing airfields must be protected as far as is possible."

That summer it was also planned to eliminate the pocketed Soviet forces in Army Group Center's rear, before implementing two offensives: with attacks by the Ninth Army from Rzhev and the Sixteenth Army from the Demiansk bridgehead toward Ostashkov to encircle the bulk of the Kalinin Front; and for the Second and Fourth Panzer Armies to pinch off the Soviet salient between Iukhnov and Bolkhov. Later, in OKW Directive No. 45 from 23 July 1942 it was stated that the operations "on the sectors of the front of Army Groups Center and North must be conducted rapidly, one after the other. In this way the dismemberment of the enemy forces and the collapse of the morale of the enemy command staff and troops will be secured." The fact that for all of 1942, the German command indeed held its largest force grouping – approximately one-third of all its divisions operating on the Soviet-German Front – here in the Rzhev – Viaz'ma salient shows its desire to retain a suitable bridgehead as a staging area for a later offensive.[9]

Thus, Army Group Center was given an auxiliary role in the *Wehrmacht's* 1942 summer campaign. With the aim of disinformation, a directive was issued about feigning preparations for an attack on Moscow. A deceptive Operation Kremlin was worked out in detail by the headquarters of Army Group Center in order to give the impression that the main offensive would be here: "Destroy hostile troops ... west and south of the enemy's capital, and firmly seize the territory around Moscow, having encircled the city." The operation was supposedly going to start several days prior to Operation Blue. Once the offensive toward the Caucasus began, *Wehrmacht* summaries over the radio and in the newspapers announced that German forces had gone on the offensive "on the southern and central sectors of the Eastern Front", but in front of Moscow the offensive operations were pursuing different goals.[10]

In reality in May-June 1942, the forces of the German central grouping did what it had been designated for them to do back in the spring. They conducted a series of offensive operations in the area of the Rzhev – Viaz'ma salient with the aim of eliminating the units of Group Belov and the partisan detachments south and southwest of Viaz'ma and the units of the 39th Army and 11th Cavalry Corps northwest of Viaz'ma, which had been operating there since the winter in the rear of the Fourth and Ninth Armies and the Third Panzer Army.

Group Belov represented the greater danger for the German forces. It was controlling territory within the triangle formed by the Viaz'ma – Smolensk, Smolensk – Zanoznaia and Zanoznaia – Viaz'ma railroads. I've already mentioned the critical importance of the railroads for supplying the troops of Army Group Center. In the words of the Soviet historian D. M. Proektor, "... the partisans and troops for more than five months had been dictating their will upon the Nazi command on the central sector of the Soviet-German front." The troops of the 39th Army and 11th Cavalry Corps fighting in semi-encirclement, using a portion of the aforementioned former defensive fortifications in this area, were diverting a significant amount of German strength. The Germans were complaining that they were compelled to have a double front, depriving the main front to the east of manpower. The frontlines here had a smaller salient centered on Kholm-Zhirkovskii protruding within the larger Rzhev – Viaz'ma salient. This inner salient, which designated troops of the Kalinin Front were occupying, is sometimes called the Belyi salient in the literature, and at other times the Kholm-Zhirkovskii salient.[11]

K. von Tippelskirch noted the anxiety of the Germans over the operations of these units operating on both sides of Viaz'ma. He mentions that two army corps consisting of several infantry divisions and one panzer division were withdrawn from the front in May 1942 for the struggle against units of Group Belov. The *Wehrmacht* operations against Group Belov received the code names "Hannover-1" and "Hannover-2". Seven divisions from the Fourth Army's two army corps and around 600 panzers took part in the offensive. At first it was intended to destroy Belov's headquarters and the headquarters of the 4th Airborne Corps through diversionary raids, and then to eliminate the entire group in the course of 2-3 days.[12]

Active offensive operations against the Soviet units within the Rzhev – Viaz'ma salient began on 24 May on several directions. The troops of the Western Front located in the enemy rear went on the defensive. Already by the end of the first day, the paratroopers were cut-off from the rest of Group Belov. Lieutenant General Belov, anticipating the start of the prepared Soviet relief operation, appealed to his commander-in-chief G.K. Zhukov: "I request the hastening of the tank group's arrival ... It is desirable to hasten Boldin's offensive [the 50th Army]..." Later P.A. Belov would write, "All of our plans in these days were based upon the firm belief that in the first days of June, no later than 5 June, a large-scale operation by the Western Front would begin." In his words, at the end of May his group together with the partisans numbered around 17,000 men. However, the Soviet operation never got underway: there was no attack by the Western Front from outside the pocket with the purpose of linking up with the encircled forces.[13]

Units of the 4th Airborne Corps and the 2nd Cavalry Division began to fight their way out to the west to link-up with the 1st Guards Cavalry Corps. They were forced to cross the Ugra River, which at that time presented a serious obstacle. On 30-31 May, they managed to make contact with the rest of Group Belov.

On 4 June P.A. Belov again appealed to the Western Front commander for permission to break out:

> The time has come to seek your counsel ... Over 12 days of heavy fighting the enemy has seized more than half of the area previously held by group. Another 24 hours of fighting and an enemy breakthrough into the center of the group and the splitting of our force is possible. Further fighting in encirclement threatens the destruction of the manpower of our forces ... I request your permission to withdraw from encirclement under the condition of the continuation of stubborn defensive fighting. The plan: to breakout east of El'nia ... with a further advance in the direction of Kirov for linking-

up with the rest of the Front. I request urgent measures, assistance and advice.

An answer from the Front headquarters arrived the next day. Two alternatives were proposed: withdrawal to the north to join Kalinin Front, or breakout to the east to the 50th Army. By a directive from Western Front headquarters, the partisans were ordered to remain in the enemy rear.[14]

General Belov, however, chose a third alternative to escape the encirclement: a withdrawal to the southeast in the direction of El'nia. The breakthrough of the ring of encircling enemy forces on 9 June was successful. By the middle of June, the escaping column had reached the Warsaw highway. In his memoirs, P.A. Belov writes that "once again, as back in January, we had to cross it, but now in a different direction and in a different place." On the night of 16 June, with extremely savage fighting, only units of the first echelon managed to break through across the Warsaw highway. They headed south and on the night of 23 June broke through to the lines of the 10th Army.

The half of Group Belov that was unable to breakthrough across the highway fell back to the north, divided into separate groups of mounted men and paratroopers, and again set off to the south. They crossed the Warsaw highway along an unpopulated stretch of the road. On 21-22 June the paratroopers and cavalrymen joined up again. The severely wounded and sick were evacuated by airplane. On the night of 24 June at an order from Front headquarters, General Belov and other senior commanders flew out from behind enemy lines. The entire remaining personnel of the group, combining into a single detachment, on the night of 27 June broke through enemy defenses and reached the friendly lines of the Western Front. Part of Group Belov became separated from the rest of the group and made its way out to the north to link-up with the Kalinin Front.[15]

F. Halder wrote in separate entries in his diary, "Unluckily, the main body of Belov's cavalry corps and of the 4th Airborne Brigade [sic] has escaped to the south. ... Cavalry Corps Belov is now floating around in the area west of Kirov." More than 10,000 men returned to friendly lines, not including the 3,000 wounded who had been evacuated earlier. Not less than 7,000 men remained behind enemy lines in the partisan units. Halder wrote further, "Quite a man [Belov] that we have to send no less than seven divisions after him." In Belov's opinion, if the four more German divisions on the containing directions are added, then 11 German divisions took part in the May fighting with his group.[16]

Despite the fact that the main body of Group Belov succeeded in escaping the encirclement, for the Red Army the outcome of this operation in an operational-strategic sense was unsuccessful: the area in the rear of the hostile troops was lost, the retention of which would have permitted the inflicting of a painful blow to the supply lines of the central German grouping.

The German "Hannover" offensives unfolded outside the boundaries of the Rzhev – Viaz'ma salient, but it is impossible to pass over the actions of General Belov's Special Group in silence. In May-June 1942 they were both a continuation and a conclusion to the winter Rzhev – Viaz'ma offensive and the first stage in Army Group Center's operations to mop-up its rear in the summer of 1942.

Much has been written about the actions of the paratroopers and cavalrymen of Belov's Special Group in the enemy rear and their breakout from enemy encirclement, although not everything. Less is known about what occurred with the Soviet forces north of Viaz'ma. There events followed a less successful scenario.

The second stage of Army Group Center's mopping-up of its rear areas was the Ninth Army's Operation Seydlitz against the units of Kalinin Front's 39th Army and 11th Cavalry Corps, which were operating between Belyi and Sychevka and occupying the Kholm-Zhirkovskii salient.[17] In a *Wehrmacht* announcement on 13 July there was mention of a large-scale offensive of German units; F. Halder made almost daily entries in his diary about the operation's progress, while General Grossmann called it a battle. These facts together with the large number of German troops committed to the operation testify to its significance for the *Wehrmacht*. No less than 12 divisions and a cavalry brigade of the Ninth Army took part in it, as well as other units.[18]

The planning of the operation began back in May. During its preparation, the commander of the Ninth Army Colonel General W. Model was wounded by a gunshot from some woods as he was flying over Soviet-occupied territory. The operation's plan featured attacks against the Soviet forces occupying the salient from four directions: first against units of the 22nd and 41st Armies holding the neck of the salient, followed two or three days later with attacks from the north and east against the 39th Army inside the salient, and finally an attack from the south two or three days after that to destroy the 11th Cavalry Corps.[19]

In H. Grossmann's opinion, by the beginning of June 1942 60,000 Soviet troops were located in the rear of the Ninth Army. According to materials of the Russian Federation Ministry of Defense's Central Archives, on 1 July 1942 Lieutenant General I. I. Maslennikov's 39th Army had eight rifle divisions, one artillery regiment, three mortar battalions, one tank battalion, and two battalions of engineers. The 11th Cavalry Corps under the command of Colonel S.V. Sokolov had four cavalry divisions on 14 May 1942, including the 18th Turkmen Cavalry Division, a mortar regiment, a mounted artillery battalion and a signals battalion.[20] These forces, fighting in semi-encirclement, had a link with the Kalinin Front and were receiving everything necessary through the "Nelidovo corridor" between the towns of Belyi and Nelidovo, which at its narrowest point was no wider than 30 kilometers, and which was being defended by units of the 22nd and 41st Armies. The defensive positions of the 41st Army's 17th Guards Rifle Division ran along the streets of Belyi.

In Russian historiography, the actions of the Soviet troops in this operation have been labeled as the "Defensive operation of the Kalinin Front's 22nd, 39th, 41st, and 3rd Air Armies in the area of Belyi, 2-27 July 1942". According to official statistics, at the start of the operation the involved Soviet forces had 187,690 soldiers and officers.[21]

The commands of the Kalinin Front and armies were aware of the German preparations for the offensive and even anticipated where the initial attacks would fall. One can judge this from discussions over a direct line in the final days of June between Front commander I.S. Konev, the commander of the 39th Army Lieutenant General I. I. Maslennikov and the commander of the 11th Cavalry Corps Colonel S.V. Sokolov. For example, Konev informed Maslennikov that "an enemy offensive from the area of Belyi to the north and northeast in the next few days cannot be ruled out." Sokolov and Maslennikov spoke about the possibility of enemy attacks at the boundary between the army and the corps, as well as at the boundary between the 39th and 22nd Armies with the aim of isolating them from each other. Maslennikov and Sokolov protested the withdrawal of divisions in their respective commands into the Front reserve, some of which were already on their way to the corridor. They reported on the situation with ammunition and food. The 11th Cavalry Corps had "one day's allotment of rifle cartridges, one-quarter of a day's allotment of artillery shells, and no mortar rounds at all. Food – 4 day's worth." The defensive fortifications were not fronted with mines and wire entanglements, because there weren't any available. The 39th Army had "3-5 days of rations and on average only one day's allotment of ammunition. In individual cases, in particular for the 150mm shells, we have a reserve of up to two daily allotments ... but for the ShVAK [heavy machine] guns only half a daily allotment. We've received machine-gun ammunition drums for the tankettes, but only three drums per machine gun ...." Both commanders requested the urgent delivery of rations and ammunition. Maslennikov said, "... I am prepared to fight on in a most disadvantageous situation, that is to say, combat in encirclement without the right to withdraw the army. For this only ammunition and food are necessary. Taking advantage of the available fortified belt, the army can conduct prolonged defensive fighting in it."[22]

Operation Seydlitz got underway on the morning of 2 July, later than planned due to bad weather. The German forces began the offensive at the narrowest sector of the corridor, attacking units of the 41st Army on the Belyi axis and units of the 22nd and 39th Armies on the Olenino axis. Soviet troops put up fierce resistance. On a number of sectors they were able to beat back the German attacks with heavy losses to the attackers.[23]

The Germans reinforced their groupings on these directions, and on 4 July launched additional attacks with active air support from the east from the Sychevka area against positions of the 39th Army's divisions. The 11th Cavalry Corps at this time was still holding its positions and repulsing attacks by small enemy groups. On 4 July, the Germans seized the village of Razboinia, where the 39th Army headquarters was located.[24]

With the commitment of fresh armor units, on 5 July the Germans added more weight to their attacks from three directions. According to German records, at 1600 on 5 July German forces attacking the narrow neck of the salient from the south and north linked-up in the village of Pushkari north of Belyi. Soviet records indicate this occurred on 6 July. The 39th Army, the 11th Cavalry Corps, as well as the left flank of the 41st Army (the 17th Guards and 135th Rifle Divisions and the 21st Tank Brigade) and the right flank of the 22nd Army (the 355th Rifle Division, part of the 380th Rifle Division, and separate units of the 185th Rifle Division) became encircled. The 22nd and 41st Armies attempted to re-open the corridor to the encircled units. The Soviet side brought up fresh units from Nelidovo to help break through the German line now blocking the salient's neck.[25]

The 39th Army command quickly made the decision to withdraw its divisions from the salient. Already on 5 July, the army's divisions and certain units of the cavalry corps abandoned their positions and retreated to the Obsha River in an area where there were some temporary bridges. On the night of 5 July and through the day of 6 July, arriving troops battled for possession of the bridges, but only several units from different divisions succeeded in crossing. Because of the impassable roads, the *Katiusha* rocket-launchers in their possession had to be blown up.

On the morning of 6 July, the remaining units of the 11th Cavalry Corps left their positions and headed to the northwest to link-up with the 39th Army. Along the way, they blew up the bridges behind them, felled trees across the forest roads, and destroyed whatever equipment they could not bring out. A German aerial reconnaissance report on that day noted a mixed column of cavalry, infantry and separate tanks that stretched for many kilometers moving along the road to the north and northwest.[26]

The German command, taking units from other sectors of the front, rushed them to the threatened crossings on the Obsha River. On 7 July the German troops attacking from east from the Sychevka area reached Belyi and created a second pocket. The Soviet forces were now split into two isolated groups, a northern and a southern. In his diary, Halder observed on 7 July, "Operation SEYDLITZ continues to develop very satisfactorily. The enemy seems to have been caught just as he was falling back. Complete success is imminent."[27]

In the northern pocket, the entire swampy, forested area between the Belyi – Olenino and Belyi – Kostritsy highways was jammed with large and small groups of Soviet commanders and Red Army troops from various divisions of the 22nd, 41st and 39th Armies and the 11th Cavalry Corps, which were striving to reach the Belyi – Olenino highway in order to escape the encirclement. Along the entire sector north of Belyi, numerous scattered, small groups of troops and individual soldiers were trying to cross the highway.

According to the recollections of those who escaped, the Germans quickly sent special groups into the woods comprised of Russian traitors and Germans who could speak Russian or one of the languages of the Caucasian and Central Asian nationalities. Dressed in the uniforms of Red Army soldiers and commanders, these groups were sent with the assignment to kill Soviet commanders and commissars, and to gather and lead the rank and file Red Army soldiers into captivity. These special teams also worked to spread false rumors and to create a sense of panic among the Soviet military men wandering through the woods and the local population. Their lies fell on fertile soil, since small groups of hungry soldiers, who by their low ranks could not know the real situation, were roaming the forests.[28]

Many recalled the terrible scenes of the encirclement. B.P. Poliakov, a signals officer in the 17th Guards Rifle Division's 26th Guards Rifle Regiment, remembered driving along the road to regiment headquarters on 5 July:

> Previously empty, it [the road] was filled with wagons and vehicles, primarily ambulances ... it was a terrible sight. I never saw anything more horrible for the rest of the war. Large shell craters already filled to the brim with water, the wreckage of wagons and vehicles strewn along the road, dead horses and human corpses. An especially dense pileup of wrecked transport and guns surrounded a small lake. The groans of the wounded carried from the direction of a wooded thicket. One heartrending voice has been burned into my memory: "Medic, medic!" It was the voice of a doomed man. Supply trains were continually hurrying along, and it cost us much exertion to make our way through the uninterrupted tangles of fallen trees and piles of equipment. The sun was setting when the last vehicles emerged from the woods a short distance away from where the regiment headquarters was located that day. Corpses were lying all around. Directly across the road I could see the torso of the chief of finances Maksimov, his legs torn away; they were quickly preparing to bury him on the spot ... Having assembled the remaining wagons, the rear services were moving further to the northwest toward a forest that was visible up ahead. Passing by Solodilovo, I spotted one of our "34"s. The tank was moving down an empty street, its turret facing the rear and sending out shot after shot ... The tank was acting as the rear guard, covering the retreat of the rear services. We hadn't yet managed to reach the woods, when German submachine gunners took the village. ... Having no communications link with the regiment, the chief of the rear services sent me to the headquarters. ... At the headquarters, an atmosphere of calm fatality reigned. You could sense that the people had done everything possible within their strength, and

> now through inertia, through the ingrained habit of duty, they were carrying their burdens to the end, to the exhaustion of their remaining strength …."[29]

Already between 7 and 9 July, units of the 41st Army were filtering out of the encirclement: around 3,000 men with mortars, machine guns and ordnance, as well as "individual men and elements" of several of the cavalry and rifle divisions of the 22nd and 39th Armies. More troops were escaping, but the Germans brought up additional forces to the breakout sector and fully sealed the ring of encirclement.[30]

In his book on the history of the German 129th Infantry Division, a veteran of the division G. Boucsein described another attempt by Soviet units to break out on the night of 10 July. His recollections allow one to see those events through the eyes of an adversary. From the stories of prisoners and deserters, intercepted radio traffic and the information from their own reconnaissance, the German command had a fairly clear picture of the condition of the Soviet troops in the northern and southern pockets and of their plans. It knew that the "woods were full of Red Army men who wanted to break out to the northwest." If initially only isolated panzers, armored cars and small groups of infantry supported by company guns patrolled the Belyi – Olenino roads, then after 8-9 July the Germans shifted additional forces from other sectors of the front and brought up heavy guns. The infantrymen took up a defense along both sides of the highway, with a front to the north and northwest against the main Russian forces, and a front to the south and east against the encircled units. The highway was studded with artillery batteries, and radio posts had been set up. The *Luftwaffe* also helped defend the road.

G. Boucsein recalls the constant attempts by Russian troops to break out of the encirclement and the help provided to them from the direction of the main Russian front. In his opinion, one breakout attempt by a large group on the night of 10 July had been thoroughly planned and prepared together with units of the 22nd Army's 380th Rifle Division outside the pocket. The encircled units maintained a continuous radio link with the division command post. The breakout attempt was coordinated down to the minute with a simultaneous attack from outside the pocket.

Around 2200, a Polikarpov Po-2 biplane [which the Germans called "the sewing machine"] heading to the southeast from the direction of the main Soviet front flew overhead. Soon the airplane returned and fired a signal rocket. It was the signal for the Soviet troops to attack. That which followed G. Boucsein called "an inferno, hell". The following combat narrative is drawn from his book.

Directly from the woods to the west, out of the mists and smoke rising from the ground, enemy infantry had closed within the range of a hand grenade toss. The Red Army men rose and rushed the German position with their battle cry of "Ura!" Hand-to-hand fighting erupted at the point of breakthrough and as far as the highway. German mortars and machine guns were firing, while artillery blasted away over open sights.

After all the attention of the Germans had been shifted to the northwest, a wedge of encircled units moved out silently from the forests on the south side of the road, out of the pocket, for an attack against the German positions. German outposts were silently eliminated in the darkness with the use of cold steel. At places, these outposts were just 30 meters from the highway. Some sound betrayed the attackers and two heavy German guns turned 180 degrees and began firing over open sights at the encircled men's positions along the edge of the forest. The encircled troops dragged up a 45mm anti-tank gun to the highway and began firing at the German guns. The attackers were approaching simultaneously from the north and the south. Artillery salvoes, the firing of mortars, the whistling shots from rifles, explosions, the rattle of machine guns and the barking shots from the main guns of tanks merged together into the cacophony of combat, in which the cries and shouts of the wounded from both sides rang out. According to Boucsein, that which was occurring was "a slice of hell". On both sides, soldiers were being killed by friendly fire. When the combat died away, both sides began retrieving their wounded, the blood trails of which were visible only with the light of day. All the wire obstacles had been breached.

At 2230, there was a second attack. The main blow was inflicted from within the pocket by a group of approximately 1,500 Red Army men led by a general. Simultaneously a second column of encircled men tried to break out of the pocket in a different place, where Soviet forces were attacking from the north to link-up with it. On the sector of one of the German battalions, 40 Red Army men succeeded in breaking through to their own side. In the process, five commissars were killed. Gaps in the German defenses were quickly filled by soldiers from the supply train.

There was a third attack at 0015 on the sector of a different German battalion. At 0300 from the southeast out of the pocket came a fourth attack, this one by a cavalry unit.

In the early light of the dawning day, a horrible scene emerged on the battlefield. The positions of the fallen on the north and south side of the road showed that they were only 30 meters away from each other. Many of the dead had terrible wounds like smashed skulls. Everywhere there were blood trails left behind by the severely wounded who had crawled away into a birch grove. Mess tins with pieces of boiled horseflesh lay among rifles with attached bayonets, submachine guns and machine guns. One Soviet shell casing was lying directly in front of a German radio operator's entrenchment.

The number of dead on the sector of III Battalion alone amounted to five commissars, 10 officers and 140 soldiers. They were unable to count the number of dead at a distance from the road, especially in the swampy forest. An anti-tank gun, four submachine guns, eight pistols, four machine guns, four sabers and approximately 40 rifles were seized as trophies. A large number of abandoned and broken weapons were lying around. Twenty-five captured horses were led away to the supply trains. Part of the surviving Soviet soldiers slipped away into swampy areas, while more were captured or killed by the Germans as they mopped up the nearby woods.[31]

The situation of the southern group of encircled units of the 39th Army and 11th Cavalry Corps turned out no less tragically. The main forces of the army and corps that approached the Obsha River on 7 and 8 July had to fight for the crossings with their last remaining ammunition and no air cover. On 8 July, the cavalry corps was subordinated to the 39th Army.

The effort to break through across the river failed, so the 39th Army's Military Council decided to preserve the remaining manpower by leading the troops into a forested area to the southeast. The eight *Katiushas* launched one last salvo of rockets and then were blown up. The men siphoned the little fuel that remained into the vehicles that were running the best, disabled the others, blew up the artillery pieces and mortars that remained without ammunition, destroyed the army's files and papers, Party documents and the army's printing equipment and headed deeply into the Smolensk area's forests and swamps. The Front headquarters lost contact with them.[32]

A note in the Kalinin Front's journal of combat operations for 9 July passes on the tragedy of the situation: "Radio communications with the 39th Army were lost at 2335 8 July; there was no response to signals from a number of the Front's radios to the radios of the 39th Army and 11th Cavalry Corps ...." The next day, the journal noted:

> In order to make contact and clarify the situation, staff officers of the Front were sent out in aircraft. Of the five officers, two returned with wounds and carried out the assignment; one has not returned and his fate is unknown; one remained in the area of Mafrinka in order to organize the withdrawal of separate groups from encirclement.

A note for 11 July records that according to a report from Lieutenant General Bogdanov, deputy commander of the 39th Army, troops had concentrated in groups in the woods in the Tupik area and were preparing to make their way out of encirclement. Regular communications with Bogdanov could not be established, because his radio had no power supply. An officer was dispatched with a power source for the radio sets.[33]

On 11-12 July, the retreating units were concentrated in the areas of Vladimirskoe, Tupik and Varvarino. Altogether, up to 7,000 men had arrived here, including up to 4,000 cavalrymen. On 13 July, a coded telegram arrived at Front headquarters with a request for food drops to be made to the encircled men, which were subsisting primarily on horse meat without salt. Local residents helped, but it was prohibited to forage among them and the order was strictly followed. Even the Germans, who were interrogating prisoners, made note of this.[34]

The command of Army Group Center, alarmed by attacks against the Second Panzer Army in the first half of July 1942 by Western Front's 10th, 16th and 61st Armies and in need of reserves, demanded the Ninth Army to accelerate the elimination of the encircled Soviet forces. After the Soviet attempt to break out on the night of 10 July failed, the Germans began to mop-up the territory. On 12 July 1942, the Ninth Army reported, "The Seydlitz offensive has been completed today." On 13 July 1942, a *Wehrmacht* announcement trumpeted the news about the encirclement and destruction of several Soviet rifle and cavalry divisions and one tank brigade. It gave a number for the prisoners taken – more than 30,000. The announcement also mentioned that 218 tanks, 591 artillery pieces, 1,300 machine guns and mortars, and other weapons and equipment had been captured or destroyed.[35]

On the following day, 14 July, Soviet newspapers published a refutation from the *Sovinformburo* under the headline "Fraudulent announcement of the Hitler command", which stated, " ... in the given case, the Hitlerites have set nothing less than a record in unpardonable lying." It informed readers:

> Between 2 and 13 July there was actual fighting in the area southwest of Rzhev. The Hitlerite forces went on the attack, trying to encircle one of our formations and cut its supply lines to the rear. As a result of combat against enemy forces superior in numbers and in the quantity of tanks, our units, having inflicted heavy damage on the Germans in personnel and equipment and suffering significant losses in return, were compelled to retreat and abandon the area they had been defending. In the course of the fighting our troops lost 7,000 killed and wounded and 5,000 missing-in-action, a significant portion of which formed partisan units ....[36]

Red Army men taken prisoner during Operation Seydlitz, July 1942. A German photograph.

Unquestionably, it was difficult to put together the entire picture of what had actually happened in those days southwest of Rzhev immediately after they occurred, and what the actual casualty toll was, but all the *Sovinformburo* announcements from the Kalinin Front in those days spoke only about the successful repulse of enemy attacks and German losses. After 19 July, the fighting in the area fell under the designation "battles of local significance".[37]

In reality even after the Germans declared Operation Seydlitz finished on 13 July, fighting continued for the forces of Kalinin Front both inside and outside the pocket. Units of the 22nd and 41st Armies attempted to break through the ring of encirclement, while separate groups continued to trickle into their lines north and south of Belyi. The main part of the encircled forces began a withdrawal from a forested area to the north toward the Obsha River. Along the road leading to the river, these units had to fight their way through enemy blocking forces. According to the recollections of S. Mikaelian, they were moving toward the point of breakthrough in large groups. They made their way through forests and swamps and marched through burning villages under enemy mortar and tank fire. They sought to avoid clashes with large enemy garrisons in the villages. Men were also moving in small groups to avoid casualties from the mortar fire.[38]

The Germans knew that large enemy forces were still present in the swampy forests. Information from deserters established that a group of approximate 1,500 men led by the General of Cavalry Ivanov was concentrated in the forests east of the Belyi – Olenino road, while on 17 July another large group of Red Army men crossed the Obsha River to the north. This group included approximately 8,000 men, including the commander of the 39th Army Lieutenant General Maslennikov, his deputy Lieutenant General Bogdanov, the 39th Army's artillery commander Major General Kuteinikov and other commanders. According to prisoner interrogations, General Maslennikov initially had wanted to move to the northwest with tanks, but due to the loss of all the tanks, he had been forced to remain with the remnants of his army until 18 July.[39]

The Kalinin Front command ordered the evacuation of the 39th Army's Military Council and a group of staff officers, which was in fact done overnight between 17 July and 18 July. According to German information, on the night of 18 July, nine Soviet U-2 airplanes flew into the pocket, three of which crashed upon landing. The recollections of the pilot who flew General Maslennikov out of the pocket have been preserved. He recalled that the 41-year-old General Maslennkov, who'd been wounded in the leg, rode up to the airplane together with General Bogdanov on horses, wearing cloaks and forage caps. Maslennikov hobbled up to the airplane with the aid of a walking stick. The pilot asked Bogdanov if he was leaving too. Bogdanov replied. "We'll break out. We need airplanes. There are a lot of wounded."[40]

A comparison with the conduct of another army commander in the exact same situation, the 33rd Army's General M.G. Efremov, suggests itself. When they sent an airplane for him in order to bring him out of the encirclement, he declined to board the plane, saying, "I came here with the soldiers and I will leave with the soldiers." He sent out unit colors with the aircraft, led the units toward a breakout, was wounded, and shot himself to avoid becoming a prisoner. I.I. Maslennikov, wounded in the leg, climbed into the aircraft and flew away.[41]

Command of the troops that remained in encirclement was laid upon the 39th Army's deputy commander Lieutenant General Bogdanov and the deputy chief of the 39th Army's Political Department, Battalion Commissar Shabalin. In the course of a day, all the scattered and disorganized units of the army were combined into a single regiment, which became part of the 256th Rifle Division. Altogether there were up to 5,000 men. The units of the 11th Cavalry Corps had a remaining strength of up to 4,000 men and 2,000 horses. The men were armed with rifles, submachine guns, a small number of light machine guns, and a heavy machine gun. Ammunition was low. There were great difficulties in finding edible food.

On this same day, encircled troops crossed the Belyi – Kostritsy road. General Bogdanov decided to make a sudden breakout attempt, under the cover of darkness, coordinating his actions with units of the 22nd and 41st Armies.[42]

From 15 July, units of the 22nd Army's 185th Rifle Division began operations to make contact with the Bodganov's encircled group at points of a possible breakout. On 18 July, the division sent a reconnaissance group through the German lines to establish contact with Bodganov, and on 20 July, launched a probing attack in the sector where Bodganov's group might emerge. The 41st Army was undertaking similar operations on its sectors. On 20 July, the Kalinin Front's air force conducted 202 individual sorties for purposes of bombing German lines, reconnaissance, and covering Bogdanov's withdrawal from encirclement. Finally, on 21 July at 1900, the 22nd and 41st Armies began operations to secure the escape of the encircled units, which started at 2200.[43]

Despite stubborn German resistance, already by 2300 3,500 men had come out of the encirclement, and by 0400 22 July – more than 10,000 men. In the documents of 22nd Army, there is a report for 22 July from a Military Council member, P.E. Smokachev:

> People are emerging in an organized fashion. Men are collapsing from utter exhaustion and the lack of food. The bulk of those who have come out have gathered at an assembly point, [and there is] heavy movement in the corridor through the German lines. Most

Lieutenant General I.A. Bogdanov, deputy commander of the 39th Army, made Major General in July 1942.

Colonel S.V. Sokolov, commander of the 11th Cavalry Corps.

of the men are armed with rifles and submachine guns. The breakthrough was highly organized. The gates were opened. Bogdanov began to form up the troops and dandily led his men out of the encirclement with the support of his closest assistant, the army's deputy chief of artillery."[44]

Lieutenant General Bogdanov himself was wounded and evacuated to a hospital in Kalinin, where he passed away. He was buried on 24 July 1942 on Lenin Square in the city of Kalinin. He was awarded the Order of Lenin posthumously, though among veterans of that fighting there is the conviction that General Bogdanov was worthy of the title Hero of the Soviet Union.[45]

From the German side, this breakout looked as follows. A shock group was formed for the breakthrough, which was to clear the way forward and secure the flanks. Then the main force was to follow it through the German lines. Between the two groupings there was a company-sized detachment of approximately 150 officers. In the twilight hours after an eight-hour march, the Russians attacked. Not long before this, a coordinated attack by Russian regiments toward the southeast began from outside the pocket. At the boundary between two German divisions, which suffered heavy casualties, a gap was created, through which many hundreds of Red Army men escaped the pocket. The Soviet side lost 460 killed, among which were many officers, and 172 taken prisoner. The Germans called Major General of Cavalry Ivanov, commander of the 18th Cavalry Division, the hero of the breakout operation. He was severely wounded in the action and died on the battlefield, despite the fact that the Germans gave him medical aid. The Germans buried him with

Guards Senior Lieutenant I.I. Zhukov, who in July 1942 flew Lieutenant General Maslennikov out of encirclement.

military honors on 22 July. According to the Germans, a large number of Soviet soldiers were unable to break out and slipped away back into the swampy forests.

Despite the fact that the German army command determined that these remaining scattered Soviet groups were unable to undertake serious operations, it decided on 22 July to form a security line opposite the large forested zone as a screen against attempts to filter out of the pocket. According to information from deserters, there were still around 8,000 Red Army men in the forest. Numerous large and small groups continued to attempt to break out to the west. They were taken prisoner at a rate of 100 a day immediately after 22 July. According to some German sources, the final stray groups held out until October. F. Halder in his diary entry for 19 July observed, "Operation SEYDLITZ is continuing satisfactorily with the new mission to mop up the forest area north of the Smolensk – Viaz'ma road."[46]

Individual groups continued to escape the pocket north and south of Belyi in the direction of Rzhev and Zubtsov until the end of July and even in August. According to the scholars M. Vorob'ev and V. Usov, approximately 18,000 men eventually made their way out of the encirclement.[47]

Losses were being calculated already during the operation. At the end of July 1942, the Kalinin Front's total losses of personnel were summed up for the month (see Table 3).

Table 3: Total personnel losses of the Kalinin Front for July 1942

Formation	Killed	Wounded	Missing-in-action	Other causes	Sick, hospitalized	Total
22nd Army	1,433	3,279	3,905	27	699	9,343
39th Army	582	269	22,749	33	14	23,647
41st Army	2,000	4,156	6,347	868	531	13,902
11th Cavalry Corps	371	316	14,071	42	30	14,830
Total	4,386	8,020	47,072	970	1,274	60,722

Source: TsAMO RF, F. 213, Op. 2002, D. 402, L. 48, 49.

The total losses of missing-in-action alone in the 39th, 22nd and 41st Armies and the 11th Cavalry Corps amounted to more than 47,000 men. It is difficult to say how many of these were actually killed, taken prisoner or remained behind to fight on in partisan units, but this number is close to the German total for the number of captured Russian prisoners. In addition, the 11th Cavalry Corps alone reported losing 9,472 horses, out of a total loss of horses equaling 15,472.[48]

Let the readers not be surprised that the loss of horses was indicated together with the human losses. In the war years, the loss of horses was tracked according to the same rules as the loss of personnel. Horses served side by side with the soldiers: they went on the attack, starved in the enemy rear, hauled pieces of artillery out of mud, carried out the wounded, and even with their deaths, their flesh saved famished men. At the same time, even if the people knew that they were losing their endurance, the horses nobly continued to do their own work.

According to German data, as a result of the entire operation, up to 50,000 Russians were taken prisoner, and 230 tanks, 58 airplanes, 760 guns of all types were destroyed or captured, as well as thousands of individual firearms. Even today, official Russian historiography attempts to reduce the Kalinin Front's losses in the operation. For example, in *Voenno-istoricheskii zhurnal*, No. 2 (1999), the total casualties in this operation were set at 20,360 soldiers and officers, of whom 7,432 were lost irrevocably, and 12,928 were wounded or sick. The number of missing-in-action is totally omitted.[49]

The losses of the units and divisions that took part in the operation were so large, that already on 13 July 1942 the 17th Guards Rifle Division was withdrawn into the second echelon for refitting and replacements. At the beginning of August, the 11th Cavalry Corps' 18th Cavalry Division was disbanded, and the 39th Army was reformed on the basis of the 58th Army. The remnants of the 373rd, 381st, 256th, the 252nd and other rifle divisions were withdrawn for reforming.[50]

The results of this operation for the Red Army were unsuccessful and even tragic. With the loss of the Kholm-Zhirkovskii salient, the Soviet troops lost an important staging area, the use of which the command was counting upon in the future to resolve strategic tasks. In I.S. Konev's opinion, this staging area "would have been very useful to us ... for implementing offensive operations ... In principle we might at any time bring up additional forces to forward positions within the salient and launch an attack that would have emerged deeply in the rear of the entire enemy grouping."[51]

Moreover, having lost this staging area, the Red Army command not only lost an opportunity to marshal reserves, as had been planned earlier, but on the contrary had to search for reserves to restore a whole number of units and divisions to combat effectiveness. The most terrible thing was the loss of tens of thousands of soldiers! They all endured the tragedy of encirclement and the majority – the hardships of combat, an unknown death or German captivity. The fate of some of them is known, but nothing is known about the fate of thousands of others. This also relates to generals. The place of burial of the deputy commander of the 22nd Army Major General A. D. Berezin, who repeatedly went back into the pocket to bring out groups of soldiers, is only presumably known. His service to the Armed Forces and the country has not received due notice and praise.

Major General P.S. Ivanov's situation in his final minutes is also still unclear. In the report of P.E. Smokachev, it is stated that he was "wounded in the leg on our side of the lines". The Germans write that they gave assistance to the wounded Ivanov, but he died on the battlefield and they buried him with military honors. However, a 1993 article in the *Voenno-istoricheskii zhurnal* about General Ivanov states, "Located inside the pocket and badly wounded, he committed suicide in July 1942." Nothing is known about his place of burial. Rzhev searchers from the "In Remembrance of the 29th Army" team assert that during a joint trip in the 1990s to battle sites in the area, G. Boucsein told them that General Ivanov was buried in the vicinity of a cemetery in "Karskoe" (possibly Klevtsovo,

Major General A.D. Berezin accepts the Guards Banner for the 17th Guards Rifle Division, near Belyi, Kalinin Oblast, 1942.

Major General P.P. Miroshnichenko, 39th Army chief of staff, killed when coming out of encirclement.

Major General P.S. Ivanov, commander of the 18th Cavalry Division, killed when coming out of encirclement in July 1942.

which is not far from the point of breakout). The *Voenno-istoricheskii zhurnal* also informed readers about Major General P.P. Miroshnichenko, the 39th Army's chief of staff: "Killed-in-action in July 1942. Buried in Tver', although according to information from the Tver' Oblast military commissariat, P.P. Miroshnichenko isn't listed among those buried within the oblast.[52]

In our view, the blame for the tragedy of the 39th Army and 11th Cavalry Corps should be placed on the Kalinin Front command, the *Stavka*, and to a certain degree, those who worked out the plan for the winter 1942 Rzhev – Viaz'ma operation. It was precisely as a result of this operation that units of the Western Front's 33rd Army (which were destroyed in April), the troops of Belov's Special Group, and the forces of the Kalinin Front's 39th Army and 11th Cavalry Corps all wound up in the German rear. It should be recalled that units of the 29th Army were also encircled within the framework of the same operation.

Likely, it was just because of these mistakes by the Soviet higher command, which led to such tragic consequences, that the fate of the 39th Army and 11th Cavalry Corps, and together with them, those who remained lying in the Belyi and Smolensk swamps or who died in German imprisonment, for many long decades was forgotten by military historians. At the end of the 1980s, the forester N.I. Gromov came upon the remains of a man and a horse in the vicinity of Belyi District's village of Verkhov'e. In the process of interring them, an Order of the Red Banner was discovered. From its number, researchers were able to determine that the Order belonged to N.N. Glushkov, the chief-of-staff of the 18th Cavalry Division.[53]

The main result of Operation Seydlitz for the *Wehrmacht* was the liquidation of the "second front" within the German Rzhev – Viaz'ma salient. The territory lying between Sychevka and Belyi had been swept clean of a large grouping of regular Soviet troops. Already

The grave of Major General A.D. Berezin, Belyi District, Kalinin Oblast.

on 6 July, the Germans re-occupied Kholm-Zhirkovskii, and on 7 July, the Andreevo areas of Smolensk Oblast.[54] Although partisan units and small groups of encircled men remained on the territory of the former Kholm-Zhirkovskii salient, they represented no serious threat to the Ninth Army.

However, the courage, tenacity, and loyalty to their duty and country displayed by the troops of the 39th, 22nd and 41st Armies and the 11th Cavalry Corps were not in vain. Here it is worth citing the words of the already mentioned *Sovinformburo* announcement from 14 July 1942: "… the Germans are losing thousands and thousands of men daily on the Soviet-German front. This, despite the temporary successes of the German forces, is gradually eroding the Nazi military machine and preparing the ground for Germany's defeat in this war."[55]

In reality, even though there are no composite figures for the German casualties in this operation and our own data for them are dubious, German historians confirm that the units that took part in Operation Seydlitz were bled white and required replacements: "… this fighting demanded such exertions from the [Ninth] army, that instead of the proposed transfer of units to the south, it required reserves itself." Those units of the Ninth Army freed up after Operation Seydlitz were compelled to remain within the Rzhev – Viaz'ma salient. H. Grossmann wrote in his book about the Rzhev battles: "Now, after eliminating the second front, the possibility appeared to gather strength and create a continuous line of defense again."[56]

In the aggregate, the troops of 23 German divisions were committed into Operations Hannover and Seydlitz, which was almost a third of the 77 divisions of Army Group Center. This allows us to assess on the whole the use of the Army Group's strength in the summer 1942 campaign. In his time, the Soviet historian D. M. Proektor expressed his opinion about why Army Group Center was not actively involved in Operation Blau:

> The troops of Army Group Center could not have taken part in a new general offensive ... because for the entire spring and summer of 1942, they were pinned down by heroic Soviet partisans [having in mind as well the regular troops of the Western and Kalinin Fronts fighting in the German rear] ... Von Kluge was forced to turn part of his forces against 'the partisans and troops between Smolensk, Viaz'ma ... and at Rzhev.' This 'complicated Army Group Center's participation in the main offensive on the southern wing of the Soviet-German front in the summer of 1942, which was then underway.'"[57]

This can be considered the main result of the defensive operations of the Western and Kalinin Fronts in May-July 1942.

One can speak boldly as well about the perceptible influence of our forces' operations on the Rzhev – Viaz'ma axis for the entire summer 1942 campaign, in addition to May-July. I.S. Konev recalled that in the latter part of the winter of 1941/1942, the General Staff had formed an intention to straighten out the frontlines in order to obtain reserves "... to liquidate those convolutions, which appeared in the course of the offensive of our forces." They had in view the salients in the areas of Demiansk, Kholm, Velikie Liuki and elsewhere. Justifying the rejection of this plan, I.S. Konev wrote:

> We became convinced of the importance of the salients on the Northwestern Front, and particularly on the Kalinin and Western Fronts. The Germans did not undertake any active operations here in the course of all of 1942, and in particular didn't do this because a threat continued to hang constantly over them ... In the complex situation during the summer and autumn of 1942, when fighting was going on at Stalingrad, the configuration of our frontlines tied up large enemy forces."[58]

At the same time, as a result of Operations Hannover and Seydlitz, in May-July the operational situation for Army Group Center improved significantly: there were no longer any regular Red Army forces in its rear. This greatly helped the German divisions to withstand the subsequent offensive launched by the armies of Western and Kalinin Fronts during the First Rzhev – Sychevka operation in July-September 1942.

4

The Second Attempt … "By the end of the second day, seize the city of Rzhev"[1] – The First Rzhev – Sychevka (Gzhatsk) Offensive, 30 July–30 September 1942

The history of the First Rzhev – Sychevka Offensive of 1942 has been covered to the present day, as a rule, according to versions that have been laid out in such, one can say, "established" multi-volume encyclopedias and reference military-historical publications of the Soviet period, as *Istoriia Velikoi otechestvennoi voiny Sovetskogo Soiuza* [History of the Patriotic War], *Istoriia Vtoroi mirovoi voiny 1939-1945* [History of the Second World War 1939-1945], *Sovetskaia voennaia entsiklopediia* [Soviet Military Encyclopedia] and others. In the four-volume *Velikaia otechestvennaia voina 1941-1945: Voenno-istoricheskie ocherki* [Great Patriotic War 1941-1945], published by *Nauka* in 1998, the operation didn't even receive mention in the chronicle of events of 1942. Out of fairness, it should be said that in the new edition of the *Voennaia entsiklopediia*, certain supplemental material has been added and clarifications have been made in the description of the operation, though fundamentally it hasn't changed.[2]

In the works mentioned above, the main goal of the Rzhev – Sychevka operation was given as tying up Army Group Center's forces on the central axis, in order to deprive it the possibility to transfer divisions to the south, where the battle for Stalingrad and the struggle for the Caucasus were unfolding. The majority of these sources say that the operation involved Kalinin Front's 29th and 30th Armies and the 3rd Air Army, and Western Front's 20th and 31st Armies with the 1st Air Army. Sometimes, the commitment of Western Front's 5th and 33rd Armies into the operation is mentioned.

Having launched the offensive on 30 July, the Kalinin Front became bogged down in fighting north of Rzhev because of frequent summer downpours. The Western Front's attack, which started on 4 August, had more success: the German defenses were breached in the area of Pogoreloe Gorodishche, and by 23 August, Kalinin Oblast's city of Zubtsov and Smolensk Oblast's village of Karmanovo had both been liberated. This date has been given as the endpoint of the operation.

The Soviet sources consider the operation a success, not only because the enemy was forced to keep units, which were ready to head south, here on the central axis, but also because the Germans had to shift reserves from other sectors of the front to stop the Soviet offensive. At the same time, though, they consider the operation incomplete, because neither Rzhev nor Sychevka was liberated. The failure to capture these objectives was attributed to the rainy weather as well as the insufficient strength and means. Almost always, one sees the words of G.K. Zhukov about the "lack of one or two armies", which prevented the destruction of the "entire German Rzhev – Viaz'ma grouping." Within the framework of the operation, participants recall the enormous meeting clashes, when both sides committed all of their troops designated for operating on the Zubtsov, Sychevka and Karmanovo directions into the fighting. The total losses of the *fronts* in the operation, according to official data, amounted to 193,683 men.

The analysis of documents from the *fronts* and armies that took part in the offensive contradicts some of the main points in the official Soviet treatment of the operation. This concerns first of all the assertion that by 23 August, "the attacking potential of the Soviet forces had been exhausted, and they went over to the defense," as well as even the cited territorial scale of the operation: Rzhev – Sychevka. I am offering my own description of the operation, based on documents of the Western and Kalinin Fronts, and of the 30th, 29th, 31st, 20th, 5th and 33rd Armies. At the same time, I don't in any way pretend to offer an exhaustive and detailed study of the course of the operation, and I emphasize that much remains to be learned about it.[3]

Let us recall, that the offensive of the Western and Kalinin Fronts that had been designated to begin in June 1942 did not take place because of the transfer of Soviet forces to the south, where a tragic situation was taking shape, as well as because Army Group Center had mopped up its rear areas. However, the "Map-solution of the commanders of the 5th, 33rd and 49th Armies for seizing Viaz'ma" and the "Map-solution of the 20th and 43rd Armies for seizing Viaz'ma" dated 17 June 1942, and the "Map-plan of the 20th Army's offensive in the Gzhatsk area" dated 21 June 1942 allow one to assert the planning for an offensive on the Western Front was still continuing, and first of all on the Gzhatsk – Viaz'ma axis that was so favored by the Western Front commander.[4] According to Zhukov's memoirs, at the beginning of July the Supreme Commander I.V. Stalin phoned him and asked "whether I could organize an offensive with the Front's forces in order to divert the enemy's attention from the Southwestern Direction, where a difficult situation for us was forming." Zhukov replied:

> Such an offensive would be useful and it could be quickly prepared. One – on the left wing of the Front from the Kirov – Bolkhov area; the other – on the right flank in the Pogoreloe Gorodishche area, which it would be desirable to conduct in cooperation with the Kalinin Front.[5]

In the wake of the discussion with the Supreme Commander, a plan arose for an offensive by the 20th Army, called Operation "Sverdlovsk", designed to destroy the enemy's Sychevka grouping. Preparations for the offensive were to begin on 19 July and be completed by 31 July. The 20th Army was to operate in cooperation with other armies of the Front. The "Map-plan of the offensive operation of the 5th, 20th and 31st Armies from 4 to 7 August 1942" confirms this, as do other materials. However, having given new axes for possible offensive, G.K. Zhukov didn't abandon his intentions to attack on the Gzhatsk direction as well.[6]

In the *Stavka* directive from 16 July about conducting an offensive in the Rzhev area, the left-wing of the Kalinin Front and the right-wing of the Western Front were assigned through joint operations to "clear the enemy from the territory to the north of the Volga River in the Rzhev area and the ground to the east of the Vazuza River in the Zubtsov, Karamzino and Pogoreloe Gorodishche areas; to seize the cities of Rzhev and Zubtsov; and to reach the Volga and Vazuza Rivers and firmly dig in along them, having first secured bridgeheads in the vicinities of Rzhev and Zubtsov" – all between 28 July and 5 August 1942.[7] The offensive was to include Major General D.D. Leliushenko's 30th Army, Major General V.I. Shvetsov's 29th Army, and Major General of Aviation M.M. Gromov's 3rd Air Army of Colonel-General I.S. Konev's Kalinin Front; and Major General V. S. Polenov's 31st Army, Lieutenant General M.A. Reiter's 20th Army, and Lieutenant General of Aviation S.A. Khudiakov's 1st Air Army of General of the Army G.K. Zhukov's Western Front.

We don't know the *Stavka* directives about the involvement of other armies, but *front* and army documents, in particular the above mentioned map, as well as the "Map-preliminary plan for the 33rd Army's offensive operation in the Gzhatsk area, 9-10 August 1942" and the "Map-plan for the 33rd Army's offensive operation in the area west of Medyn' for 11 August" allow us to assert that the commander of the Western Front planned from the outset to use Lieutenant General I.I. Fediuninsky's 5th Army and Lieutenant General M.S. Khozin's 33rd Army; moreover, the 33rd Army was given a large role in the offensive. It was to penetrate the enemy's defenses and, "developing the success in the Ostroluch'e, Silenki, and Gzhatsk direction, to destroy the enemy's Gzhatsk grouping in concert with units of the 5th Army." The 5th Army in the Western Front's operation was to launch a secondary attack and "reach the line Gorodok, Karmanovo, Samuilovo, where in cooperation with the 20th Army it was to destroy the enemy grouping north of the Titovka and Yauza Rivers, after which, pivoting its front to the south, it was to reach the Gzhatsk area and to the west of it with its main forces." To support the 5th and 33rd Armies, it was planned to regroup the greater portion of the Front's artillery of reinforcement from the 31st and 20th Armies to previously prepared positions, at first in the 5th Army sector, and then the 33rd Army's sector. There was also the intention to redirect a significant amount of the Front's aviation to support these armies' operations.[8]

It should be noted that these armies attacked with only a portion of their forces. The 5th Army, on the direct axis to Moscow, was ordered to maintain a solid defense, since here was the shortest distance between the front lines and the capital. Later, after the 20th Army concluded its Pogoreloe Gorodishche operation, it was planned to introduce a mobile group of the Army (consisting of the 2nd Guards Cavalry and 8th Tank Corps) under the command of Lieutenant General Tiurin to destroy the enemy northwest of Gzhatsk with a subsequent link-up with troops of the 33rd Army. In the order to the army on 31 August, after breaking through the enemy's defense and emerging west and northwest of Gzhatsk, the pivoting of this group to the east was foreseen "in order to envelop Gzhatsk from the west and to destroy the Gzhatsk grouping" in cooperation with units of the 5th and 33rd Armies. Later, in the Front's documents, the actions of the 5th and 33rd Armies would be called as being "along the Viaz'ma direction." Thus, still one more objective of the operation was the liberation of Gzhatsk. Therefore in the future, this operation would become known as the Rzhev – Sychevka (Gzhatsk) operation.

Later in 1979, a map of the operation's design showing the planned participation of the 5th and 33rd Armies was published in A. I. Radzievsky's book *Proryv* [Breakthrough].[9] From it one can see that it is fully possible to call the operation the Rzhev – Gzhatsk offensive. However, since the results of the offensive in the direction of Gzhatsk were minimal and failed to obtain that designated objective, in the future this part of the overall operation was simply forgotten.

As already related above, the operation was planned to be swift – just ten days. Already "by the end of the second day of the operation", the 30th Army was to seize Rzhev. The 29th Army was to reach the Volga on the third day, while on the second day of the offensive the 20th Army was to reach the line of the Vazuza and Gzhatsk Rivers. The 5th Army was given only three days to complete its part of the operation.[10] The Kalinin Front was to launch the operation first on 28 July, followed by the Western Front's offensive on 31 July. The hopes for a swift operation rested on the fact that by the end of July 1942, a powerful Soviet grouping had assembled at the center of the Soviet-German front.

Before the start of the offensive the armies that were supposed to take part in it received reinforcements. On the Western Front, the 20th and 31st Armies created mobile groups based upon tank brigades, as well as the 6th and 8th Tank and 2nd Guards Cavalry Corps. Divisions and units of the 7th and 8th Guards Rifle Corps also participated in the offensive, the former in the sector of the 33rd Army and the latter in the sector of the 20th Army. As a result by the beginning of August 1942 a grouping had been created on the approaches to Moscow that consisted of six combined-arms armies and two air armies of the Kalinin and Western Fronts, which included (beyond those in the Guards rifle corps) 43 rifle divisions, up to 72 rifle brigades, at least 21 tank brigades, 67 artillery units, 37 battalions of Guards mortar (*Katiusha*) battalions and other units. Altogether, excluding the Guards rifle corps, this grouping numbered more than 486,000 soldiers and officers. Moreover, these figures aren't definitive; they vary in the documents of the *fronts* and armies, which creates difficulties when summing them.

The 20th and 31st Armies and the 6th and 8th Tank Corps had 949 tanks of all types

Acceptance into the Party before a battle, summer 1942.

on the Sychevka axis. On the Gzhatsk direction, the 5th Army had 120 tanks and the 33rd Army had 256 more, for a total of 376 tanks. On the Rzhev axis, the 30th Army alone had 390 tanks. Thus, excluding the 29th Army, the two *fronts* could hurl 1,715 tanks against the Germans.[11]

The density of artillery on the axes of main attacks in the 33rd Army was 40-45 guns per kilometer and in the 20th Army – 122 guns per kilometer. The Kalinin Front had 115-140 artillery pieces per kilometer of the front.[12]

In the attack sectors of the Kalinin and Western Front's shock groupings, the Soviet side managed to obtain a significant superiority in troop strength, tanks and artillery (see Table 4).

Table 4: Correlation of forces prior to the First Rzhev – Sychevka (Gzhatsk) offensive 30 July 1942-30 September 1942 on sectors of the attacking armies

	In breakthrough sectors					
	30th Army	29th Army	31st Army	20th Army	5th Army	33rd Army
In "infantry", "active fighters", "active bayonets"	3:1	"Overwhelming superiority"	4:1	6.9:1	7:1	3.5:1
In artillery	2:1	"Overwhelming superiority"	6:1	6.2:1	7:1	1.6:1
In armor	2:1		22(?):1[a]	7.2:1	"Complete superiority"	

Notes:

[a] The figure for the correlation of forces in armor for the 31st Army is dubious, although the author has checked repeatedly; most likely, it is missing a decimal point, so 2.2:1 is correct.

Source: Compiled from TsAMO RF, F. 208, Op. 2511, D. 1044, L. 187; D. 1463, L. 46ob, 80, 119ob, 164; D. 1464, L. 8.

According to data in the latest edition of the *Voennaia entsiklopediia*, around 1,100 aircraft were available to support the Soviet offensive.[13]

In the course of the operation, due to the combat losses and the departure of separate units, the combat strength of the six armies dwindled, and on 5 September they totaled 334,808 men, 2,947 field guns, 412 tanks and 571 rocket-launchers, but despite the fact that the Germans brought up fresh reserves, on the whole the Soviet side retained its numerical advantages in men and equipment. For example, the chief of staff of the 5th Army noted that in its sector, it held a 2:1 advantage in men, 2.3:1 in artillery and 1.5:1 in tanks. At the same time, though, he expressed regret over these correlations, since in his opinion, they were adequate to break through an enemy defense, but were insufficient to exploit the breach.[14]

By 10 September, combat attrition had dropped the aggregate strength of the six Soviet armies even further, which now amounted to 184,265 men, 3,340 field guns and 306 tanks, but the Soviet forces continued to hold advantages: 1.9:1 in men and 2.7:1 in artillery. In tanks, for the entire front of the six armies, the numerical superiority in tanks was minimal.[15]

The 30th, 29th, 31st and 20th Armies at the start of the operation faced nine infantry and motorized divisions of the German Ninth Army. Nine infantry divisions of the Third Panzer Army were opposite the 5th and 33rd Armies, but in the front line of the designated breakthrough sector, only six infantry regiments, with two more in reserve. In the course of the operation, however, the enemy grouping grew significantly with the arrival of reserves and reinforcements.[16]

The existing literature on the Rzhev – Sychevka operation notes the successful set of measures taken by the Soviet side to achieve the factor of surprise for the offensive.[17] However, this wasn't so. F. Halder made a number of entries in his diary on the days leading up to the offensive, noting the build-up of Soviet forces:

> 10 June -- ... in Ninth Army sector, the enemy is evidently dispersing his forces on the northern front. Evidently, the Russians are bringing up fresh forces ...
> 11 June -- ... Situation in enemy line facing northern front of Ninth Army is unclear. (Railroad movements, concentration of armor.) Nor is there any clear picture of what the enemy facing the northeastern front is up to (increase in enemy artillery).
> 26 July – The enemy regrouping, including in front of the Ninth Army, allows one to assume that new attacks are being prepared.[18]

Both Soviet and German veterans of the fighting, recalling the summer of 1942, claimed that on the eve of the offensive, the Soviet side broadcast messages about the offensive being readied, which even included information about the jumping-off date. It is difficult to explain this fact from any rational standpoint, but these messages prompted the local civilians to evacuate before the offensive, particularly from the city of Rzhev, giving clear notice to the Germans that something was up. Thus, the Soviet offensive on the

Moving up into position, Kalinin Front, summer of 1942. Photo by B. Vdovenko.

Flamethrowers of the 1245th Rifle Regiment before the battle, summer of 1942.

central sector of the Soviet-German front could not have been a surprise for the Germans.[19]

On the 30th of July, the Kalinin Front's offensive began with a powerful artillery preparatory barrage. The Front's artillery commander Colonel General N.M. Khlebnikov recalled, "The power of the fire attack was so great, that after several tentative attempts to answer the fire, the German artillery fell silent. The two forward positions of the enemy's main defensive belt were smashed, and the troops occupying them were almost completely wiped out."[20] By the end of the first day, units of the 30th Army had broken through on a front of 9 kilometers and to a depth of 6-7 kilometers.

On the morning of the first day of Kalinin Front's offensive, heavy rains began which continued for several days. The roads became quagmires of mud, and the small streams in the area, of which there are many, turned into wide and raging rivers. N.M. Khlebnikov shared his impression of those days:

> Whoever attacked back then in the lowlands and swamps in the vicinity of Rzhev will scarcely ever forget these days. Rain was coming down in torrents, instantly filling the freshly dug entrenchments. Your feet became stuck so firmly in the black, viscous glop that it would trap boots like claws ... The muck was our main adversary.[21]

Under these conditions, units of the 30th Army became bogged down in bitter fighting in the area of Polunino north of Rzhev, and its offensive ground to a halt.

The 29th Army failed to penetrate the German lines. An after-action report explains why:

Katiusha rocket launchers announce the opening of Western Front's offensive, 4 August 1942.

German prisoners, Western Front, August 1942.

> In view of the heavily saturated soil after the downpours, the tanks became mired, and the infantry became pinned down. ... Only after an hour had passed did the division commander continue ... the offensive without the tanks. The rallied infantry advanced again and ran into enemy firing positions that opened up a withering fire; as a result, the infantry suffered heavy losses and became pinned down again in a zone beaten by enemy artillery and mortar fire. The offensive sputtered to a halt.[22]

Because of the muddy roads, the Western Front didn't begin active offensive operations until 4 August. As a result, the interval of time between the start of the two *fronts*' offensive increased to five days. The Western Front's initiation of the offensive, as with the case of its neighboring Kalinin Front, began with a powerful artillery preparation, as a result of which more than 80 percent of the enemy's weapons were knocked out. The German defenses were penetrated on both sides of Pogoreloe Gorodishche, and the mobile groups of the armies rushed into the breaches: the 31st Army's toward Zubtsov, the 20th Army's toward Sychevka. By the evening of 6 August, the breach in the German front had expanded up to 30-kilometers wide, and Soviet troops had penetrated to a depth of 25 kilometers. Attacking troops were closing upon the line of the Gzhatsk and Vazuza Rivers.[23]

Paying tribute to the heroism and selflessness of the Soviet troops, it is also worth mentioning here the measures taken to carry out the well-known Order No. 227 from 28 July 1942 – the "Not a step back!" order. On this same day, the Western Front command ordered the formation of blocking detachments and penal companies to begin. Later in his report on the operation, G.K. Zhukov wrote:

> In order to prevent the lagging behind of separate elements and for the struggle against cowards and panic-mongers, officers specially appointed by the armies' Military

Rations being delivered to the front on horses due to the muddy quagmire caused by the heavy rains. The Pogoreloe Gorodishche area, 10 August 1942.

Crossing a river line, Kalinin Front, summer of 1942.

> Councils followed behind each separate attacking battalion of the first echelon in a tank. As a result of all the undertaken measures, the troops of the 31st and 20th Armies successfully broke through the enemy's defense.[24]

Here we can also mention the appearance of a *Stavka* directive regarding the results of the two *fronts*' aviation in the first four to five days of the operation. Of the 400 fighters assigned to take part in the operation, "given the complete absence of enemy aviation on the first day of the offensive, and the thrice-fold numerical advantage over the enemy on subsequent days", 140 aircraft were put out of action: 51 fighters due to combat losses, and 89 – due to mechanical problems. The *Stavka* viewed this as a "sign of plain sabotage, of saving one's own skin on the part of some of the flight staff, who ... were striving to avoid combat." It was proposed to create penal squadrons and penal infantry companies from such pilots.[25]

On 5 August, "in connection with the commonality of the tasks being conducted in the Rzhev area by the troops of the Western and Kalinin Fronts, and in order to direct them in the future toward a single, common goal", the *Stavka* of the Supreme High Command appointed General of the Army G.K. Zhukov in command over all the operations in the Rzhev region. Zhukov proposed to liberate Rzhev with the forces of the Western Front's 31st Army and Kalinin Front's 30th Army as soon as 9 August; the 20th Army intended to liberate Sychevka on 7 August, on the same day that units of the 5th Army were to go on the attack and link-up with the left-flank units of the 20th Army by 9 August.[26]

On these days, alarm appears in F. Halder's war diary about the large breach in the Ninth Army's sector, and measures are noted for closing it. K. von Tippelskirch wrote: "A breakthrough was averted only by the fact that three panzer and several infantry divisions,

A downed German Heinkel He 111 bomber, Kalinin Front, summer of 1942.

A disabled Lend-Lease American M3A1 Stuart light tank being towed through a Russian village back to a field repair shop, August 1942.

German vehicles destroyed during the Pogoreloe Gorodishche operation, Western Front, August 1942.

which were already prepared to transfer to the southern front, were detained and committed first to localizing the penetration, and then for a counterattack as well."[27]

The German counterattack came from the directions of Sychevka and the Karmanovo area. A heavy meeting engagement developed, as each side threw into the fighting all the troops that had been pre-designated for operating on the Zubtsov, Sychevka and Karmanovo directions. On the latter half of 9 August and throughout 10 August, the bitter fighting reached its apogee. According to data given by the chief of staff of the 20th Army Major General Sandalov, the Western Front introduced 800 tanks of its three mobile groups into the fighting, which were countered by 700 tanks on the Germans side. The air force of both sides took active part in this battle.[28]

Unfortunately, even with the presence of such a large number of tanks, which were the basis of Western Front's three mobile groups, "the forces were unable to develop the tactical success into an operational one."[29] The groups lacked the necessary signals equipment and command facilities; there was no combat teamwork between the headquarters of the mobile groups; the infantry units hadn't been trained to cooperate with the tank units; and the mobile groups didn't have attached artillery, primarily anti-tank artillery. As a result, one of the mobile groups alone received four contradictory orders within the span of 9 hours on 7 August, another lost communications with its own army for two days, while the third lost its bearings and for several days operated in complete isolation. Some of the units were thrown into battle without prior reconnaissance, from the march, against the enemy's well-organized anti-tank defenses and suffered heavy losses. Because of weak support from engineers, one of the units alone lost more than 20 tanks while attempting to cross a swollen stream.[30]

A counterattack by the German Ninth Army was repulsed by the Soviet forces,

A mortar team in action near Rzhev, summer of 1942.

but they in turn were unable to make any great headway. To be sure, the Ninth Army commander Colonel General Model on 16 August sent something close to an ultimatum to his superior, Army Group Center commander Field Marshal von Kluge: "The Ninth Army is about finished and needs three more divisions." He warned if those could not be given, the army group will have to assume responsibility for the consequences and "provide detailed instructions as to how the battle is to be continued."[31] Model received his needed reinforcements.

On 13 August, units of the 33rd Army joined the operation, but because the start of its attack had already been delayed since 9 August, the factor of surprise was lost: "the enemy had time to withdraw the bulk of men and equipment out from under the attack and to bring up reserves", and the attack quickly faltered.[32]

Along the entire front of the offensive, Soviet troops became enmeshed in savage, bloody fighting, complicated by the weather conditions. For example, the assault group of the 30th Army's 243rd Rifle Division, having seized the village of Kopytikh, repulsed 14 enemy counterattacks, and went on the attack itself eight times.[33]

According to the memoirs of Lieutenant Colonel A. Kopin, the former chief of operations in the headquarters of the 139th Rifle Division, which was under the command of the 30th Army at the beginning of August, "fighting went on for every hill, crossroads, isolated building, shed, and fold in the ground. The Germans had adapted all of these for a lengthy defense and points of resistance ... There were cases when after seizing enemy bunkers, German soldiers were found who had been chained to the machine guns – penal suicide fighters."[34]

Only after 20 August were some successes achieved: divisions of the Kalinin Front's

A German artillery crew in its firing position in the Rzhev area, summer of 1942.

30th Army on 21 August finally liberated the ill-fated village of Polunino and closed upon the outskirts of Rzhev, while units of the 29th Army reached the Volga River between Rzhev and Zubtsov. On 23 August, divisions of the Western Front's 31st Army in concert with units of the 29th Army liberated Zubtsov, while units of the 20th and 5th Armies shattered the enemy's Karmanovo grouping and took possession of that town.

As already mentioned above, 23 August – a day of visible successes – is considered by Soviet and Russian historiography as the final day of the Rzhev – Sychevka operation. With full responsibility I can assert that in the materials of the *fronts* and armies, other than the 5th Army, I could find no orders about going over to a defense on this date. Only the attacking units and formations of the 5th Army shifted to the defense on 25 August, although even then it continued to conduct local attacks. The assertion that after 23 August "the opposing sides conducted no active combat operations" is simply not the true. The offensive continued beyond 23 August with no diminution of effort. Repeated Soviet attacks sparked bitter fighting and continued until the middle of September west of Zubtsov, and until the beginning of October around Rzhev. German sources place the end of the summer battle for Rzhev in the middle of October.[35]

In the Kalinin Front's journal of combat operations for 23 August 1942, it was noted: "The 30th Army commander decided to go on the offensive ... with the assignment to destroy the enemy's Rzhev grouping in concert with the 29th Army and to take Rzhev." After a limited regrouping, at 0530 24 August units of the 30th Army resumed the offensive north and east of Rzhev following an artillery preparation and air strikes, while units of the 29th Army went on the attack south of the city. General H. Grossmann, commander of the 6th Infantry Division that was defending Rzhev at the time, wrote: "On this day of 24 August,

Soviet infantry dash along a street in Karmanovo. Western Front, August 1942.

as the Caucasus was reached on the southern part of the Eastern Front and a German military flag was unfurled on Mt. Elbrus, at Rzhev it was a day of heavy fighting."[36]

B.S. Gorbachevsky went on the attack toward Rzhev on this day in the 30th Army's 215th Rifle Division. The description of the battle that he gives in his memoirs allows one to understand why the fighting at Rzhev remained in the memory of Soviet soldiers as "the Rzhev meat grinder":

> We're attacking head on, in echelons, and my company is advancing in the second line. Other men are hurrying in front of us and behind us; whoever is lucky tries to follow the tanks; but they are in front of us, as we still haven't caught up with the tanks. Forward, forward, about 300 meters to the heights remains, as we've already overcome half the distance! ... and at that moment, the German trenches speak up. A growing, destructive fire sweeps up and down the attacking lines with a storm of machine-gun fire. The hoarse coughing of mortars follows the machine guns. Artillery starts to roar. Enormous geysers of earth toss the living and the dead high into the air. Thousands of shell splinters, like poisonous hornets, rip into the men, tearing bodies and the earth. How can this be? It appears that our artillerymen didn't reconnoiter the enemy's firing positions; did they just pound vacant space for thirty minutes?
>
> Never mind! The tanks are moving forward with infantry on board. Having successfully navigated the minefields, they are now moving with all their mass and firing on enemy positions – they'll fix everything; they're just about to reach the German trenches, where our infantry will toss their hand grenades, while the tanks crush the German positions.
>
> Suddenly Stuka dive bombers appear above the battlefield from the direction of Rzhev. Confidently and impudently they head straight for the tanks. One tank ... a second ... a third explodes from the direct attacks, turning into large black-and-crimson bonfires, but the remaining tanks, quickly dispersing, continue to advance on their objective. The bombers are flying in flights. The lead plane, turning on its siren, gracefully goes into a dive and, having released its bomb on its target, soars skyward

In the liberated village of Pogoreloe Gorodishche, August 1942.

again. After it, in single file, dives a second, a third, a fourth ... a tenth, forming a unique carousel above the hastily scattering tanks. The bloody feast of the vultures, occurring in eyesight of the charging soldiers, causes a commotion: where are our fighters – why haven't they arrived to protect the tanks and infantry?

... the infantry ... despite the dense curtains of machine-gun fire from the front and the flanks, continues the attack, and our first ranks are approaching the first line of the enemy's trenches. However, they aren't able to reach it in the first rush, and our fighters, lying behind shrubs and little mounds, hiding in little hollows and gullies, open fire on the enemy's firing points from under cover.

...

'Forward! Forward!' shout the officers who are still alive, many just before dropping dead among their own soldiers. The men are mechanically moving forward, and many are dying – but we now no longer belong to ourselves; we have all been seized by the incomprehensibly savage element of battle. Shell bursts, shell fragments and bullets are sweeping away the infantry lines, shredding the living and the dead. ... The ranks of the attackers are thinning, but even more new units are filling in the gaps. The remnants of former companies and battalions have turned into a senseless mass of onward-charging, desperate men. The din of battle swallows the cries of the wounded; medics, risking their own lives, rush about, caught between the wall of heavy fire and these terrible cries. Trying to help those they can, the medics drag the maimed and bleeding to the nearest shell craters. In the howl and shriek of shells, we stop recognizing one another. Faces have become pale, lips compressed. Many men are trembling from fear. Some men are vomiting. Some are crying as they advance, and the tears, mixed with sweat and filth, stream down their faces and blind their eyes. Some men have involuntarily urinated or defecated from the shock. Wild swearing

Residents of a liberated village greet their liberators, autumn of 1942.

and curses fills the air. One man is trying to cross himself on the run, gazing upwards with a prayer. Someone is calling for his beloved Marus'ka.

...

Attacking waves of men followed one after another. The conflict flared up, the piles of corpses grew. We drew even nearer to the enemy trenches. This is the most difficult moment of battle. The night before, our sappers had cleared passageways through the minefields, and now remnants of the attackers were rushing through them. I saw the first soldiers as they reached the trenches, broke into them; now frenzied hand-to-hand fighting with bayonets and fists ensued. But I was not able to rush up to join it. The last thing I heard was some sort of senseless cry. With this cry I felt, painfully and sharply, something cold, slippery and blunt strike me in the back of the neck, stunning me and slamming my head forward against my chest. The strong jolt rocked me sharply, threw me forward, and I crashed face-first to the ground. But I never lost consciousness. I could feel that I was suffocating, that my nose and mouth were filled with earth and dirty grass; I spat it out, and it became easier to breathe. Lifting my head with difficulty, I saw fighters, who were running past a large crater. I had to reach it. I crawled over and slid down into it. ...

When I came to ... a terrible sight appeared before my eyes. Opposite me, covered in blood and grime, lay a soldier with a split skull and already glazed eyes; it was evident that he had been mortally wounded somewhere close to the crater and had managed somehow to slip down into it. Quite close to my right, half-sitting, leaning against the slope of the crater, was another man. He was unconscious. His abdomen had been ripped apart by a shell fragment, and his intestines had spilled out onto the ground. With an arm bloody up to his elbow, he was mechanically striving to stuff them back in again.[37]

Petr Mikhin, another veteran of the 30th Army from the 52nd Rifle Division, recalled the moment in the battle, when he managed to run up to the enemy trench:

> In the trench, the water was almost up to our knees, and there were the corpses of our guys and Germans beneath the surface; something soft and slippery was still moving underfoot, and you, balancing yourself on the uneven footing on the bottom of the trench, dodge death-dealing blows and with all your might deliver one in return. It was *Kto kogo* [Who whom]. This time our guys took the trench. The Germans were driven back. However, there were few of us remaining. We hadn't yet managed to catch our breath, when the Germans were attacking again with fresh forces. We again are crawling back across the corpse-strewn field to our own trenches. The Germans are shooting at our backs, and fresh corpses add to the carnage on the field. In distinction from the old corpses, the fresh bodies of the dead are lying as if they're still young, living boys who've just fallen asleep ... This was repeated several times a day.[38]

In his excellent memoirs, Mikhin thought back on these terrible days of the August 1942 offensive:

> On one of these hot August days the rifle battalion, which had only 50 men left out of 200, assaulted German earthworks in front of the village of Polunino on orders of superiors. The entire field, over which the infantrymen charged, was littered with the corpses of our men who had fallen in previous attacks. .... I took part in many battles during my three years at the front, but again and again my thoughts and painful memories return me to the fighting at Rzhev. It is horrifying to think of how many people died there! The Rzhev battle was a meat-grinder and the city of Rzhev was the focal point of this carnage ... So a new prolonged, hopeless and doomed offensive began with the remaining worn-out divisions. The result was the same: *fields of corpses, "Groves of Death", "Valleys of Death"* [author's emphasis] – across which our men attacked from out of the swamps, storming the Germans' fortified high ground. The Germans also took casualties, as we fought selflessly, but their losses were incomparably smaller than our own ...[39]

On the Western Front, the 31st Army had already been ordered on 22 August to prepare to resume the offensive. All the regiment commanders were forewarned that "they would answer with their heads for a failure of the offensive". The attack would begin at 0545 on 24 August after an artillery preparation.[40] The 33rd and 20th Armies also resumed the offensive on 24 August. F. Halder noted in his diary on this day, "In *Center*, heavy attacks against Second Panzer Army (eastern flank), Third Panzer Army (penetrations) and Ninth Army, where enemy made local gains. The situation remains difficult despite arrival of 72nd Infantry Division. On the western [sector of the] front, an attack on Belyi was beaten off."[41] Halder is writing about an attack in the Belyi area, on the western side of the Rzhev – Viaz'ma salient. Apparently, certain forces of the Kalinin Front were also attacking here. Halder's assertion about a Soviet offensive at this time in the Belyi area requires confirmation through further analysis.

On 26 August 1942, G.K. Zhukov was appointed Deputy Supreme Commander, while Colonel General I.S. Konev took over command of the Western Front, and Colonel General M.A. Purkaev assumed command of the Kalinin Front. On 27 August, the *Sovinformburo*'s first official communiqué about this operation appeared in the newspapers' regular feature "In the last hour". It said, "Fifteen days ago, forces of the Western and Kalinin

Fighting for a village, August 1942.

Fronts went on the offensive on the Rzhev and Gzhatsk – Viaz'ma directions", and asserted that "the enemy's defense was breached on a front with an extent of 115 kilometers." The communiqué went on to list the successes, captured spoils, and gave the last names of the commanders of the *fronts* and the armies, including those of Fediuninsky and Khozin. This is further confirmation that forces of the 5th and 33rd Armies took part in the operation, and moreover on the Gzhatsk – Viaz'ma axis. Everything else in the communiqué only partly corresponds to reality.[42]

On 25-26 August, units of the 30th Army reached the Volga River 5 to 6 kilometers west of Rzhev, and then were able to force a crossing of the river on 29 August and create a bridgehead on its right bank. Over all of these days, the Kalinin Front's artillery was bombarding the city, which was also being subjected to bombing raids. H. Grossmann wrote, "Day after day, fighting for Rzhev ... After four weeks it is now impossible to recognize a single building or street. Just like on the Somme in the First World War, a cratered landscape has arisen in place of the city."[43] F. Halder on 30 August wrote: "In Ninth Army, trouble again at Zubtsov and north of Rzhev. *Grossdeutschland* released for commitment."[44]

In the combat orders of the 30th Army throughout the end of August and beginning of September, the phrase "30th Army continues to exploit the success to take possession of Rzhev" repeatedly appears. However, there was no success: it could not take the city. By a *Stavka* directive from 29 August 1942, Kalinin Front's 29th and 30th Armies were

A *Wehrmacht* soldier, vicinity of Rzhev, August-September 1942.

Knocked-out Soviet tanks loom over a German trench, Rzhev area, August 1942.

transferred to the Western Front "with the aim of the most rapid destruction of the enemy Rzhev grouping, seizure of the city of Rzhev, and for facilitating command of the forces."[45]

A 5 September report from the new Western Front commander to the Supreme Commander observed that in the course of the offensive:

> The infantry is dwindling in number and there are few shells ... It would be advisable to suspend the operation temporarily, accumulate shells, restore order to the troops, put damaged tanks and aircraft back into service, and organize a new attack by the 29th and 31st Armies from the southeast and the 30th Army from the northwest. Close the encirclement ring south of Rzhev.[46]

The Front commander requested the *front* be strengthened with aviation "by the start of the Rzhev operation," and that the 30th and 31st Armies receive replenishments and M-30 and M-20 rocket-launchers. He also proposed a halt to the Gzhatsk operation.[47]

The Gzhatsk operation in fact was soon stopped. As already mentioned, units of the 5th Army's shock grouping went on the defensive back on 25 August, though "units of the Army's northern grouping in cooperation with the left-flank units of the 20th Army" continued to attack the enemy's Samuilovo grouping. In the beginning of September, there was an attempt to resume the offensive of the 5th and 33rd Armies.[48] G.F. Denisenko, who was serving at the time in the 5th Army "not far from Gzhatsk" noted on 4 September:

> Today, somewhat before 0600, an artillery preparation for an offensive began. Work for it has already been done to prepare for it for around the last ten days. The artillery and mortars began to fire. The enemy began to open up in response. A continuous thunder. The hissing of fragments, and long bursts of machine-gun fire. The ground shakes, and the walls of the dugout are perceptibly swaying ... In short intervals of eerie silence, the distant rumble of guns and the drone of aircraft are audible. Our infantry, attacking, have been digging-in, but they haven't advanced very far. As always in these cases, conversation focuses on the horrors: the enemy has 7 rows of entrenchments. A tremendous intensity of artillery ... The fighting on 4 and 5 September was very bitter .....[49]

Isolated offensive operations by the 5th Army continued until the end of September; the 33rd Army halted offensive actions on 7 September. The 20th Army after unsuccessful attempts to penetrate the enemy front and attack Gzhatsk from the west also went on the defensive on 8 September. The precise days that the armies went on the defensive may need clarification.[50]

However, heavy fighting continued on the right flank of the Western Front in September. Just as it was a matter of prestige for the *Wehrmacht* to seize Stalingrad, it was a matter of prestige for the Red Army to liberate Rzhev. General Leliushenko's 30th Army, which had been fighting directly for the city and had lost more than 80,000 men in the August battles (almost its entire effective combat strength at the start of the operation), on 30 August again had on its roster 11 rifle divisions and one motorized rifle division, one rifle and six tank brigades (100 tanks), 13 artillery and mortar units, and other units. Its effective combat strength on this day was 70,494 men.[51]

On 9 September, after a 90-minute artillery preparation, divisions and units of the

30th Army launched a fresh assault on Rzhev at 0700. The 29th Army "at dawn on 8.9.42 in cooperation with the 31st Army went on a determined offensive ... with the mission to seize the southern part of Rzhev." The 31st Army on these days conducted resolute attacks in order to encircle Rzhev from the south together with the 30th Army.[52] A German military doctor in the 161st Infantry Division, which was fighting on the Zubtsov axis, in several letters home recalled 9 September with horror, when Russian forces [of the 31st Army] attacked throughout the entire day, from early morning until late evening.[53]

On 14 September, once again "after an artillery barrage units of the army [the 30th Army] went on the attack ... By 1630, having broken through to the brick factory, they took possession of the first line of trenches ... northeast of Rzhev."[54] In the words of a veteran of the 215th Rifle Division I. Maslennikov:

> It began on the morning of 14 September. The roar became such that nothing was audible from a man standing next to you, talking, or more accurately, shouting ... The smoke screen allowed a swift approach to the enemy line, but the wall of fire prevented the attackers from reaching the buildings on the outskirts and initiate street combat. ... On 14 and 15 September the regiment went on the attack several times, but still failed to reach the first buildings.[55]

On 16 September the 31st Army temporarily suspended its attacks, but on 21-23 September the Army again attempted to attack with the three divisions on its right flank.[56]

The 30th Army fought longer for Rzhev than the others. Its ten rifle divisions with the support of several tank brigades on 21 September at 1000 began a new assault on the city after an artillery preparation. Divisions and units on its left flank achieved success: from the march several blocks in the city' northeastern outskirts were taken.[57] Savage street fighting flared up and went on for every street and each building. On 24-25 September, German forces attempted to drive the Soviet divisions out of the city with counterattacks. Participants in the fighting from both sides recalled the bitterness and intensity of the combat over these days.

A veteran of the German 6th Infantry Division remembered:

> On 24 September the prolonged struggle on the northeastern outskirts of Rzhev reached a new critical point ... Of all the days of combat for Rzhev, this was the severest. It cost enormous losses of guns and men, especially officers and non-commissioned officers. However, enemy losses were even greater ... The companies at the point of breakthrough ... were so depleted, that it was ordered to pull the division out of the line and replace it ....[58]

M. K. Sushkov of the 215th Rifle Division wrote: "The Germans launched a counterattack on 25 September. ... On this day both sides fought with exceptional fury; I never witnessed such fighting until the end of the war, even on such directions as Orsha, Smolensk and Minsk, and in East Prussia."[59]

The 29th Army also supported the 31st Army's offensive. In the Museum of the Kalinin Front, there are five fragments of notebook paper, badly worn, scorched, with missing sections, possibly from the 246th Rifle Division's journal of combat operations, found by searchers in the northern part of Zubtsov District. On one page there is an entry for 21

Fighting in Rzhev, September 1942.

September 1942. The recreated text reads approximately as follows: "The division after an artillery preparation went on the attack at 0945 toward Point ... [illegible] ... After two attacks, overcoming barrier fire and enemy counterattacks, units of the division reached a line north of the village by 1000. Regiments' losses ... 908th – 171 killed and wounded, 915th – 59 killed, 80 [82?] wounded, altogether 453 men."

The capture of Rzhev was anticipated from day to day. An important foreign guest, Wendell Willkie, one of the leaders of the American Republican Party who was visiting the USSR as a personal envoy from the President, was allowed to travel to the 30th Army. On 23 September he met with Stalin, and on 24 September he was in the Rzhev area, where he had a conversation with the commander of the 30th Army Lieutenant General D. D. Leliushenko. His arrival near Rzhev was reported rather widely: even in the newspaper of the Kalinin Oblast's Staritsky District, there was a large article about his trip.[60]

In its intensity, bitterness and the casualties it produced, newspapers on both sides in those days compared the August-September battles in the Rzhev area to the fighting in Stalingrad. Ilia Ehrenburg, who had been in Rzhev in September, later wrote in his memoirs, using front-line reporting:

> I never managed to be in Stalingrad ... However, I'll never forget Rzhev. Perhaps there were offensives that cost more human lives, but there was never another, it seems, so tragic – for weeks fighting went on for five-six devastated villages, for a wall of a shattered building and for a puny little knoll ... Our guys were occupying an airfield, but its military encampment was in the Germans' hands. ... In the headquarters there were maps showing blocks of the city, but at times there was not a trace left of the streets. ... Several times I heard German singing and fragments of conversation. The Germans were messing around in their trenches....[61]

The German combat journalist J. Suddekopf in October 1942 wrote in an article entitled "The locking bar Rzhev":

> The German offensive in the East has reached two places on the Volga River: the walls of Stalingrad and Rzhev. ...That which is happening at Stalingrad ..., has been going on on a smaller scale at Rzhev for almost a year now. Almost to the day a year ago the Germans reached the Volga for the first time ... Since that time, three major battles have developed for each clump of earth on the upper course of the Volga – and a fourth is going on now, the most bitter yet, which has been unceasing for more than the past two months.[62]

In order to support the 30th Army's operation, on the night of 23 September, "three partisan detachments and six diversionary groups numbering a total of 240 men were dropped by parachute on the enemy supply lines in the Rzhev, Belyi, Iartsego, Viaz'ma, Gzhatsk and Sychevka areas."[63] F. Halder in his diary on 24 September noted a Russian landing of 300-400 parachutists in an area southwest of Sychevka in order to organize a major diversion against the Viaz'ma – Sychevka railroad.[64]

In addition, on 19 September the *Stavka* of the Supreme High Command confirmed the plan of operations of the Kalinin Front's 39th Army [the 30th Army's right-hand neighbor] to destroy the German 87th Infantry Division west of Rzhev. It was proposed to call the operation "Venus". The phase of the *Stavka*'s enthusiasm to name operations after planets had begun! On 26-27 September, divisions and units of the 39th Army fully swept the northern bank of the Volga River clear of the German division.[65]

At the end of September-beginning of October, the German command launched repeated counterattacks, but the Germans were unable to regain the northeastern blocks of

German soldiers occupied with a too-familiar task: killing lice. Rzhev area, summer-autumn 1942; a captured German photograph.

Rzhev. By the beginning of October, the fighting finally began to subside, and the Soviet armies in the Rzhev area also went over to the defense – the 29th Army on 25 September, the 30th Army on 1 October. In the Western Front's journal of combat operations for the month of September 1942, when summing up the results for the month it was noted that the Front's main forces conducted "stubborn and protracted fighting during the month" for Rzhev, and "on a number of sectors (the 20th, 5th, 33rd, 16th and 61st Armies and the 3rd Tank Army), battles of local significance"; the journal also observed that all the armies of the Front had settled into defensive positions.[66] Having entered the operation at different times, the armies also exited it at different times. Following logic, if the start of the operation is dated from when the first armies began the offensive, then its end should be dated from when the last army that took part in the operation went over to the defense. Thus, 30 September 1942 should be considered the conclusion of the Rzhev – Sychevka (Gzhatsk) operation. Of course, this is open to debate.

The results of the operation for the Soviet side were insignificant. Unquestionably, three panzer and several infantry divisions of Army Group Center that were ready to move to support the operations in the south were detained. Moreover, 12 German divisions were transferred to the Rzhev – Viaz'ma salient from other sectors of the front, even from the south, and at the end of August the *Grossdeutschland* Division as well, which had been marked for shipment to France. The losses of Army Group Center were quite significant: in total, the 16 German divisions lost 50 to 80 percent of their personnel. In his book on the history of the 6th Infantry Division's 18th Grenadier Regiment, Reich discusses the event of this period under the headings "The Regimental Path of Sacrifices" and "The Regiment Loses Blood", and asserts that in the August-September fighting in the Rzhev area, the regiment lost all its veterans that had entered Russia in 1941. An appendix to H. Grossmann's book about the history of the 6th Infantry Division reveals that between 1 and 22 August 1942 alone, the division lost 3,294 men. The Germans don't report aggregate numbers of their casualties in this operation, but certain German authors have written that at times, matters reached the point that even "construction units of labor conscription ... that were working in the East" entered the fighting, which prior to the summer of 1942 hadn't made an appearance on the fronts of the Second World War. The Germans explained this by the "special conditions of the war in Russia." German armor losses were also "highly unpleasant", which F. Halder had written back on 13 August in his diary.[67]

Army Group Center command's declination to conduct planned operations toward Kirov and Sukhinichi that were preempted by the First Rzhev-Sychevka (Gzhatsk) operation can also be regarded as a success,[68] as well as the liberation of part of the territory of Kalinin and Smolensk Oblasts: the city of Zubtsov, the town of Karmanovo, and a large number of villages and hamlets were liberated. Troops of the 30th Army were occupying city blocks on the northeastern outskirts of Rzhev by the end of the operation.

However, at the same time the Western and Kalinin Fronts suffered enormous casualties in the operation (see Table 5).

The total losses of personnel (killed, wounded, missing-in-action) amounted to no less than 300,000 men. The total from Table 5 does not include the losses of the separate corps or the air armies, so it cannot be considered conclusive. Moreover, the total casualties according to documents from the armies are often higher than those obtained from *front* documents. For example, the 31st Army reported losing a total of 81,737 men in the month of August, but the corresponding figure for it found in documents of the Western

Front from 4 August to 31 August is 30,683, a difference of 50,000 men. Naturally, this complicates the compilation of figures (given the fact that several of the figures came from data found in *front* documents). The loss of tanks in the 30th Army for the month of August alone amounted to 261 tanks, and in the 5th Army – 100 tanks; the armies and corps on the Sychevka axis lost 680 tanks, of which 311 had to be written off, for a total of 1,085 tanks. This figure does not include data for all the armies. According to information from General Grossmann, the Russians over the entire period of the operation lost 380,000 killed and wounded, 13,700 prisoners, 2,956 tanks, 227 mortars, 781 machine guns and 870 aircraft.[69]

Table 5: Total Soviet personnel losses in killed, wounded and missing-in-action in the First Rzhev-Sychevka (Gzhatsk) offensive

Formation	Total losses in personnel	
30th Army	For August-September:	99,820
29th Army	For August-September:	16, 267
31st Army	For period 4 August – 15 September:	43,321
20th Army	For period 4 August – 10 September:	60,453
5th Army	For period 7 August – 15 September:	28, 984
33rd Army	For period 10 August – 15 September:	42,327
	Total:	291,172

Veterans of the fighting around Rzhev recalled the terrible scenes of those August days. Former commander of a mortar platoon of the 114th Separate Rifle Battalion L. M. Vol'pe: "I passed through the entire war, but I never happened to see so many of our own dead anywhere else. The entire field (four kilometers deep by six kilometers wide) was strewn with corpses ...." The writer A. Tsvetkov in notes he took at the front wrote that when their tank brigade was transferred to the area of the village of Deshevki (north of Rzhev and Polunino), when climbing out of their vehicles and glancing around, the tanker were struck with horror: the entire area was covered with soldiers' corpses. There were so many corpses, it was as if they were grass that someone had cut down with a scythe and left scattered there. Platoon commander Tarakanov, heavily sighing, related, "Our sappers suffered most of all. ... There were thousands of them there, those corpses ...They fought with no quarter asked or given, to the death. It seemed as if matters had reached the point of hand-to-hand fighting ... a cruel scene, like one I'd never seen."[70]

The operation was unable to achieve its final goal: "the seizure of Rzhev, Sychevka, Gzhatsk", as set forth in the Western Front's journal of combat operations for September 1942. The advances made by the Soviet troops on a number of sectors were quite insignificant. The 30th Army was able to sweep the enemy from a sector of the front 24-kilometers wide, to a depth of 10 kilometers on the right flank and to 20 kilometers on the left flank. The 31st, 20th, and right flank of the 5th Army advanced 35-40 kilometers, while the 33rd Army made gains of 20-25 kilometers to the west and northwest.[71]

All the armies stressed the difficult weather conditions in their reports, when as a result of the heavy rains, the roads turned into quagmires and even the smallest brooks became flooded. However, obviously the enemy was suffering under the same weather conditions, and it had to struggle against them to bring up reserves to the front. From the very outset of the Soviet offensive, the German command began to shift forces to the Moscow axis, trying to retain a good staging area for a subsequent offensive toward Moscow. By the end of September 1942, the enemy forces were concentrated against the Western Front on the Rzhev – Sychevka axis and the Viaz'ma axis. Respectively, they consisted of up to 16 infantry and three panzer divisions on a sector of 135 kilometers (8.5 kilometers per infantry division on average) and 11 infantry divisions and one panzer division on a sector of 148 kilometers (10.5 kilometers per infantry division on average).[72]

Subjective causes, connected with the "human factor" were no less significant in the failure of the operation. Foremost among these were the Red Army's rules and methods of conducting combat operations that existed at that time, which the formations and unit commanders were compelled to employ at the front. In the opinion of the operations departments of the headquarters of the 5th, 33rd and 29th Armies, "the main shortcoming of the operation that was conducted in August was the reserves of manpower and combat means in the deployment of the regiments' combat formations (2-3 echelons), in particular at the start of the offensive ..."; the infantry during the offensive operated "in densely-packed formations, both across the front and in the depth, from which it suffered excessive losses ... there was almost no coordination between fire and maneuver, which gave the enemy the possibility to conduct fire with impunity at close ranges at the packed, advancing combat formations and inflict painful losses to them"; "regiment and battalion commanders ... sent their units head-on against the enemy or directly into kill zones. The combat formations were too tightly compressed, fearing that the second echelons wouldn't have time to enter the battle at the moment they were needed, and [the second echelons] were kept within the zone of enemy artillery and mortar fire."[73]

This experience from the costly and unsuccessful infantry operations during the summer-autumn 1942 offensive was taken into account when developing the new "Combat Infantry Manual of the Red Army", which came out in November 1942. This can be considered one of the positive outcomes of the operation.

When analyzing the causes for the operation's failures, the actions of all types of troops came under criticism. The reports described the Germans' powerful, deeply echeloned belt of defensive fortifications, only the first line of which was penetrated by Soviet forces. Reconnaissance provided information about the forward edge of the enemy's defense, but had no information about the depth of the defenses, although the operation's planning stage had been rather lengthy. In this case, is it possible to say that the operation was well-prepared? In the first stage of the operation, the artillery carried out its assignment to crack the enemy's defense, but the enemy's system of fire in the depth of the defenses was scarcely touched. In addition, problems arose with ammunition supplies in the following stages of the operation, because its planners hadn't considered that it would continue for such a prolonged time. All the descriptions of army-level operations note the poor cooperation between the infantry, tanks, air force and artillery.[74]

The ineffective employment of the armored forces in the operation has already been discussed above. An article about this operation in the newest edition of the *Voennaia entsiklopediia* notes the Western Front command's creation of the mobile groups as a positive aspect. The authors preferred to ignore a document published back in 1999 among a collection of documents from the series *Russkii arkhiv. Velikaia Otechestvennaia. General'nyi shtab v gody Velikoi Otechestvennaia voiny. Dokumenty i materialy 1942* [Russian archive. The Great Patriotic War. The General Staff in the years of the Great Patriotic War. Documents and materials 1942], in which the General Staff subjected the operations of these groups to serious criticism: "All these mobile groups failed more than once to carry out their assignments on behalf of their infantry, did not reach [their objectives], suffered exceptionally heavy losses and were disbanded." The improvised nature of the creation of these groups was called the primary reason for their failure. The document ended with the words, "I request that the Front commander be notified about the inexpediency of using improvised tank groups in the future."

The clumsy employment of the tanks and the absence of coordination with the infantry were noted on other directions as well. The tank units were frequently reassigned, shifted around, thrown into combat hastily, without preliminary reconnoitering, in piecemeal fashion, and operated in forest combat without support. Radio communications were almost absent. As a result, the large number of tanks did not lead to achieving the operation's ultimate goals, which was recognized by the command of the Western Front's armored and mechanized forces and the Front command.[75]

On 26 May 1943, Major General A.F. Bychkovsky was placed under arrest, accused in particular that during the 31st Army's offensive in August 1942 "as commander of a mobile tank group, he had criminally organized the carrying out of the tasks it had been given, as a result of which the operation was unsuccessful, and the materiel of the tank group that he commanded was destroyed by the enemy."[76] They had found a scapegoat! Unquestionably, it is difficult to agree with the justification for Bychkovsky's arrest, since he alone wasn't responsible for everything that happened in August 1942.

Air operations prompted many criticisims. We'll recall the already cited *Stavka* directive from 4 August, which incidentally has been published. In the opinion of L.M. Sandalov, the 20th Army's former chief of staff, the air force operated effectively at the outset of the operation, but subsequently it lacked close communications with the ground troops. The pilots hadn't mastered their new aircraft, and rarely provided more than 15-20 minutes of cover for the ground forces.[77]

When analyzing the cavalry's operations, L.M. Sandalov acknowledged the inexpediency of introducing them into the breakthrough given the presence of major enemy panzer forces.[78] Should it really have taken a year of war to understand that a cavalryman armed with a saber is ineffective against a tank?

Command over the troops at every level came in for criticism. In the Western Front's journal of combat operations for August 1942, there is discussion of the wide separation between the shock groupings; the uncoordinated operation of various types of forces; the tardy introduction of exploitation forces into the breakthrough; the indecision, passivity, and the lack of initiative of various high-ranking commanders. One of the causes of the ineffective leadership over the troops was the blind execution of orders from above. The majority of commanders at every level were either unable or unwilling to assume personal responsibility, to make use of maneuver, to by-pass enemy strongpoints, and to show flexibility in command of their units. The divisions and units under the direction of such commanders spent weeks and months fighting for one location, expending men and without achieving success.

The fighting for the village of Polunino north of Rzhev can serve as confirmation of this, when the units of the division attacking here spent almost 20 days in the effort to capture it, always attacking from the north. When a new commander was appointed in charge of the division, who had personally investigated other routes of approach to the village, it was liberated in a savage battle, but one that lasted only two hours, as the Red Army soldiers attacked it from the north and the south. Later at a meeting with the Front commander, attempts were made to criticize this division commander for his incorrect employment of tanks. A neighboring division assaulted the village of Galakhovo south of Polunino every day between 5 August and 26 August.[79] As a result, a fraternal grave containing the remains of more than 12,000 Soviet soldiers is located in Polunino; another 11,500 of the dead lay in the ground of Moscow Hill in the city of Zubtsov.

The command and control of the armies and subordinate formations depended much upon the ways the *front* headquarters operated, and the performance of the General Staff as well. For example, one can express surprise that the powerful force grouping that was assembled by August 1942 on the central axis of the Soviet-German front was split up and operated on three different directions: Rzhev, Sychevka and Gzhatsk. They drove head-on into strong, deeply-echeloned enemy defense. Colleagues of the Western Front commander observed the dispersion of strength and means: I.S. Konev, who replaced G.K. Zhukov in command of the Front, immediately proposed a conclusion to the Gzhatsk operation. Certain armies were operating in two completely different directions: the 29th Army to the north, toward Rzhev, and to the south, toward Zubtsov; the 5th Army – to the north, toward Karmanovo, and to the south, toward Gzhatsk. The *fronts* and armies were introduced into the operation at different times, thereby throwing away the factor of surprise. Really, would the introduction of "another one or two armies" resolve all the above-listed problems?

The reasons for the operation's failures even to the present day agitate the common soldiers who participated in these events. They were the ones who paid for the mistakes and absence of professionalism of their commanders with their lives and well-being. A veteran of the 30th Army's 52nd Rifle Division Kh.A. Shakirzhanov argues:

> Why did each step forward around Rzhev come to us at the cost of so much blood? Is it because we fought poorly? No and again no; our combat spirit was high, though many of us lacked weapons, ammunition and experience. The lack of qualified officer cadres was telling, and the solution of a number of tactical questions at Rzhev from the direction of the higher command was inept. Just who primarily was occupying lower command posts at the start of the war? They were former directors of schools, businesses and factories.[80]

P. P. Shekhovtsev, a signalman in the 30th Army's 215th Rifle Division believes:

> There was no worse place for an offensive than Rzhev anywhere else on the entire Kalinin Front. An attack upon the city had to cross the Volga River, and the city itself stood on its higher bank ... and the technical resources that we had during the offensive could not have any chances for success and led to excessive losses ... Really, couldn't our Supreme Command have found a better place for an offensive?[81]

★★★

Thus, on 30 September 1942, the next "unfinished" Soviet offensive operation in the area of the Rzhev – Viaz'ma salient came to an end. It developed parallel with the Stalingrad defensive operation. However, if the *Wehrmacht* forces were attacking actively on the southern sector of the Soviet-German front in the summer of 1942, then in the center the German forces, with the exception of mopping up their rear areas and operations on the flanks of its central grouping, which were necessary, were conducting an active defense. They were forced to adopt such a strategy by the Soviet operations. One can say that on the central sector of the Eastern Front, despite the overall failures, the strategic initiative remained in the hands of the Red Army. Its operations pinned down a significant amount of German strength and prevented them from undertaking their own offensive operations. In order to retain its positions in the center of the Eastern Front, the German command repeatedly had to commit reserves there and bring in divisions from other sectors of the front, including from Europe. As a result, the armies of the Western and Kalinin Fronts assisted the defense of Stalingrad and the Caucasus, and operations of our forces on other fronts of the Great Patriotic War. Moreover, in the words of G.K. Zhukov, the "active operations of our forces in the summer and autumn of 1942 on the Western Direction against the German Army Group Center, according to the *Stavka*'s calculations, were to disorient the adversary, to create the impression that it was just here, and nowhere else, where we were preparing the winter campaign."[82] Already in September 1942, the Soviet command was developing a new offensive operation in the area of the Rzhev – Viaz'ma salient under the code name "Mars".

5

Operation Mars – The Second Rzhev – Sychevka Offensive, 25 November–20 December 1942

Although the Rzhev – Viaz'ma salient had withstood the repeated sledgehammer attacks from Kalinin Front and Western Front in the summer and autumn of 1942, in the words of K. von Tippelskirch, it still "presented particularly favorable opportunities for surrounding the German forces and for a large advance to the west" to the Russian forces.[1] The Red Army command planned to accomplish these objectives with Operation Mars. It was developed and executed in parallel with Operation Uranus – the Soviet offensive at Stalingrad. Cast into the shadows of the triumph of victory in the south, Soviet and Russian historiography has been silent about Operation Mars for long decades. For the sake of justice, I should point out that the operation's plan was partially indicated on Sketch Map No. 2 in an appendix to Volume 6 of *Istoriia Vtoroi mirovoi voiny*. A. I. Radzievsky back in 1979 presented a short analysis of the operation's plan and course, and several Soviet military commanders have mentioned it in their memoirs.[2] However, the *Stavka* directive that spelled out the objectives and assignments for Operation Mars still remains unpublished today, which creates difficulties in studying it and leads to arguments and needless speculation. It can be assumed that disclosure of this document, or the *Stavka* documents related to the operation, might be dangerous to the official version of the operation. However, that appeared only at the end of the last century, following the publication in Russia of the American historian David Glantz's book *Zhukov's Greatest Defeat* about Operation Mars. The archival documents that are available, as well as the reasoned assertions of a few scholars, do not appear to support fully the official version and assessment of Operation Mars.[3]

According to official historiography, Operation Mars was an offensive by the Northwestern Front in the Demiansk area, in conjunction with an offensive by the Kalinin and Western Fronts in the areas of Velikie Liuki and the Rzhev – Viaz'ma salient, designed to pin down the enemy forces and to draw his reserves to these directions. The Rzhev – Sychevka offensive of 25 November – 20 December 1942 was the centerpiece of the entire operation. A.I. Radzievsky's version of the operation's plan did not include the offensive of the Northwestern Front in the Demiansk region.[4]

At present, the majority of scholars and authors refer to the Second Rzhev – Sychevka operation of November-December 1942 as Operation Mars. At one time, the author of these lines was informed that "the name 'Second Rzhev – Sychevka offensive' itself" was not official or commonly accepted, but a name conceived by authors. To clarify, we're speaking about the offensive that followed after the Rzhev – Sychevka (Gzhatsk) operation of 30 June – 30 September, which was discussed in the previous chapter. In the latest edition of the *Voennaia entsiklopediia*, the description of the 1942 Rzhev – Sychevka operations was presented in one article under a single name.[5] The operations followed one after the other; thus it is fully logical to number them as "First" and "Second". On the other hand, if the preceding offensive against the Rzhev – Viaz'ma salient is named the "Rzhev – Gzhatsk" operation, that alone would be sufficient to distinguish it from the following "Rzhev – Sychevka" operation.

Representatives of the Soviet high command described Operation Mars as a diversion, designed to keep the *Wehrmacht* from sending divisions to the southern sector of the front, and called Operation Uranus the main offensive. Official historiography even today adheres to this view. As a confirmation of this version, one can cite the words of I. Stalin, which appeared in his correspondence with W. Churchill and F. Roosevelt. On 27 and 28 November 1942 respectively, Premier Stalin wrote to them in almost identical words: "... We've decided to undertake an operation on the central front as well, in order to impede the enemy from sending forces to the south ...."[6]

D. Glantz maintains that in its level of preparation, scale and scope, Operation Mars was as significant, if not more so, than Operation Uranus. He calls these operations "twins": it was planned to encircle and destroy von Paulus' German Sixth Army at Stalingrad, and Model's Ninth Army at Rzhev. In his book *Zhukov's Greatest Defeat* about Operation Mars, Glantz cites the text of a radio message from London that was intercepted by German intelligence: "Moscow has informed us about a major Russian offensive on the central front, which has been conceived as a most crushing blow against the enemy, in certain respects surpassing the offensive at Stalingrad."[7] General Grossmann called the *Wehrmacht's* combat operations inside the Rzhev – Viaz'ma salient in the winter of 1942 the "winter battle around the Ninth Army's block."[8]

A comparison of the Red Army's strength of forces on the Stalingrad and Moscow directions compels one to pay heed to Glantz's opinion. At the same time, it should be stressed that these figures were published back in Soviet times in Volume 6 of *Istoriia Vtoroi mirovoi voiny*. Fragments of tables from this volume are given below in Table 6.

Table 6: A comparison of the Red Army's concentration of strength and means on the sectors of strategic directions by 19 November 1942, in real numbers and as percentage of totals on Soviet-German Front

	Sector length, km (% of total)	Manpower (% of total)	Guns and mortars (% of total)	Tanks and self-propelled guns (% of total)	Combat aircraft (% of total)
Kalinin and Western Fronts and Moscow Zone of Defense	1,050 (17)	1,890,000 (31.4)	24,682 (32.0)	3,375 (45.9)	1,170 (38.6)
Southwestern, Don and Stalingrad Fronts	850 (14)	1,103,000 (18.4)	15,501 (20.1)	1,463 (19.9)	928 (30.6)

Source: *Istoriia vtoroi mirovoi voiny*, Vol. 6, p. 35.

From the table it is evident that on an extent of 17 percent of the Eastern Front, there continued to be a powerful (to be more precise, the most powerful) grouping of Soviet forces, superior to the grouping on the Stalingrad direction in its strength of forces.[9] However, an examination of the Soviet forces on broader stretches of the front shows that the central sector had a little fewer men and combat equipment than the southern sector (see Table 7).

Table 7: Replenishments committed to the fronts in October-November 1942

	Personnel	Guns and mortars	Tanks and self-propelled guns
Kalinin, Western and Briansk Fronts	102,350	2,895	242
Voronezh, Southwestern, Don and Stalingrad Fronts	105,211	3,391	376

Source: *Istoriia vtoroi mirovoi voiny*, Vol. 6, p. 34.

A.V. Isaev's calculations, given in his article "*Poteriannoe zveno*" ["Lost echelon"] in the Foreword to the Russian-language edition of Glantz's book, support the conclusion that a larger grouping of Soviet forces was to take part in the Second Rzhev – Sychevka operation, than in the Stalingrad offensive operation: the nine armies (excluding the air armies) of the Kalinin and Western Fronts had a combined 702,924 men and 1,718 tanks; the ten armies of the Southwestern, Don and Stalingrad Fronts had a total of 667,478 men and 1,318 tanks. In his calculations, A.V. Isaev used the data in a statistical reference book published by the Ministry of Defense's Institute of Military History in 1997: "Boevoi i chislennyi sostav Vooruzhennykh sil SSSR v period Velikoi Otechestvennoi voiny (1941-1945)" ["Combat and numerical strength of the USSR Armed Forces in the period of the Great Patriotic War (1941-1945*)"*] *Statisticheskii sbornik*, No. 5 (20 November 1942).[10]

Even according to the official version, Operation Mars was to involve 46 divisions, 16 rifle and 32 tank (mechanized) brigades, six separate tank regiments and several dozen artillery and mortar regiments, and other units for a total of more than 545,000 men, 1,355 tanks, and 10,900 artillery pieces and mortars. According to the same official version, three armies on the left wing of Colonel General Purkaev's Kalinin Front (the 41st, 22nd and 39th Armies), plus the 1st and 3rd Mechanized Corps and part of the 3rd Air Army were to participate in the Second Rzhev – Sychevka operation. Colonel General I.S. Konev's Western Front was to contribute three of its right-flank armies to the offensive (the 30th, 31st and 20th Armies), plus the 5th and 6th Tank Corps, the 2nd Guards Cavalry Corps, and part of the 1st Air Army.[11]

However, as archival documents and A.I. Radzievsky's map of the plan show, the operation was to include the Western Front's 5th and 33rd Armies. In the files for the Western Front there is a "Map-solution of the 33rd Army Commander for an offensive south of Gzhatsk" dated 14 November 1942. A.V. Isaev cites Directive No. 00315 on 19 November from the headquarters of the Western Front, which directs the 5th and 33rd Armies to destroy the enemy's Gzhatsk grouping. On 25 November, the entry of these armies into the offensive was postponed until 1 December.[12] However, due to the failures of the first stage of the operation, the offensive of these armies never took place.

Archival documents also give evidence as well about the planned participation and eventual involvement of the Western Front's 29th Army in the operation. In particular, there is a 28 November order from the Front headquarters to the 29th Army commander:

"The start of the Samuilovo operation [will be] on the morning of 4 December; the operation is named 'Mars'", as well as the "Plan of the 29th Army's operation for seizing Sychevka" dated December 1942.[13]

In Operation Mars, the main forces of Army Group Center, which by November 1942 had 79 divisions under its command, opposed the forces of the Kalinin and Western Fronts. All of the divisions in the Army Group were German, which comprised 41 percent of all the *Wehrmacht's* divisions on the Soviet-German front. This testifies to the significance of the central sector of the front and the advantageous Rzhev – Viaz'ma staging area for the *Wehrmacht* command.[14]

Colonel General W. Model's Ninth Army was defending the territory of the Rzhev – Viaz'ma salient itself against the Soviet attacks. According to official sources, on 25 November 1942 it included 19 divisions (16 infantry, two panzer and one motorized) numbering a total of 140,000 men, 1,900 artillery pieces and mortars, and 125 tanks. Already in the first days of the Soviet offensive, the Ninth Army was strengthened with three panzer, one cavalry and one motorized divisions. Altogether in the course of operation against the Rzhev salient, ten divisions from the reserves of Army Group Center and the OKH arrived from other sectors of the Soviet-German front to counter the Soviet offensive. As a result, the Ninth Army's roster of divisions grew by more than 50 percent.

At the outset of the operation, the correlation of forces on the axes of the main attacks was in favor of the Soviet force: 4 to 1 in personnel, 2 to 1 in artillery, and 10 to 1 in tanks. In the course of the operation these advantages decreased, but nonetheless remained in favor of the attackers.[15]

On individual sectors, the correlation of strength could be greater in favor of the Soviet side. According to documents of the Kalinin Front's 39th Army, which attacked on the Olenino axis, on the main sector of the Army's offensive, it had concentrated 10,561 "active bayonets" against 2,423 Germans, 95 tank of all types (81 of which were lost in the operation) against none for the Germans, six artillery battalions against none for the Germans, and 205 aircraft against 42 German.[16]

Interesting materials of the 20th Army show both the initial superiority it held over the enemy on its sector, but also how that advantage dwindled over time (See Table 8). Casualties and arriving German reinforcements reduced the favorable correlations, but did not reverse them.

The authors of the article on the Second Rzhev – Sychevka operation in the latest edition of the *Voennaia entsiklopediia* assert that the objective of the forces of the Kalinin and Western Front was the encirclement of the German Ninth Army and the liquidation of the Rzhev salient.[17] Judging from the record of the *Stavka's* activity in the preceding operations around the salient, when it met the initial failures of the attacking troops with repeated demands that the originally assigned goal be carried out, one can state that the final goals of this operation were more ambitious. If the planned participation of the 5th and 33rd Armies on the Gzhatsk direction is recalled, then the well-known *Stavka* directive from 8 December 1942 allows us to assume that the destruction of the entire Rzhev – Gzhatsk – Viaz'ma enemy grouping and re-occupation of the old 1941 fortified line that had been lost to the Germans in their Operation Typhoon the year before was the objective. We'll recall that the *Stavka* had demanded the achievement of this very same goal in its directives back on 16 February and 20 March 1942. That is to say, at the end of 1942, the troops of the Kalinin and Western Fronts were tasked with the same objectives that they'd been given at the beginning of the year.

Table 8: Correlations of forces and means with the enemy at start of and during Operation Mars, according to documents of the 20th Army

	On 25 November 1942		On 15 December 1942	
	Our forces	Enemy forces	Our forces	Enemy forces
Personnel	5.4	1	2.5	1
Rifles	6.0	1	4.1	1
Submachine guns	6.3	1	4.8	1
Light machine guns	3.8	1	1.5	1
Heavy machine guns	3.6	1	1.5	1
Anti-tank rifles	17.2	1		
Anti-tank guns	6.0	1		
Field guns	3.4	1	3.0	1
Mortars	10.0	1	3.9	1

Source: TsAMO RF. F. 423, Op. 6631, D. 56, L. 21, 47.

In the first stage of Operation Mars, a concentric attack was envisioned, exploiting the arrangement of the front lines around the Rzhev salient. Western Front, from its lines on the Vazuza and Osuga that it had reached by the end of the summer-autumn battles, was to attack with its armies on its right wing. The left wing of the Kalinin Front on the opposite side of the Rzhev salient was to attack from the northwest and the area of Belyi in the general direction of Kholm-Zhirkovskii. The two attacking groupings were to link-up in the German rear, thereby encircling the German Ninth Army. Model's army would then be subjected to dismemberment and destruction. Simultaneously, Kalinin Front's 3rd Shock Army with the participation of long-range aviation was to launch the Velikie Liuki offensive operation with the goal of encircling and destroying the enemy on the left flank of Army Group Center.

In the words of G.K. Zhukov, he was standing at the headwaters of Operation Mars. In his memoirs he wrote that in order to prevent the Germans from transferring forces to the south from other sectors of the front, in particular from Viaz'ma, during the Soviet offensive at Stalingrad, it was necessary first to destroy the Germans in the Rzhev salient. He claimed that in a conversation with Stalin on 13 November, he said, "Vasilevsky can coordinate the operations at Stalingrad while I take charge of the preparations for an offensive by the Kalinin and Western Fronts." On 17 November G.K. Zhukov, in his words, was summoned to the *Stavka* "to work out the operation in detail" and "Between November 20 and December 8 the planning and preparation of this operation were finalized."[18]

Today it is known that G.K. Zhukov was dissembling; preparation for Operation Mars actually began back in September 1942. Additionally, according to historians who reject the official point of view, initially the date for when the troops would go on the offensive was set for between 21 and 23 October. The scholar S.I. Isaev, when analyzing G.K. Zhukov's combat travels during the war, noted that he visited the Kalinin Front in order to assess the situation with the goal of a forthcoming operation in the Belyi area between 21 and 29 October 1942.[19] K.N. Galitsky, the former commander of the 3rd Shock Army, wrote in his memoirs about the preparations for an offensive by the forces of the Kalinin and Western Fronts in October 1942, which received the code name "Mars".[20] As confirmed by David Glantz, the *Stavka* of the Supreme High Command sent the first directives for Operation Mars to the *front* headquarters on 28-29 September.[21] The 20th Army's "Description of combat operations, 25 November-18 December 1942" states that the Army command on 1 October received Directive No. 0289/op from the Western Front commander, which specified the Front's task as "the destruction of the enemy's Rzhev – Sychevka grouping with the forces of the 29th, 30th, 31st and 20th Armies together with units of the Kalinin Front." The 20th Army was to be ready to jump-off on 12 October, and it was planned for it to capture Sychevka by 13 October.[22]

However, no matter when the operation began, Deputy Supreme Commander G.K. Zhukov, who quite recently had commanded the Western Front and at different times had commanded the forces of both the Western and Reserve Fronts and the entire Western Direction, and thus must have been very familiar with the both the terrain of the salient and the situation there, took the most direct part in the implementation of Operation Mars. During the operation itself, with the exception of 6-9 December, he spent more than a month in the headquarters of the *fronts* and armies on the Western Direction.[23]

The offensive, which had been planned for October, "due to the rainy weather and poor trafficability of the roads", was postponed until the ground hardened with the arrival of freezing temperatures. It is possible to assume that there was another reason to push back the start date of the offensive: it was very difficult for the armies of the Western Front to prepare for a new offensive, since it had just – in September – ended the preceding costly offensive. In any case, more than a month passed before the Operation Mars finally began.[24]

According to a version offered by NKVD Lieutenant General P.A. Sudoplatov, who in the war years had worked in the NKVD's Fourth Directorate, on 4 November 1942 "the Germans were tipped off about our offensive on the Rzhev direction by the [NKVD] double agent "HEINE"-"MAX", and G.K. Zhukov wasn't aware of the "radio game" being played by the NKVD. David Glantz also writes about MAX's dispatch.[25] It is possible that such a message was in fact transmitted, but the German command knew about the preparations underway for the Soviet offensive well before 4 November. Back on 22 September, Halder had noted in his diary: "Relentlessly intensive train movements on the railroad sectors from Moscow in the direction of Zubtsov and from Bologoe toward Velikie Liuki ..." and on 24 September, "Heavier railroad traffic on the territory of the entire area in front of Army Group Center ... The possibility should be considered that the enemy is concentrating new shock groupings opposite the entire front of the Ninth Army."[26] K. von Tippelskirch wrote that in the middle of October, German aerial reconnaissance had spotted a major concentration of Russian forces between the cities of Toropets and Kalinin.[27] On 15 October, in the German "Bulletin of assessments of the situation" it was noted: "The enemy, apparently, is conducting preparations for a major winter offensive against Army Group Center, for which it must be ready by approximately the beginning of November. ... "[28] Quite astonishing is an intelligence assessment from the Ninth Army's Ic (chief of the intelligence branch) Colonel G. Buntrock dated 29 October, in which he identified the full intent of the forthcoming Russian offensive with striking accuracy: "The enemy would mount a major offensive against the Ninth Army, striking both the east and west faces of the [Rzhev] trapezoid. ... The objective was to break into the trapezoid from both sides, annihilate the Ninth Army, crack open the front, destroy Army Group Center, and seal this victory by advancing in triumph to recapture Smolensk."[29] The latter words, incidentally, corroborate that the goals of Operation Mars were more ambitious than those purported by the official historiography.

It is also difficult to agree with the Deputy Supreme Commander's ignorance of the NKVD's radio transmissions to the Germans. Let us recall Zhukov's words already cited above, that the offensives in the summer and autumn of 1942 had been designed to focus the Germans' attention on the central axis and mislead them as to where the Red Army would launch its winter offensive. Judging from the *Wehrmacht's* reaction, the Soviet high command's efforts were more than successful: the head of *Fremde Heere Ost* [Foreign Armies East, German General Staff intelligence organization], Colonel R. Gehlen stated in his 6 November intelligence assessment, "Before the German east front, the point of main effort of the coming operations looms with increasing distinctness in the area of Army Group Center." For the troops of the Kalinin and Western Fronts, who would be taking part in Operation Mars, this had tragic consequences. The German forces worked intensively to strengthen their positions and to prepare to meet the Russian offensive. In the autumn of 1942, the German command directed the bulk of its reserves to reinforce Army Group Center. In the month of October alone, the Army Group received an additional army corps headquarters and eight divisions, seven of which arrived from Germany. In total, by the beginning of November, 12 divisions had been transferred to Army Group Center to reinforce it. In the course of the operation, as mentioned above, the enemy continued to build up his strength in the Rzhev salient.[30]

Before the German positions, west of Rzhev, November 1942.

Thus, after more than a month of delays and preparations, at the end of November 1942 the forces of the Kalinin and Western Fronts went on the offensive. The Velikie Liuki operation was the first to begin: on 24 November the Kalinin Front's 3rd Shock Army jumped-off. Already by 28 November, the German grouping in Velikie Liuki had been encircled. Combat with German units that had been sent to this sector in the attempt to free the trapped grouping continued throughout the month of December.

The Second Rzhev – Sychevka Operation got underway on 25 November. After an artillery preparation, Soviet troops went on the offensive on the eastern, northern and western faces of the Rzhev salient. As had been the case in the summer, weather conditions complicated the beginning of the operation: "from the morning there was snow, developing into a snowstorm", which deprived the artillery and tanks of the possibility to conduct aimed fire, greatly hampered air operations, and "disrupted coordination and control over the forces."[31]

Major General N.I. Kiriukhin's 20th Army of the Western Front, which launched the main attack from the east, was unable to breach the enemy defenses and only pushed the Germans back from the front line to a depth of 10 kilometers in a sector just 3-4 kilometers wide. Units of the second echelon (the 8th Guards Rifle Corps) and the 20th Army's mobile group (the 2nd Guards Cavalry and the 6th Tank Corps) were pushed forward and concentrated in order to break through the German defenses. Unfortunately, only two narrow roads led into the concentration area. What happened next to these breakthrough forces was reported by the military procurator of the 2nd Guards Cavalry Corps to the military procurator of the Western Front:

> The area, insignificant in size, was jammed with troops, wagons, transport, ammunition, artillery, cavalry and other types of forces. In addition, the terrain was open and there were no woods. As a consequence of which the units, supply trains, transport, artillery and cavalry became jumbled and crowded together into a draw. ... The enemy is sweeping our combat formations to their depth with artillery and mortar fire from the left and the right, and bombing them from the air. Our units have no cover, and packed together in dense mobs in the draw and on the open fields, are suffering colossal losses in men, horses and equipment. The gullies in several places are piled with thousands of corpses and dead horses; a number of regiments ... are almost combat-ineffective as a result of the colossal losses in men and horses. In my view, there is no unified, centralized command over the units and formations located in the indicated sector.[32]

The units of Major General V.V. Kriukov's 2nd Guards Cavalry Corps and the 6th Tank Corps (temporarily commanded by Colonel P.M. Arman, because Major General A.L. Getman was ill) were forced to make their own breach in the enemy's defense at the cost of heavy losses. For example, the 6th Tank Corps lost 50-60 percent of its tanks and personnel in the fighting on 26 November. Nevertheless, on 27 November, separate units of the 6th Tank Corps and 2nd Guards Cavalry Corps that had fought their way through the German defenses were now moving into their depth. They managed to cut the Rzhev – Sychevka railroad, but wound up encircled. Here the 6th Tank Corps had only 20 tanks left; on 29 November a few more broke through to join them.[33]

Units of the Western Front's 31st Army, commanded by Major General V.S. Polenov,

The battlefield after an attack by mounted Cossacks on German positions east of Osuga, December 1942. A captured German photograph.

which was securing the 20th Army's right flank, in the course of three days of repeated attacks were unable to penetrate the German defenses despite heavy losses. On 28 November, the Soviet offensive on the eastern side of the Rzhev salient came to a temporary halt. On the night of 29 November, remnants of the 6th Tank Corps managed to break out of their encirclement with the assistance of an attack by the main forces outside the encirclement ring, but in the process lost almost all of its remaining tanks and a large part of its personnel. The cavalry units, which managed to destroy a section of the Viaz'ma – Rzhev railroad and a railroad bridge, were unable to fight their way back to friendly lines. The commander of a German armored train, which traveled up and down the on the sector of railroad between Viaz'ma and Osuga, stated that a Russian cavalry formation mounted a classic cavalry charge against the armored train, totally exposed across the open snow with their sabers waving in the air, but in the process it was almost totally destroyed.[34] Remnants of the cavalrymen were forced to escape into the woods to the west.

On 1 December, the 20th Army, which had acquired the two left-flank divisions of the 31st Army after the latter had assumed a defensive posture, managed to pierce the enemy defenses on an 8-kilometer sector to a depth of 6 kilometers, but it was unable to expand the penetration. On 3 December, Major General V.Ia. Kolpachki's 30th Army of the Western Front entered the operation with attacks northwest of Rzhev in the direction of Chertolino. After four days of bitter fighting, units of the 30th Army managed to establish a small bridgehead on the southern bank of the Volga River, which protruded into the forward edge of the German defenses.[35]

The offensive of the armies of the Kalinin Front on the western face of the Rzhev salient developed somewhat more successfully. Major General S.I. Povetkin's 6th Stalin Volunteer Rifle Corps, which had formed in Siberia, was to penetrate the German defenses south of

Dead Red Army men after an attack on positions of the 129th Infantry Division; Rzhev area, December 1942. German photographs.

Belyi. In its units there were many men who had been deported to Siberia in the 1930s, who had now volunteered to go to the front. The corps had been unlucky from the very start of its time with the Kalinin Front. From its detraining stations, it had been forced to make a long march to its assembly area through places that had already been devastated by the war, and somehow it was "out of the loop" for obtaining food rations. The corps' march covered 170 kilometers in 30 days. Each day the soldiers only received 400 to 700 grams of bread. Famished men dropped out of the column due to exhaustion, and there were fatal cases of "strokes due to cardiac insufficiency". When the corps finally arrived at its assembly area, the emaciated men were restored to good condition in urgently created "Rest Homes".[36]

So this somewhat rested corps, which had become part of Major General G.F. Tarasov's 41st Army, on 25 November with the support of tank battalions from Major General M.D. Solomatin's 1st Mechanized Corps attempted to breach the German defenses. According to recollections of participants in the fighting, not all of the soldiers were armed. They were to pick up a weapon from the battlefield. Not everyone was wearing winter camouflage clothing. The chosen location for a breakthrough was not a good one: a narrow valley about 1-kilometer wide, overlooked by heights occupied by German units. Today, a Memorial of Honor to the Siberian soldiers stands over the remains of 12,500 men who fell in this "Valley of Death".

The losses during the breakthrough attempt were so great, that due to the threat of the offensive's collapse, the entire 1st Mechanized Corps was thrown into the fighting ahead of schedule. Its mass of armor punched through the German lines; mechanized units penetrated 20 to 25 kilometers, and cut the Belyi – Vladimirovskoe highway supplying the German troops in Belyi before being halted at the beginning of December by rapidly

Interrogation of a German prisoner, Kalinin Front, end of 1942.

On the attack. Soldiers of the 158th Rifle Division, Kalinin Front, west of Rzhev, November 1942.

Another view of soldiers of the 158th Rifle Division on the attack, Kalinin Front, west of Rzhev, November 1942.

shifted German reserves.[37] Other units of the 41st Army attacked north and south of Belyi, but the attempts to encircle the city were unsuccessful.

Divisions and units of Major General V.A. Iushkevich's 22nd Army, which was operating in the valley of the Luchesa River north of the 41st Army, slowly but stubbornly ground its way forward to the Olenino – Belyi highway with the support of Major General M.E. Katukov's 3rd Mechanized Corps. At the cost of high casualty figures, it managed only to make an 18-kilometer penetration into the German defenses. From the north, divisions and units of Major General A.I. Zygin's 39th Army assisted them with an attack toward Olenino. They were unable to break through the German defenses, but, having suffered heavy casualties, managed to push the Germans back a short distance by 30 November.[38] The fighting on all the sectors was extremely bitter and bloody. One of the German participants in the defense against the 39th Army recalled, "On my sector the sights were terrible. Fallen Russian and German soldiers lay quietly side by side. It was an apocalypse of death. ..."[39]

By the beginning of December, the Kalinin Front's offensive was already bogging down. There were no reserves to throw into the battle, because this Front was simultaneously conducting the Velikie Liuki offensive.

The German command, despite its advance knowledge of the looming Russian offensive, nevertheless at a certain moment experienced feelings of discomfiture. An episode from the history of the 6th Infantry Division's 18th Grenadier Regiment is evidence of this, when one of its battalions on 29 November received six contradictory orders in a row because of "enemy penetrations on different sectors of the front."[40] The text of an ABC Sydney news report, intercepted by German intelligence, stated, "The Rshew battle exceeds all previous in violence. Whatever meaning one in Germany attaches to this battle, the fact remains clear that Hitler himself sent a telegram to the commander of the Rshew Army, Colonel General Model, in which he stated that the position must be held at all costs." The report claimed that Hitler recognized that "a Russian breakthrough will open the way to Berlin."[41]

After a rapid and skillful regrouping, and having received fresh reinforcements, the German command launched counterattacks against the Kalinin Front's penetrations on the western face of the salient. As a result of one counterattack northeast of Belyi, the 41st Army's 47th Mechanized Brigade was destroyed, while southeast of Belyi on 7 December, units of the 1st Mechanized Corps and remnants of the 6th Rifle Corps were encircled.[42]

On 8 December, the Kalinin and Western Fronts received a *Stavka* directive that reiterated the orders to destroy the Rzhev – Sychevka – Olenino – Belyi enemy grouping by 1 January 1943. The directive went further, though, proposing after a regrouping of the *fronts'* forces to destroy the entire Gzhatsk – Viaz'ma – Kholm-Zhirkovskii enemy grouping and a return to the old Rzhev – Viaz'ma line of fortifications by the end of January 1943. The operation was to conclude with this and the seizure of Viaz'ma.[43] The impression is such that the higher command had no understanding of the actual situation!

The Western Front's 20th Army was reinforced, partially at the expense of the grouping designated for the Gzhatsk operation, which was again ordered to be postponed. In particular, the 20th Army received the 5th Army's 5th Tank Corps, commanded by Major General K.A. Semenchenko.[44]

Dissatisfied with the initial results of the operation, G.K. Zhukov, its supervisor in his role as *Stavka* Representative and, in general, its direct leader cashiered several army and formation commanders. On 4 December, Lieutenant General M.S. Khozin replaced Major

General Kiriukhin in command of the 20th Army; on 15 December, Lieutenant General V.A. Iushkevich was dismissed from his post in command of the 22nd Army and replaced by Major General D.M. Seleznev; and on 11 December Colonel I.I. Iushchuk replaced Colonel P.M. Arman in command of the 6th Tank Corps. On 14 December, according to David Glantz, G.K. Zhukov took personal command of the 41st Army after relieving Major General G.F. Tarasov of his duties, although officially Tarasov's dismissal didn't come until after 20 December.[45]

On 11 December, the reinforced 20th Army, as well as the 31st and 29th Armies, resumed the offensive along the entire front. The main forces of the 5th and 6th Tank Corps were committed into the fighting, the latter after being hastily reformed between 30 November and 11 December. Several units were replenished at the expense of the rear services, which were ordered to be stripped of personnel "to the absolute minimum necessary." Officers who'd been previously certified as being unfit for command duties due to poor health or age were called up to fill the vacant posts in the acting units.[46]

One can assess the power of the Soviet offensive from the diary found on a German prisoner:

> In the morning, an unimaginable firing of artillery, Stalin's organs [*Katiushas*] and of tanks at our positions began. ... It seemed as if the world was coming to an end. We were sitting in our trenches, hoping that a direct hit wouldn't blow us all away. This hell continued for a full hour. When the artillery preparation ended, I wanted to climb out, but had to take cover again, since tanks were advancing on us. From my fighting position I counted up to forty heavy tanks. Two of them were heading directly toward my position, one behind the other. It was enough to drive one insane. We thought that we would perish, but were saved by a long-barreled assault gun. I never will forget this day.[47]

The Soviet attacks continued in this sector until 18 December.

On the western face of the salient, remnants of the 6th Rifle Corps and the 1st Mechanized Corps under the command of Major General M.D. Solomatin were fighting in encirclement. From 8 until 14 December, troops of the 41st Army repeatedly tried to break through the 3-5 kilometers that separated them from the encircled forces. According to the memoirs of corps commander Solomatin, each morning the Hitlerites announced through loudspeakers to the encircled troops that the corps command had flown off to the rear, abandoning them to the will of fate, and suggested they surrender. By 14 December, ammunition was running out for the encircled troops: each tank, field gun and mortar had only 5-6 shells left, each machine gun and submachine gun had only 10-15 cartridges remaining, and each rifle was down to 5 cartridges. Aircraft dropped some ammunition, but it wasn't enough, and moreover the entire area occupied by the corps was being raked by enemy artillery fire.[48] In the circumstances when the 20th Army, which according to the plan was to break through from the east to link up with the troops of the 41st Army, had in fact failed to penetrate the enemy's defenses, it was senseless to continue the corps' operation in the enemy rear.

According to the memoirs of N.M. Khlebnikov, while General Solomatin's corps was in encirclement, G.K. Zhukov spent almost the entire time at the headquarters of the 41st Army.[49] In the 1st Mechanized Corps' journal of combat operations there is an

Major General M.D. Solomatin; in 1942 the commander of the 8th Tank Corps (August-September) and the 1st Mechanized Corps (November-December).

entry: "General of the Army Zhukov has ordered: on the night of 15.12.42 to destroy the equipment, and to break out back to friendly lines with the personnel."[50] This entry, albeit indirectly so, corroborates the words of D. Glantz about the dismissal of the 41st Army commander by G. K. Zhukov.

The breakout attempt began at 2300. For 30 minutes prior to the start of the night attack, units of the 41st Army conducted an artillery preparation, and then gave one interdiction barrage on the flanks of the breakthrough. In the village of Klemiatino, which lay in the direction of the break out, three large fires were lit in order to guide the escaping troops. On the night of 15 December M.D. Solomatin executed the breakout and withdrew his remaining units from encirclement.[51]

By the middle of December Operation Mars, which in the words of D. Glantz had become "butchery", finally died out, which Stalin, the *Stavka*, and possibly even Zhukov himself all recognized. The following fact speaks to the unwillingness of the *Stavka* Representative to see reality: having visited the 39th Army, he sent its commander Lieutenant General A.I. Zygin and Military Council member V.P. Boiko personalized watches: "I am awarding you with watches for taking the city of Olenino and wish you further successes. General of the Army G.K. Zhukov. 13.12.42."[52] In fact, the town of Olenino wasn't liberated until 4 March 1943.

The date 20 December is considered the final day of Operation Mars. Its final act was the withdrawal of units of the Western Front's 2nd Guards Cavalry Corps out of encirclement into the lines of the Kalinin Front on the opposite side of the Rzhev salient

Fighting of the 158th Rifle Division for the village of Kondrakovo; Kalinin Front, west of Rzhev, December 1942.

Fighting for the village of Sverkuny west of Rzhev; Kalinin Front, December 1942.

in January 1943. Having concealed themselves in woods after the unsuccessful attempt to break out to friendly lines at the end of November 1942, in the same area where back in July cavalrymen of the 11th Cavalry Corps had also operated in encirclement, they at first conducted diversionary operations, attacking German garrisons in settlements and villages. However, their situation deteriorated. The men were living in hovels in conditions of hard freezes, deep snow, and insufficient food for the men or forage for the horses: men began to fall ill, horses collapsed, and there were many wounded and frostbitten men. In order to subsist, the cavalrymen removed straw from the roofs of huts, raked the snow and cut the exposed dried grasses with knives, and gathered moss and leaves from trees. For a spell they were helped out by rations and food items they had seized during an attack on the German garrison in Kholm-Zhirkovskii. However, they quickly exhausted this limited supply and things began to worsen again. They began to head west, moving from one partisan detachment to the next. The Germans were tightening the encirclement ring. On 24 December remnants of the 20th Cavalry Division and other units moved toward the front lines to unite with regular troops. The author of a book about the 20th Cavalry Division, N.P. Kudinov wrote:

> Exhausted by many days of combat, the haggard, hungry, frozen fighters were confident that their commanders would find a way out of the situation. But the commanders themselves at times didn't know which way to lead the troops: scouts sent ahead didn't always return … . They moved primarily at night, guided only by compass and avoiding populated places. … They often came under hostile fire. They would again head deep into the forests and again would wander without rest, without food, almost without ammunition. The men understood that it was necessary to escape the encirclement at whatever the cost ….[53]

In January 1942 they encountered a group of scouts from one of the divisions of the Kalinin Front that had been sent to meet them. One unit of the encircled cavalrymen broke out by itself, while tankers of the 3rd Mechanized Corps were sent to extract the second group. Even the *Sovimformburo* on 3 February 1943 reported the escape from the enemy rear of Colonel Kursakov's cavalry group.[54]

The latest offensive operation of the Kalinin and Western Fronts against the Rzhev salient – the Second Rzhev – Sychevka Operation – again met failure. The operation's main goal – the elimination of the Ninth Army and the salient itself – was not achieved. In an announcement to the troops, the Ninth Army command stated, "The Ninth Army 'block' with the bulwarks of Sychevka, Rzhev, Olenino and Belyi, remains solidly in German hands …"[55] The territorial gains made by the Soviet forces were minimal: on the Kalinin Front up to 50 kilometers, on the Western Front, even less – in the course of the most bitter fighting, the 20th Army was only able to penetrate the German defenses to a depth of 6 kilometers on a sector 11-kilometers wide. The words of D.A. Dragunsky, who later would become a Colonel General of Tank Forces and twice Hero of the Soviet Union, but in those days was serving in the 3rd Mechanized Corps, can serve as an overall assessment of the operation, even though they were spoken about the "successes" of one *front*: "Our successes on the Kalinin Front in comparison with the glittering victories achieved by the Red Army on the Volga looked quite modest. Over two weeks of the offensive we advanced no more than 50 kilometers. This was murderously little." And this was said given the operation's highest daily casualty rate of all the operations of the second and third periods of the war: every 24 hours the troops of the Kalinin and Western Fronts lost on average 8,295 men.[56]

The casualties in the armies, formations and units that took part in the operation were horrifyingly enormous. The 20th Army lost 58,524; the 8th Guards Rifle Corps over five days of combat lost 6,068 men; the 6th Tank Corps essentially lost its entire authorized strength twice over; the 5th Tank Corps lost its entire authorized complement of tanks in three days of fighting; the 6th Rifle Corps – 25,400 men; the entire 41st Army – 50,636 men; the 1st Mechanized Corps – 8,180 men; the 39th Army – 36,158 men; and the 19th Mechanized Brigade lost 2,446 men out of its starting 3,618 men. According to official data, the total losses of the two *fronts* amounted to 215,700 men, of which 70,400 were killed or missing-in-action, and 1,366 tanks. One can judge the equipment losses of the formations from a document of the General Staff dated 25 December 1942 about replenishing the losses of the 1st Mechanized Corps and the 6th Siberian Rifle Corps with the following weapons: 12,000 rifles, 6,000 submachine guns, 400 anti-tank rifles, 500 light machine guns, 250 heavy machine guns, 100 45mm guns, and 50 long-range field guns.[57]

In the opinion of D. Glantz, German estimates of the total Soviet personnel losses in the operation were more accurate and equaled 335,000 men.[58] According to German calculations, the losses of personnel of the Soviet rifle formations that participated in combat operations amounted to 50-80 percent, more than 200,000 men killed and wounded, 1,847 tank and 127 aircraft.[59]

Operation Mars failed. This is affirmed not only by D. Glantz, whose opinion is impugned because of his criticism of G.K. Zhukov. Such is the opinion as well of the authors of the 4-volume collection of essays on the history of the Great Patriotic War, published in 1998 by the *Nauka* publishing house.[60] However, official historiography on the operation places greater emphasis on its positive results: the troops of the Kalinin and Western Fronts pinned down up to 30 enemy divisions here, and drew those enemy reserves upon themselves that might have been sent to the south.[61] We'll add, and not only to Stalingrad. In his time the English historian B. Liddell Hart wrote that Hitler had to cancel an airborne landing at Batumi that he had designated for October 1942, because "then the Russian offensive at Stalingrad took place, followed by a new Russian attack at Rzhev… Hitler was so alarmed at the dual threat that he cancelled his last bid for Batumi, and ordered the parachute forces to be rushed north by rail to Smolensk, as a reinforcement to the central front."[62] Incidentally, by speaking about a "twin threat", Liddell Hart puts the Soviet offensives at Stalingrad and Rzhev on the same level of importance.

For the German Ninth Army, the fighting in November-December didn't pass without consequences: its forces in the Rzhev – Viaz'ma salient had been battered and the troops were utterly exhausted. D. Glantz cites the testimony of one of the German defenders, who wrote:

> All of the committed troops were completely exhausted; often superiors fell asleep next to their men. Only with difficulty did they hold out. During the night they constructed positions, digging into the ground in order to reduce their losses and occupying them during long periods of darkness (1500 to 0600 hours); this required the last ounce of the troops' strength. And then, during the day, would come the battle and the strong and continuous enemy fire.[63]

In the words of Glantz, Model's forces in these battles "had endured unprecedented privations and suffered immense losses, at least by German standards."[64]

Unfortunately, having estimated the losses for the Soviet forces, neither D. Glantz nor H. Grossmann offer any figures for the Ninth Army's losses in their books. However, they were significant. For example, the 1st Panzer Division after 4-6 weeks of fighting lost 1,793 men and was withdrawn from combat for reforming. The 5th Panzer Division over just ten days of fighting lost 1,640 men and 30 tanks, while the 18th Grenadier Regiment of the 6th Infantry Division between 28 November and 25 December 1942 lost 13 officers and 407 soldiers. D. Glantz calls the German victory in this operation "Pyrrhic". He writes: "As they grimly counted the tens of thousands of Russian casualties and tallied the hundreds of their own, Generals Hilpert and Weiss of the XXIII and XXVII Army Corps wondered how long their steadily weakened forces could continue to defend the Rzhev salient in this appalling war of attrition."[65]

A.V. Isaev cites figures for the combat strength of the German Ninth Army, which show that this "attrition" had not in fact been offset with replacements by the summer of 1943. In his opinion, as in the opinion of D. Glantz, Operation Mars had an indirect, but fully tangible influence on the 1943 summer campaign. Having passed through the meat grinder at Rzhev, the Ninth Army could not replace all its losses: not by May 1943, which forced Hitler (among other reasons) to postpone Citadel, nor by July of the same year had the German divisions that repulsed the Soviet offensive at Rzhev reached an acceptable level of combat-effectiveness. This became one of the reasons why the offensive by the Ninth Army on the northern shoulder of the Kursk bulge quickly sputtered out.[66]

The causes for the failures of Soviet operations have been analyzed both during the war and after it.[67] No matter how paradoxical it may see, we can cite the same miscalculations, mistakes and shortcomings to explain the failure of Mars as we gave for the preceding operations against the salient. Among the objective reasons, weather again played a major role. However, in the case of Operation Mars, subjective reasons are first and foremost: alongside the courage, heroism and self-sacrifices of the soldiers and officers directly at the front, there were the ineptitude, errors and miscalculations of the *front* commands and the higher leadership.

G.K. Zhukov, analyzing the causes for the operation's failure, wrote: "... the main factor was the underestimation of the rugged terrain in the theater selected by the Front command for the main attack ... In the given case, the rugged terrain occupied by the German defenses, which were well-sheltered behind reverse slopes, was not taken into account."[68] This is a surprising comment, and sounds like the viewpoint of someone who might be engaged in field work of some sort, like exploration or an expedition. A *Stavka* representative, who took direct part in the preparations for operation, probably should have familiarized himself with the terrain and German positions facing the *fronts* before launching the operation, which, incidentally, an apologist for G.K. Zhukov's military talent, M. A. Gareev, also corroborates. Citing the words of Vasilevsky, Chief of the Red Army General Staff, he acknowledged that "... separate plans of the *fronts* and armies were examined in the *Stavka* or by its representative Zhukov."[69] Besides, G.K. Zhukov wasn't simply a passive onlooker for the Western Front – he was the *Stavka* Representative. Two months previously, his armies of the Western Front had conducted an offensive in practically these same places. For practically the entire first half of 1942, as we can suppose, a map of the relatively compact area of the Rzhev – Viaz'ma salient, where his troops were operating, was in front of G.K. Zhukov as Front commander. A talented fellow could have memorized this map within the span of several months. As Zhukov would have it, however, the former Western Front commander either didn't know the details of the terrain, or didn't bother to look into details of the operation as it was being readied, and wasn't responsible for the selection of the designated breakthrough places.

Another reason for the operation's failure, in the *Stavka* Representative's opinion, "was the shortage of supporting armor, artillery, mortars and aircraft to pierce the enemy defenses."[70] It is impossible to agree with this, if the enormous amount of men and material that had been assembled for this operation is recalled. In the view of military specialists, here we see directly the inept employment of this assembled force, and this is the fault first of all of those who planned the operation. For example, A.I. Radzievsky writes that the creation of 13 smaller assault groupings led to the multiplicity of attacks and a dissipation of support fire for the attacks.[71]

As always, after the operation, the armies' operations departments generated analyses of how it was executed, wherein they also gave reasons for any failures. Among these reports, the main reason specified was the month and a half-long period of preparation for the operation, which "gave the enemy the opportunity to decipher the command's plans, as a result of which the factor of surprise was lost ...." The enemy amassed forces, especially artillery, on the shock groupings' directions of attack and positioned operational reserves on the flanks of the breakthrough sectors.[72]

Again, the operations of all types of forces were analyzed. The conclusions of the 20th Army's analysis of the operation stated:

> The attacking infantry crowded together, its support weapons were often inactive; the attacking tanks, which became separated from the infantry ... would come to a stop, not maneuver on the battlefield, and not search for enemy firing points to destroy. ... The units had a sufficiently complete picture of the enemy's first line of defense ... there was almost no available information about the second line of defense ... During the offensive, reconnaissance was not conducted. There was no clear notion of the enemy's troop strength. Cooperation among all the types of forces ... has been insufficiently rehearsed and organized ... There is no common language between the infantry and the aviation, the infantry and the tanks, or between the aviation and the tanks ....[73]

This is almost a word for word repetition of the shortcomings when conducting the preceding offensive!

The operations of the mechanized and tank formations came in for serious criticism. Again, just as in the case of the preceding operation, it was stated that the large mass of tanks failed to carry out their assignments. When analyzing the experience of the combat operations back during the war, it was said that neither the Kalinin Front nor the Western Front used the tanks for a massed attack to destroy the enemy's manpower. Certain entries in the documents of the 20th Army practically repeat entries that were made about the summer-autumn operation:

> Commanders of tank subunits didn't understand their actions with the infantry, didn't familiarize themselves with the terrain, as a result of which tanks repeatedly blew up on our own minefields ... Tank units didn't know the enemy, his weapons ...

> During combat the tanks were poorly supported by artillery fire ... The tanks often became exposed and lacked infantry support.[74]

The authors of the article about the operation in the latest edition of the *Voennaia entsiklopediia* note the improper employment of the tank and mechanized corps, which were thrown into the fighting prematurely in order to break through the enemy's defenses, which led to large tank losses. Even they, representatives of official historiography, were compelled to acknowledge that "Miscalculations were made by the *front* headquarters when planning the offensive ... Enemy strength was underestimated ...."[75]

Back on the eve of the Soviet offensive, the chief of the German General Staff intelligence department R. Gehlen, who after the war headed the West German intelligence apparatus, when addressing specific likely directions of Soviet attacks, wrote that "the Russians had often set objectives too distant for the forces they used."[76] The Ninth Army's intelligence staff attributed the overall failure of Operation Mars to poor enemy leadership. It's intelligence summary stated:

> *The enemy leadership*, which demonstrated skill and adaptability in the preparation and initial implementation of the offensive ... and once again, displayed its former weaknesses as the operation progressed. Indeed the enemy has learned much, but he has again shown himself to be unable to exploit critical favorable situations. The picture repeats itself when operations, which began with great intent and local successes, degenerate into senseless, wild hammering at fixed-front line positions once they encounter initial heavy losses and unforeseen situations. This incomprehensible phenomenon appears again and again.[77]

In Glantz's opinion, the blame for the failure of the operation, and first of all for the terrible human losses, lies on the *front* commands and on G.K. Zhukov personally. If we recall the Deputy Supreme Commander's statement that he was indeed "standing at the headwaters" of the operation, and was its overall leader, we have to agree with this opinion. G.K. Zhukov himself, who later criticized generals that didn't mention their own failures, in his own memoirs discusses only selected episodes of the fighting at Rzhev in November-December 1942, remaining silent about the entire course of the operation and its frightening results.[78]

★★★

As has been already mentioned, the Second Rzhev – Sychevka Operation of the Kalinin and Western Fronts took place side by side with the Stalingrad offensive operation. However, if at Stalingrad von Paulus's Sixth Army was encircled and eventually ceased to exist, then there the Red Army achieved a strategic success, while at Rzhev General Model's Ninth Army withstood the test, and the operation for its destruction ended in failure. The rest of Army Group Center was also firmly holding their positions. There was no success in inflicting a defeat upon it in 1942. To both sides it was clear that the battle for the Rzhev – Sychevka salient was not finished and would be continued. Already in December 1942, even while the Second Rzhev – Sychevka Operation was still underway, work was going on in the *Stavka* on a plan for an operation by the Western, Kalinin, Northwestern, Volkhov and Leningrad Fronts in December 1942-February 1943.[79] From the end of December 1942, positional fighting began around the entire perimeter of the Rzhev – Viaz'ma salient.

6

The Dénouement – The Liquidation of the Rzhev Salient – The Rzhev – Viaz'ma Offensive Operation, 2-31 March 1943

At the beginning of the new year of 1943, there was still a powerful grouping of German forces on the central sector of the Soviet-German front: Army Group Center, which consisted of 77 divisions and brigades, more than half of which were occupying the Rzhev – Viaz'ma salient just 150-220 kilometers from the capital of the Soviet Union. In January-February 1943, fighting continued all around the perimeter of the salient without any significant successes. Small, local operations were conducted on a number of sectors of the front. For example, on 25 January, units of the 30th Army's 215th Rifle Division tried to liberate completely the municipal forest and the portion of Rzhev on the left bank of the Volga River, but had no success.[1]

After the liberation of Velikie Liuki on 17 January 1943, Soviet forces were now 240 kilometers to the west of Rzhev. This development significantly and adversely affected the situation of all the German units that were located in the Rzhev – Viaz'ma salient. In the words of B. Liddell Hart, "As a result the danger, not only to Rzhev, but to the whole fist, became more manifest."[2] The command of both the *Wehrmacht* and the Red Army clearly saw this danger. In the words of one German prisoner from the 87th Infantry Division, "Officers were always telling us that the danger of encirclement was constantly threatening us from the direction of Velikie Liuki."[3] Indeed the entire situation on the Eastern Front had turned against the Germans after the conclusion of the Stalingrad battle on 2 February 1943. Both sides separately reached a decision to liquidate the Rzhev – Viaz'ma salient almost simultaneously.

On 26 January 1943, the commander of Army Group Center General von Kluge had recommended to Hitler to abandon the Rzhev salient in order to straighten the lines on this sector of the front and to prevent the possible encirclement of the weakened Ninth and Fourth Armies. The Chief of the General Staff Colonel General Zeitzler also repeatedly insisted on this. As was expected, Hitler at first categorically rejected the idea, but after the catastrophe at Stalingrad, the difficult situation on the Eastern Front forced him to agree with the Generals' proposals. On 6 February, he at last authorized the withdrawal of the Ninth Army and part of the Fourth Army to the Dukhovshchina – Dorogobuzh – Spas-Demensk line.[4] In the words of Liddell Hart, "Much as the Leader hated any withdrawal, and particularly one that would be a step back from Moscow, he was induced to agree that the front must be straightened on that sector, to avoid a collapse and to free reserves."[5]

The operation to withdraw the troops from the salient received the code name *Büffel* [Buffalo, sometimes also seen as *Büffelbewegung* (Buffalo Movement) or *Büffelstellung* (Buffalo Position)]. For the Ninth Army, this operation consisted of multiple tasks: before the arrival of the muddy season, the construction of a new line of defense in the rear and the establishment of intermediate defensive lines for the staged withdrawal; "clearing the army zone to a depth of more than 100 kilometers"; constructing a new 200-kilometer road for motorized vehicles and a 600-kilometer road for sledges and animal-drawn traffic; the removal of "economic goods" and combat equipment; the evacuation of 60,000 Russian civilians to the west "at their desire"; the demolition of 1,000 kilometers of railroad tracks and the rolling up of 1,300 kilometers of communications cable; the laying down of 450 kilometers of cable anew; and the development of a plan of movement for the separate corps.[6]

The *Stavka* of the Supreme High Command also had worked out a plan at the end of January 1943 for several successive operations on the Western Direction, all linked by a single strategic conception. It was proposed to use the forces of the Kalinin, Western, Briansk, and Central (recreated on the basis of the Don) Fronts in order to execute the *Stavka* plan. The following sequence of *front* operations was planned: first the Briansk and the left wing of the Western Front would attack to encircle and destroy the enemy's Orel grouping (the 2nd Panzer Army); then the armies of the Central Front, which was yet to deploy between the Briansk and Voronezh Fronts, would develop the offensive toward Briansk and Smolensk, emerge in the rear of the enemy's Rzhev – Viaz'ma grouping, and together with the Kalinin and Western Fronts, encircle and destroy the main forces of Army Group Center.[7] In this manner, in January 1943 the *Stavka*, just as it had in January 1942, again set an ambitious task: in the words of K.K. Rokossovsky, "in the course of an operation beautiful by its design", inflict a defeat upon Army Group Center.[8]

It was a case of *déja-vu*; the only difference is that a year before, the longest arrows on the map of the plan pointed to the south and southeast, while this time, they were aimed to the northwest. Yet this despite the fact that the Central Front, which was assigned to execute the deep penetration, still didn't even exist. The operations of the Kalinin and Western Fronts directly in the area of the Rzhev salient were only part of this strategic design.

On 6 February 1943, *Stavka* directives on the preparation of an offensive on the central axis of the Soviet-German front, "with the aim ... of emerging in the rear of the enemy's Rzhev – Viaz'ma grouping", went out to the commanders of the *fronts* on the Western axis. The Briansk Front, which acquired the 61st Army from the Western Front, was assigned to prepare on offensive set to start on 12 February 1943 in the direction of Orel and Briansk. The Western Front's 16th Army was to support this offensive with an attack from the north. It was intended to complete the encirclement and destruction of the enemy's Orel grouping by 15-17 February. The Central Front (which still existed only on paper) was ordered on the morning of 15 February to go on the offensive and to seize Briansk by 23-25 February together with forces from other *fronts*. Then from the Briansk – Gomel line, Central Front was to go on the offensive toward Smolensk and Mogilev. The directive to the commander of the Central Front stated: "Simultaneously with the launch of your forces toward Smolensk, the Western Front will go on the offensive toward Roslavl' and further on toward Smolensk; the Kalinin Front – toward Vitebsk, Orsha and with part of its forces toward Smolensk, to meet up with your main attack."[9]

Thus, judging by the design, the intent was to fragment the German forces on the central and Moscow directions into several isolated pockets. From the very beginning, it was planned to stagger the introduction of the Soviet *fronts* into the operation.

The ambitiousness of the goals, the speculative hopes for the impetus and success of the offensive, and simultaneously – the unpreparedness, are apparent even to a non-military person. The Soviet Supreme Command was falling into the same trap as it had before! Colonel General K.K. Rokossovsky's attempts to convince the *Stavka* that the start date for the Central Front's offensive was totally unrealistic were not heard.[10]

On 12 February 1943, two armies of the Briansk Front went on the attack, trying to envelop Orel from the southeast and south. However, by this time the enemy had already shifted seven divisions from the Rzhev – Viaz'ma salient to this sector of the front, which put up exceptionally stubborn resistance to the attacking Soviet forces. Over two weeks of fighting, the Briansk Front's armies were only able to make an advance of 10-30 kilometers, and by 24 February the front here became stabilized. On 22 February, divisions of the Western Front's 16th Army started their offensive toward Briansk from the north, but were only able to advance to a depth of 10-13 kilometers before the attacks were halted.[11]

Naturally, there cannot be any talk at all about on offensive on 15 February by the armies of the Central Front, because they were simply didn't have time to reach their assembly area and get ready for combat operations. The explanation for the causes of this by Front commander K.K. Rokossovsky, who was supposed to whisk his armies to the assembly area from the south, is well-known:

> We had available for our use only a single-track railroad ... It, of course, was insufficient for the rapid movement of an enormous number of troops. The plans for the movement went all to pieces ... Requests for trains were not satisfied. ... The NKVD was instructed to take measures to speed up the troop movements. Workers of this People's Commissariat, who zealously took to carrying out this assignment, overdid themselves and in places put so much pressure on the railroad administration that it didn't know whether it was coming or going. Indeed, if before this intervention a certain timetable had existed, then now not even a trace of one remained. Jumbled formations began to arrive at the assembly area. The artillery's guns and materiel were being unloaded from the trains according to orders, but the horses and vehicles were all still back at the former location. ... The equipment was being unloaded at one station, but the troops – at a different station. Trains came to a standstill at stations and on sidings for several days.[12]

One more omission, in K.K. Rokossovsky's opinion, was the troops' unfamiliarity with the ground in the assembly area. As he wrote in his memoirs, "Even the higher organs that planned the operation of the newly created *front* forgot about this .... As a result, the arriving divisions wound up in a difficult situation – without roads, without transport."[13] In the troops, an acute deficit of everything – food, fodder, fuel and ammunition – was palpable.[14]

As a result, the Central Front began its offensive ten days later than scheduled, on 25 February, and with only part of its forces. Initially, things went well: by 6 March 1943, units of the armies had advanced up to 30-60 kilometers and had cut the Briansk – Konotop railroad; General Kriukov's mounted rifle group penetrated 100-120 kilometers into the depth of the enemy's defenses and on 10 March reached the Desna River. However, in the words of K.K. Rokossovsky, the enemy "plainly outstripped us in assembling and deploying forces."[15] Enemy strength on the Orel and Briansk directions increased. S.M. Shtemenko writes that up to 16 enemy divisions had already been shifted to this area from the Briansk and Rzhev regions. The enemy attacked the cavalry group that had penetrated to the Desna from the flanks and rear, and it was forced to fight its way back out of encirclement to the west.[16]

The task of the Central Front was changed: together with forces of the Briansk Front and the left wing of the Western Front, the armies of the Central Front were to crush the enemy's Orel grouping. The Front became enmeshed in fighting with this grouping, and now there was no longer any talk about an advance toward Smolensk. K.K. Rokossovsky wrote in his memoirs: "Undertaking such a grandiose operation as the encirclement of the enemy's entire Orel grouping, the *Stavka*, apparently, failed to take something or other into account."[17] What then could be said about the *Stavka* on the matter of its even more grandiose plans to crush the enemy's entire Rzhev – Viaz'ma –Briansk grouping?!

At the same time when the formations of almost nine armies of the Briansk, Central and Western Fronts, not including the air armies, were enmeshed in savage fighting in February 1943, trying to execute their assignments of the first stage of the operation to destroy Army Group Center, 12 armies of the Kalinin and Western Fronts were standing idly around the perimeter of the Rzhev – Viaz'ma salient, waiting for something. Perhaps, for the emergence of Central Front's armies on the Briansk, Gomel line?

In the history of the Great Patriotic War, the operations of the Kalinin and Western Fronts in March 1943 received the name of the "Rzhev – Viaz'ma Offensive Operation". In the historical literature it has been rather calmly presented and treated as a pursuit operation. However, there are secrets and mysteries in its story, which haven't been disclosed to the present point.

As already mentioned above, the offensive of the armies of the Kalinin and Western Fronts were planned to be only part of a grand strategic operation to destroy Army Group Center. Due to take part in it were Lieutenant General K.D. Golubev's 43rd Army, Major General I.M. Managarov's 41st Army, Major General D.M. Seleznev's 22nd Army (commanded by Lieutenant General V.A. Iushkevich after 5 March), and Lieutenant General A.I. Zygin's 39th Army with the support of Major General of Aviation M.M. Gromov's 3rd Air Army, all from Colonel General M.A. Purkaev's Kalinin Front; and Lieutenant General V.Ia. Kolpachki's 30th Army, Major General V.A. Gluzdovsky's 31st Army, the 20th Army (temporarily commanded by Major General, from 28 April Lieutenant General N.E. Berzarin between January and 17 March, and subequently by Major General A.N. Ermakov between March and August 1943), Lieutenant General V.S. Polenov's (from 27 February) 5th Army, Lieutenant General V.N. Gordov's 33rd Army, Lieutenant General I.G. Zakharin's 49th Army, Lieutenant General I.V. Boldin's 50th Army, and Lieutenant General V.S. Popov's 10th Army with the support of Lieutenant General of Aviation S.A. Khudiakov's 1st Air Army, all from Colonel General I.S. Konev's Western Front. This was a powerful grouping, which according to official data numbered 876,000 men at the start of the operation.[18] The correlation of forces with the opposing side, although not to the same extent as it had been in the summer and winter of 1942, still favored the Soviet side, which was documented later in analyses of the operation (see Table 9).

In the armies, preparation for the offensive began on 6 February. Originally, combat orders set the date by when each army should be ready to attack: the 30th Army – by 20, 21 February; the 31st Army – by 20, 21 February, the 5th Army – by 22 February, the 33rd Army – by 21 February, the 50th and 10th Armies, by *Stavka* directive – by 25 February.[19] The armies of the Kalinin Front were also supposed to be ready to attack at the end of

February.

The 30th Army's description of the operation states, "The Front commander is giving an order about the army's forces going over to a decisive offensive." In accordance with this, on 19 February, and then on 20 and 21 February, combat orders for an offensive went out to the army's formations and units: "The army's task – timely detect the beginning of the enemy's withdrawal or the partial removal of forces from the army's front ... With the discovery of the main forces' withdrawal, break through the covering screen left behind by the enemy with strong detachments and resolutely pursue him." By plan, the 30th Army's divisions were to launch the main attack toward Monchalovo and to encircle Rzhev. It was emphasized: "A frontal attack on Rzhev is least advantageous."[20] They had learned something after all!

Table 9: Correlation of forces with the enemy at the start of the 1943 Rzhev-Viaz'ma operation

<table>
<tr><th></th><th>Enemy</th><th>43 A</th><th>41 A</th><th>22 A</th><th>39 A</th><th>30 A</th><th>31 A</th><th>5 A</th><th>20 A</th><th>33 A</th></tr>
<tr><td></td><td></td><td></td><td></td><td></td><td></td><td colspan="3">On breakthrough sectors</td><td></td><td></td></tr>
<tr><td>Personnel</td><td>1</td><td>1.4</td><td>1.2</td><td>1.6</td><td>2.3</td><td>2.3</td><td>1.5</td><td>1.8</td><td>4.0</td><td>1.8</td></tr>
<tr><td>Rifles</td><td>1</td><td>1.7</td><td>1.2</td><td>1.3</td><td>2.7</td><td></td><td></td><td></td><td>3.3</td><td></td></tr>
<tr><td>Heavy machine guns</td><td>1</td><td>0.4</td><td>1.6</td><td>1.1</td><td>2.8</td><td>2.6</td><td rowspan="2">All, 0.6</td><td rowspan="2">All, 1.3</td><td>1.0</td><td rowspan="2">All, 1.7</td></tr>
<tr><td>Light machine guns</td><td>1</td><td>0.6</td><td>0.6</td><td>0.8</td><td>1.4</td><td>2.8</td><td>1.2</td></tr>
<tr><td>Submachine guns</td><td>1</td><td>1.2</td><td>2.2</td><td>3.3</td><td>3.2</td><td></td><td>2.3</td><td></td><td>4.9</td><td></td></tr>
<tr><td>Anti-tank rifles</td><td>-</td><td>683[a]</td><td>883[a]</td><td>475[a]</td><td>685[a]</td><td></td><td>5.6</td><td></td><td>9.6</td><td></td></tr>
<tr><td>Field guns</td><td>1</td><td>1.2</td><td>1.6</td><td>2.2</td><td>2.2</td><td>2.5</td><td>3.4</td><td>1.2</td><td>2.3</td><td>1.6</td></tr>
<tr><td>Anti-tank guns</td><td>1</td><td>1.0</td><td>0.8</td><td>0.8</td><td>0.8</td><td>5.5</td><td>0.9</td><td>1.1</td><td></td><td></td></tr>
<tr><td>Mortars</td><td>1</td><td>2.5</td><td>1.8</td><td>3.4</td><td>3.9</td><td>13.0</td><td>2.4</td><td>2.1</td><td>4.0</td><td>2.8</td></tr>
<tr><td>Tanks</td><td>-</td><td></td><td>31[a]</td><td>9[a]</td><td>56[a]</td><td>5.6</td><td></td><td>3.1</td><td>2.1</td><td></td></tr>
<tr><td>Rocket launchers</td><td>-</td><td>14[a]</td><td>8[a]</td><td>23[a]</td><td>24[a]</td><td></td><td></td><td></td><td></td><td></td></tr>
</table>

Note: Blank cells in the table denote the absence or lack of complete data for these parameters in the archival documents that the author consulted.

a Figure indicates actual count, not correlation.

Sources: Taken or calculated from TsAMO RF, F. 208, Op. 2511, D. 2605, L. 113, 40, 49; D. 2606, L. 25, 163, 164; F. 354, Op. 5806, D. 256, L. 7; F. 213, Op. 2002, D. 971, L. 63.

In the combat order issued by the 31st Army commander from 18 February, it was noted: "Authorizing the very same task (the destruction of the enemy's Rzhev grouping), which determined the army's combat operations throughout all of 1942, the commander of the 31st Army has decided to penetrate the enemy defenses ..., [and] in concert with units of the 30th Army as well to destroy the enemy Rzhev grouping ...." In the documents of both armies, there is mention that the offensive should be a surprise for the enemy. Planning the attack for 20 February, the 30th Army headquarters ordered: "Conduct the attack suddenly (without artillery preparation), using the artillery to support the attack and to back up the combat in the depths. Upon taking possession of the forward trenches and strongpoints, continue an impetuous offensive forward ... Bypass stubbornly defending strongpoints, suppressing and destroying them with detached groups."[21]

Measures were designated in all the armies: active reconnaissance and observation in order promptly to detect the enemy's withdrawal; creation of pursuit groups comprised of submachine gunners and ski groups with machine guns and field guns mounted on skis or sledges; preparation of means for mobile communications, sapper groups, road construction units and materials for bridge-building, etc. The main task of the two armies was to prevent an enemy withdrawal.

Meanwhile, the German troops in the Rzhev – Viaz'ma salient were carrying out their own measures as set forth in Operation Buffalo: in the span of four weeks, a new rear defensive line was constructed and a set of intermediate defensive lines was prepared; economic goods and combat equipment were transported away; mines were laid; and other work done. In particular, everything that the Germans couldn't take away was destroyed. For example, after the liberation of Briansk, our soldiers found it in rubble and ashes. Everything was mined and booby-trapped, except for the German military cemetery in the city center. The Germans "managed to destroy all the road bridges and pedestrian bridges; saw down the telegraph poles; shoot up everything at the petroleum storage depot down to the last tank, cistern and drum; and to demolish all the track switches on the railroad tracks, blow up the tracks at the joints, and tear down the signal lights.[22]

As the month of February 1943 progressed, there were increasing signs that the Germans were pulling out of the Rzhev – Viaz'ma salient. Already between 10 and 15 February, the westward movement of enemy groups and vehicles was spotted on certain sectors of the Soviet armies. On the sector of the 5th Army, on 13 February a westward movement of a supply train and a herd of cattle (presumably belonging to a division) was noted. From the middle of February 1943, observations began to appear in the reports of scouts that the enemy was clearing roads, separate units were pulling out of the line in a

German flamethrowers in action, Rzhev area, January 1943.

Wehrmacht units on the move to a new position, February 1943.

westward direction, some of the artillery was being moved closer to roads, and some of the bunkers, bridges, buildings and the railroad bed were being prepared for demolition. H. Grossmann even writes that already on 18 February, the Russians were broadcasting over loudspeakers, "Ninth Army, gather your suitcases and get ready for a withdrawal."[23]

More reports poured in suggesting an enemy withdrawal: on 20 February at 1200, "the central church was blown up" in Belyi; the church had contained a German artillery observation post. On 22 February, five railroad trains – 35 box cars, 10 tank cars and 15 platform cars in all – were seen moving from Chertolino toward Monchalovo (west of Rzhev). On the night of 23 February, "up to 20 large explosions were detected" in Belyi; the following day, the water tower and railroad bridge at Mostovaia Station, not far from Olenino, were blown up. On 25 February, a flour factory was blown up. The enemy was firing off his excess ammunition: on 24 February, the combat positions of the 134th and 362nd Rifle Divisions were struck correspondingly by up to 1,800 and 1,000 artillery shells and mortar rounds. The situation was the same on the sectors of other armies.[24]

Prisoners and deserters were confirming the enemy's withdrawal. On 16 February, prisoners taken in the sector of the 5th Army talked about a withdrawal to a new line of defense and asserted that the 35th Infantry Division had already been withdrawn to the Viaz'ma area. A prisoner captured on 17 February in the sector of the 30th Army, stated, "In February an order was given about sending the supply trains, extra ammunition and non-essential military property well to the rear, as well as the evacuation of all the sick and wounded." German soldiers taken prisoner on 24-25 February in the sector of the 31st Army declared that "preparation for a troop withdrawal began back on 15.2.43 (all their footgear had been exchanged, they'd been issued 4 days of rations and a lot of ammunition) ...." One of the prisoners explained the reason for the withdrawal in this way: "Discussions are going on among the soldiers about the fact that so many German soldiers were killed in Stalingrad, that there aren't enough replacements for this sector of the front, and that they

The central church in Belyi – a symbol of the city. March 1943.

A graveyard of tanks between the Soviet and German positions in the northeastern portion of Rzhev. Early 1943.

cannot withstand the pressure of the Russians, and therefore, fearing encirclement, the German command is withdrawing its units with the aim of shortening the front lines."[25]

Already in the last ten days of February, it was clear that the German Ninth and Fourth Armies were abandoning the Rzhev – Viaz'ma staging area. So it is all the more strange that the forces of the Kalinin and Western Fronts remained passive. Why? This in fact is one of the puzzles of the Rzhev – Viaz'ma operation. It will be possible to figure it out only after going through the documents of the *Stavka* and the General Staff, and a lot of other materials to which ordinary scholars still have no access. The "Supervisor" of this axis, Deputy Supreme Commander and former commander of the Western Front G.K. Zhukov, who had tried throughout all of 1942 to defeat Army Group Center, in February 1943 traveled off to the Demiansk area, where he oversaw the operations to liquidate the German salient there. Why there, and not at the Rzhev – Viaz'ma salient? It is another puzzle.

In the documents of the 31st Army there is an attempt to explain why the start of the offensive was postponed: "In connection with the fact that on 17-20 February 1943 the enemy in front of the army unusually increased its artillery fire, while reducing signals traffic and other changes, the scheduled jumping-off date for the offensive was postponed, and measures were taken to clarify the enemy's intentions." Another document says that as a result of reconnaissance and observation it was established that "the enemy is preparing to withdraw its main forces from the Rzhev – Sychevka line in the direction of Viaz'ma, Dorogobuzh and Smolensk." The withdrawal had been designated to begin on 18 February, but the activity of our scouts forced the enemy "to remain in place and fire off his reserves of shells." The withdrawal of enemy troops became "definitely clear" on 23-24 February.[26] It would seem that the moment had arrived when it was necessary to attack, but the armies only activated their observation and reconnaissance, including combat probes, with the aim of clarifying enemy intentions. It is astonishing!

For the sake of justice, it must be said that there nevertheless was an attempted attack by Soviet formations in the region of the salient in February 1943. On one of the sectors of the 5th Army, a shock group consisting of the 29th Guards Rifle Division and the 35th Rifle Brigade attempted to breach the enemy's defenses on 22 February 1943. Several companies managed to penetrate the enemy's first and second line of trenches. The 153rd Tank Brigade and a ski battalion were introduced into the fighting. The tankers had no success, but the skiers, having slipped through enemy positions and seized a small settlement, wound up encircled and were wiped out. When the Soviet advance finally began, on 4 March at the place of the ski battalion's final stand, a sole survivor from this battalion was discovered.[27]

The already mentioned "elderly soldier" from the 352nd Rifle Division, G.F. Denisenko, left a story about this attack:

> On the morning of the 22nd [February] ... around 10:00 the artillery preparation for our attack began. The thunder of artillery ... the din and rustle of artillery shells passing high overhead, smoke, mist. Tanks headed toward the front. Dozens of tanks of an American model. The powerful machines flew by along the snow road. Later I found out that almost all of them were knocked out and burned. And the tankers? How often back then I witnessed the unkind fate of the tankers!
>
> ... Scattered firing on the morning of the 23rd. Then it intensified. The attacks began again. A fierce engagement. The same picture on the 24th. On this day all the reserves were moved up into the fighting, including an anti-tank rifle company, even

> though from the very first day, the attacks' lack of success was apparent. ... Many soldiers of the company, seeing the attackers' thin ranks, the feebleness of the artillery preparation, didn't actually carry out the attack order. A hard memory. The rifle companies were almost wiped out to the last man in the fighting. Later (4 March), during the general offensive, we saw piles of riddled and frozen corpses in front of the German trenches. Probably the Germans had thrown them together: they couldn't have been killed in such a position during the attack. ... The entire division in the fighting between 22 and 24 February suffered colossal losses. Later, Morozov, the company sergeant major, said that only one man remained alive in one company, but they found fault in him – because he remained alive – and shot him. Later I spoke with the officer-in-charge of the Special Department about this case .... He confirmed that this man actually had been shot, because he had repeatedly fled the battlefield. The division's entire leadership was replaced. The commander of our regiment was also replaced ....[28]

On 27 February 1943, the commander of the 5th Army Colonel General Ia.T. Cherevichenko was also relieved of his duties, because he had been "unable to cope with the fulfillment of his combat assignments." On this same day by a different order of the *Stavka*, the commander of the Western Front Colonel General I.S. Konev was removed from his post with just the same stern wording: "unable to cope with the Front's leadership tasks." The Western Front's chief of staff Colonel General V.D. Sokolovsky assumed command of the Front in Konev's place.[29] Were they removing those who had tarried with the start of the offensive of the Front's armies and had allowed the Germans to escape, or those who had jumped the gun and attempted to attack on one sector? Is really I.S. Konev alone the guilty party, when Army Group Center withdrew its forces from the salient on other sectors of the front? Why didn't the General Staff and the *Stavka* intervene, ultimately? Or did they overlook the signs of a German withdrawal, and decided to make I.S. Konev a scapegoat? The answers to these questions are buried under seven seals in the Ministry of Defense's Central Archives. One can only assume that the failures of the Western Front in the 1942 winter offensive didn't play the last role in the dismissal of Front commander I.S. Konev.

On 28 February 1943 the German command reached its final decision to evacuate the Rzhev – Viaz'ma salient. H. Grossmann writes that an order arrived in the units: the withdrawal of the main forces was to begin at 1900 on 1 March. This was done very stealthily. Rear guard detachments remained in Rzhev until the evening of 2 March. Before pulling out, they blew up the bridge across the Volga River in Rzhev. According to Grossmann, Adolf Hitler heard this explosion in his headquarters: "For this purpose, a telephone line was laid down that connected the *Führer* headquarters with the blasting apparatus. Everything went according to schedule, and Hitler listened over the telephone to the rumble as the bridge blew up." A symbolic act that for the Germans marked the endpoint of their defense of the staging area in front of Moscow, which in their opinion they abandoned unvanquished. The German soldier G. Pabst wrote in his diary: "Farewell, Rzhev, cable fabricators and churches. Little is left of you. We are leaving you without combat, but the foe will understand that he cannot make a virtue of this stone from our bastion."[30]

According to documents, the 31st Army was the first to go in pursuit of the retreating

German units pulling out of Rzhev, March 1943.

Another view of Germans withdrawing from Rzhev, March 1943.

The mortar crew of Senior Sergeant M. Deev in action, Rzhev area, early 1943.

enemy units, followed by the 39th, 22nd and 30th Armies. On the sector of the Western Front's 31st Army, the withdrawal of the enemy's main forces began at 0300 on 2 March. Units of two divisions of the 31st Army went on the attack at 0350 and seized the first line of trenches. Then other of the Army's divisions advanced and bumped into serious enemy resistance. The army's initial task was to break through the enemy's defenses with a shock group on its right flank and enter the city of Rzhev from the south.

At 0830 on the morning of 2 March, the Kalinin Front's left flank with forces of the 39th Army and part of the 22nd Army went on the attack. Later that day at 1430, divisions of the Western Front's 30th Army went on the attack west of Rzhev.[31]

At 1715 2 March, a *Stavka* directive was issued, which raises many questions. In it, there is a statement about the start of an enemy troop withdrawal from in front of Kalinin Front's left wing and Western Front's right wing. Had the *Stavka* really not received any of the intelligence about this back in February? It says that "the pursuit of the withdrawing foe is being conducted sluggishly and indecisively." Had there ever been a *Stavka* directive about going on the offensive? The directive ordered measures to be taken for an energetic pursuit of the enemy's retreating forces, for which purpose "mobile pursuit detachments from various types of forces" were to be created. Was the *Stavka* really unaware that such pursuit detachments had already been created in the armies in the last ten days of February? The directive declared that "the general pursuit of the enemy must not follow the routes of his withdrawal, but according to our offensive plan." Does that mean there really was an offensive plan? And given the presence of this plan, they merely watched as the enemy withdrew, and didn't attack? This directive ordered the *front* commands to have a plan ready for an offensive with the left wing of the Kalinin Front and the right wing of the Western Front no later than 2300 of that same day. Prepare another plan, if one already exists? Indeed, is it really possible to prepare a serious plan in just six hours? Finally, a copy of this *Stavka* directive was addressed to G.K. Zhukov. This is understandable; after all, he was overseeing the Northwestern and Western directions, but he was currently located in the area of the Demiansk salient. Was that a more important sector of the front, or did G.K. Zhukov not want another failure?[32]

In the face of the most acute deficit of information about the activities of the *Stavka* of the Supreme High Command and the General Staff, familiarity with their documents is necessary, but also still tightly restricted. However, even the Western Front's journal of combat operations for the period of January-March 1943 was still kept classified in the Central Archives as of 2006.

Only after the cited *Stavka* directive from the afternoon of 2 March did the forces of the two *fronts* begin active pursuit of the retreating enemy. On 3 March, Rzhev was finally liberated by units of the 30th Army. Directly in the area of the city, the enemy pulled out of the first trenches completely unnoticed. M.T. Burlatov, who commanded the sanitation platoon of the 220th Rifle Division, recalled this day: "... there was a certain strange silence. There was not a sound, either from the direction of the Germans, or from our side. Gradually the soldiers began to clamber out of the trenches and shelters; such brave hearts slowly but steadily grew in number. Just then I heard a shout: 'Fritz has skedaddled!'"[33] Kh.Kh. Iakhin, a signaler with the 215th Rifle Division, remembered that on 2 March a reconnaissance group of 22 men had left to probe the German line. They ran into an ambush, and only one man survived. He continues by describing the morning of 3 March:

> Sitting by the telephone apparatus, I paid attention to the voice of the general [division commander Kupriianov] as he spoke with the commander of the 711th Rifle Regiment, Major Gutarga. The voice of the division commander pricked up my ears, since he was talking in an agitated tone not typical of him. He was saying that other reconnaissance scouts had not found any Germans not only in Rzhev, but also along the approaches to Olenino. Immediately over the battalion net, orders went down to the company commanders, and soon we were getting reports from them that there was nobody in the German trenches. Struck by what had been heard, I handed the phone to my battalion commander. He just couldn't believe that only 2-3 hours before, an entire reconnaissance group had perished.[34]

The write E. Rzhevskaia, who had been a translator with the 30th Army headquarters during the war, recalled that its commander Lieutenant General Kolpachki, even having received intelligence about the withdrawal of the German forces, for a long time couldn't decide to issue the order that would put the army on the offensive:

> Our offensives had so many times come to nothing around Rzhev; even now, after the victory at Stalingrad, when all the attention of Moscow was focused here, he dared not miscalculate and procrastinated. He needed a guarantee that this time the much talked about Rzhev would fall and would be taken. ... Everything was decided by a night phone call from Stalin. He called and asked the army commander whether he would soon take Rzhev ... So the army commander replied, 'Comrade Commander,

The demolished bridge across the Volga River in the city of Rzhev, early spring 1943.

tomorrow I will be reporting to you from Rzhev' – and he moved out his troops."[35]

In the city itself, and to the west and south of it, our advancing units frequently clashed with enemy rear guard detachments, a fact mentioned in numerous documents and memoirs.[36] In the *Sovinformburo*'s official report "In the last hour" from 3 March 1942, it was said: "Several days ago our forces launched a decisive assault on the city ... Today, 3 March, after prolonged and bitter fighting, our troops have seized Rzhev."[37]

On 3 March, the offensive of the 39th and now of the entire 22nd Army continued. Aerial reconnaissance spotted a 16-kilometer "mixed" enemy column: its tail was in Olenino, while the head of it was approaching Kostritsa. On 4 March, Soviet troops entered Olenino. On this same day, the 41st Army went on the offensive. It was ordered on 6 March together with the 22nd to encircle and destroy the enemy's Belyi grouping. They were unsuccessful in doing this, but on 10 March Belyi was liberated.[38]

The 31st Army on the morning of 3 March was ordered to alter its direction of advance and attack to the south and southwest. On 8 March, units of the army liberated Sychevka.

On 4 March, the 20th, 5th and 33rd Armies also began pursuit of the retreating enemy. On 6 March, the city of Gzhatsk was liberated, and then on 12 March – Viaz'ma. At the base of the Rzhev-Viaz'ma salient, the 43rd and 50th Armies began an active advance only at the concluding stage of the operation.[39] The scholar D.E. Komarov writes that enemy forces on the sectors of the front of these armies remained in place and were receiving a steady stream of reinforcements from the withdrawing units. In addition, the Soviet armies didn't have sufficient strength for a powerful attack.[40]

The Soviet advance was slow. The "offensive" turned into a pursuit of a withdrawing foe. The causes of this were the meticulous forethought and preparation given by the enemy to the withdrawal from the salient, and the organized nature of the retreat. This was remarked

The banner of liberation waves over the city of Rzhev, 3 March 1943.

В последний час

I.

Наши войска заняли город Ржев

Несколько дней назад наши войска начали решительный штурм города РЖЕВА. Немцы давно уже превратили город и подступы к нему в сильно укреплённый район. Сегодня, 3 марта, после длительного и ожесточённого боя наши войска овладели РЖЕВОМ.

По неполным данным, взяты следующие трофеи: танков — 112, орудий разного калибра — 78, паровозов — 35, вагонов — 1.200, складов разных — 5, а также много снарядов, мин, пулемётов, винтовок и другого военного имущества.

Противник оставил на подступах к городу и в самом Ржеве убитыми до 2.000 солдат и офицеров.

Первыми ворвались в город части генерал-майора тов. КУПРИЯНОВА А. Ф., генерал-майора тов. ОЛЕШЕВА Н. Н. и полковника тов. ШУЛЬГА В. П.

Sovinformburo's announcement from 4 March 1943. The headline reads: "In the last hour: Our troops have occupied the city of Rzhev."

The shattered city of Rzhev, March 1943, as seen from a low-flying aircraft.

In liberated Rzhev, March 1943.

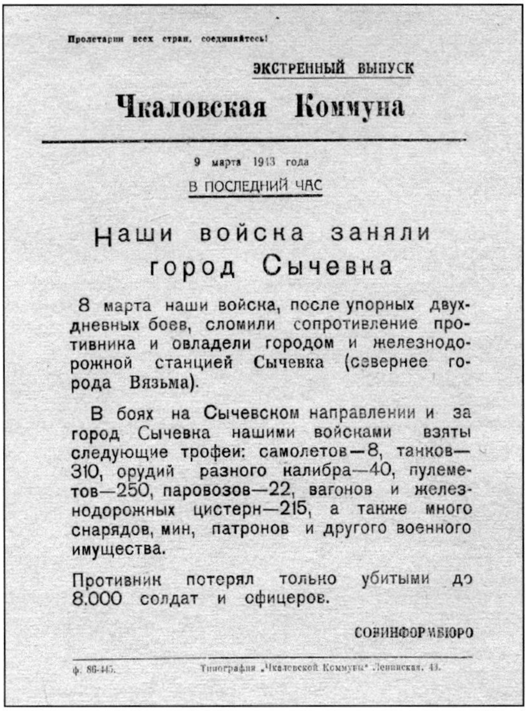

Пролетарии всех стран, соединяйтесь!

ЭКСТРЕННЫЙ ВЫПУСК

Чкаловская Коммуна

9 марта 1943 года

В ПОСЛЕДНИЙ ЧАС

Наши войска заняли город Сычевка

8 марта наши войска, после упорных двухдневных боев, сломили сопротивление противника и овладели городом и железнодорожной станцией Сычевка (севернее города Вязьма).

В боях на Сычевском направлении и за город Сычевка нашими войсками взяты следующие трофеи: самолетов—8, танков—310, орудий разного калибра—40, пулеметов—250, паровозов—22, вагонов и железнодорожных цистерн—215, а также много снарядов, мин, патронов и другого военного имущества.

Противник потерял только убитыми до 8.000 солдат и офицеров.

СОВИНФОРМБЮРО

ф. 86-445. Типография „Чкаловской Коммуны" Ленинская, 43.

Sovinformburo 9 March 1943 announcement about the liberation of Sychevka in the *Chkalovskaia Kommuna* newpaper.

upon in the documents of practically all the advancing armies. Documents of the 31st Army give a thorough description of the tactics used by the withdrawing adversary. Covering groups (rear guards) were detached from each infantry division, composed of a battalion or regiment with the support of two or three mortar batteries, one or two batteries of 75mm field guns and one or two batteries of 105mm howitzers. The rear guards, covering the withdrawal of the main forces, would hold up our units' advance, striving to allow the main forces to escape as far as possible to the rear; then under the cover of darkness they would themselves break contact from our pursuing units.

The main forces would withdraw in bounds of 40-45 kilometers for the divisions. In their turn, the divisions would also withdraw their regiments in bounds of 20-25 kilometers. Intermediate defensive lines were set up in advance every 10-12 kilometers on average, on commanding heights, along roads, on the outskirts of settlements and villages, behind rivers, and on the margins of groves and woods. Engineered works on the given lines consisted primarily of snow barriers and paired foxholes. Artillery and mortar shells would be left behind here for the arriving field guns and mortars; having expended this ammunition, the artillery would withdraw. On a few of the intermediate lines there were Soviet earth-and-timber emplacements that had been abandoned unfinished in 1941. In the Dnepr region, the enemy also made use of our system of fortifications from 1941 (trenches, barbed wire barriers).

On the sector of the 31st Army, there were 13 such intermediate lines. When defended by the Germans, the Soviet advance would come to a halt. The strength of the rear guard

German artillery on an intermediate defensive line, March 1943.

detachments increased as the Germans continued to fall back. At the final intermediate lines, the Germans had self-propelled guns and tanks, which they would skillfully maneuver to counter Soviet threats on one sector of the front or another. The Germans increasingly launched counterattacks, accompanied by the fire of howitzers and mortars and supported with assault guns.[41]

Minefields created great problems. The Germans blew up all the bridges as they withdrew and mined all the roads. The lands west of the Dnepr River were turned into a barren zone. On the Moscow – Minsk highway, all the bridges and overpasses were blown up, and in many places the elevated roadbed as well, where the highway passed through swampy terrain. The railroad was totally demolished.[42]

From the middle of March 1943, the spring muddy season arrived: melting snow, early seasonal flooding that affected the numerous streams and gullies that interlaced the area. All this taken together created an adverse situation for the pursuing Soviet troops. G.F. Denisenko noted in his diary:

> Since 10 March, the sun gets warm in the afternoon. The roads are becoming a mess ... 13 March a Road to Cavalry through Viaz'ma. Mud already in front of the city. Wagons jam the road. We don't move for a long time. The bridge has been blown up. ... Our felt boots are soaked and our feet don't dry out. ... We spend the night of 13/14 March on the road by a campfire. A ceaseless stream of men and equipment. ... Things are animated, like on the streets of Moscow."[43]

The *Stavka* ordered more energetic operations from the *front* commands, to use

Red Army infantry on the march, March 1943.

outflanking maneuvers to cut off his routes of retreat rather than simply pushing the Germans back. Unit commanders were ordered to make "broader use of outflanking maneuvers and envelopment, categorically forbidding frontal strikes and attacks", and demanded "to conserve manpower to the maximum through the use of skillful fire and maneuver."[44] However, the pace of advance for the attacking forces was slow, amounting to only 6-7 kilometers a day.

In the latter half of March, the Western Front command undertook an attempt to snap out of the plodding course of events. The 5th Tank Corps attempted to attack in the direction of El'nia, while the 1st Tank Corps, bypassing Spas-Demensk to the west into the enemy rear, attempted to cut off the retreating German units of the Orel – Briansk grouping and to break into operational space. However, neither corps was able to cope with its assignments. Their numerously repeated attacks led only to heavy losses. Over several days of fruitless fighting, the tank corps lost a combined 132 combat vehicles.[45]

As a result of the withdrawal, by 22 March the enemy had consolidated on a previously prepared and fortified line running from Dukhovshchina through Dorogobuzh to Spas-Demensk with 17 divisions of Army Group Center. Here there was an elaborate network of well-built trenches and communication trenches, a large number of bunkers and armored turrets, a continuous line of wire obstacles and expansive mine fields.[46]

On 22 March 1943, Soviet forces neared this line. All the armies were complaining that the artillery and rear services had fallen far behind, that ammunition and rations weren't reaching the frontline units because they had outdistanced their sources of supply and because they lacked a sufficient quantity of transport vehicles. In their reports, they also noted a shortage of men. For example, on 20 March the regiments of the 31st Army averaged approximately only 120 men each, while the 33rd Army's regiments only had 100-150 men each. The 31st Army's 42nd Guards Rifle Division, for example, numbered only

3,432 soldier and officers. At the same time, only a trickle of replacements was flowing into the armies. Between 1 March and 1 April, the 33rd Army received a total of 587 men. On 12 March, the 20th Army was withdrawn into the reserve by order of the Front commander for rest and refitting.[47]

At the same time, as is noted in the documents of the 31st Army, the enemy's situation in this respect was the opposite. One report states: "The combat formations of the enemy's rear guards have become notably more solid since the line of the Viaz'ma River. Their activity has increased ... the enemy's firepower has grown especially strong, because of the filling out of the combat formations as well as an increase in the amount of artillery and mortars."[48] Enemy resistance on the fortified line grew stronger.

The Soviet forces were forced to halt the offensive. On 24 March, armies of the Kalinin Front went over to the defense. After conducting a regrouping of forces, the Western Front tried to continue the offensive until the end of the month and to penetrate the German Dukovshchina – Spas-Demensk line, but was unsuccessful. So on 1-2 April 1943, its armies also began to dig in on the lines they occupied. The date 31 March is considered the day that the 1943 Rzhev – Viaz'ma operation ended.[49] The front lines on this axis stabilized right up to August 1943, when the Smolensk offensive operation began.

Captain I. P. Maslennikov, the assistant chief of staff of the 30th Army's 618th Rifle Regiment of the 215th Rifle Division, wrote about the final days of the Rzhev – Viaz'ma operation:

> We advanced through the Viaz'ma forests and crossed over the Vop' River just before the ice broke up. About 7 kilometers beyond it we stood on the defense. We attempted to attack, but the Germans had entrenched. We were played out. On 30 March we received an order to defend. Hard work throwing up defensive fortification began. The muddy season brought all transport to a stop until 22 April. We sustained ourselves on whatever we received by air drop. There was no tobacco, and just 100-150 grams of sugar and 100 grams of flour for soup. It was a hard time.[50]

The primary result of the Rzhev – Viaz'ma offensive operation was the liquidation of the German Rzhev – Viaz'ma bridgehead at the end of March 1943. The front lines had been pushed back from Moscow another 130-160 kilometers, and the length of the front on this sector had been reduced by 350 kilometers. The lengthy threat to the capital posed by Army Group Center's Rzhev staging area had finally been eliminated, which was a strategic success. The Soviet command was able to withdraw into *Stavka* Reserve two combined-arms armies and a mechanized corps.[51]

However, the 1943 Rzhev – Viaz'ma operation was not successful. Its ultimate aim, as in the case of all the other offensives on this sector of the front – the destruction of Army Group Center – was not achieved. Army Group Center was indeed thoroughly worn down, but it hadn't been destroyed. The English correspondent A. Werth, wrote:

> Now, in March 1943, fearing to be outflanked by the Russians from the south (and, eventually, of being trapped in that great 'twixt-Moscow-and-Smolensk' encirclement which the Russians had failed to carry through in February 1942) the Germans simply pulled out of the 'Moscow springboard', though with some heavy rearguard actions, notably at Viaz'ma, and destroying as much as time would permit them.[52]

As a result of Operation Buffalo, the front of Army Group Center shrank by up to 200 kilometers. The Army Group command obtained reserves – more than 20 German divisions, which were immediately sent to other sectors of the Soviet-German front. The transfer of 15 of these divisions to the Orel axis enabled the Army Group command to halt the offensive of the Briansk and Central Fronts.[53]

Moreover, despite the fact that the Rzhev – Viaz'ma operation was largely a pursuit operation and continued for only a month, the *fronts'* losses were rather large. According to official data, 138,577 soldiers and officers were lost during the operation.[54]

In the opinion of the officers of the operations departments of the armies' headquarters, when conducting the operation many shortcomings that had been revealed in the preceding offensive operations were taken into account, but at the same time, a host of reasons are given for why they failed to inflict a defeat on the enemy. First of all, there were the enemy's thorough preparations for the withdrawal and its careful implementation according to plan; the intermediate lines of defense that they had created, and the tough resistance the German troops put up. Naturally, they also point to the weather conditions and the poor quality of the roads. Finally, they offer the almost complete lack of mobile units – tanks, self-propelled guns, cavalry, and motorized infantry. The use of propeller-driven sledges in this operation was plainly inadequate.[55] In his 2004 article about the operation in the *Voenno-istoricheskii zhurnal*, D.E. Komarov maintains that partisans who were operating within the salient "kept the Soviet command fully-informed about the condition of the German units, their rear services, and any German movements." If this was in fact so, then what we have here is the ineffective use of this information about the enemy: in the armies' documents, there is talk about the absence of aerial reconnaissance, the ill-defined actions of tactical reconnaissance, and the reconnaissance units lack of radios, as a result of which "the attacking units didn't always have a clear view of the enemy." The artillery reconnaissance and the ineffective operations of the limited number of tanks that was available came under criticism. Despite the fact that even before the operation and in the course of it, unit commanders were warned against frontal attacks, they were nevertheless identified in the analysis of the causes for the operation's failure. In addition, the reports mention the not always effective operations of the mobile groups.[56]

In the research literature, the operation's failures are explained by the crude blunders in decision-making and command at the high level. As confirmation of this, the authors of the 1998 military-historical essays cite the words of I.Kh. Bagramian, who in his memoirs wrote:

> Almost all the offensive operations on the western direction in the spring of 1943 were marked by haste and urgency. At the time, the glittering victories of the Red Army achieved at Stalingrad were still fresh in all of our minds... It seemed that the enemy's morale had cracked and if we didn't allow him to recover, if we constantly attacked in more and more new directions, then soon he would be decisively crushed... Even some of the *front* commanders had the mistaken conviction and persistent desire to achieve successes like the Stalingrad triumph more quickly.[57]

Combat operations on the Orel – Briansk axis continued in March 1943. The actions of the Supreme Command here also prompt great surprise. On the one hand, here, as already mentioned, the offensive operations of the Briansk and Central Fronts were continuing.

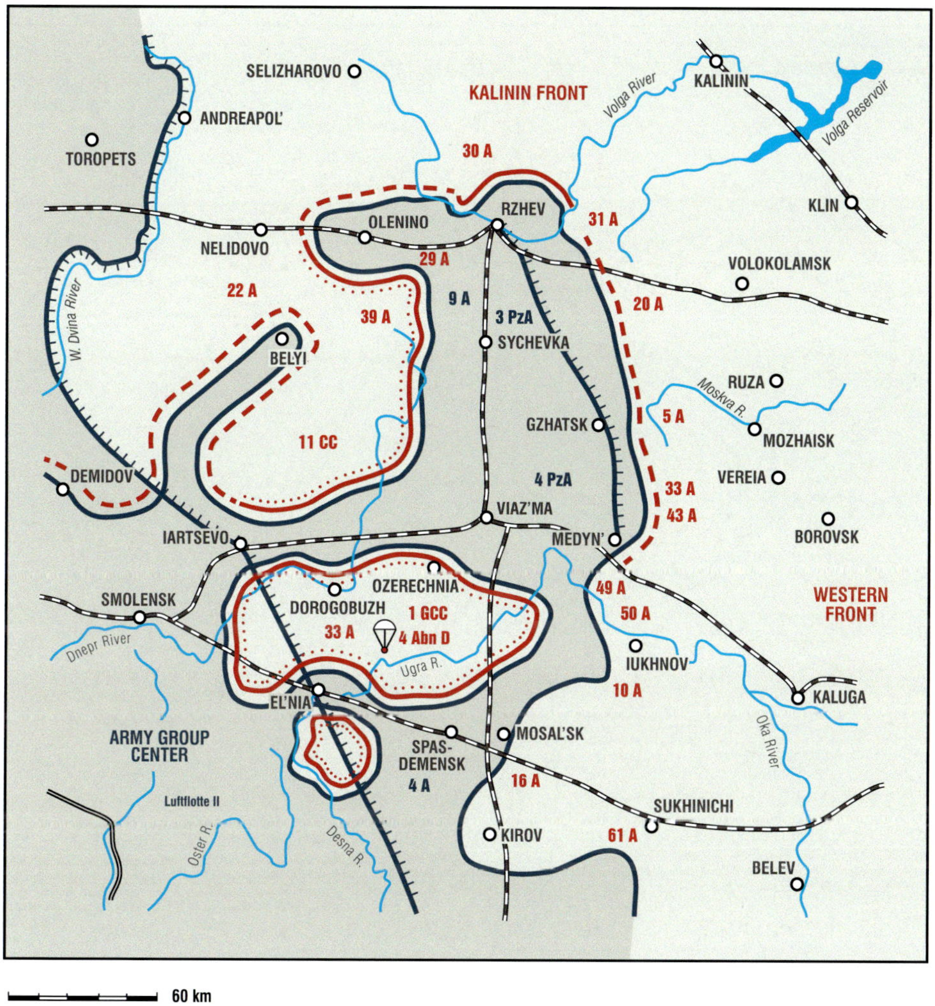

The Rzhev-Viaz'ma salient in the line of the Soviet-German front, first half of 1942.

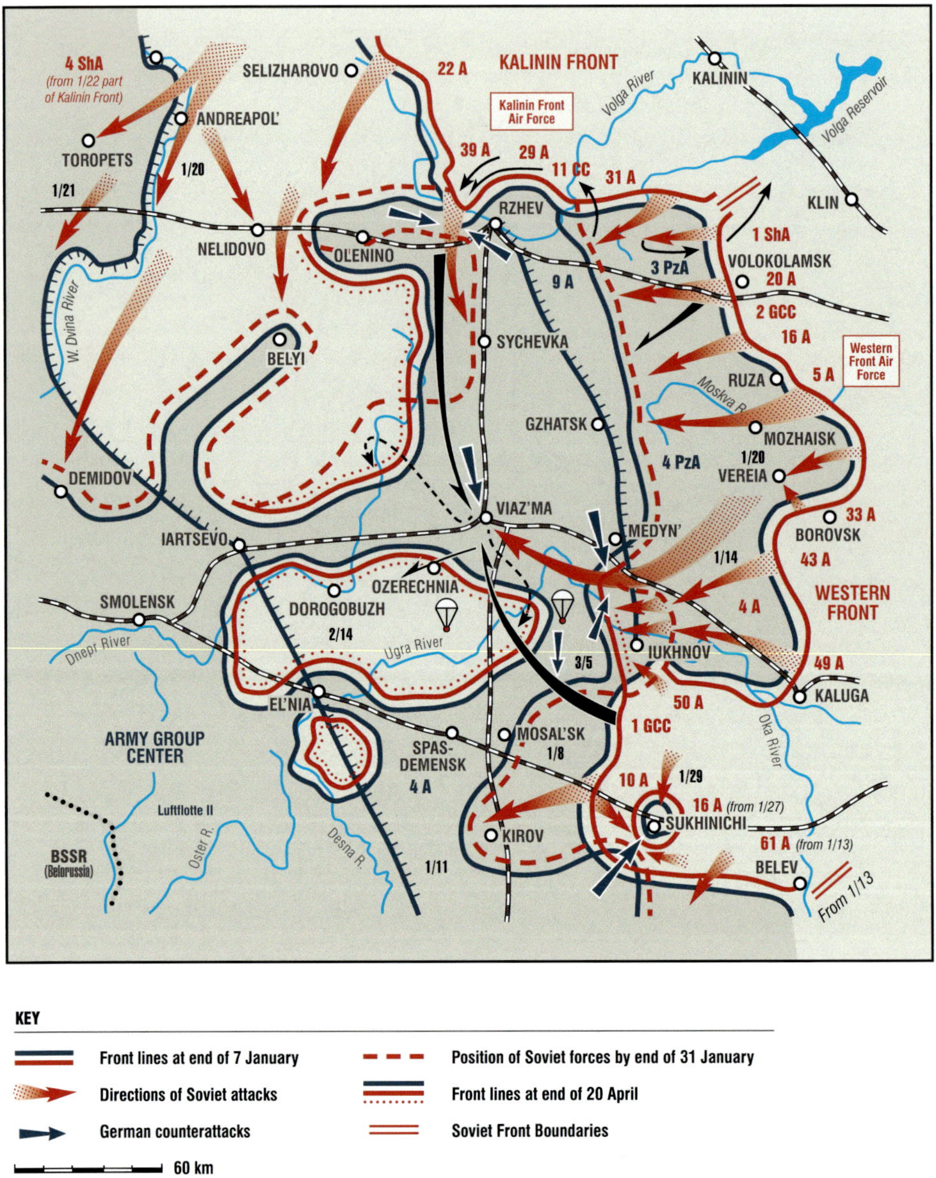

The Rzhev-Viaz'ma Offensive, 8 January–20 April 1942.

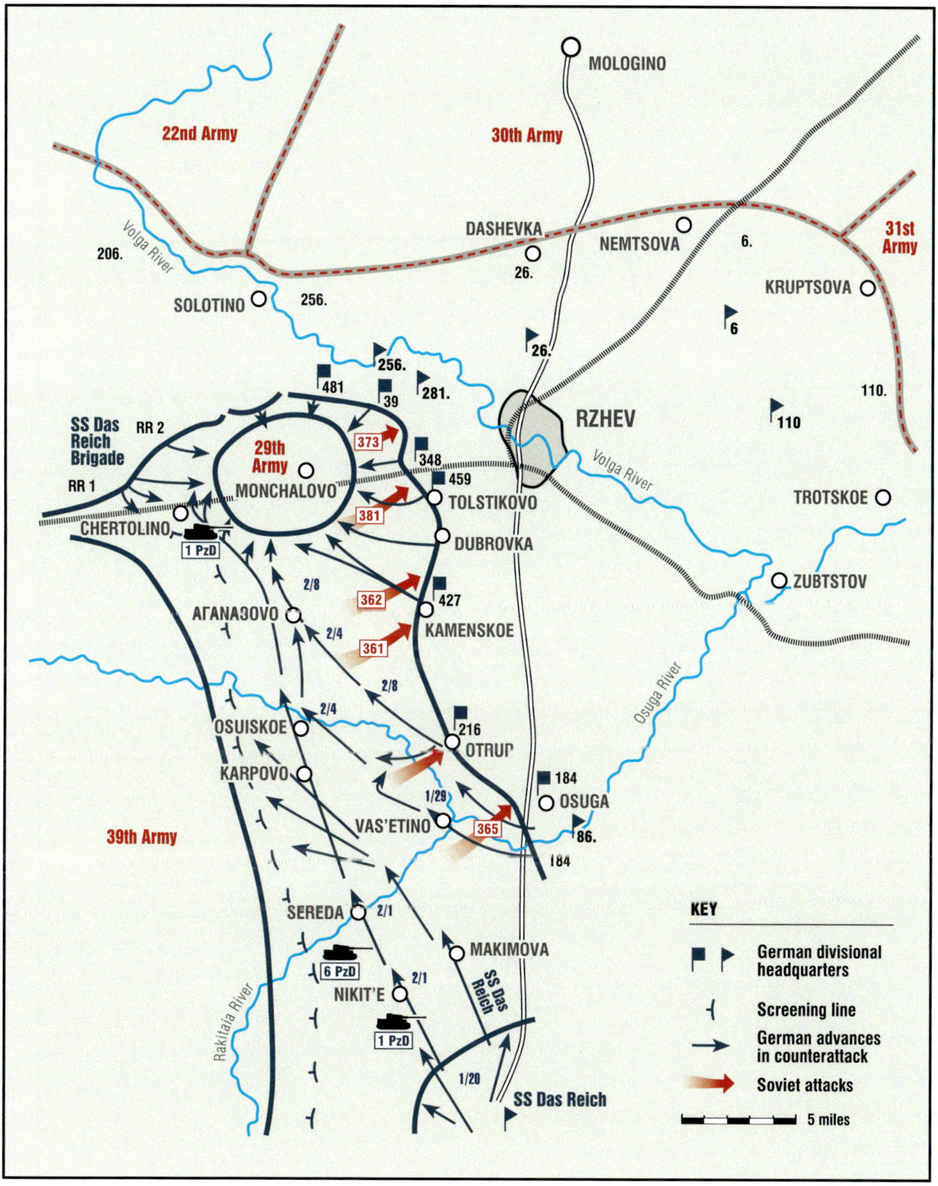

Encirclement of the 29th Army in February 1942.

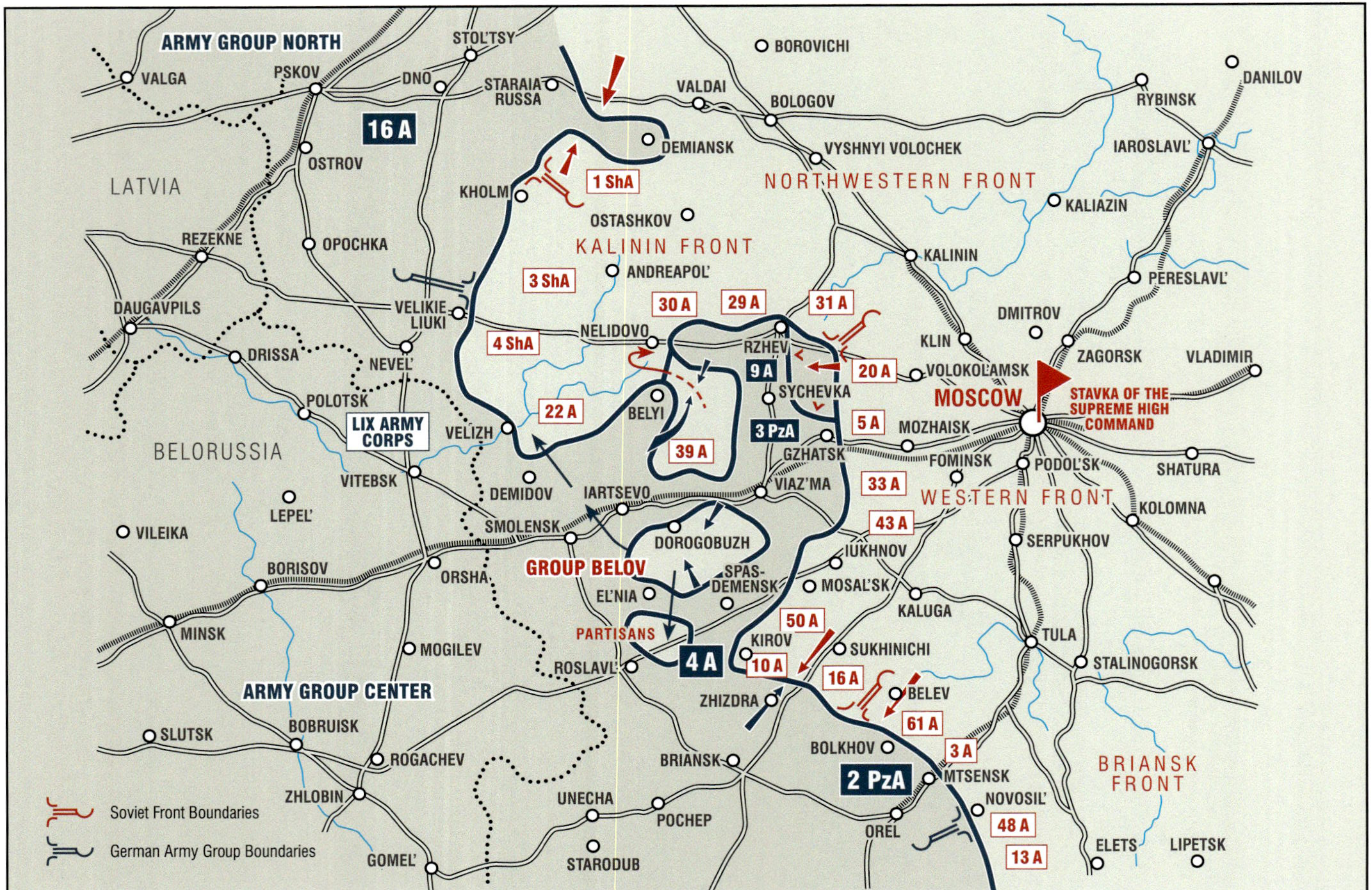

Combat operations in the area of the Rzhev-Viaz'ma salient in May–June 1942.

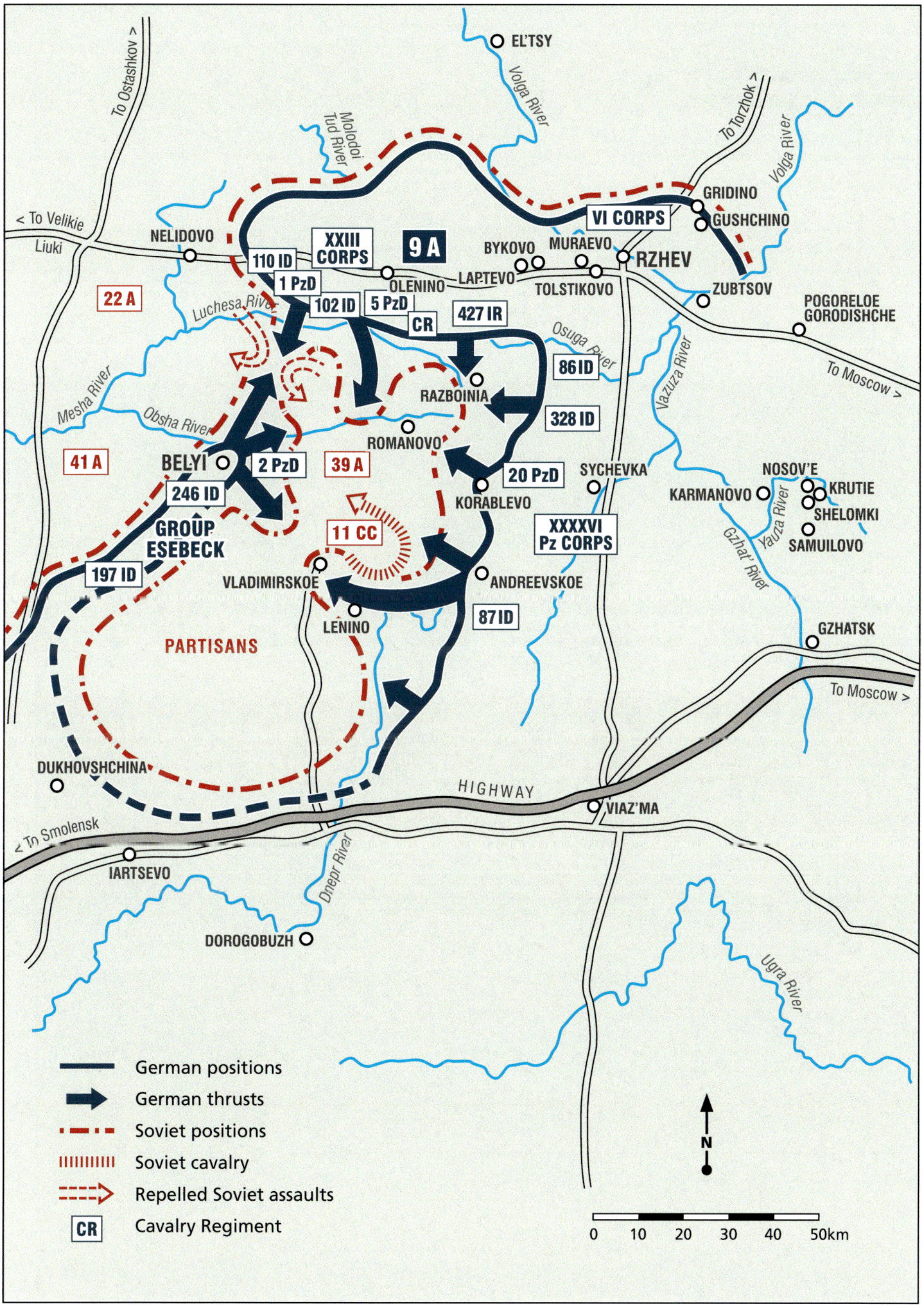

Operation Seydlitz, July 1942. The summer combat between Rzhev and Belyi.

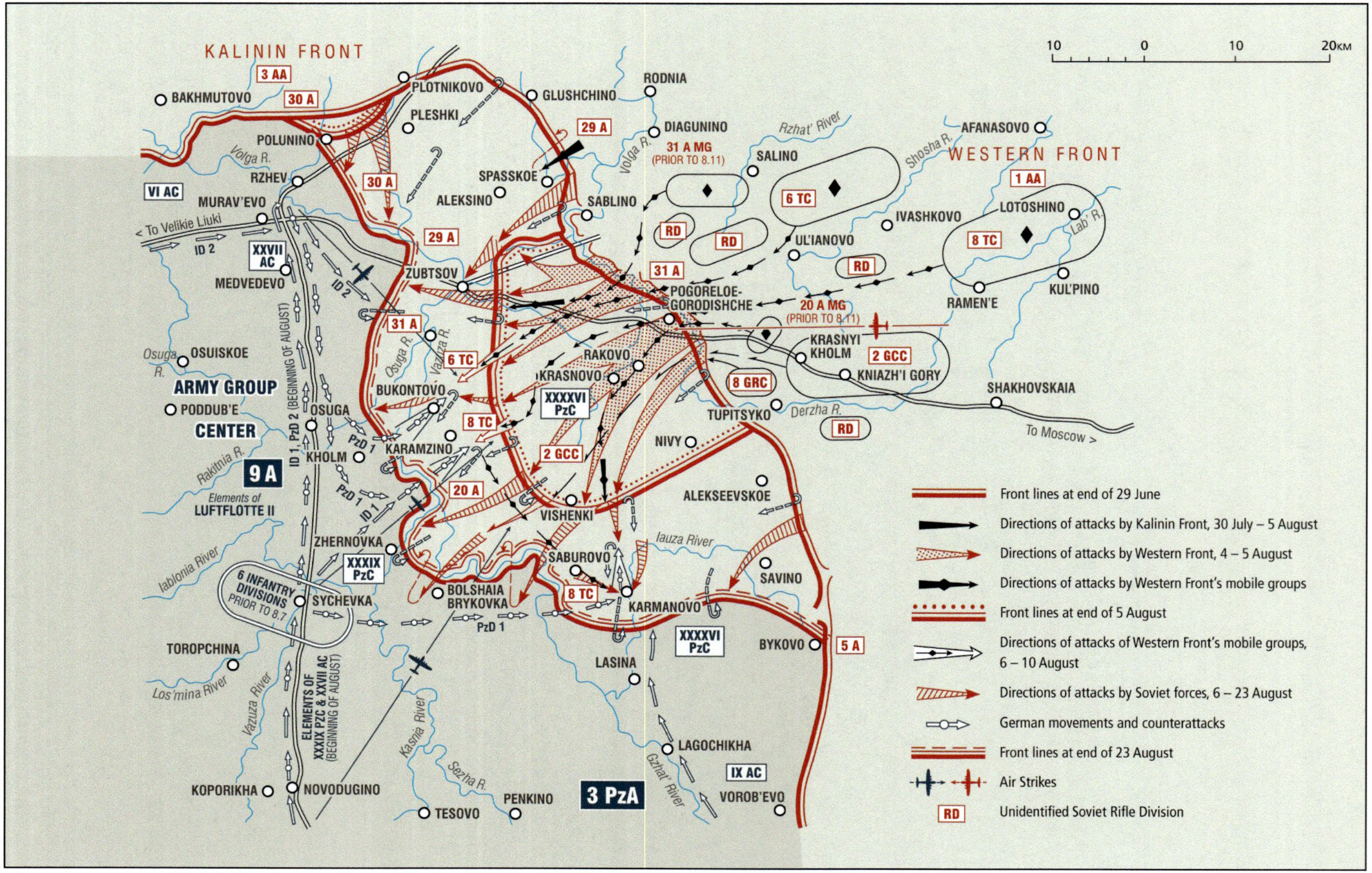

The First Rzhev-Sychevka Offensive, 30 July–23 August 1942.

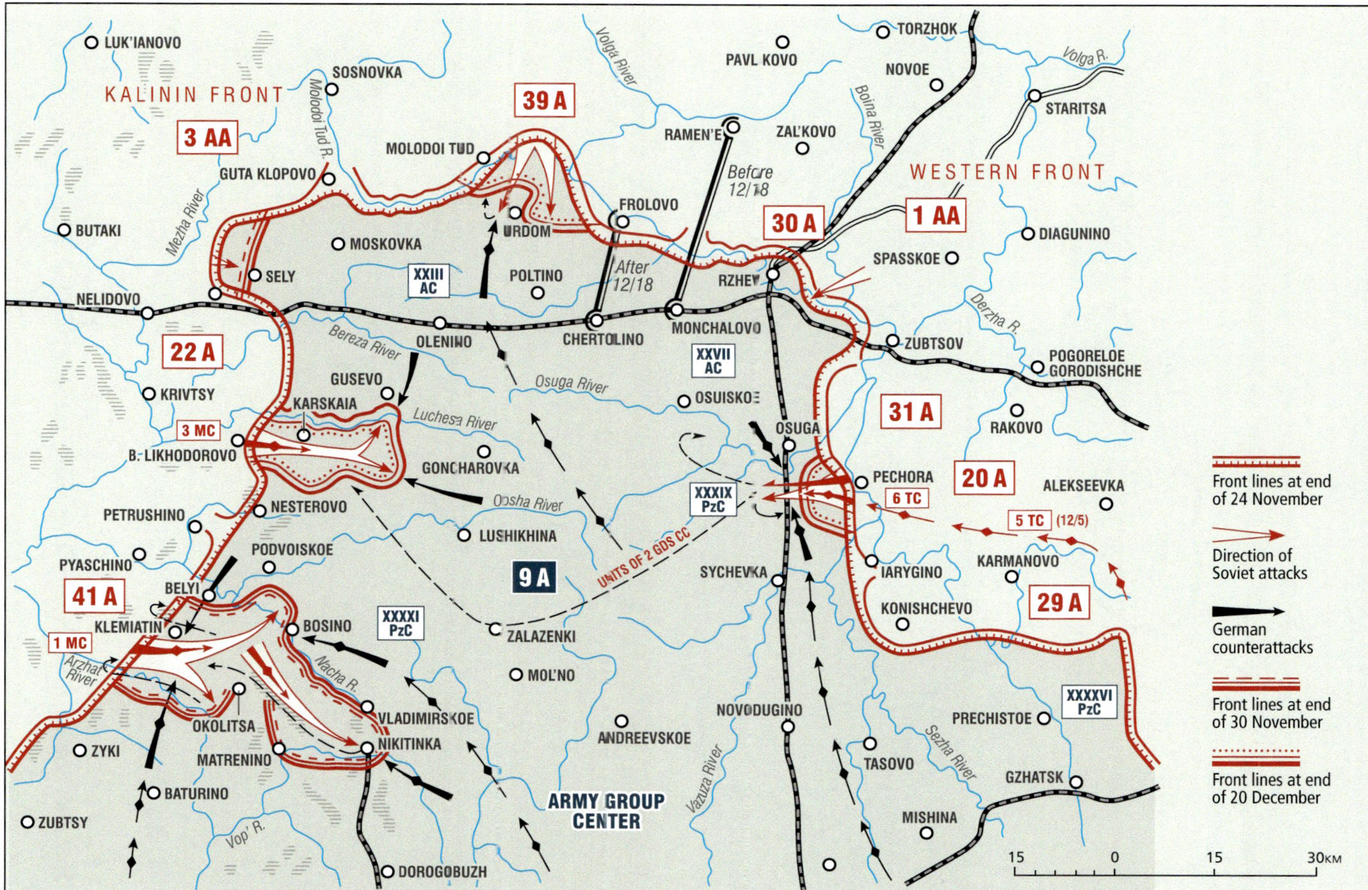

Operation Mars, the Second Rzhev-Sychevka Offensive, 25 November–20 December 1942.

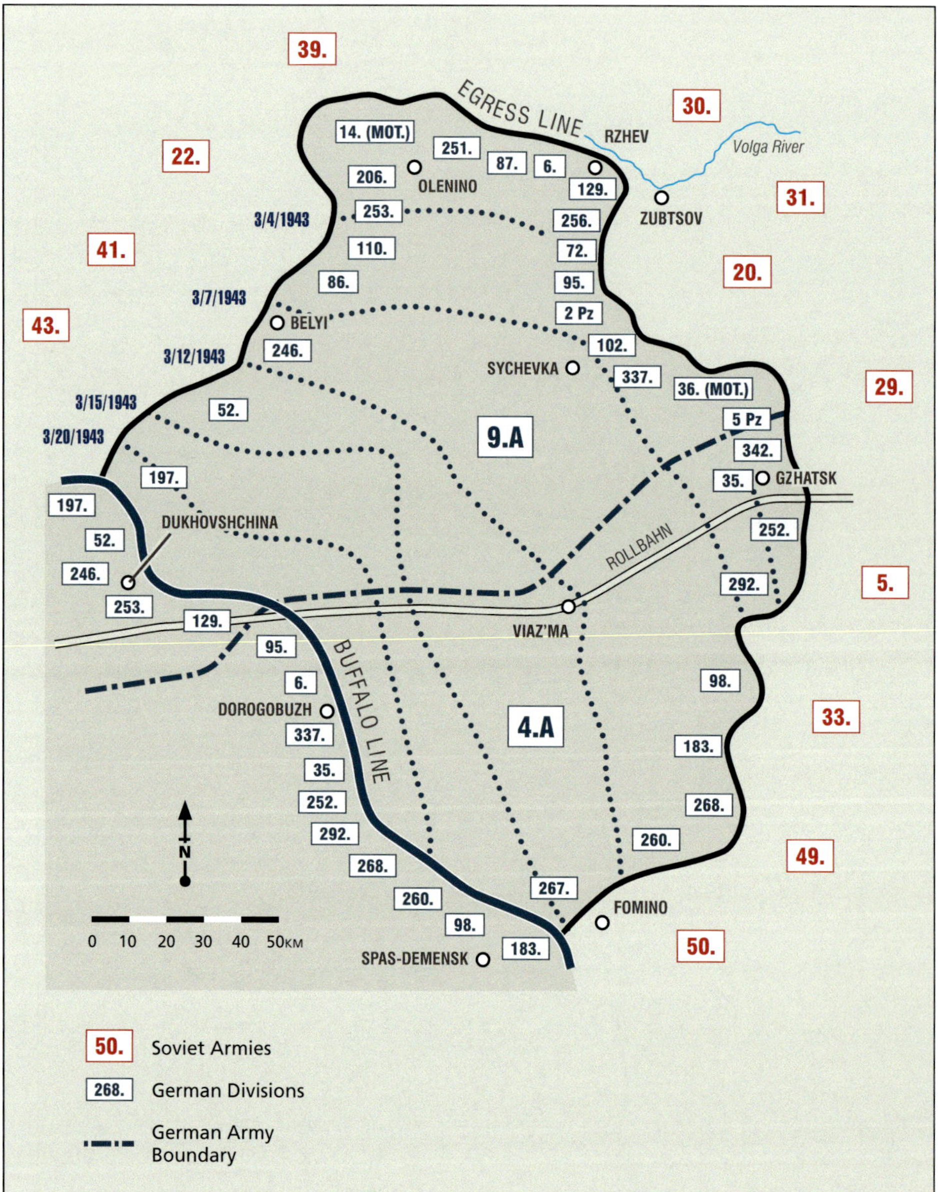

Operation Buffalo, the German withdrawal from the Rzhev Salient, 1–21 March 1943.

Moving to another position, spring 1943.

On the other hand, the *Stavka* "was toying around" with the *fronts* and "shuffling" the armies: on 12 March the Briansk Front was disbanded; on 23 March a Reserve (Kursk) Front was created, followed by the creation of the Reserve (Orel) Front on 27 March; on 28 March the Briansk Front was reconstituted. On the same date that the Briansk Front reappeared, the 21st Army was transferred from the Central Front to the Voronezh Front. It is no wonder that the operations of the Soviet forces on this sector of the front didn't yield results. On 28 March the Central Front's offensive operation was halted, and the *fronts* here went on the defense. Another attempt to defeat the German Army Group Center had ended with yet another failure.[58]

The authors of the six-volume *Istoriia Velikoi Otechestvennoi voiny* give Stalin's underestimation of the enemy's strength and capabilities, the serious shortcomings in the *Stavka*'s and the General Staff's planning of separate operations, the Red Army's dispersion of efforts, and the placement of unrealistic tasks in front of the *front* commands as the reasons for the Red Army's lack of success in the 1942/1943 winter campaign.[59] This list repeats almost word for word the reasons for the failures of the 1942 Rzhev – Viaz'ma operation (see above)! The impression is such that the Soviet Supreme High Command and the leadership of the country had learned nothing over a year of war?!

The sole major strategic result of the offensive of the Soviet *fronts* on the western direction in February-March 1943 was the liquidation of a direct threat to Moscow. The 1943 Rzhev – Viaz'ma offensive operation surpassed the results of all the offensive operations of 1942 on the central – Moscow – axis of the Soviet-German front: the Rzhev – Viaz'ma salient in the front lines was eliminated, and with it the enemy staging area close to the capital. The *Werhmacht* command had to abandon the idea of a new offensive on this axis, launched from this staging area. Long-suffering Russian cities, which for more than a year had been German strongpoints in the staging area – Belyi, Olenino, Rzhev, Sychevka, Gzhatsk, Viaz'ma – were at last liberated. Their liberation, which had been planned back at the beginning of 1942, managed to be achieved only in March 1943. Life began to return to the cities, which had been almost completely demolished not only by the enemy, but also by the Red Army's shelling. The struggle to liquidate the hostile staging area close to the capital had come to an end.

7

Results of the Battle – "This large and lengthy battle ..."

After the description of the combat operations in the region of the Rzhev – Viaz'ma salient between January 1942 and March 1943, it is fully natural, resting on the existing conceptual apparatus, to give them an evaluation, to determine their scale, and to establish whether or not they constitute a Battle of Rzhev, on par with the Battle of Moscow or the Battle of Stalingrad.

Familiarity with the operations of the *fronts* and armies on the Moscow axis in the course of three campaigns of the first and second stages of the Great Patriotic War doesn't permit us to call these operations simply *boi*, or combat actions on a tactical scale. Even a simple chronological description of the course of combat operation in area of the Rzhev – Viaz'ma salient allows one to see that they go far beyond the definitional boundaries of *boi* and *srazheniia* (military engagements), as official domestic historiography has maintained and continues to maintain. Viewing them as separate, disconnected Soviet offensive operations also doesn't reflect the magnitude of what happened in the area around the Rzhev bridgehead between January 1942 and March 1943. Facts testify that over the period of the winter 1941/42, summer-autumn 1942, and winter 1942/1943 military campaigns on the Moscow axis, a battle unfolded between major force groupings of both warring sides for the achievement of strategic goals. In this battle one side – the Soviet side – was attempting to defeat an enemy grouping on the western strategic axis that was standing at the walls of the capital of the Soviet state. The other side – the German side – was attempting to hold a strategically advantageous staging area in the center of the Eastern Front. Stemming from the definitions, such operations must be construed as strategic military operations, and they simply classically fit the Russian concept of *bitva*, or battle.

In the course of a prolonged time – 15 months – on one of the sectors of the central (Moscow) strategic axis, Soviet forces conducted four major offensive operations one after the other, all united by a single aim. Front and army operations were part and parcel of these operations. The separate operations of these *fronts* were supported simultaneously by offensive operations of neighboring *fronts* and armies. Several *front* operations on an operational scale were also conducted here. All of these operations were linked territorially by the configuration of the front: they were conducted in the region of the Rzhev – Viaz'ma salient.

Defensive and offensive operations of the *Wehrmacht* forces opposed these Soviet operations. In the given work, they are listed according to the interpretation of General H. Grossmann in his book *Rzhev: The Cornerstone of the Eastern Front*, which originally came out in Germany in 1962, before being translated into Russian and published in Rzhev in 1996. The book discusses several sequential engagements or battles in the area of the Rzhev salient, though in the German language, both *srazhenie* (engagement) and *bitva* (battle) are called by the same word (*Schlacht*). Despite certain slight discrepancies, the Soviet operations and the German engagements in 1942-1943 essentially coincide in date. It should be clarified that it is possible to disagree with the general on many points. For example, he also calls the quashing of resistance of isolated, retreating Soviet units in October 1941 in the area of Rzhev a *Schlacht*.

Table 10: German and Soviet timelines of respective operations in the Rzhev-Viaz'ma region

Soviet operations	German Operations and Combats
	1. Capture of Rzhev (Operation Typhoon) – October 1941
1. **Rzhev-Viaz'ma offensive operations of the Kalinin and Western Fronts, 8 January-20 April 1942**. Simultaneously: Briansk Front's Bolkhov operation and the Northwestern (later Kalinin) Front's Toropets-Kholm operation.	2. The winter fighting for Rzhev. January-February 1942.
Defensive operation of Western Front's Group Belov in May-June 1942	Operations Hannover-1 and Hannover-2 in May-June 1942. (H. Grossmann doesn't discuss these in his book.)
Kalinin Front's defensive operation in the Belyi area, 2-27 July 1942	3. Operation Seydlitz, 2-12 July 1942
2. **1st Rzhev-Sychevka (Gzhatsk) operation of the Western and Kalinin Fronts, 30 July-31 September 1942**.	4. Summer fighting for Rzhev. End of July – middle of September 1942
3. **2nd Rzhev-Sychevka offensive operation (Mars) of the Western and Kalinin Fronts, 25 November-20 December 1942**. Simultaneously, the Velikie Liuki operation of part of Kalinin Front's forces, 24 November 1942-20 January 1943	5. Winter fighting around Ninth Army's positions, 25 November-15 December 1942
	Army Group Center's withdrawal from the salient – Operation Buffalo, February 1943
4. **Rzhev-Viaz'ma offensive operation of the Western and Kalinin Fronts, 2-31 March 1943**. Simultaneously, the Briansk and Central Fronts' offensive	6. Fighting in March 1943.

Official military-historical history only considers one of the four Soviet offensive operations in the region of the salient a strategic operation. This prompts surprise, since according to the current definition of a strategic operation – the encirclement and destruction of an enemy grouping[1], both the Second Rzhev – Sychevka Operation and especially the 1943 Rzhev – Viaz'ma Operation due to their intent, goals and tasks, territorial scale and numerical strength of the participating groupings were practically repetitions of the 1942 Rzhev – Viaz'ma Operation.

In 1986, the *Voenno-istoricheskii zhurnal* conducted a discussion about strategic operations. Several authors protested against the assignment of the 1943 Rzhev – Viaz'ma Operation to the category of strategic operations, because it turned into a pursuit operation and didn't achieve its designated objective – the encirclement and destruction of the enemy grouping.[2] But after all, the 1942 Rzhev – Viaz'ma Operation didn't achieve this goal either.

Such strange, dual approaches! Or perhaps they reflect the inaccuracy or inadequacy of the definitions?

Doubtlessly, the Rzhev – Viaz'ma salient in 1942 was one of the "most important directions or theater of combat operations." However, it is difficult to agree with the assertion that both the 1942 Rzhev – Sychevka and the 1943 Rzhev – Viaz'ma operations "were now no longer conducted on the campaign's main axis of attack, but on secondary directions." In their opinion, "after May 1942 ... the main events were occurring not on the central axis, but on the southern wing of the Soviet-German front." If this opinion is accepted, then even all three above named operations that were conducted against the Rzhev – Viaz'ma salient taken together do not meet the Russian concept of "battle" (*bitva*).[3]

Even to a person untrained in the military science, it is obvious that an "axis of a campaign's main attack" and a "strategic direction" are different things. The assertion that the Rzhev salient was a "secondary axis", most likely, would have been taken with surprise by the leaders of the two warring states and the command of the armed forces of both sides. They considered this axis to be very important and thus kept up to a third of their strength on the entire Eastern Front here, even when heavy fighting was underway in the south.

The Soviet offensive operations in the region of the Rzhev salient were linked by a single concept: three of the four operations were an attempt to encircle the enemy forces and destroy them in a piecemeal fashion. The operations were mutually connected in terms of both the objective and the assignments. It is possible to recall their goals and tasks once again, as determined by the *Stavka* of the Supreme High Command: 7 January 1942 – "encirclement of the Mozhaisk – Viaz'ma grouping ..., destruction of the enemy's Rzhev grouping"; 16 February 1942 – "smash and destroy the enemy's Rzhev – Viaz'ma – Gzhatsk grouping ..."; 16 July 1942 – "clear enemy from the territory to the north of the Volga River in the Rzhev, Zubtsov area and from the territory of the Vazuza River in the Zubtsov, Karazino, Pogoreloe Gorodishche area; seize the cities of Rzhev and Zubtsov; reach and firmly dig-in on the Volga and Vazuza Rivers ..."; 8 December 1942 – "smash the enemy's Rzhev – Sychevka – Olenino – Belyi grouping ..., and subsequently ... destroy the enemy's Gzhatsk – Viaz'ma – Kholm-Zhirkovskii grouping ...". Since the *Stavka* directive regarding the operation of the Kalinin and Western Fronts in February 1943 has not been made public, we'll recall the words from the *Stavka* directive to the commander of the Central Front, which was to operate "with the aim of emerging in the rear of the enemy's Rzhev – Viaz'ma – Briansk grouping ..." In order to meet the advance of the Central Front, "the Western front will go on the offensive toward Roslavl' and further on toward Smolensk; the Kalinin Front – toward Vitebsk, Orsha and with part of its forces toward Smolensk."[4]

Thus, the main goal of all the operations was to inflict a defeat upon the main forces of the Germans' Army Group Center in the Rzhev – Viaz'ma area; and to liberate the cities of Rzhev, Sychevka, Viaz'ma and others, and thereby eliminate the Rzhev salient. The territorial extent of the operations varied: in the beginning of 1942 – along the entire front of the salient; in the summer and at the end of 1942 – combat operations were limited to the Rzhev – Sychevka – Belyi portion of the salient; in March 1943 – again along the entire front encompassing the salient. However, they were always conducted within the bounds of the salient. Even when combat operations extended beyond the boundaries of the salient, for example, Group Belov's fighting in May-June 1942, they were all still closely connected with the situation in the expanse of land between Rzhev and Viaz'ma.

The operations unfolded in the wide territories of the Moscow, Tula, present-day

Kaluga, Kalinin (now Tver') and Smolensk Oblasts. As has been mentioned above, the extent of the front lines in the area of the Rzhev – Viaz'ma salient varied between 550 and 700 kilometers. The latest edition of the *Voennyi entsiklopedicheskii slovar'* sets them at 530 kilometers.[5]

Combat operations here were of an intense and bitter nature: in the course of 8 of the 15 months, the Soviet forces conducted active offensive operations resulting in heavy losses on both sides. Major force groupings of both sides always took part in the combat operations around the salient. On the Soviet side, troops of the Kalinin and Western Fronts were operating here, supported on the flanks by the troops of the Northwestern, Briansk and Central Fronts. According to rough estimates, troops of no less than 40 armies (including air armies) of the two *fronts* took part in the four named offensive operations alone; moreover, with stubborn persistence, the list of the involved formations never varied. On the enemy side, forces of Army Group Center took part – the Ninth Army, and at various times the Fourth Army, as well as the Third and Fourth Panzer Armies and part of the Second Panzer Army.

The *Stavka* of the Supreme High Command and the Supreme Commander himself always exerted overall leadership over the operations, as documents testify (see the Appendices). Practically the same men and organizations planned and worked out the operations: the General Staff (the chief of which was B.M. Shaposhnikov between 1941 and May 1942, and A.M. Vasilevsky between June 1942 and February 1945) and the *front* commands. General of the Army G.K. Zhukov was in command of the Western Front between January and September 1942, of the Western Direction between February and May 1942, and commanded both the Kalinin and Western Fronts in September 1942. He was also the *Stavka* Representative at the Kalinin and Western Fronts in November and December 1942. Almost all this time, General V.D. Sokolovsky was the Western Front chief of staff or the chief of staff of the Western Direction. From the start of the Battle of Rzhev and practically until its end (27 February 1943), Colonel General I.S. Konev commanded the Kalinin Front and then the Western Front. General M.V. Zakharov was chief of staff of the Kalinin Front between January 1942 and April 1943.

Although the central German grouping was in fact never crushed, by the battle's conclusion a significant result had been achieved – both strategic and political. The enemy's dangerous staging area in close proximity to Moscow was liquidated, and the danger of a new German offensive on the Moscow axis was eliminated. The liberation of Rzhev and of other cities within the salient became a matter of prestige for the Soviet leadership and had an international significance: Supreme Commander I.V. Stalin mentioned the names of the cities in his correspondence with the British Prime Minister W. Churchill. In a letter from W. Churchill to I. Stalin on 4 March 1943, the Prime Minister had written, "Accept my most fervent congratulations on the occasion of Rzhev's liberation. From our discussion in August, it became known to me what great significance you were giving to the liberation of this point." On 6 March I. Stalin answered W. Churchill and boasted of another victory: "Thank you for your congratulations on the occasion of the taking of Rzhev by our troops. Today our troops took the city of Gzhatsk." On 13 March 1943, the Prime Minister of Great Britain again congratulated Stalin: "I sincerely congratulate you on the matter of Viaz'ma ..."[6]

Incidentally, March 1943 wasn't the first time that events on the central sector of the Soviet-German front were a topic in the correspondence of the leaders of the Allied governments. In the latter days of November 1942, Stalin had reported to both Prime Minister Churchill and President Roosevelt about the "'active operations on the Central front that were underway", which testifies to the significance of the combat operations against the salient to the Supreme Commander.[7]

Thus, practically all of the conceptual underpinnings of the word "battle" (*bitva*) are distinctly evident in the combat operations in the area of the German Rzhev-Viaz'ma staging area in the period January 1942 – March 1943. It follows that these military operations can be viewed as a battle with full justification. Indeed, this is not only the opinion of the author of this book. Back in the war years, the words of Lieutenant General D.D. Leliushenko, commander of the 30th Army rang out, to be sure, as represented by journalist and publicist I. Ehrenburg. They had met in the vicinity of Rzhev in October 1942. Ehrenburg wrote about the general:

> Young, unsophisticated, energetic. Under the dim light of a lamp, he is explaining the battle for Rzhev over a map that has been mauled by colored pencils. This is not a local battle; it is a large and lengthy battle. Of course, the Germans don't value the ruins of the second-rate city. Rzhev is a gateway. It can be opened to the east and the west. One prisoner told me: "How does Rzhev come into the picture? ... It begins with trifles, but it can end with Berlin ....[8]

Incidentally, in this phrase, albeit in a figurative fashion, the strategic significance of Rzhev both as a symbol and as the eponymic city of the entire battle is reflected.

The Supreme Commander also already during the war placed the combat operations at Rzhev on par with the most significant battles and engagements of the early war years. In the order of the Supreme Commander from 23 February 1943, there is the statement, "Our people will forever remember the historic defense of Sevastopol and Odessa, the stubborn fighting in front of Moscow and in the foothills of the Caucasus, in the area of Rzhev and in front of Leningrad, and the greatest clash in the history of warfare at the walls of Stalingrad."[9]

It is unequivocal: on the approaches to Moscow in January 1942 – March 1943, a prolonged, bitter and bloody battle unfolded. It flared up at times of Soviet offensive operations and subsided during inactive periods. The city of Rzhev became the symbol of the battle on the approaches to Moscow. In the names of all the aforementioned major Soviet offensive operations, there is the term "Rzhev"; in the cited order of the Supreme Commander the phrases "the stubborn fighting in front of Moscow" and "in the region of Rzhev" are mentioned separately. According to German veterans of the war, in the *Grossraum Rshew* [large expanse of Rzhev], they were defending Olenino, Rzhev, Zubtsov, Sychevka and Viaz'ma, and moreover in H. Grossmann's book, Rzhev is "the cornerstone of the Eastern Front". Although he is discussing the combat operations of the Ninth Army, the maps in the book show the entire Rzhev – Viaz'ma salient.[10] It is fully logical to call the battle by the name of the city that became its symbol for both sides – Rzhev. As it happened, this name arose on its own accord. War veterans, politicians, local and regional historians actively use this term – the Battle of Rzhev.

However, official historiography categorically rejects the existence of a "Battle of Rzhev". One of its main arguments is the absence of an operational pause between the Moscow offensive and the 1942 Rzhev – Viaz'ma operations. According to contemporary official views, the 1942 Rzhev – Viaz'ma operation is part of the Battle of Moscow. We'll remind the reader that this leaves the three later major Soviet offensive operations "hanging in the air".

One way out of this situation has been proposed above: to consider the beginning of January as the end of the Battle of Moscow. The Battle of Rzhev begins with the *Stavka* directive from 7 January 1942, when the Rzhev – Viaz'ma direction was first mentioned, and it continued until the elimination of the salient. The task of liberating the cities, which became German strongpoints in the salient, was assigned by this directive in January 1942, and was fulfilled only in March 1943.

A second way out is also possible, in which all of the operations on the Moscow axis receive their precise placement: the Battle of Moscow ended with the liquidation of the Rzhev – Viaz'ma salient in March 1943, when German forces were pushed back from Moscow, in general, by more than 300 kilometers. Such a proposal flashed through the public utterances of the well-known military chief, but wasn't heard.

One detail of the Battle of Rzhev was the fact that in the entire second half of 1942, it unfolded in parallel with the Battle of Stalingrad. The First Rzhev – Sychevka (Gzhatsk) offensive and Stalingrad defensive operations began in July 1942. There was combat directly inside Stalingrad on 17 and 30 September, and in Rzhev – on 13 and 21 September. Already in the war years, people spoke of the similarity and uncommon intensity of the fighting in the cities. Both in Stalingrad and in Rzhev, savage street fighting was going on, when both sides struggled for each building and for every street. Frontline war correspondent B. Iampul'sky wrote in *Izvestiia* in October 1942 about the fighting in Rzhev:

> Frames and doors go flying from a blast wave. Roofs are blown skyward and walls are collapsing. Soldiers are running through the burning street with pike poles, ladders and ropes, like firemen. And through the walls and fences – onto the roofs via downspouts and cornices, into the windows, into holes and gaps in the walls. First a grenade, and after it – with bayonets and knives – into the blast wave, into the smoke, rumble, toward the German moans and cries. Now combat is going on inside the buildings, in narrow and dark corridors, between the bedroom and dining room, between the chest of drawers and the armoire, from the attic down to the basement. One phrase alone from the German *Luftflotte* 4's journal of combat operations for 22 September gives an impression of the fighting in Stalingrad: "Insignificant success: from ruin to ruin, from cellar to cellar."[11]

The Stalingrad offensive Operation Uranus and the Second Rzhev – Sychevka offensive (Operation Mars) began one week apart – on 19 and 25 November respectively. On 2 February 1943 the Battle of Stalingrad came to an end; on 6 February 1943, because of a lack of reserves as a consequence of the defeat at Stalingrad, Hitler issued an order for the abandonment of the Rzhev – Viaz'ma salient. The fighting at the center of the Soviet-German front had an influence on the fighting in the south, while the results of the battle in the south in the most direct manner told upon situation in the center.

The attitude of the leadership of the warring governments and the commands of the Red Army and the *Wehrmacht* toward Rzhev and Stalingrad as symbols of the battles were identical: the attacking forces were supposed to capture a city at whatever the cost, while the defenders were to hold their positions and not yield a city to the enemy. For A. Hitler it became a matter of prestige to take Stalingrad and not surrender Rzhev; for I. Stalin – to take Rzhev and not give up Stalingrad. The date by which the cities had to be taken were issued repeatedly: Stalingrad – by 20 October, or by 10 November 1942; Rzhev – by 8-9, 11, 12 January, prior to 14 January, no later than 21 January, no later than 5 April, by 31 July-1 August, 9 August, 23 December 1942. In reaction to failures, the conduct of members of the command of both sides was also similar: they refused to see things objectively; that which was desired was taken for reality. For example, in a speech in Munich in the beginning of November 1942, Hitler said, "We wanted to take Stalingrad ..., and there's no reason to be modest: it has already been taken."[12] As already described above, G.K. Zhukov awarded the commanders of the 39th Army personalized watches in December 1942, for "taking the city of Olenino", even though the small town of Olenino wasn't liberated until 4 March 1943.

If we speak concretely about the cities, then Rzhev and Stalingrad stood on opposite sides of the front line: Soviet forces defended Stalingrad and never yielded it to the Germans; German forces held Rzhev for 14 months and didn't give it up even in periods of the most active Soviet offensive operations, and moreover, they abandoned the salient of their own volition. When today many war veterans and the mass press call Rzhev "the second Stalingrad", this is in essence inaccurate and testifies to ignorance of the real events. Rzhev was the German Stalingrad. Just as in our country, people who passed through the hell of the bloody battle at Stalingrad, who withstood the terrible experiences and in the process carried out their duty, are called "Stalingraders", in Germany in the war years there was a prevailing concept of "*der Rshew-Kämpfer*" – the "Rzhev fighter", which signified a soldier who had carried out his military duty to the end.[13]

From this arises the converse nature of the very essence of the Battles of Stalingrad and Rzhev. In the first case, the Soviet troops withstood the onslaught of a powerful adversary, and then crushed him. In the second case, the adversary stood firm against several major Soviet offensives, did not allow himself to be destroyed, and in addition withdrew from the city voluntarily. It is this that explains historiography's veil of silence over the combat operations in the region of the Rzhev – Viaz'ma salient in Soviet times and today.

The simultaneity of the battles fully naturally leads to their comparison. For official history of the war this is blasphemy, an attack upon fundamental principles. Academician A.A. Samsonov compared the Battle of Stalingrad with the battle for the Caucasus: "The indisputable similarity of the two battles, which began almost simultaneously (17 and 25 July) existed from the very beginning."[14] With no less justification, the same thing can be said about the Stalingrad and Rzhev battles. Their comparison allows one to draw some interesting conclusions (Tables 11, 12).

According to German data 76 divisions of various designations were committed at Stalingrad. Primarily on the defensive at the Rzhev – Viaz'ma staging area, the *Wehrmacht* committed up to 57 divisions.

The data in the tables show that the combat operations in the area of the Rzhev – Viaz'ma salient, by the number of participating troops, by the size of the territory, by their extent, by the losses, by the attention given to them by the military leadership of the opposing sides are not only comparable to the Battle of Stalingrad. In a number of instances, they exceed it.

Table 11: The strength of the Soviet forces at the start of the operations

	Battle of Rzhev					Battle of Stalingrad		
Operations	**Rzhev-Viaz'ma 1942**	**1st Rzhev-Sychevka**	**2nd Rzhev-Sychevka**	**Rzhev-Viaz'ma 1943**	**Total**	**Defensive**	**Offensive**	**Total**
Armies	14	6	6	12	38			
Rifle, Motorized Rifle, Cavalry, Tank Divisions	90	33	54	53	230	37	74	111
Rifle, Motorized Rifle, Tank Brigades	35	29	42	25	131	22	34	56
Personnel	1,059,200	345,100	545,000	876,000	2,825,300	547,000	1,143,500	1,690,500

Source: The number of divisions and brigades involved in the Battle of Rzhev have been calculated from *Obshchevoiskovye armii i ikh boevoi sostav za 1942 v Velikoi Otechestvennoi voine* and *Obshchevoiskovye armii i ikh boevoi sostav za 1943 v Velikoi Otechestvennoi voine*, both from the TsAMO Library. Corps, artillery and aviation formations and units are not included. Only combined-arms armies are indicated, but formations and units of the *fronts'* air forces always took part, and after May 1942 – the 1st and 3rd Air Armies. The number of divisions and brigades involved in the Battle of Stalingrad, as well as the number of personnel involved in all the operations, are taken from Krivosheev, ed. *Grif sekretnosti sniat: poteri Vooruzhennykh sil SSSR v voinakh, boevykh deistviakh i voennykh konfliktakh XX veka* (Moscow: Voennoe izdatel'stvo, 1993).

Table 12: Length of front, duration and losses of the battles of Rzhev and Stalingrad

	Battle of Rzhev	Battle of Stalingrad
Length of front	As the battle unfolded, the front shrank from more than 700 kilometers in length down to 550 kilometers	As of 19 November 1942, 850 kilometers
Duration	15 months	7 months
Total casualties	1,324,823 men (according to official data for the four offensive operations over eight months)	1,129,619 men

Sources: See Kondratjew O.A. *Die Schlacht von Rshew: Ein halbes Jahrhundert Schweigen*. Arethousa Verlag. Műnchen, 2000, pp. 105-112; *Velikaia Otechestvennaia bez grifa sekretnosti: Kniga poteri* (Moscow: Veche, 2009), p. 115.For the dimensions of the Rzhev salient, see *Velikaia Otechestvennaia voina 1941-1945. Entsiklopediia* (Moscow 1985), p. 612; *Velikaia Otechestvennaia ... Ocherki*, Book 2, p. 242; *Istoriia vtoroi mirovoi voiny*, Vol. 6, p. 35; *Rossiia i SSSR v voinakh XX veka*, pp. 277, 279, 281, 312, 313. The new book *Velikaia otechestvennaia bez grifa sektretnosti* on pages 104, 179, 180, 181 gives the respective losses for the operations.

In the official version of the Great Patriotic War, and indeed of the entire Second World War, the Battle of Stalingrad is considered the most bloody. However, the analysis of combat operations on certain sectors of the Soviet-German front, which at times heated up during offensive operations, then became quiet for some time, as happened, for example, in the areas of the Rzhev – Viaz'ma salient and Leningrad, permit one to speak about the more significant human losses, naturally, with regard to the losses in all the operations conducted there.

"Rzhev – It is the Abyss. Will anyone ever add up how many it swallowed?"

E. Rzhevskaia, a former translator on the staff of the 30th Army headquarters, wrote in the days of the fighting at Rzhev, "Rzhev – It is the Abyss. They are hurling more and more men into it. Will anyone ever add up how many it has swallowed?"[15] Such calculations were needless to the leadership of the Soviet country, both after the elimination of the enemy bridgehead at the walls of the capital and after the war. The casualty figures, as recorded in the documents of the *fronts* and armies that fought in the region of the Rzhev salient, were kept classified in the Ministry of Defense's Central Archive. They emerged only in step with the divulgence of facts from the history of combat operations in the Rzhev – Viaz'ma expanse. The process was gradual, and the figures that appeared were plainly understated.

At present, the official point of view about the casualties has been made manifest in the book *Rossiia i SSSR v voinakh XX veka: Statisticheskoe issledovanie* [*Russia and the USSR in the Wars of the XX Century: A statistical analysis*], published by the OLMA-PRESS publishing house in 2001. Here, the figures for total casualties (irrecoverable – killed, mortally wounded, missing and captured; and medical – wounded and sick) of the participating *fronts* were published for the four offensive operations against the Rzhev-Viaz'ma salient:

Rzhev – Viaz'ma 8 January – 20 April 1942	– 776,889
Rzhev – Sychevka 30 July – 23 August 1942	– 193,383
Rzhev – Sychevka 25 November – 20 December 1942	– 215,674
Rzhev – Viaz'ma 2 – 31 March 1943	– 138,577

The total casualties over approximately eight months of fighting (out of 15 months between the start and endpoint of the operations) amounts to 1,324,823 men, which is a higher number than the total Soviet losses in the Battle of Stalingrad. The irrecoverable losses over this time at the Rzhev salient comprised 433,037 men, in the Stalingrad battle – 478,741 men, which is also fully comparable.[16]

In the 1990s and the present decade, individual scholars, including foreign scholars, who disagreed with the official casualty figures, tried to estimate the Soviet losses in the separate operations. As already mentioned previously, S.N. Mikhalev placed the losses of the Soviet armies in the 1942 Rzhev – Viaz'ma operation at 948,000 men. According to H. Grossmann, Russian casualties in the summer-autumn fighting of 1942 amounted to 380,000 men; according to incomplete data in the possession of the author of these lines, Soviet operational losses in August-September 1942 were more than 300,000 men. D. Glantz agrees with the German estimate of Russian casualties in the Second Rzhev – Sychevka Operation, which puts them at 335,000 men. These calculations and estimates increase the total casualties in the four operations to up to 1,700,000 men.[17]

This figure is not conclusive, since the number of Soviet missing-in-action and prisoners-of-war have not been determined. Moreover, none of the official figures include the casualties over the seven months when there were no offensives underway – over May-July and October-November 1942, and January-February 1943, and they, as already noted above, were frequently significant. Let's recall at least the losses in the defensive operation of the Kalinin Front in July 1942 in the Belyi area, when approximately 50,000 alone were taken prisoner. With the inclusion of casualties from these seven months between offensives, as one can assume, the human losses of the Red Army in the fighting at the

Rzhev – Viaz'ma staging area might possibly even exceed 2,000,000 men.

In March 1998, in the Tver' Oblast and city of Rzhev newspapers, a speech by Rzhev's Head of Administration A.V. Kharchenko on the occasion of the 55th anniversary of the city's liberation was published. In it, he gave a new figure for the losses of the Red Army on the Rzhev – Viaz'ma axis – 2,060,000 men. The number of "more than two million men, including 913,000 irrecoverably" was repeated at a conference dedicated to the history of the Battle of Rzhev, at the Central Museum in Moscow. The information about the losses was given by the Institute of Military History in response to a question from Marshal of the Soviet Union V.G. Kulikov, a participant in the fighting at Rzhev, and an honored citizen of the city. A detailed breakdown of this figure was being kept (is being kept?) by the Rzhev city administration, unfortunately without any public release of the data or the endorsements, but with references to the book *Grif sekretnosti sniat* [The Seal of Secrecy has been Lifted] and several files from the Central Archive's Collection No. 213 (the operations department of Kalinin Front's field headquarters). Marshal Kulikov said that "the operations at the staging area can logically be assigned to the category of slaughters, that is to say, to battles with a large quantity of victims."[18]

The human losses of the Soviet forces in the Moscow strategic defensive operation (30 September – 5 December 1941), in the counteroffensive at Moscow (5 December 1941 – 7 January 1942), that is, when the Rzhev – Viaz'ma salient didn't yet exist, as well as the 1942 Rzhev – Viaz'ma the Rzhev – Sychevka (30 July – 23 August 1942), and the 1943 Rzhev – Viaz'ma operations all contributed to the given casualty figure. It does not include the troop losses in May-June 1942, including those in Kalinin Front's defensive operation in the Belyi area, nor those from the end of August to December 1942, including in the Second Rzhev – Sychevka operation (Mars), or those in January-February 1943. Including the official casualty figures in the excluded operations, the total losses approach 2,300,000 men.

The information about the casualties on the Rzhev – Viaz'ma axis, given to Marshal Kulikov in the Institute of Military History, is interesting in another respect. Having aggregated the human losses in all the operations on the Moscow axis, in both the Moscow and in the Rzhev operations, the unknown author – an employee of the Institute – perhaps unwillingly gave support to one of the two versions for assessing the combat operations on the Rzhev – Viaz'ma direction that I laid out above; namely, that these operations were linked and comprise a unified whole.

In March 2000 in his presentation at the International Conference "Rzhev: two views on the battle" in the Central Museum of the Great Patriotic War in Moscow, Marshal of the Soviet Union V.G. Kulikov again gave the figure for the total losses of the Soviet forces on the Rzhev –Viaz'ma direction – more than 2,000,000 men. However, at three conferences dedicated to the Rzhev battle that took place in Moscow at the end of the 1990s and the beginning of the 2000s, the number of killed-in-action alone was given as ranging from 800,000 to 913,000 men.[19]

Here, perhaps, it is fitting to speak a bit about the fact that at the given moment, the official methodology for calculating the losses in operations is restricted to considering only irrecoverable losses – the killed-in-action, prisoners and missing-in-action. In the opinion of historians that represent the official point of view, the wounded returned to duty after recovering, while prisoners-of-war returned to the country after the war. At the view of an unprofessional military historian, there are large "holes" in such a methodology. If the

Search team members at work. Tver' Oblast, 1990s.

discussion concerns the irrecoverable losses of the Armed Forces, then a fighter who lost an arm or a leg at Rzhev never returned to the ranks of the Red Army.

At the end of March 2007, one such participant in the battle, I.A. Khrenov, passed away. In August 1942, he lost an arm outside of Rzhev, found himself in civilian life after the war, and he lived it very commendably. However, he never served again in the Red Army, so for it he was an irrecoverable loss, though his wound placed him in the category of medical losses (wounded or sick).

Those who were taken prisoner by the Germans in the combat operations, naturally, never took part with the Red Army again in the fighting, but at the same time, they were not killed-in-action. Moreover, immediately after the operations, formations and units were sent to be reformed, or were disbanded due to all their losses, and not just due to their killed-in-action. For example, there was the case of the Kalinin Front's 11th Cavalry Corps. At the beginning of August 1942 it was disbanded, because its killed, wounded, missing-in-action, sick and other losses amounted to 14,830 men, of which the missing-in-action alone numbered 14,071 men.[20] Replacements in the course of the fighting arrived in the formations and units to offset total losses. Nobody waited for when those wounded in the fighting would return after being discharged from a hospital. Nevertheless, it is possible that a simple person isn't given to understand the official methodology.

The cited material on the human losses speaks to the fact that the question of the human toll of the fighting around the Rzhev – Viaz'ma salient hasn't been researched to the end, and the precise answer as to how many of its compatriots Rzhev "swallowed" is still in the future.

According to the Tver' Oblast Military Commissariat in response to a query from the Tver' State Consolidated Museum, by the end of 2002 on the territory of the Belyi, Zubtsov, Olenino and Rzhev districts, around 150,000 fallen Red Army soldiers and officers had been counted. By the same time, according to data of the Smolensk Oblast Military Commissariat, approximately 68,000 of the fallen had been counted on the territory of the Viaz'ma, Gagarin (formerly Gzhatsk), Sychevka, Ugra and Kholm-Zhirkovskii districts – a figure with which the staff of the Oblast Military Commissariat themselves disagreed. In a letter accompanying the report, it was written that this number was approximate: "the figures are increasing every year. With the work of search teams in the field and according to archival documents, each year we are memorializing somewhere around 5,000 more of the dead."[21]

To the present day, at combat locations throughout the entire Rzhev – Viaz'ma salient rest the unburied and uncounted remains of Soviet soldiers. Numerous search teams, both local and from other oblasts, are working in the Smolensk and Tver' Oblasts to recover the remains of fallen soldiers, perhaps identify them, and give them a proper burial. In Tver' Oblast, the public organization "Scientific-Historical Military-Patriotic Center 'Deed'" has been conducting such search work since 1987. Between 1988 and 2003 in Tver' Oblast, the remains of more than 22,000 soldiers were recovered and interred with military honors and religious ceremony; the identities of more than 3,000 of the remains managed to be established.[22]

While working in the field, search team members have encountered things that disclose cruel scenes from the war. Smolensk searchers once found a large pit in the woods, in which the drivers, medical staff and patients of an entire ambulance wagon train were at rest – about fifty remains. On the bones there were signs of splints, amputations and wounds. The

Artifacts found by a search team, 1990s.

A Red Army helmet found by a search team, Rzhev area, 1990s.

Nazis had obviously attacked the small convoy and killed everyone.[23] In the field notes of the Borzovy family search team from Moscow, who worked in the Gzhatsk area, there is horrifying information about the traces of combat that they uncovered in the soil and in interviews with local residents:

> "It seems they were unable to make it across the field," recalls Aunt Fenia; "The remains were lying side by side. Back in the day, there was nothing for us old ladies to wear on our feet, so those who were a bit bolder would shake the bones out of a pair of boots and put those same boots on their own feet." A peasant male, about 50-years-old, continues her story:
>
> "They never in fact collected the bones from those fields. In places a bulldozer had scraped them together, in other places they simply plowed right through the bones. It happened, you'd start the tractor and look straight ahead into the distance at some birch tree, so that you wouldn't veer off-line and wouldn't have to see what was going on under your tractor. If I'd known that you needed helmets, I could have brought you a trailer full of them from Kostrovo; I was plowing over there today. There you don't even need to search for them; they're lying in every crater. You know, we have here hoes made from sapper's shovels in every household."

The Borzovy field notes continue, "Now and then in the spruce forest you come across helmets, mess kits, gas mask canisters ... It is something like a city of the dead. It stretches as far as you can see. I wanted to take a mess kit or a tin cup, but everything is full of holes,

Remains found by a search team, Tver' Oblast, 1990s.

A funeral service for the remains of Red Army soldiers at the Memorial complex in Rzhev, 2002.

МЕДАЛЬ „В ПАМЯТЬ 50-ЛЕТИЯ МОСКВЫ“

Петухов
Сергей
Михайлович

НАГРАЖДЕН(А)

МЕДАЛЬЮ „В ПАМЯТЬ 850-ЛЕТИЯ МОСКВЫ“

М. П.

Президент Российской Федерации

Б № 0141371

Указ от 26 февраля 1997 года

Удостоверение руководителя Ржевского поискового отряда "Память 29-й армии"

An award to the leader of the Rzhev search team "Memory of the 29th Army".

shot through ... The evident density of fire is horrifying. Canisters, boxes – everything is riddled."[24]

The activity of the search teams permits the recovery and honorable reburial of the remains of thousands of Soviet soldiers, who were at one time "forgotten" on the battlefield. Through the results of their work over five more years, as well as a consequence of additional processing and clarification of archival records, on the territory of the four districts of Tver' Oblast named above, another 17,000 men (and women) who were killed in the war were counted; the number of those remains found on the territory of the Rzhev district alone that were re-interred increased by almost 10,000. Even more striking are the numbers from Smolensk Oblast. If in 2002 they put the number of those who'd been killed on its territory between 1941 and 1943 and whose remains had been located and reburied at 198,318, then by 2002 this number increased to more than 349,000. In 2006 alone, 82 search teams were working in Smolensk Oblast. Within Kalinin Oblast's Iukhnov District, by April 2007, the remains of 20,954 Red Army soldiers and officers, who were killed in the Great Patriotic War, were found and reburied.[25]

It is now hardly possible to establish a precise figure for the human losses in the Rzhev – Viaz'ma region, and now even more impossible to identify the names of all those who fought, were killed, or went missing-in-action in those places. One must agree with the opinion of D. Glantz that a cult of sacrifice and the unwillingness or incapability to consider human losses are both totally inherent to a totalitarian regime.[26]

The disregard for the individual person, the attitude toward a human as merely a tiny

Dead German soldiers of the 129th Infantry Division in the church in the village of Romanovo, Christmas Day 1941, Kalinin Oblast.

A German cemetery in the Rzhev area, spring of 1942.

A graveyard of approximately 2,000 German soldiers on the eastern outskirts of Rzhev, first half of 1942.

A German cemetery outside a hospital in the southern part of Rzhev, July 1942.

Another German cemetery at Bocharovo, Rzhev area, winter 1942-1943.

cog in an enormous state machine, led to the fact that even today, 60 years after the war, we're continuing to operate on the basis of approximate figures for the total casualties, while the words "No one is forgotten ..." remains only a declaration.

There are also no accurate aggregate figures for the *Wehrmacht's* human losses in the battle for the Rzhev – Viaz'ma staging area, at least in the author's possession. As a rule, German materials provide information for individual combat units and formations over a certain period of time. For example, the losses in the 6th Infantry Division's 18th Infantry Regiment for August 1942 amounted to 746 men, of which 23 were officers; the total losses of this division between 1 and 22 August 1942 numbered 3,294 men. According to information from the National Union of Germany for the Care of Military Graves, the Ninth Army in the battle for the Rzhev bridgehead in the Belyi – Olenino – Rzhev – Zubtsov – Sychevka area lost 120,000 men killed, while the number of wounded significantly exceeded this quantity. In the words of German veterans who fought at Rzhev, in the fighting for the bridgehead 350,000-400,000 German soldiers and officers were killed. These numbers lack substantiation by references to documentary sources. E. Rzhevskaia in 1985 in one of her books cited an article in the Hamburg newspaper *Die Welt*: "In the fighting for Rzhev, as many Germans were killed as there are residents, for example, in Cottbus or Ingolstadt." She didn't indicate when this article was published, but as of 1992, approximately 98,000 and 129,000 people respectively were living in these two cities, which is in the neighborhood of the figure offered by the National Union of Germany for the Care of Military Graves for the Ninth Army's human losses.[27]

Precise figures for the human losses on the German side in the battle for the Rzhev – Viaz'ma staging area also still remain to be tabulated.

The Lost Victory

Just who won and who lost the Battle of Rzhev? The question is not at all a simple one. Upon examining this question, the Battle of Rzhev is reminiscent of the Battle of Borodino; even today, historians still argue over who won that battle. In both battles, the sides didn't achieve their ultimate objectives, but at the same time fulfilled specific assignments. Several scholars believe that the Battle of Borodino had no victor, but gave a morale boost to the Russians. The results of the Battle of Rzhev in a certain way are similar to this situation, but with a minus sign on the Russian side with respect to morale.

The Soviet forces in 1943 made significant territorial gains. Unquestionably, the elimination of the dangerous German staging area in the center of the Soviet-German front and the simultaneous removal of a constant threat to the Soviet capital must be viewed as an important result and one with strategic significance. The liberation of Rzhev and other cities and towns in the German salient, which the Soviet forces had been unable to take for many months, was an important political result. But this victory was far from triumphal in the way of the Battle of Stalingrad: the primary objective of all the operations in the area of the Rzhev – Viaz'ma salient – the destruction of the main forces of Army Group Center – was not achieved.

The German forces voluntarily withdrew from the salient, unbeaten and unbowed on this sector on this sector of the front. They did of their own volition what their opponent had been trying to force them do for more than a year, and in the process conserved their strength for future operations. However, at the same time the *Wehrmacht* could no longer hold on to the salient, and it lost its strategically advantageous staging area at the center of the Eastern Front. The Germans were compelled to abandon Rzhev, this eponymic city, which personified the defense of a large territory, this "gateway to Berlin".

For both one side and the other, this was a lost victory. But for both sides, this victory was even more a pyrrhic one.

The Rzhev salient, the "Rzhev bulge" became for both armies a "black hole" that sucked in and swallowed large numbers of troops. In the memory of the Soviet soldiers that served there, it remained the "Rzhev meat grinder", the "Abyss". To the present day, in the villages of many districts around Rzhev, the expression "herded at Rzhev" still circulates. This actually was a Moloch, which devoured their children. The heroism and self-sacrifice of some stood side-by-side with the negligence, oversights, blunders and at times even criminal behavior of others. The problem with material-technical supply, the mistakes in planning the combat operations on the whole and in separate operations, the shortcomings in controlling the forces, the leadership of the country and the Red Army's Supreme Command tried to resolve at the expense of the "human factor". The striving to achieve victory "at any cost", at the expense of enormous human losses does not give evidence of the ability to fight according to Suvorov's dictum – "Not with numbers, but by skill." The acquisition of combat experience by the Red Army command and the leadership of the country came at too high a price.

P. Mikhin, a former platoon commander in the 1028th Artillery Regiment of the 30th Army's 52nd Rifle Division wrote back at the beginning of this century:

> We learned to fight on the land of Rzhev, while our great commanders learned how to execute their forthcoming victories at our expense. For 15 months we battled for Rzhev and accomplished almost nothing, until the Germans left it themselves. Let us

> assume that these were victories for the enemy, but these were also our most terrible tragedies. The war didn't develop on successes alone. But the history of it should be complete and credible, no matter how bitter it was. War was this bitterness after all, so costly to many, who passed through the 'Rzhev meat grinder'. The Germans were turning the handle, and we poured and poured thousands and thousands of soldiers into it.[28]

However, the Rzhev – Viaz'ma salient became a "black hole" for the German forces as well. German veterans to the present day recall with horror the fighting in the *Rshew Grossraum*. The "irreplaceable losses" of the *Wehrmacht* here "were kept hidden from the unknowing population, and they cast a pall over the assessment of Operation Buffalo as 'a military achievement'". Colonel-General Model, who directed the defense, subsequently gained the reputation of an "expert of retreats".[29]

The Battle of Rzhev was one of the bloodiest battles of the Great Patriotic, and perhaps of the entire Second World War: the total losses on both sides were enormous. The Soviet forces, although in fact they had no big success on this sector of the front, they pinned down a large number of German troops here, and on a daily basis ground down the enemy's manpower and equipment. This eroded the Nazi military machine and laid the basis for Germany's defeat. Historian A.N. Mertsalov calls the collective feat of the Red Army's units and formations here one of the sources of victory over fascism: "This is heroism of a different sort – prolonged and hard, this was the military labor of millions of Red Army men under conditions of constant mortal danger … ."[30] P. Mikhin wrote:

> Our 52nd Rifle Division attacked toward Rzhev from the north, through Polunino, head-on against the enemy. Over six month of fighting we advanced 6 kilometers. We liberated four piles of ashes and left behind us two fraternal graves with up to 13,000 men in each … Nobody wanted to die, but kept advancing forward at a run – attacking and dying. So many "valleys of death", "groves of death" and "swamps of death" we baptized and left behind us! But nevertheless we kept advancing, but measured our progress in meters. Recalling the past, I see the fields around Rzhev, strewn with the corpses of our guys and the Germans.[31]

In the vicinity of Rzhev, Sychevka, Viaz'ma, Zubtsov, Belyi, Olenino and at Gzhatsk, Soviet soldiers with their daily military work kept drawing closer to Victory over the foe and thus are worthy of respect and remembrance no less than those who marched all the way to Berlin.

The military operations of the Soviet forces in the region of the Rzhev – Viaz'ma salient had a large influence on the *Wehrmacht's* entire strategy on the Eastern Front in 1942: the German forces did not conduct active offensive operations on the central sector of the front. Here, for all of 1942 they were compelled primarily to defend, even in the period of the 1942 summer-autumn campaign, which Soviet military science has assigned to the category of defensive campaigns. This is evidence that the strategic initiative on the central sector of the Soviet-German front, which had been intercepted in the Battle of Moscow, remained on the Red Army's side for all of 1942, despite the *Wehrmacht's* own limited offensives to clear the salient of Soviet-held pockets and penetrations resulting from the 1941/42 Moscow counteroffensive.

The name of the German general H. Grossmann's book *Rzhev: The Cornerstone of the Eastern Front* isn't quite accurate. In German newspapers of the second half of 1942, this phrase was expressed differently: "the cornerstone of the German line of resistance", or "the Führer's impenetrable line".[32] German generals already in the war years called the operations of their forces around Rzhev in January-February, August-September, and November-December 1942 "Rzhev's defensive engagements" – *Abwehrschlacht von (bei) Rshew*. In the opinion of the author of the book on the history of the 129th Infantry Division H. Boucsein, all of the Ninth Army's military operations at this time within the boundaries of Army Group Center could be called "defensive engagements in front of Moscow".[33]

In both domestic historical literature and in the public's perception, the battles in the area of the Rzhev – Viaz'ma salient in the summer, autumn and winter of 1942 assisted the operations of the Soviet forces at Stalingrad. Interestingly, the Germans also said that they were defending Rzhev, in order to obtain victory in the south. The task of both sides at Rzhev was to tie up enemy forces there and prevent their transfer to the south, to Stalingrad and the Caucasus axis. That is undoubtedly the case. However, to speak only about assistance to Stalingrad means to minimize the significance of the Battle of Rzhev, which to a certain degree affected combat operations on both other sectors of the Soviet-German front as well as on other theaters of combat operations of the Second World War, thereby making a most significant contribution to the achievement of victory over fascism. German divisions and units were removed not only from the south, but also from other directions, and transferred to the center of the Eastern Front over the entire time of the Battle of Rzhev, which for some reason is often forgotten.

For example, in January 1942, 12 German divisions and two brigades were transferred here from Western Europe – from France, Belgium, Yugoslavia and other countries occupied by Germany. In May 1942, two army corps consisting of several infantry and one panzer division were removed from the front in order to eliminate the threat posed by the units of Group Boldin behind their lines. In July, a large portion of Ninth Army was occupied with the fight against Kalinin Front's 39th Army and 11th Cavalry Corps.[34] We'll recall D.M. Proektor's words that "this circumstance for a long time excluded the forces of Army Group Center from overall fascist strategy."[35] In August 1942, the *Wehrmacht* command was forced to keep three panzer and several infantry divisions on the Zubtsov axis, which were poised to transfer to the south. Moreover, 12 divisions from other sectors of the front were transferred to Army Group Center's sector of the front, including from the south.[36] At the same time, the Soviet command was able to send a portion of its forces from this sector of the front to the south.

In the same summer of 1942, Army Group Center received the *Grossdeutschland* Division, which had been scheduled to go to France, as well as an infantry division which was on its way to Leningrad.[37] D.M. Proektor wrote that the appearance of the S.S. Division *Das Reich* at Rzhev must be seen as a real assistance to the English, who would soon conduct their landing at Dieppe. Moreover, because of the Soviet Rzhev – Sychevka (Gzhatsk) operation in the summer of 1942, the Army Group Center command could not implement its limited offensives toward Kirov and Sukhinichi that were part of the *Wehrmacht's* original summer plans in the East.[38]

On 30 October 1942 in order to reinforce Army Group Center in connection with the looming Russian offensive in the center, von Manstein and his headquarters was transferred to Mogilev from the Leningrad area at Hitler's order. D.M. Proektor wrote that after this,

Field Marshal H.G. von Kluge, the commander of Army Group Center in 1941-1943. A 1942 photograph.

Colonel General W. Model, commander of the Ninth Army, 1941-1944.

the "question about an assault on Leningrad essentially dropped away".[39] Of course, to be honest, when the Soviet counteroffensive began at Stalingrad, von Manstein was sent to the south. In that same October, the Germans moved a panzer, a motorized and an infantry division to Velikie Liuki area from the Leningrad region, seven divisions from France and Germany to the Vitebsk and Smolensk areas, and two panzer divisions from Voronezh and Zhizdra to the areas of Iartsevo and Roslavl', for a total of twelve divisions.[40]

Among the divisions transferred to the center was a division from the North Caucasus. We'll remember that according to Liddell Hart, Hitler in October 1942 had planned an airborne landing in the Batumi area, but after the Stalingrad and Rzhev offensives, the "twin threat" they posed forced Hitler to cancel the operation and order the urgent movement of the paratroop division by rail to the north, to the Smolensk area.[41]

In the opinion of D. Glantz and I.V. Isaev, the Second Rzhev – Sychevka Operation had an indirect, but fully tangible influence on the 1943 summer campaign. The Ninth Army, which had taken heavy casualties at Rzhev while stopping Operation Mars, was unable to replace those losses it incurred in the fighting. The German divisions defending the Rzhev bridgehead were unable to reach an acceptable level of combat-effectiveness, neither by May 1943, which was one of the reasons why Hitler postponed Operation Citadel, nor by the time of the Kursk offensive in July 1943. This became one of the reasons why the offensive against the northern shoulder of the Kursk bulge quickly ran out of steam.[42]

All these facts plainly support the opinion that the operations of the Soviet forces at Rzhev influenced the situation not only at Stalingrad, but also in the Caucasus, at Leningrad, and on other sectors of the central front. To a certain degree, they also affected the situation on the Western Front, thereby rendering assistance to the Allies.

General of the Army G. K. Zhukov, November 1942.

Lieutenant General V.D. Sokolovsky, the Western Front's chief of staff in July 1941-January 1942, and again from May 1942 to February 1943. A 1941 or 1942 photo.

However, even with the extra divisions that the *Wehrmacht* directed to the Rzhev – Viaz'ma salient, it was ultimately unable to retain the promising staging area, and the *Wehrmacht* forces were forced to abandon it. Indeed, this doubtlessly is a victory of the Soviet Armed Forces as a whole. This is both the result of the exhaustion of the enemy strength directly in the region of the salient, and the result of the victorious operations of Soviet forces in the south.

However, this was also an undoubted failure of the Soviet high command and of those military chiefs and commanders that directed the strategic force operations here: I.V. Stalin, B.M. Shaposhnikov, G.K. Zhukov, V.D. Sokolovsky, I.S. Konev and M.V. Zakharov. Although A.M. Vasilevsky was Chief of the General Staff from June 1942, he was only partly connected with the operations against the Rzhev salient, since G.K. Zhukov was always supervising this axis, and from September 1942 he was the Deputy Supreme Commander. The strategic conception of the *Stavka* of the Supreme High Command and the General Staff – to encircle and destroy the main forces of Army Group Center in the Rzhev – Viaz'ma salient – suffered a complete failure. They were unable to turn Rzhev into a second Stalingrad.

The duel with the *Wehrmacht* higher command, as well as directly with the commander of Army Group Center Field Marshal von Kluge and the commander of the Ninth Army Colonel General W. Model on this sector of the front was lost by the Soviet commanders.

Marshal Zhukov, who in our days is called "The Marshal of Victory" and "The Conqueror", understood this. The Rzhev – Viaz'ma salient occupies a large space in his military career: for eight months – from January to August 1942 – he was directly commanding the Western Front, while at the same time commanding the Western Direction, directing the operations of both the Western and Kalinin Fronts. At the end of 1942, he practically led Operation Mars. However, in February 1943, when the *Wehrmacht* command was in the process of withdrawing its forces from the Rzhev – Viaz'ma staging area, G. K. Zhukov preferred to be with the Northwestern Front, where Soviet forces were trying to eliminate the enemy's Demiansk salient. Zhukov chose to avoid direct participation in the next operation of his "own" Western and Kalinin Fronts, likely fearing another failure. As the first deputy of the Supreme Commander, he probably could himself choose the *front* of his own assignment. But G.K. Zhukov didn't risk traveling to the "accursed" Rzhev – Viaz'ma salient, which can be viewed as an indirect acknowledgement by the Marshal of his previous failures in this region.

In his postwar memoirs, G.K. Zhukov describes the fighting in the Rzhev area selectively, with distortions and omissions, in which the reader can be convinced, since in this book the Marshal's memoirs have been cited multiple times.

I.S. Konev also didn't want to recall the combat operations at Rzhev. In his post as commander of first the Kalinin Front and then the Western Front, he spent 14 months located in this sector of the front – from January 1942 until March 1943. However, his memoirs "Zapiski komanduiushchego frontom" ["Notes of a Front Commander"] begins only in the summer of 1943. In his recollections published in the journal *Znamia* in 1987, he dedicated only one paragraph to his time here, which I cite here in full:

> In August 1942 I was again appointed commander of the Western Front. Throughout the autumn and winter of 1942 and the beginning of 1943, the Western Front primarily was resolving tasks of defending the lines, which had been reached at the beginning of 1942. We conducted local operations, pinning down enemy forces in order to exclude the possibility of their transfer elsewhere. At this time, as is known, the fighting at Stalingrad was unfolding. It should be noted that the German-fascist command didn't transfer a single division from the Western strategic direction or, in particular, from the sector opposite the Western Front, to the Stalingrad axis. The foe was plainly counting upon the fact that after the successful operation at Stalingrad, a favorable situation would again appear for outflanking Moscow from the south and for launching a frontal assault with the major grouping, which was positioned in defense opposite the Western Front. The Soviet high command, on its side, devised and developed a plan, in accordance with which, in case of an enemy approach, the Soviet forces would impetuously go on the offensive. Shock groupings were created and given directions of attack, but unfortunately, I didn't get the opportunity to carry out this assignment. At the direction of the *Stavka* of the Supreme High Command, I was transferred to the Northwestern Front, in order to replace the Front commander Marshal Timoshenko.[43]

Any commentary is unnecessary!

Out of fairness we'll note that in the Soviet Union, they wrote only what they were permitted to write. It is possible, therefore, that the chiefs of staff V.D. Sokolovsky and M.V.

Colonel General I.S. Konev, commander of the Kalinin Front (October 1941-August 1942) and the Western Front (August 1942-February 1943). A 1942 photo.

Major General M.V. Zakharov, Kalinin Front chief of staff in the period January 1942-April 1943. A 1941 or 1942 photo.

Zakharov didn't even leave behind memoirs.

Many Soviet military commanders, who later became famous, commanded armies, corps, divisions and lower-level units that fought at Rzhev and Viaz'ma: P.A. Belov, A.Kh. Babadzhanian, M.E. Katukov, A.L. Getman, M.M. Gromov, M.S. Khozin, S.A. Khudiakov and others. Their commands varied in fortune; some achieved results that weren't bad. General of the Armies V.S. Polenov and M.A. Reiter penetrated the German defenses in the area of Pogoreloe Gorodishche in August 1942; General M.D. Solomatin not only fought courageously in encirclement, but even broke out of the enemy ring. P.A. Belov showed himself to be a talented commander. Several of the named military commanders wrote about the operations of their units and formations in postwar memoirs.

Others were less fortunate: the armies of I.I. Maslennikov, V.I. Shevtsov and K.D. Golubev didn't always perform well. D.D. Leliushenko achieved no success at Rzhev. The 30th Army under his command between January and November 1942 – 10 months in combat, a long time – fought savagely to take Rzhev, but were unable to seize it. In September 1942, General Leliushenko's divisions were already fighting in the streets of the city, but .... In his memoirs *Moskva – Stalingrad – Berlin – Prague: Notes of an Army Commander*, D.D. Leliushenko identified several divisions and units that distinguished themselves in the fighting at Rzhev and provided the names of certain commanders and soldiers, but nothing more. This list didn't even take two pages![44]

The hushing up of those events by famous Soviet commanders and military chiefs is evidence that there were no major successes on this sector of the front. The remembrance of those battles on the part of the government and the people was different.

Supreme Commander I.V. Stalin.

Photocopy of a sketch made by an unknown artist, "Stalin surveys the city of Rzhev, 4-5 August 1943". The original sketch cannot be located.

Colonel General A.I. Eremenko, commander of the Kalinin Front, in front of the home (on the left) where he had just met with the Supreme Commander. The Rzhev area's village of Khoroshevo, 5 August 1943. Photo by B. Vdovenko.

Remembrance

The government's remembrance was brief. After an order from the Supreme Commander dated 23 February 1943, where the events at Rzhev were placed on the same rank with the most significant battles and engagements of the first years of the war, many years of silence set in. To be honest, 3-5 August 1943 the Supreme Commander personally traveled around the territory of the Rzhev – Viaz'ma salient. He met with the command of the Western Front on 3 August in Iukhnov, and on 5 August met with the command of the Kalinin Front in the village of Khoroshevo. This was practically his only trip to the front, although the front lines were already well to the west of here. N.N. Voronov, the Red Army's chief of artillery who was a participant in the meeting with Stalin in Iukhnov, later called this trip "strange, unnecessary". He wrote:

> Why was it necessary to drive so many kilometers over a road that had been chewed up by the tanks and tractors, in places was impassable, and to stop in a small town that was so far behind the front lines? There was nothing he could see from here, and he didn't meet with anyone else here but us. It was much more difficult to communicate with the *fronts* from here than it was back in Moscow.[45]

The same thing regards Rzhev as well, which had been completely destroyed by the fighting. They were only able to find undamaged residences in the village of Khoroshevo, which lay 3 kilometers from the city, where Stalin spent the night of 4 August 1943 in a rural home.

"Stalin's Home" in the village of Khoroshevo, Rzhev area, at the end of the 1990s.

The interest of the Supreme Commander for the cities "on the nearest approaches" to Moscow can be explained only by the fact that he wanted personally to see the places of bitter fighting on the approaches to the capital, to see Rzhev, this "thorn" that couldn't be removed from in front of Moscow for over a year.

This trip likely made a strong impression on the Supreme Commander. There was a reason why I. Stalin mentioned it, though without naming the places, in his communications to both Churchill and Roosevelt. He wrote Roosevelt on 8 August 1943, "Only now, upon my return from the front, I can respond to your letter from 16 July ... I had to spend some time personally on various sectors of the front"; on 9 August he wrote to Churchill, "... I've had to travel to the forces more frequently than usual, to one or another sector of our front." S.M. Shtemenko and A. I. Eremenko mentioned Stalin's trip to the front while naming the concrete places he visited while there. This trip is mentioned as well in several scholarly works. Despite this, in Soviet times the fact of this trip was regarded skeptically, and only fresh publications in the 1990s, including the memoirs of people who had accompanied Stalin on this trip, dispelled the disbelief.[46]

In Rzhev itself there was never any doubt about Stalin's trip. In the Rzhev Museum of Regional History, there is a resolution of the Kalinin Oblast Executive Committee from 23 August 1945 about preserving the home where Stalin spent the night.[47]

There exists an exquisite legend: supposedly the residents of the city after the war appealed to Stalin himself with a proposal to create a museum in the house where he stayed the night. Stalin purportedly replied that people don't frequent museums, so let there instead be a library in the home. They indeed opened a Stalin Library in the residence, while they built a new residence for the homeowner in Rzhev. The Library is still open today, and there is a small display there about the events. The virtually totally demolished ancient Russian cities, which had been converted into strongpoints by the enemy in the Rzhev salient, were recreated from the ashes after the war through the people's labor. However, only Viazm'a alone was included in the special decree of the USSR Council of People's Commissars about the resurrection of 15 of the oldest Russian cities. In 1946, a monument to General M.G. Efremov was unveiled.

The Soviet state's ideological machine, which held a monopoly over the interpretation of history, divulged information about the combat operations in and around the salient in driblets. The reason is understandable: any public discussion of them would have to address the failures of world-renowned victorious military commanders and authorities. The well-known historian V.M. Kulish in one of his works cited the words that the chief of the Main Political Directorate of the Soviet Army and Navy A.A. Epishev told them in a meeting with V.M. Kulish and N.G. Pavlenko in 1967: "... They are saying, 'Give them the full truth.' Why the hell do we need this, if it brings us no advantage?"[48]

The splitting of history into the advantageous and the disadvantageous; the ignoring and hushing up of failures, defeats, miscalculations; the portrayal of defeats as victories; and the government's disregard for the individual led to the fact that many generations of politicians and military men in our country after the Great Patriotic War were nurtured on the idea that losses could be justified by lofty patriotic and nation-wide goals and expressions, such as "We were victorious, and the cost is unimportant", "Death on the battlefield is an honor" and "The great laws of war have not been written."[49]

However, despite the strict censorship, even that which nevertheless was published in the memoir literature; which could be read between the lines in scholarly works; the oral and unpublished stories of veterans and local residents, and of enthusiasts, who buried the dead; and the number of names and the figures on the plaques standing above fraternal graves all allow one to envision the bloody meat grinder that was at work in the Rzhev, Belyi, Zubtsov, Sychevka, Viaz'ma, Gzhatsk, and Iukhnov forests and swamps. After the war, district military commissariats and military archives were deluged with thousands of letters from people who were seeking the graves of their loved ones who were killed or went missing-in-action. Relatives in the thousands traveled to the places of the battles. Those who fought here were also constantly drawn to return to the battlefields of their youth.

E.M. Rzhevskaia made many trips back to Rzhev. On one of her trips to the village of Zaimishche in the Rzhev district, she jotted down the story of a driver named Sasha, introducing it with the words "Here the dead are still waiting for when the living will bury them.":

> Sasha told me a story he heard from his mother: She and some other women were walking toward distant fields to reap them. They suddenly came upon a soldier wearing a greatcoat and a helmet, sitting in an overgrown foxhole. The women were stunned: They burst into tears and rushed to him, but as soon as they touched him, he disintegrated.[50]

The silence of the authorities gave rise to bewilderment and indignation. It is possible that this explains why in 1978 – on the 35th anniversary of the city's liberation – Rzhev was the only one of the cities in the territory of the salient to be awarded with the Order of the Patriotic War 1st Degree.

The people have never forgotten about the "Rzhev Abyss". Examples of the people's memory of the fighting at Rzhev as a bloody slaughter were brilliantly expressed in poems that appeared after the war. Doubtlessly, the first and most impressive of them was A. Tvardovsky's "Ia ubit podo Rzhevom" ["I was killed in front of Rzhev"]. It dates back to 1945 or 1946. In August 1942 the author was in the vicinity of Rzhev, but that which he witnessed there he could only express much later:

I was killed near Rzhev,
in a nameless swamp.
...
The front was burning without subsiding
Like a sword-cut to the body.
...
I was killed and do not know
Is Rzhev ours, at last?
...
In the summer of forty-two,
I was buried without a grave.

The actor M. Nozhkin created a sketch about the fighting near Rzhev according to the stories of his father who fought there. In 1985, M. Nozhkin wrote a song, the lyrics of which also reflect the people's image of the bloody fighting that developed around the Volga city:

Near Rzhev the grass for a long time

The fraternal grave in the village of Polunino, Rzhev area, 1990s.

Was reddish-brown from all the blood.
...

And under the ground there
Lying in three layers, three layers, three layers
Were soldiers, soldiers, soldiers of Russia.
....

Then these examples were repeated in a variety of ways in the poems of other authors: "My father has remained unburied/Near the forbidding Rzhev ... (N. Ignat'ev, Tver'); "A battalion perished near Rzhev/Seven men remained/But it didn't give up the village/ named Kosmarikha ..." (G. Rozova, Rzhev).[51]

In the 1950s, a series of mass military burials were conducted: from hundreds of thousands of individual gravesites and small group burial sites, the remains were shifted to large fraternal graves in populated places. Frequently this was done formally. Volunteers appeared who began to establish the identities of the fallen. For example, the teacher A.M. Kaloshina was able to establish the names of a thousand soldiers, who were buried in a

The Church of Nikolai Chudotvorets at the Memorial in honor of Iakut soldiers, Rzhev area, circa 2000.

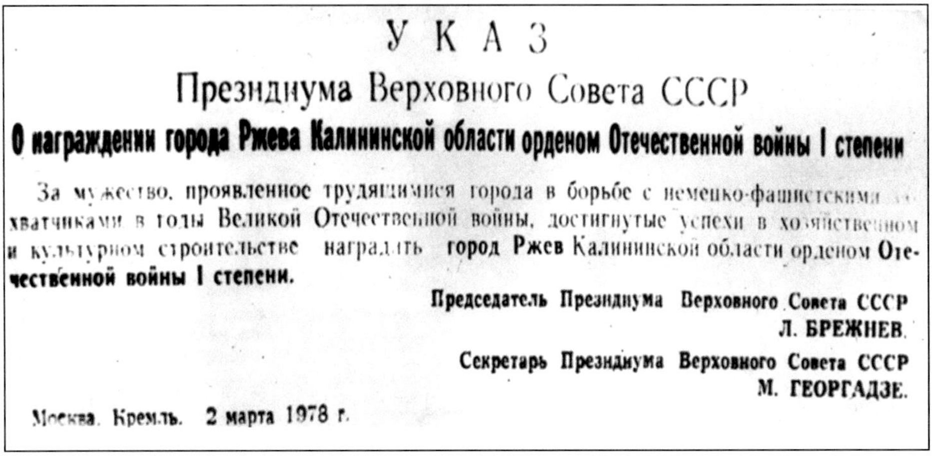

УКАЗ

Президиума Верховного Совета СССР

О награждении города Ржева Калининской области орденом Отечественной войны I степени

За мужество, проявленное трудящимися города в борьбе с немецко-фашистскими захватчиками в годы Великой Отечественной войны, достигнутые успехи в хозяйственном и культурном строительстве наградить **город Ржев** Калининской области орденом **Отечественной войны I степени.**

Председатель Президиума Верховного Совета СССР
Л. БРЕЖНЕВ.

Секретарь Президиума Верховного Совета СССР
М. ГЕОРГАДЗЕ.

Москва, Кремль. **2 марта 1978 г.**

A photo of the bulletin announcing the awarding of the Order of the Patriotic War 1st Degree to the city of Rzhev on 2 March 1978. The award states, “For the courage displayed by the workers of the city in the struggle with the German-fascist aggressors in the Great Patriotic War, and the achievements in economic and cultural construction ...”

The Memorial of Honor to the Siberian soldiers in the village of Ploskoe, Belyi District, Tver’ Oblast, at the end of the 1990s.

fraternal grave in the village of Polunino, north of Rzhev. According to data for 2006, the remains of 12,538 troops are now at rest here, whose names are all known. Monuments have been established at many of these mass grave sites, and obelisks have been erected.

At the end of the 1970s, the search team movement re-arose. In 1988, the first *Vakhta Pamiati* [Remembrance Watch] took place. The results of the search teams, their discovery and burial of thousands of soldiers who had not received a proper burial in their own time, or who had been listed as missing-in-action, and their criticism of the official figures of the losses in the war years became a reason for why the government was compelled not simply to make empty declarations, but to pay practical attention to matters of perpetuating the memory of the fallen.

Representatives of all the nations and peoples of the Soviet Union took part in the fighting for the Rzhev – Viaz'ma salient. In the 1980s and 1990s, residents and authorities of individual, wealthier regions began to raise monuments to their native sons and daughters on the various battlefields at their own expense. For example, the government of the Republic of Sakha-Iakutiia financed the creation of a Memorial in honor of the Iakut soldiers, which was opened in August 1994 in the village of Filkino in the Rzhev area. In 2005 the Memorial was reconstructed, again through funding from Iakutiia.[52]

At the end of the 1980s, six Siberian regions – the oblasts of Novosibirsk, Tomsk, Omsk, and Kemerov, as well as the Altai and Krasnoiarsk Krai [districts] signed an Agreement to Raise Funds for a Memorial of Honor to the Siberian soldiers. The Tver' Oblast also took part in the Agreement. Over several years, funds were raised, the project was worked out and construction began. On 14 August 1996, the Memorial was opened in the village of Ploskoe in the Belyi area, where back in November 1942 in the course of Operation Mars, the soldiers of the units and formations that had been formed in Siberia broke through the German defenses.

Every year on this date, delegations from Siberia arrive in the Belyi area. Local residents, veterans, Siberian search team members, relatives and fellow countrymen of those who fought gather in the village of Ploskoe. They recall the 12,500 men, who were buried in the "Valley of Death". Today the Memorial on Belyi land has "outgrown" its local significance and is considered a monument to all the Siberians, who fought on the various fronts of the Great Patriotic War.[53]

Political processes in the country in the 1990s contributed to an explosion of information, in particular, in historical studies of the Great Patriotic War. The publication of new documents and studies led to the appearance of new facts, which on top of existing information, shattered the entrenched official version of the war and permitted the possibility to treat the military operations in the area of the Rzhev salient as a separate battle with sufficient confidence. The change in the political situation in Russia also allowed the German side to initiate activity to perpetuate the remembrance of their fallen compatriots. In Russia in the 1990s, German military cemeteries began to be created in places of the heaviest fighting. Debates about the possibility of creating such a cemetery in Rzhev quickly expanded beyond the boundaries of the district and exploded onto the pages of oblast (and not only Tver' Oblast) and Russian newspapers. Thousands of people wrote protest letters to the State Duma, and to the Tver' Oblast, Rzhev city and district government agencies.

In 2000, the general director of the Association of International Military-Memorial Cooperation appealed to the chairman of the Russian Federation government with a request

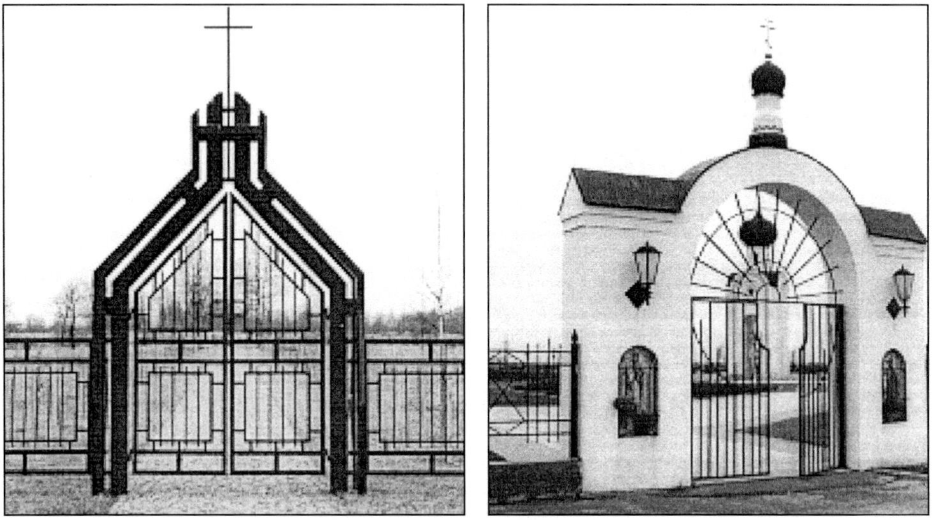

Entrances to the German cemetery (left) and the Russian Memorial (right), Rzhev 2005.

Memorial to the Soviet Troops, Rzhev, 2005.

Veterans of the war at the opening of the Rzhev Memorial, May 2005.

to finance the construction of a cemetery for German soldiers in Rzhev. As practice has indicated, this would have permitted the easing of tensions, "and at times the open resistance of various social groups and public organizations", that were stirred by the development of a German military cemetery. At the beginning of 2001, a plenipotentiary of the President of the Russian Federation in the Central Federal District, who was disturbed by the "growing negative public reaction" and the "persistent negative public opinion that has taken shape", sent a similar request to the leadership of the Russian government. In September 2002 the opening of two cemeteries in Rzhev took place, where the formal burial of the remains of the fallen began to be conducted. Through the joint financing of the Russian and German governments, a Russian Military Memorial was built, which opened in May 2005.[54]

In these same years veterans, as a rule, who served on different sectors of the front, public organizations, regional authorities and individual citizens of Rzhev began to campaign for the immortalizing of the Battle of Rzhev by awarding the city with a title, if not the title of "Hero City", then the title "City of Military Glory" (there were editorial calls for one or the other). The protests from direct participants in the fighting and the regional historians that it was impossible to call what happened at the Rzhev – Viaz'ma salient "glorious" were not heeded. People who didn't know the true history of events wanted to honor the fallen, but simply didn't see any other alternatives than what was the convention in Soviet times. A paradoxical situation arose: that, which Soviet authorities had preferred not to remember, because it wasn't a victorious page in Soviet history, mass public conscience at the end of the 1990s began to call "glorious". This is a clear example of how historical memory changed the evaluation of the events from a minus to a plus.

Proposals to establish by law the title of "City of Military Glory" and its bestowal upon several cities, including Rzhev, came to the attention of the President of the Russian

Federation. The public pressure was so heavy, that in May 2006 a Federal law was adopted "On the honorific title 'City of Military Glory' of the Russian Federation". In February 2007, the administrations of Tver' Oblast, the city of Rzhev, and the legislative assembly of Tver' Oblast sent a petition to the Russian Federation government about awarding this title to the city of Rzhev. Similar documents have been prepared or are being prepared in Viaz'ma and Iukhnov.

How far does the genuine history of the events match its present-day assessment? Cities that were formerly enemy strongpoints, and which were not taken by our troops until the enemy voluntarily left them (this doesn't apply to Iukhnov) – are these truly "Cities of Military Glory"? The fulfillment of military duty no matter what, the sacrifice and heroism displayed, independently of the outcome of the fighting, doubtlessly are worthy of remembering and honoring. But is it ethical to call the deaths of an enormous number of troops and the failure of commanders "glorious"? Is it possible that there are other ways to perpetuate the memory of the deed of those Soviet soldiers who fought and died at the Rzhev salient?

Postscript, 2009

On 8 October 2007, the President of the Russian Federation signed Decree No. 1345 "On the awarding of the honorific title 'City of Military Glory' to the city of Rzhev" with the following substantiation: "For the courage, resolve and the mass heroism, displayed by the defenders of the city in the struggle for the freedom and independence of the Fatherland, the city of Rzhev is thereby awarded the honorific title 'City of Military Glory' of the Russian Federation."[55] These words are extremely ambiguous: just who did the President have in mind when he used the words "defenders of the city", if the city was being defended by German troops, while troops of the Red Army were trying to liberate it?

Conclusion

Thus, the facts have been laid out, conclusions have been drawn, and a point of view has been expressed. It is possible to agree with it or to dispute it, but it is hardly possible to ignore it. It is possible that the author's not always professional military language will give rise to the indignation of professional military historians. Alas, even more so, the supporters of the official version of the war will disagree with the author's conclusions, which do not correspond to the established treatment of the events.

However, the author is not alone in the non-traditional interpretation of wartime events. In our day, bookstore shelves are filled with dozens of books on various questions of military history, which frequently refute existing stereotypes and have often not even been written by historians. There is a mass of new interpretations and points of view; some are interesting and well-reasoned, others are naïve and amusing. There also some that can be viewed as myths, and others that prompt protest. However, this mass of literature has turned up a multitude of new facts, numbers and names, which allow a fresh look at a large variety of episodes from military history.

In this enormous amount of work to re-evaluate the historical past, official historiography, at the very least on questions of the history of combat operations in the region of the Rzhev – Viaz'ma salient, is on the defensive and in the role of trying to regain lost ground. After long years of a monopoly in interpreting the events of the Great Patriotic War, official military-historical science has ceased to be a leader in the generation of fresh historical knowledge.

For example, the official description of Operation Mars appeared only after the publication of D. Glantz's work on the subject. It would have seemed much simpler to publish the documents of the *Stavka* and the General Staff on this operation, in order to forestall the appearance of multiple interpretations. However, the monopoly on access to these official sources remains in the hands of the few, and this select few accuse critics of the official version of Operation Mars of falsifying the historical past, of besmirching famous names, and of attempting to discredit the Great Victory. Differing opportunities in obtaining original data allow some to interpret past events accurately, while others are left to assume and make conjectures. We will be forbearing to official historiography of the war: it is at the service of the state and writes whatever is beneficial to it. One must agree with the assertion of many historians and sociologists that today the government is attempting to make remembrance of the war its monopoly. In the opinion of certain politicians, the history of the Great Patriotic War can today become a bulwark of national consciousness and unity.

But facts are facts. Even the official science must reckon with them. It is possible to assert that the accumulated mountain of facts and the new, obvious interpretation of them by historians, local historians and veterans have reached that critical mass, which compelled a representative of official science, a staff member of the Institute of Military History and a leading specialist on the study of combat operations on the Moscow axis B. Nevzorov to agree in the *Voenno-istoricheskii zhurnal* in February 2007 (at the time of this book's writing) that the date of 20 April 1942 as the end point of the Battle of Moscow was debatable. Having listed the Soviet offensive operations in the region of the Rzhev – Viaz'ma salient, which has been the subject of this book, he wrote: "Of course, it would be more logical to shift the conclusion of the Battle of Moscow to 31 March 1943, when the 1943 Rzhev – Viaz'ma Operation was completed."[56]

These words are recognition of the right of the author of the given work and its supporters, first of all, to evaluate the combat operations against the Rzhev salient as a battle. One must acknowledge the courage of this representative of official historiography, who agreed to "extend" the Battle of Moscow, and for all intents and purposes tossed aside thousands, and perhaps even tens of thousands of works, studies and memoirs about the victorious conclusion of the battle for the capital in December 1941.

Thus, officially the Battle of Moscow lasted until April 1943, but whether the combat operations from January 1942 until April 1943 were part of the Battle of Moscow, or a self-contained Battle of Rzhev remains a subject of academic discussion.

Appendices

Documents of the *Stavka* VGK [Supreme High Command] and the General Staff regarding matters of the combat operations in the area of the Rzhev – Viaz'ma salient (as published in the collected volumes of documents from the series *Russkii arkhiv: Velikaia Otechestvennaia*).

I *Stavka* VGK Directive No. 151141 to the Commanders of the Western and Kalinin Fronts about the Encirclement of the Enemy's Mozhaisk – Gzhatsk – Viaz'ma Grouping

7 January 1942, 20 hr 40 min

The *Stavka* of the Supreme High Command orders the Western and Kalinin Fronts to direct further efforts toward the encirclement of the enemy's Mozhaisk – Gzhatsk – Viaz'ma grouping, for which:

1. The commander of the Kalinin Front is to detach part of its force in order to smash the enemy's Rzhev grouping and to occupy Rzhev, and with a shock grouping in strength of two armies consisting of fourteen-fifteen rifle divisions, a cavalry corps and a large number of tanks, to attack in the general direction of Sychevka, Viaz'ma with the task, having seized the railroad and major Gzhatsk – Smolensk road west of the railroad, to deprive the enemy of his main communications. Next, encircle and then capture or destroy the enemy's entire Mozhaisk – Gzhatsk – Viaz'ma grouping jointly with the Western Front.
2. Without waiting for the approach of the cavalry corps and the full assembly of all the forces of the shock grouping in the area of Rzhev, with the available forces of the 39th Army as the primary force of the main grouping, develop the offensive immediately in the Sychevka, Viaz'ma direction, while keeping the remaining forces as a second echelon behind the main grouping, with the intent of emerging in the Sychevka area and occupying Sychevka no later than 12 January 1942.
3. The commander of the Western Front is to destroy the enemy's Iukhnov – Mosal'sk grouping no later than 11 January, to launch the main attack with the forces of Group Belov and the 50th Army toward Viaz'ma, and then to complete the encirclement of the enemy's Mozhaisk – Gzhatsk – Viaz'ma grouping in cooperation with the forces of Kalinin Front's shock grouping.
4. Simultaneously with the forces of the 20th Army penetrate the enemy's front and attack in the direction of Shakhovskaia, Gzhatsk; direct part of the army from Shakhovskaia into the rear of the enemy's Latoshino grouping and encircle and destroy it in cooperation with Kalinin Front's 30th Army.
5. Confirm receipt.

Stavka of the Supreme High Command
I. Stalin
A. Vasilevsky

Source: TsAMO, F. 148a, Op. 3763, D. 130, L. 1, 2

II *Stavka* VGK Directive No. 170007 to the Commander of the Kalinin Front about the Liberation of Rzhev

11 January 1942, 01 hr 50 min

In connection with the fact that the enemy's further possession of Rzhev creates a threat of a flank attack to the *front*'s main shock grouping, which is attacking in the Sychevka, Viaz'ma direction, the *Stavka* of the Supreme High Command orders:

1. Seize Rzhev in the course of 11 January and in no case later than 12 January, and for this purpose call upon part of the strength of the 39th Army (two-three rifle divisions) for an attack from the south and southwest, and the entire strength of the 29th Army for an attack from the west, north and east.
2. The *Stavka* recommends the maximum use of available artillery, mortar and air power in this area for this purpose and to hammer the entire city of Rzhev, not stopping before serious damage to the city.
3. Confirm receipt, report on the execution.

Stavka of the Supreme High Command
I. Stalin
A. Vasilevsky

Source: TsAMO, F. 148a, Op. 3763, D. 97, L. 153.

III *Stavka* VGK Directive No. 170035 to the Commander of the Kalinin Front about a Change of the Front's Roster and Specification of Tasks

19 January 1942, 21 hr 15 min

The *Stavka* of the Supreme High Command orders:

1. Transfer to the control of Kalinin Front from 0600 22 January 1942 Northwestern Front's 3rd and 4th Shock Armies, consisting of:

   3rd Shock Army – the 23rd, 33rd and 257th Rifle Divisions; the 20th, 27th, 31st, 42nd, 45th and 54th Rifle Brigades; the 141st and 146th Tank Battalions; the 429th and 613th Artillery Regiments (Army); the 106th, 107th and 205th Guards Mortar Battalions; seven ski battalions; and the 803rd Motorized and 5th Horse-Drawn Transport Battalions.

   4th Shock Army – the 332nd, 334th, 358th, 360th and 249th Rifle Divisions; the 21st, 39th, 48th and 51st Rifle Brigades; the 170th and 171st Tank Battalions; the 270th and 421st Artillery Regiments (Army); nine ski battalions; the 109th and 204th Guards Mortar Battalions; and the 611th and 802nd Motorized Transport Battalions.
2. Additionally to strengthen: 3rd Shock Army – the 390th and 130th Rifle Divisions and the 154th and 86th Rifle Brigades; complete their transfer along the railroad to the Krestsov and Liubitsy area [by] 29 January. 4th Shock Army – 155th and 158th Rifle Divisions; complete their transfer along the railroad to the Ostashkovo area [by] 1 February.
3. Move the Kalinin Front headquarters by the morning of 22 January to an area to be determined by the Front commander.
4. Have the boundary line with the Northwestern Front from 0600 22 January: Edrovo, Shumilov Bor (15 km northwest of Demiansk), Ratcha (35 km northwest of Kholm), Vydumka (8 km northwest of Novosokol'nikov), Novokhovansk Station (15 kilometers southwest of Nevel'; all points excluded for the Kalinin Front.
5. The Front's tasks:
   (a) with resolute operations of the 30th Army and the cavalry corps in the direction of Semlevo Station (west of Viaz'ma), strengthened in the future by operations of the 30th Army [though I believe it is a typo and could be the 39th Army], jointly with troops of the Western Front attacking toward Viaz'ma from the direction of Mosal'sk, encircle and then capture or destroy the enemy's Gzhatsk – Viaz'ma grouping. The cavalry corps, reinforced with a tank brigade and a motorized rifle division, is to reach the area of Semlevo Station no later than 21 January;

   (b) with the forces of the 29th and 31st Army no later than 21 January seize the cities of Rzhev and Zubtsov;

   (c) developing the offensive with the 3rd Shock Army from Kholm toward Velikie Liuki and further toward Vitebsk and with the 4th Shock Army from Toropets toward Velizh, Rudnia, the indicated armies are to reach the Vitebsk, Orsha area, having isolated Smolensk from the west, and thereby ensuring the capture of Smolensk.
6. The separate and high-priority task of the 3rd Shock Army: with operations of part of its force from Staraia Rusa to Kholm, to block the enemy's path of retreat from the Demiansk

area and in cooperation with the Northwestern Front's 34th Army to liquidate him.

7. Confirm receipt; present the concrete plan of your operations in execution of the present directive to the *Stavka*.

Stavka of the Supreme High Command
I. Stalin
A. Vasilevsky

Source: TsAMO, F. 132a, Op. 2462, D. 233, L. 2, 3.

IV *Stavka* VGK Directive No. 170038 to the Commander of the 30th Army about the Confirmation of the Decision of the Kalinin Front Commander to Conduct a Regrouping

23 January 1942, 03 hr 15 min

In the given situation, the Rzhev – Viaz'ma axis has primary significance; the success of the entire operation depends upon the rapid success on it, and on the contrary, the 30th Army's direction as of now has become secondary.

Hence I consider Comrade Konev's decision correct; it is necessary to apply all efforts to its most rapid implementation.

I. Stalin

Source: TsAMO, F. 148a, Op. 3763, D. 131, L. 10.

V *Stavka* VGK Directive to the Commander of the Kalinin Front about the Liquidation of the Enemy Breakthrough West of Rzhev

31 January 1942, 21 hr 45 min

The enemy with his penetration west of Rzhev between the 30th and 29th Armies has cut off the troops of the 29th and 39th Armies from their supply lines, in view of which it is necessary to supply them from the air and this at a moment when the foe has been smashed and almost encircled.

The clumsiness and negligence of the 29th Army, and in part of the 30th Army as well, in the matter of liquidating this enemy, and the connivance in this on the part of the Kalinin Front commander is a disgrace for us.

The *Stavka* of the Supreme High Command orders:

1. The Kalinin Front commander immediately to depart to area of the enemy's breakthrough and take personal direction over the liquidation of it.
2. In order to carry out the indicated task, call upon the 30th Army for an attack from the north and no less than three divisions of the 29th Army for a meeting attack from the south.
3. Complete the liquidation of the penetration no later than 3 February and by the same time restore the general front of the 39th and 29th Armies with the forces of the 30th Army, open a supply route for them and organize regular supply by land.
4. Report on the execution [of these orders].

Stavka of the Supreme High Command
I. Stalin
B. Shaposhnikov

Source: TsAMO, F. 132a, Op. 2642, D. 12, L. 177

VI *Stavka* VGK Directive to the Commanders of the Western and Kalinin Fronts about Re-establishing the Post of Commander-in-Chief of the Western Direction

1 February 1942, 21 hr 45 min

In view of the common tasks of the Western and Kalinin Fronts and the need for the closest cooperation between them, the *Stavka* of the Supreme High Command orders:

1. To re-establish the post of Commander-in-Chief of the Western Direction with the task of organizing uninterrupted concert of action between the Western and Kalinin Fronts.
2. To appoint the commander of the Western Front General of the Army Comrade Zhukov as Commander-in-Chief of the Western Direction, while retaining him in the post of commander of the Western Front.
3. To appoint the commander of the Western Front's 10th Army Lieutenant General Golikov as deputy commander of the Western Direction while relieving him of command of the army.
4. The task of the Western Direction in the next few days, together with the task of taking Viaz'ma, is considered to be the encirclement and capture of the enemy's Rzhev – Sychevka group, or in case of a refusal to surrender, the extermination of this group.
5. The commander of the Red Army Air Force is to subordinate the 521st Aviation Regiment of Iak-1s, the 61st Aviation Regiment of Il-2s, the 314th Aviation Regiment of Pe-2s, and the 641st Aviation Regiment of U-2s to the commander of the 39th Army. Base the indicated regiments within the 39th Army's area of operations no later than 2 February.
6. The commander of the Air Defense Organization of the country's territory Comrade Gromadin is to subordinate one fighter regiment with skis to the commander of the 39th Army. The regiment is to restage to the 39th Army's area of operations no later than 2 February.
7. The chief of the Main Directorate of the Civilian Air Fleet Comrade Molokov is to transfer to the commander of the Red Army Air Force an additional 10 transport aircraft (PS-84) for transporting ammunition and fuel.
8. The commander of the Red Army Air Force is to use the 10 transport aircraft accepted from the Civilian Air Fleet and the 5 transport aircraft previously transferred to the Kalinin Front in order to airlift ammunition and fuel to the 29th and 39th Armies at the indications of the Kalinin Front commander. Compel the flight staff of these aircraft to land the aircraft mandatorily in the area of operations of these armies to deliver the loads.

   Use return trips of the transport aircraft without fail for the evacuation of wounded from the armies. Immediately charge the flight staff that refuse to carry out these demands with the failure to execute a combat order.

Stavka of the Supreme High Command
I. Stalin
B. Shaposhnikov

Source: TsAMO, F. 132a, Op. 2642, D. 12, L. 180, 181.

VII *Stavka* VGK Directive No. 01542 to the Commander-in-Chief of the Western Direction on the Destruction of the Enemy's Rzhev – Viaz'ma – Iukhnov and Bolkhov – Zhizdra – Briansk Groupings

16 February 1942, 01 hrs 50 min

The *Stavka* of the Supreme High Command orders:

1. The forces of the Western Front, with the cooperation of the Kalinin Front's 39th, 29th, 22nd, 30th and 31st Armies, plus the 11th Cavalry Corps, to defeat and destroy the enemy's Rzhev – Viaz'ma – Iukhnov grouping and by 5 March reach and consolidate upon our old Olenino – Oletskoe – Bulashevo defensive line with the prepared anti-tank ditches and further along the Dnepr River through Blagoveshchenskoe as far as Dorogobuzh, (excl.) Usviat'e, El'nia and further along the Desna River to Snopot'.
2. Also by 5 March 1942 the forces of the Western Front are to smash the enemy's Bolkhov – Zhizdra – Briansk grouping, and having destroyed it, to occupy Briansk and dig-in along the old defensive line with the prepared anti-tank ditches along the Desna River from Snopot' to Iadrovo and further along the line to Vysokoe, Krasnoe, Sosnovka.
3. By order of the Deputy People's Commissar of Defense Comrade Shchadenko, in the course of the period between 16 and 25 February, in addition to those picked up along the way, to dispatch 60,000 trained replacements to points indicated by the Commander-in-chief of the Western Direction.
4. By order of the chief of the Main Directorate of Armored and Tank Forces in the course of the period between 16 and 25 February, to send to the Western Front 40 KV tanks, 80 T-34s and 80 T-60s to points indicated by the Commander-in-Chief of the Western Direction.
5. The commander of the Red Army Air Force in a two-day period is to transfer to the Western Front 20 Il-2 aircraft and 20 Iak-1 aircraft without crews. Send crews for all of the indicated aircraft at the order of the Commander-in-Chief of the Western Direction.
6. The commander of the Airborne Forces on 17 February is to transfer the 9th and 214th Airborne Brigades to the command of the Commander-in-Chief of the Western Direction for the Iukhnov operation; the deputy commander of the Air Force Comrade Novikov and the Deputy People's Commissar of Defense Comrade Gromadin are to make provisions for the airborne landing at the indications of the Commander-in-Chief of the Western Direction.
7. For the conducting of the operation to destroy the enemy's Bolkhov – Zhizdra – Briansk grouping, subordinate the 5th Guards Rifle Corps and the 97th, 116th and 149th Rifle Divisions upon their arrival at their detraining points to the Commander-in-Chief of the Western Direction no later than 25 February.

Stavka of the Supreme High Command
I. Stalin
B. Shaposhnikov

Source: TsAMO, F. 132a, Op. 2642, D. 95, L. 27, 28.

VIII *Stavka* VGK Directive No. 170124 to the Commander-in-Chief of the Western Direction about Confirming the Decision to Break Through the Enemy's Defense on the Motaevo, Kostrovo Sector

25 February 1942, 16 hr 45 min

Your decision to organize a breakthrough on the Motaevo, Kostrovo sector with the combined forces of the 20th and 5th Armies has been confirmed by the *Stavka* of the Supreme High Command.

At the order of the *Stavka* of the Supreme High Command
Chief of the General Staff Shaposhnikov

Source: TsAMO, F. 48a, Op. 3408, D. 71, L. 54.

IX *Stavka* VGK Directive No. 170157 to the Commander of the Red Army Air Force on the creation of a Strike Air Group of the *Stavka* of the Supreme High Command

CC: Commander-in-Chief of the Western Direction

17 March 1942, 19 hr 35 min

In order to smash the enemy, which has cut off the 1st Guards Cavalry Corps, Efremov's 33rd Army and the 4th Airborne Corps, in concert with ground troops of the 43rd, 49th and 50th Armies, the *Stavka* of the Supreme High Command orders:

1. Create Strike Aviation Group No. 4 of the *Stavka* of the Supreme High Command consisting of two regiments of LaGGs from the *Stavka* Reserve, the 198th Regiment of Il-2s from the *Stavka* Reserve, which is operating at the given moment with the Western Front, the Western Front's 62nd Regiment of Il-2s, and 20 long-range bombers from Comrade Golovanov's aviation.
2. Place first deputy commander of the Red Army Air Force Lieutenant General Comrade Novikov in command of Aviation Group No. 4, giving him the right in necessary cases to call upon the air forces of the Western Front and the above-indicated armies.

   Appoint Major General of Aviation Comrade Golovanov to assist Comrade Novikov in directing the operations of the long-range bombers.
3. Strike Aviation Group No. 4 of the *Stavka* of the Supreme High Command is to become operational on 18 March.

Stavka of the Supreme High Command
I. Stalin
B. Shaposhnikov

Source: F. 132a, Op. 2642, D. 31, L. 150, 151.

X *Stavka* VGK Directive No. 153589 to the Commander-in-Chief of the Western Direction about Hastening the Destruction of the Enemy's Rzhev – Viaz'ma – Gzhatsk Grouping

20 March 1942, 22 hr 35 min

The liquidation of the enemy's Rzhev – Viaz'ma – Gzhatsk grouping has been dragged out impermissibly.

The 1st Guards Cavalry Corps, Efremov's 33rd Army and the 4th Airborne Corps continue to remain isolated from their rear services and from other armies of the Front.

The rear areas of the 39th Army and the 11th Cavalry Corps as before remain under threat of isolation.

The *Stavka* of the Supreme High Command orders:

1. Destroy the enemy's Rzhev – Viaz'ma – Gzhatsk grouping and no later than 20 April reach and dig-in on our previous defensive line along the line Belyi, Bulashevo, Dorogobuzh, El'nia, Snopot', Krasnoe.
2. The Fronts' tasks in the next several days:
   (a) Western Front – with the combined efforts of the 43rd, 49th and 50th Armies, reinforced with five rifle divisions and two tank brigades from the Supreme High Command Reserve, clear the 33rd Army's and Group Belov's supply routes of the enemy no later than 27 March, link-up with them, and then destroy the enemy's group in the Ryliaki, Miliatino, Viaz'ma area; simultaneously with the forces of the 5th Army conduct a breakthrough northeast of Gzhatsk and take the city no later than 1 April, after which with an attack toward Viaz'ma it is to cooperate with the 43rd, 49th and 50th Armies in the enemy's destruction in the Viaz'ma area;

   With the 16th and 61st Armies continue the destruction of the enemy's Zhizdra – Bolkhov grouping, with the future task of seizing Briansk.

   (b) Kalinin Front – with the combined forces of the 39th Army and the 30th Army, which have been reinforced with six rifle brigades and two tank brigades from the Supreme High Command Reserve, no later than 28 March isolate the enemy's Olenino group from the Rzhev group and link-up with each other, after which detach part of the 30th Army's strength under the command of this army's deputy commander in order to liquidate the enemy in the Olenino area jointly with the 22nd Army, while the main forces of the 30th Army are to pivot to the east for an attack together with the 29th and 31st Armies against the enemy's Rzhev grouping and to envelop the city of Rzhev no later than 5 April.

   For an attack against the enemy in the Belyi area, create a Front shock group consisting of 22nd Army's 119th and 179th Rifle Divisions, and the 134th, 135th and 234th Rifle Divisions from 4th Shock Army's reserve. Put General Kolpachki in command of the group under the subordination to the Front.
3. With the 4th Strike Aviation Group of the *Stavka* of the Supreme High Command, render all possible assistance to the 43rd, 49th and 50th Armies in the destruction of the enemy in their front, as well as by means of systematic bombing of the enemy's air fields and supply

lines in the indicated region.

4. The commander of Long-Range Bomber Aviation Comrade Golovanov is to detach an additional 20 DB-3 aircraft with a special assignment of intensively bombing and overflying Viaz'ma, Rzhev, Gzhatsk and Sychevka.
5. The commander of the Red Army Air Force Comrade Zhigarev is urgently to reinforce Aviation Group No. 5 of the *Stavka* of the Supreme High Command, which is operating in front of the 5th Army, by adding up to seven aviation regiments, including one U-2 regiment, to its roster.

   Commander of Long-Range Bomber Aviation Comrade Golovanov is to assign 10-15 DB-3 bombers to this group.

Stavka of the Supreme High Command
I. Stalin
A. Vasilevsky

Source: TsAMO, F. 132a, Op. 2642, D. 95, L. 31-33.

XI *Stavka* VGK Directive No. 170183 to the Commander-in-Chief of the Western Direction Regarding Changes in the Composition of the Western Front

21 March 1942, 22 hr 30 min

CC: Chief of the Main Directorate of Formations

The *Stavka* of the Supreme High Command orders:

1. Take under your command five rifle divisions from the Supreme High Command Reserve that are located in the Tula area (58th, 146th, 42nd, 69th and 298th) for the 50th Army in the period between 22 March and 3 April 1942.
2. Withdraw from the Western Front into the Supreme High Command Reserve:
   (a) in the period from 25 April to 30 April of this year – five rifle divisions: 108th – to Ruza, 144th Rifle Division – to Mozhaisk, 154th Rifle Division – to Maloiaroslavets, 340th Rifle Division – to Kaluga, and the 322nd Rifle Division – to Serpukhov for refitting, resupply and collective combat training;
   (b) in the period from 25 March to 5 April of this year – six rifle brigades: 36th Rifle Brigade – to Kolomna (Moscow Military District), 18th Rifle Brigade – to Tambov (Volga Military District), 55th Rifle Brigade – to Riazhsk (Moscow Military District), 19th Rifle Brigade – to Michurinsk (Volga Military District), 40th Rifle Brigade – to Griaz' (Volga Military District) and the 34th Rifle Brigade – to Ranenbrug in order to form on their basis six rifle divisions.
3. Withdraw the rifle divisions and brigades in full with their available personnel, weapons, motorized and animal-drawn transport, horses and property, forbidding any removals prior departure from the front;
4. The chief of the Main Directorate of Formations:
   (a) by 20 April of this year is to provide sufficient personnel to create rifle divisions on the basis of the withdrawn rifle brigades;
   (b) by 5 May of this year is to bring the withdrawn rifle divisions back up to table strength;
5. The chiefs of the Main Directorates of the People's Commissariat of Defense by the deadlines indicated in the fourth point are to furnish the authorized equipment for the divisions, which ... are forming on the basis of the rifle brigades.
6. The chief of the Red Army's Main Artillery Directorate is to assign the authorized armament:
   (a) to the divisions, which have been withdrawn for refitting, by 15 May of this year;
   (b) to the divisions that are forming on the basis of the rifle brigades, by 20 May of this year;
7. Report to the General Staff and the Main Directorate of Formations regarding the rifle brigades by 27 March, and by 27 April regarding the rifle divisions, and the combat strength and number of personnel as of the 25th day of the corresponding month.
8. Confirm receipt. Report on fulfillment.

Stavka of the Supreme High Command
I. Stalin
B. Shaposhnikov

Source: TsAMO, F. 148a, Op. 3763, D. 124, L. 160.

XII *Stavka* VGK Directive No. 170182 to the Commander of the Kalinin Front Regarding Changes in the Front's Composition

CC: Commander-in-Chief of the Western Direction, Chief of the Main Directorate of Formations

22 March 1942, 01 hr 30 min

The *Stavka* of the Supreme High Command orders:

1. Take under your command six rifle brigades for the 30th Army from the Supreme High Command Reserve that are located in the Moscow area (116th, 132nd, 121st, 136th, 130th and 131st) in the period prior to 30 March.
2. Withdraw from the Kalinin Front into the Supreme High Command Reserve:
   (a) in the period from 25 March to 15 April of this year four rifle brigades: 48th Rifle Brigade – to Riazan', 51st Rifle Brigade – to Orekhovo-Zuevo, and two rifle brigades from the 3rd Shock Army, of which one brigade – to Babushkin and one brigade – to Kovrov for forming on their basis four rifle divisions;
   (b) in the period from 20 April to 30 April of this year, the [following] rifle divisions from the 30th Army: 371st Rifle Division – to Kalinin, 375th Rifle Division – to Likhoslavl' for refitting, resupplying and collective combat training.
3. Withdraw the rifle divisions and brigades in full with their available personnel, weapons, motorized and animal-drawn transport, horses and property, forbidding any removals prior departure from the front;
4. The chief of the Main Directorate of Formations is to:
   (c) by 20 April of this year provide sufficient personnel to create rifle divisions on the basis of the withdrawn rifle brigades;
   (d) by 5 May of this year bring the withdrawn rifle divisions back up to table strength;
5. The chiefs of the Main Directorates of the People's Commissariat of Defense by the deadlines indicated in the fourth point are to furnish the authorized equipment for the divisions, which ... are forming on the basis of the rifle brigades.
6. The chief of the Red Army's Main Artillery Directorate is to assign the authorized armament:
   (a) to the divisions, which have been withdrawn for refitting, by 10 May of this year;
7. 7. Report to the General Staff and the Main Directorate of Formations regarding the rifle brigades by 27 March, and by 27 April regarding the rifle divisions, and the combat strength and number of personnel as of the 25th day of the corresponding month.
8. 8. Confirm receipt. Report on fulfillment.

Stavka of the Supreme High Command
I. Stalin
B. Shaposhnikov

Source: TsAMO, F. 148a, Op. 3763, D. 124, L. 159.

XIII *Stavka* VGK Directive No. 170363 to the Commanders of the Western Front and the Red Army Air Force Regarding Measures for Holding and Expanding the Staging Area, Occupied by Belov's Operational Group

8 May 1942, 2 hr 10 min

With the aim of holding and expanding the staging area, occupied by Comrade Belov's group, and using this staging area for influencing the enemy's communications, railroads, and his supply bases in the Smolensk, Iartsevo, Viaz'ma and Pochinka areas, the *Stavka* of the Supreme High Command orders to reinforce Comrade Belov's group:

1. With one mixed aviation division consisting of two U-2 regiments, a regiment of fighters, a regiment of ground attack aircraft and an Il-4 regiment, with their dispersal among airfields within Comrade Belov's staging area, at the order of the Red Army Air Force commander Comrade Novikov.
2. Transfer by air to Comrade Belov's group:
   (a) personnel in the quantity of 9,000 soldiers and officers in accordance with Comrade Belov's request;

76mm PA [field artillery] with limbers and ammunition	– 16;
76mm DA [long-range artillery]	– 12;
45mm anti-tank guns with limbers and ammunition	– 150;
120mm mortars with limbers and ammunition	– 40;
82mm mortars	– 200;
50mm mortars	– 200;
PPSh [submachine guns]	– 2000;
Heavy machine guns	– 140;
Light machine guns	– 200;
PTR [anti-tank rifles]	– 600;

   Anti-tank mines – 15,000; anti-personnel mines – 15,000; explosives – 25 metric tons with a gross weight of 120 metric tons.

   Deliver all the artillery, mortars and heavy machine guns with trained crews;

   (b) summer uniforms, kits – 25,000;
   (c) fuel for supporting the motorized transport, tractors and tanks;
   (d) food – daily not less than 10,000 daily rations.

   Provide all of the deployed personnel with a personal weapon, uniform, footgear, rations (dried) for 15 days, medications ... and 1.5 standard loads of ammunition.

   Take all the items due to be airlifted to Comrade Belov's group from the resources of the Western Front. Send a request to the General Staff of the Red Army for any deficit items.
3. The Military Council of the Western Front will assume responsibility for the leadership and organization of the airborne operation: General of the Army Comrade Zhukov and Comrade Bulganin. Place deputy commander of the Western Front's air force Colonel Kuldin in direct charge of the operation for the deployment by air.

4. In order to carry out the airlift operation, the Western Front commander will receive the following aircraft:
   (a) from the commander of the Red Army Air Force Comrade Novikov – 20 PS-84;
   (b) from the commander of Long-range Aviation of the *Stavka* of the Supreme High Command Comrade Golovanov – 30 TB-3;
   (c) from the Western Front – 50 U-2 and 20 P-5.
5. The commander of the Airborne Forces Comrade Glazunov is to give the commander of the Western Front load slings, containers and instruction staff to oversee the loading process.
6. Commander of the country's Air Defense Forces Comrade Gromadin is to be responsible for covering the airfields while the heavy lift aircraft are being loaded at the requests of the Western Front commander.
7. Begin the airlift operation on 10 May 1942 and complete it by 25 May 1942.
8. Conduct the operation from the following air bases:
   (a) TB-3 and PS-84 – Kubinka, Drakino;
   (b) light aircraft – at the decision of the Western Front commander.
9. The Western Front Military Council is responsible for preparing airfields in the staging area of Group Belov to receive the aircraft.
10. Present the plan for organizing and conducting the airlift operation to the Chief of the General Staff by the end of 9 May 1942.
11. Evacuate all the wounded from Group Belov with the aircrafts' return flights.

Stavka of the Supreme High Command
I. Stalin
B. Shaposhnikov

Source: TsAMO, F. 132a, Op. 2642, D. 41, L. 130, 131

XIV *Stavka* VGK Directive No. 170394 to the Commander of the Western Front Regarding the Front's Reinforcement

18 May 1942, 14 hr 30 min

The *Stavka* confirms your ideas regarding the plan of Western Front's operation to link up with Group Belov and to retain the staging area occupied by it.

In order to conduct the operation, the Western Front is receiving from the *Stavka* Reserve: seven rifle divisions, two heavy artillery regiments (203mm), four-five artillery regiments (152mm) of the Supreme Command Reserve, two anti-tank artillery regiments (45mm).

Additional instructions will follow regarding the number of tank brigades and aviation regiments.

At the authorization of the *Stavka* of the Supreme High Command
Chief of the General Staff A. Vasilevsky

Source: TsAMO, F. 48a, Op. 3408, D. 99, L. 212.

XV *Stavka* VGK Directive No. 170433 to the Commander of the Kalinin Front on the Preparation of an Operation to Smash the Enemy's Olenino Grouping

3 June 1942, 00 hr 40 min

The *Stavka* of the Supreme High Command orders:

1. With the aim of simplifying the situation on the lines of communications of the 3rd and 4th Shock, and the 41st and 39th Armies, in the next couple of days withdraw no less than five rifle divisions and two tank brigades into Front reserve, concentrating them in the Ostashkov, Selizharovo, Sukhodol, Kuvshinovo area.
2. Submit to the *Stavka* the plan for an operation to destroy the enemy Olenino grouping, for which purpose the use of the divisions designated for the Front reserve is authorized.
3. Withdraw the 2nd Guards Rifle Corps from its current lines to the eastern bank of the Lovat' River, having established contact with the Southwestern Front's 1st Shock Army at the boundary between the *fronts* in the Varskie, Luki area.
4. Bring the rear line on the Selizharovo, Sukhodol sector into readiness for a defense.

Stavka of the Supreme High Command
I. Stalin
A. Vasilevsky

Source: F. 132a, Op. 2642, D. 32, L. 108

XVI *Stavka* VGK Directive No. 170514 to the Commanders of the Kalinin and Western Fronts about Conducting an Offensive Operation in the Rzhev Area

16 July 1942, 22 hr 00 min

The *Stavka* of the Supreme High Command is ordering in the period between 28 July to 5 August to conduct an operation with the combined efforts of the Kalinin Front's left wing and Western Front's right wing with the mission to clear the enemy from the territory north of the Volga River in the Rzhev, Zubtsov area and the territory to the east of the Vazuza River in the Zubtsov, Karamzino, Pogoreloe Gorodishche area, to seize the cities of Rzhev and Zubtsov, and to reach and firmly dig-in on the Volga and Vazuza Rivers, having secured bridgeheads in the Rzhev and Zubtsov areas, for which:

1. The Kalinin Front is to create a main grouping consisting of the 30th Army with a strength of no less than eleven rifle divisions, three rifle brigades, eight tank brigades, and ten artillery regiments of the Supreme Command Reserve, and is to attack from the Novo-Semenovskoe, Plotnikovo front in the general direction of Polunino and Rzhev, with the assignment to penetrate the defensive front, and having secured itself on the right with an attack of three rifle divisions and on the left with an attack of not less than two rifle divisions, with the main forces it is to seize the city of Rzhev, crossings over the Volga River, and the railroad hub.

   The further task for this grouping is to attack to the east with the aim of conclusively clearing the northern bank of the Volga River jointly with the 29th Army.

   The Front is to launch a secondary attack with the left flank of the 29th Army in strength of no less than three rifle divisions, one tank brigade, and three artillery regiments of the Supreme Command Reserve along the northern bank of the Volga River in the general direction of Zubtsov.

   Readiness for the operation – 28 July.
2. The Western Front, having taken operational control of the 31st Army from the Kalinin Front, consisting of three rifle divisions, two artillery regiments of the Supreme Command Reserve and two tank brigades with all of the army's facilities, units and transport, with the forces of the 31st and 20th Armies consisting altogether of no less than fourteen rifle divisions, four rifle brigades, ten tank brigades and twenty artillery regiments of the Supreme Command Reserve is to launch an attack from the Aleshevo, Vasilevskoe front in the general direction of Zubtsov.

   The immediate task of the Front is to breach the enemy's defense and, securing itself from the south, to reach the Vazuza River and to dig-in firmly.

   Readiness for the operation – 31 July.
3. In order to reinforce the indicated *fronts*, the chief of the General Staff by 26 July is to transfer and give:
   (a) five rifle divisions, six tank brigades, two artillery regiments (152mm) of the Supreme Command Reserve, four artillery regiments of USV [the 76mm divisional gun Model 1939, also known as the F-22-USV], and ten M-30 [*Katiusha*] battalions for the

Kalinin Front;

(b) one rifle division, six tank brigades, 16 M-30 battalions and the 2nd Cavalry Corps for the Western Front.

4. The commander of the Red Army Air Force Comrade Novikov jointly with the chief of the General Staff no later than 19 July is to submit a plan for the use and combat operations of aviation in the indicated operation with the participation in it of not less than 1,100 aircraft, of which 600 are to be fighters – taken from the Kalinin and Western Front's air forces and the aviation of the *Stavka* of the Supreme High Command.

Stavka of the Supreme High Command
I. Stalin
A. Vasilevsky

Source: TsAMO, F. 132a, Op. 2642, D. 41, L. 207-209.

XVII *Stavka* VGK Directive No. 170549 to the Commanders of the Western and Kalinin Fronts and the Red Army Air Force on Measures to Eliminate the Causes of the Impermissibly High Breakdowns of Aircraft

CC: Commanders of the Fronts' forces, the 7th Separate and Air Armies, and *Stavka* Representatives

4 August 1942, 21 hr 50 min

According to a report from Comrade Novikov, commander of the Red Army Air Force, of the 400 fighters assigned for participation in the operations of the Kalinin and Western Fronts, over four-five days of operation up to 140 aircraft have been lost due to mechanical breakdowns.

According to this same report, given the complete absence of the enemy air force on the first day of fighting and given a three-fold superiority over the enemy on subsequent days, our combat losses amounted to 51 fighters; 89 fighters are considered non-operational due to technical defects.

Considering it improbable to have such an impermissibly high percentage of aircraft, which have become disabled in the course of 4-5 days due to technical reasons, the *Stavka* sees in this the presence of plain sabotage and the saving of one's own skin on the part of some of the flight staff, who are striving to avoid combat by searching for isolated small defects in the aircraft.

The disgraceful technical supervision and control over the materiel, as well as over the execution of combat missions by the pilots, that has been established in the aviation units, not only permits, but even contributes to these criminal, intolerable manifestations in the army.

The *Stavka* of the Supreme High Command orders:

1. Immediately have responsible and experienced persons check each non-operational aircraft separately; identify the genuine causes of the defects and those directly responsible for them.
2. Immediately remove pilots who are responsible for sabotage from the units, bring them together into penal aviation squadrons and under the direct supervision of the commanders of the aviation divisions, use them for carrying out the most important missions on the most dangerous axes, thereby giving them the opportunity to atone for their guilt.
3. Immediately remove unreliable, malicious cowards from the aviation units, strip them of their rank, and send them into penal infantry companies as privates in order to carry out the most difficult assignments in the ground units.
4. Report the receipt [of this order], the results of the inspection, the measures taken to implement the present order, and the list of the flight staff sent into the penal squadrons and penal companies.

Stavka of the Supreme High Command
I. Stalin
A. Vasilevsky

Source: TsAMO, F. 148a, Op. 3763, D. 107, L. 220-222.

XVIII *Stavka* VGK Directive No. 994146 to the Commander of the Kalinin Front about Unifying the Commands of the 39th and 58th Armies

CC: Deputy People's Commissar of Defense, Chief of the Main Directorate of Communications

5 August 1942, 5 hr 30 min

The *Stavka* of the Supreme High Command has ordered:

1. By 6 August of this year, unify the field command of the 39th Army and the field command of the 58th Army into one command and call it the "field command of the 39th Army".

   Use the command and headquarters staff officers, who are left without posts as a result of the merger, to fill open positions in the Kalinin Front's army and subordinate headquarters.
2. 2. Use the 58th Army's rear units, logistics units and service facilities to replenish the 39th Army's rear units, logistics units and service facilities, but those in better shape – include in the Kalinin Front's reserve.

   Report on execution.

At the authorization of the *Stavka* of the Supreme High Command
Chief of the General Staff A. Vasilevsky

Source: TsAMO 48a, Op.3408, D. 72, L. 105.

XIX To the Commander of the Western Front, to the Commander of the Kalinin Front

5 August 1942, 19 hr 30 min

In connection with the common tasks of the operations being conducted in the Rzhev area by the forces of the Western and Kalinin Fronts, and in order to direct them in the future toward the single, overall objective, the *Stavka* of the Supreme High Command is ordering:

1. From 23.00 5 August 1942, General of the Army Comrade Zhukov will assume leadership over all the operations in the Rzhev area.
2. Upon receiving this, the commander of the Kalinin Front Colonel General Comrade Konev is to report immediately to Comrade Zhukov in order to receive personal directions and orders from General of the Army Zhukov regarding the further conducting of the operation.
3. Report upon the execution.

Stavka of the Supreme High Command
I. Stalin
A. Vasilevsky

Trasmitted by Vasilevsky 05.08.42 at 21.00

Source: TsAMO, F. 96a, Op. 1711, D. 7a, L. 73-77.

XX To Kalinin Front's Chief of Staff about Shortcomings in the Organization of the 30th and 29th Armies' Combat Operations

6 August 1942

During battles, the 30th and 29th Armies have revealed a number of substantial shortcomings.

30th Army:

(a) Control over the troops on the part of the headquarters of divisions and regiments is weak;
(b) The army's force operations are uncoordinated with respect to time;
(c) Tanks, attached to the divisions, are committed into the fighting in penny-packets;
(d) Ammunition supplies are being brought up slowly, as a result of which the artillery cannot fully support all of the infantry's requests.

29th Army:

(a) The combat formations of the shock grouping are deployed in a single echelon, with all the divisions in a single line;
(b) The infantry offensive is not receiving adequate artillery fire support;
(c) Tanks are not being active.

I request that you report on the measures undertaken to eliminate the observed shortcomings.

Ivanov
Bokov

No. 156511

Source: F. 48a, Op. 3408, D. 111, L. 376.

[Author's Note: V. D. Ivanov – Deputy Chief of the General Staff; F. E. Bokov – Commissar of the General Staff]

XXI *Stavka* VGK Directive No. 170558 to the Commander of the Western Front Regarding the Plan of the Operation in the Rzhev Area

6 August 1942, 21 hr 00 min

The *Stavka* of the Supreme High Command approves your ideas regarding the plan of the operation in the area of Rzhev, with the envelopment of the latter by forces of the 30th Army from the north and the 31st Army from the south [by] 9 August.

Stavka of the Supreme High Command
I. Stalin
A. Vasilevsky

Source: TsAMO, F. 148a, Op. 3763, D. 126, L. 143.

XXII *Stavka* VGK Directive No. 170591 to the Commanders of the Western and Kalinin Fronts about the Reassignment of the 29th and 30th Armies

29 August 1942

With the aims of the most rapid destruction of the enemy's Rzhev grouping, of encircling the city of Rzhev and of simplifying control over the forces, the *Stavka* of the Supreme High Command is ordering the transfer of the 29th and 30th Armies from the Kalinin Front to the Western Front from 24.00 30 August.

Stavka of the Supreme High Command
I. Stalin
A. Vasilevsky

Source: TsAMO, F. 148a, Op. 3763, D. 124, L. 252.

XXIII *Stavka* VGK Directive No. 170606 to the Commander of the Western Front Regarding the Working Out the Plan of the Gzhatsk Operation

9 September 1942, 22 hr 40 min

The *Stavka* of the Supreme High Command approves your suggestions.

1. Work out a plan of the Gzhatsk operation jointly with the General Staff and submit it for *Stavka* approval.
2. Withdraw the 3rd Tank Army in full to the Kaluga area into the *Stavka* Reserve.

Stavka of the Supreme High Command
I. Stalin
A. Vasilevsky

Source: TsAMO, F. 148a, Op. 3763, D. 12, L. 257.

XXIV *Stavka* VGK Directive No. 170651 to the Commander of the Kalinin Front about Reinforcing the Front

13 October 1942, 03 hr 50 min

The *Stavka* of the Supreme High Command has ordered to transfer additionally to you for the forthcoming Operation Mars:

1. In order to reinforce the 43rd Army – the 5th Guards Rifle Corps, consisting of the Rifle Corps' headquarters, begins loading at Uvarovo Station of the Western Front 14.10; the 9th Guards Rifle Division begins loading at Riazan' Station 13.10; the 46th Guards Rifle Division from the Voronezh Front, begins loading 14.10 and the 357th Rifle Division, begins loading 15.10 at Naro-Fominsk Station.
2. For Front reserve in the Sablovo area – the 8th Estonian Corps consisting of the Corps headquarters, the 7th and 249th Estonian Rifle Divisions and the 19th Guards Rifle Division. The Corps begins movement in the wake of the 5th Guards Rifle Corps from the Egor'evska area and the 19th Guards Rifle Division from the Volkhov Front. Do not use the Corps without *Stavka* authorization.
3. The plan of the rail movements will come in a following message.

At the authorization of the *Stavka* of the Supreme High Command
Chief of General Staff A. Vasilevsky

Source: TsAMO, F. 48a, Op. 3408, D. 72, L. 262.

XXV To the Chief of Staff of the Western Front Regarding the Inexpediency of Using Improvised Tank Groups for Exploiting a Breakthrough

13 September 1942, 23 hr 00 min

The experience of combat on the Rzhev – Sychevka direction has demonstrated that the practice of using improvised tank groups, which have been designated for exploiting a breakthrough, is untenable. In this period, three so-called mobile groups were created: Bychkovsky's, Arman's and the 32nd Army's tank group (17th, 34th, 212th, 145th, 188th and 101st Tank Brigades). All of these groups failed in carrying out their tasks, they didn't once move out behind the infantry, as is demanded of mobile groups, they suffered exceptionally heavy losses and were disbanded.

The main reason of these groups' lack of success was the improvisation during their creation. The hastily formed tank groups:

1. Didn't possess the necessary means and organs of control.
2. Good combat teamwork with the commanders and headquarters subordinated to the group was lacking.
3. The infantry units that were included in the groups had not been trained to operate jointly with the tank units.
4. The groups didn't have attached artillery and assets, especially of anti-tank artillery; the groups' were weak in engineering assets.
5. The headquarters of the armies and the groups didn't know how to organize cooperation with supporting air groups.

As a consequence, the following most scandalous shortcomings in the combat operations of the indicated mobile groups took place:

1. 1. In a period between 3.00 and 12.00 on 7 August, the 92nd Tank Brigade received four contradictory orders from the headquarters of Bychkovsky's group.
2. 2. On 5 August, the 145th Tank Brigade of this same group was thrown into the battle without prior reconnaissance, from the march against an organized enemy anti-tank defense and suffered heavy losses in tanks.
3. 3. Engineering support for Bychkovsky's group was set up exceptionally poorly: during the course of the operation, the group sank more than 20 tanks at river crossings.
4. 4. The headquarters of one mobile group lost communications with the 20th Army for a period of more than 48 hours and in essence ignored radio messages, while the 11th Tank Brigade of this group went astray and wound up in the sector of the 8th Rifle Corps. The group headquarters could not establish communications with it, and in view of this the 11th Tank Brigade operated for several days in isolation from the group.
5. 5. The 31st Army's tank group, over 31 August and 1 September alone, operating in the area of Martynovo, as a result of poorly organized cooperation with artillery and aviation, lost up to 40 tanks.

I request you report to the Front commander about the inexpediency of using improvised tank groups in the future.

Ivanov
Ryzhkov

No. 157133

Source: TsAMO, F. 48a, Op. 3408, D. 112, L. 288, 289.

[Author's note: I. N. Ryzhkov was the military commissar of the General Staff's Operations Department.]

XXVI To the Commander of the Kalinin Front about Expanding the Area of the Unloading of the Motorized Units

10 October 1942, 19 hr 10 min

The unloading of the operational trains in the areas of Selizharovo, Soblago and Toropets is proceeding extremely slowly. The timetable for the operational assembly is plainly breaking down. Enemy air activity is compelling a move to decisive measures in order to accelerate the unloading. However, you are conducting the unloading of all the trains only south of Soblago and moreover are letting through a large number of supply trains and *front* trains.

All this might drag out the concentration [of forces] for an undetermined period and give rise to excessive losses in trains from enemy aviation.

It is proposed:

1. Immediately expand the area of unloading the motorized and mechanized units and start the unloading trains at Ostashkov Station and south of that point (except for the trains ferrying tanks, which are to move through to the Toropets area).
2. At a minimum, cease the movement of *front* and supply deliveries, allowing the possibility to complete the operational assembly.
3. Regarding the supply deliveries, implement only those that are necessary for on-going support of the troops. Conduct the creation of needed reserves upon the completion of the operational assembly.
4. Report on the measures taken.

Vasilevsky
Karponosov

No. 990109

Source: F. 48a, Op. 3408, D. 100, L. 249.

[Author's note: A. G. Karponosov was the chief of the General Staff's Organizational Directorate.]

XXVII To the Chiefs of Staff of the Northwestern, Kalinin and Western Fronts and of the Main Intelligence Directorate about Strengthening Reconnaissance

17 October 1942

Over recent days, the following has been observed:

1. Increased enemy movement along the railroads: Dno – Nevel' – Vitebsk, Pskov – Polotsk, Dvinsk – Polotsk – Vitebsk, Minsk – Borisov – Orsha – Smolensk, Zhlobin – Mogilev – Orsha, Gomel' – Unecha – Briansk, Briansk – Roslavl' – Smolensk;
2. The enemy is accumulating strength in the Nevel', Vitebsk, Smolensk, Viaz'ma areas and is concentrating forces of unknown strength and means directly before the *fronts*:
   (a) In front of the Kalinin Front – in the areas Belyi, Olenino; Demidov, Vitebsk, Rudnia;
   (b) In front of the Northwestern Front – in the Dno, Porkhov, Dedovichi areas;
   (c) In front of the Western Front – in the Gzhatsk, Novodugino, Viaz'ma area.

In connection with this it is necessary:

1. to conduct uninterrupted aerial reconnaissance daily of the unloading and assembly of forces at the front and in the depth:
   (a) Northwestern Front – as far as the line Dno, Porkhov, Novorzhev (all inclusively);
   (b) Kalinin Front – as far as the line Nevel', Vitebsk, Smolensk, Iartsevo;
   (c) Western Front – as far as the line Smolensk, Roslavl', Briansk (all inclusively); aviation of the High Command will conduct aerial reconnaissance over the railroad west of these lines both day and night;
2. to conduct reconnaissance probes and to establish the presence of new units on the front line through captured prisoners;
3. through the network of agents to determine the composition and strength of the enemy in his assembly areas;

I ask you to report everyday in the intelligence summaries about the measures you have taken and the results of reconnaissance.

Ivanov

No. 157577

Source: F. 48a, Op. 3408, D. 113, L. 227, 228.

XXVIII An Order of the Supreme Commander to the *Stavka* Representative about Reinforcing the 20th Army

[4] December 1942

Your proposal about improving the 20th Army's operation is being confirmed by the *Stavka*.

Kiriukhin is relieved of command of the 20th Army. Lieutenant General Khozin is to assume temporary leadership over the operations of the 20th Army. The Gzhatsk operation may be postponed. You are assigned to take the needed number of rifle divisions and the 5th Tank Corps from the Gzhatsk operation's group of forces, and to transfer them to the 20th Army as reinforcements. 150 tanks will be placed at Stepanov's disposal.

Vasil'ev

Source: TsAMO, F. 148a, Op. 3763, D. 126, L. 198.

[Author's note: Vasil'ev was Stalin's code name.]

XXIX *Stavka* VGK Directive No. 170700 to the Commanders of the Western and Kalinin Fronts on the Assignments Pertaining to the Destruction of the Enemy's Rzhev – Sychevka – Olenino – Belyi Grouping

8 December 1942, 22 hr 15 min

The *Stavka* of the Supreme High Command is ordering:
Through the combined efforts of the Kalinin and Western Fronts, by 1 January 1943 to destroy the enemy's Rzhev – Sychevka – Olenino – Belyi grouping and to firmly dig-in on the front Iarygino, Sychevka, Andreevskoe, Lenino, Nov[oe] Azhevo, Dentialevo, Svity.

The Western Front when conducting the operation is to be directed by the following:

(a) In the course of 10-11 December, breakthrough the enemy's defense on the sector Bol[shoe] Kropotovo, Iarygino and seize Sychevka no later than 15 December; on 20 December, withdraw no less than 2 rifle divisions to the Andreevskoe area for organizing the sealing of the encircled enemy together with Kalinin Front's 41st Army;

(b) After breaching the enemy's defense and the main grouping reaches the line of the railroad, pivot the Front's mobile group and not less than four rifle divisions to the north for an attack into the rear of the enemy's Rzhev – Chertolino grouping;

(c) The 30th Army is to break through the defense on the sector Koshkino, road junction northwest of Burgovo and no later than 15 December is to reach the railroad in the Chertolino area; upon reaching the railroad, establish combat cooperation with the Front's mobile group and attack toward Rzhev with a strike along the railroad with the assignment to seize Rzhev by 23 December.

The Kalinin Front when carrying out assignments is to be directed by the following:

(a) Continue to develop the attack of the 39th and 22nd Armies in a general direction toward Olenino with the task to destroy the enemy's Olenino grouping, and no later than 16 December the armies are to reach the Olenino area.

With a portion of the 22nd Army, launch a secondary attack in the direction of Egor' with the aim of assisting the 41st Army in the destruction of the enemy's Belyi grouping;

(b) b) The 41st Army by 10 December is to destroy the enemy's penetrating grouping in the Tsytsyno area and to restore the lost position in the Okolitsa area.

No later than 20 December, with a portion of the forces reach the Mol'nia, Vladimirskoe, Lenino area with the assignment to seal from the south the encircled enemy grouping together with units of the Western Front.

No later than 20 December, seize Belyi.

In the future, have in view, after the regrouping of the forces of the Kalinin and Western Fronts, the destruction of the enemy's Gzhatsk – Viaz'ma – Khol'm-Zhirkovskii grouping by the end of January 1943 and the emergence on our old defensive line.

With the capture of Viaz'ma and the emergence on last year's defensive line west of the Rzhev – Viaz'ma line, consider the operation completed and move the troops into winter quarters.

Confirm receipt, report on the execution.

Pass the given order down to the regiment commanders inclusively.

Stavka of the Supreme High Command
I. Stalin
G. Zhukov

Source: TsAMO, F. 148a, Op. 3763, D. 126, L. 203, 204.

XXX To the Chief of Staff of the Kalinin Front about Shortcomings in the Organization of the Defense

4 January 1943, 1 hr 30 min

According to information available in the General Staff, the following shortcomings are present in the forces of the Kalinin Front.

1. The boundaries between the armies and within the armies – between divisions – are weakly secured. Units, guarding the boundaries, in a number of places have no connection at all between each other.
2. The forces' defensive lines are not fortified and adapted to winter conditions everywhere. This observation is especially in regards to sectors occupied by our forces as a result of the offensive. The old defensive positions, occupied by our forces prior to the offensive, have been abandoned; firing positions and communication trenches are drifted over with snow and are not prepared for conducting combat.

   In the new defensive lines, many units and formations lack battle plans. Military units and formations do not have and are not striving to create the needed reserves, which are extremely necessary.
3. Ski battalions in the divisions have so far not been fully staffed and equipped. The contingent that has been detached for the ski battalions does not meet the demands for a whole number of reasons. Preparation of the ski battalions is being implemented unsystematically, while in the 39th Army, there have been no exercises at all with the ski battalions since 25.11.1942. In battle, the ski battalions are being used as regular line subunits, as a result of which they are suffering heavy losses, while in the 373rd Rifle Division, the ski battalion fully ceased to exist after several combat actions.
4. Primarily only people in the rear units and facilities have been provided with warm items, while at the same time the soldiers and officers of the combat units have not received winter uniforms (the 185th, 238th and others).
5. Weapons, as a consequence of the lack of care in the combat units, are rusty, filthy, rifles lack foresights; many of the automatic weapons no longer fire automatically because of defects, and heavy machine guns are not operable (185th, 362nd, 238th Rifle Divisions and others).

   It is necessary to take urgent measures to eliminate the shortcomings noted above.

   Report regarding the measures you have taken by 7 January 1943.

Antonov

No. 11029

Source: TsAMO, F. 48a, Op. 3409, D. 26, L. 12, 13.

XXXI *Stavka* VGK Directive No. 30040 to the Commander of the Western Front about the Transfer of the 61st Army to the Briansk Front and the Assignment for Cooperation between the Fronts

6 February 1943, 01 hr 40 min

The *Stavka* of the Supreme High Command orders:

1. 1. Transfer the 61st Army on the morning of 08.02.43 to the Briansk Front. From the moment of the 61st Army's transfer, the boundary line between the Briansk and Western Fronts will be: Kozel'sk, Khvostovichi, Zhurinichi (all for the Western Front).
2. 2. With the aim of cooperation with the Briansk Front in seizing the Briansk area by 12.02.1943, prepare an offensive of the 16th Army, reinforced by the 9th Tank Corps, in the general direction through Zhizdra toward Briansk. The time of the shift to the offensive will be indicated especially.
3. 3. By 25.02.1943, prepare an offensive of the 50th and 10th Armies, reinforced by two tank corps, in the general direction toward Roslavl', but with part of the force – toward El'nia.
4. 4. Use part of the divisions of the 1100 series, which are joining the Front from the *Stavka* Reserve, to reinforce the 50th and 10th Armies.
5. 5. Report your decision in person to the *Stavka* on 8.02.1943.

Stavka of the Supreme High Command
I. Stalin
G. Zhukov

[Source: TsAMO, F. 148a, Op. 3763, D. 103, L. 255, 256.]

XXXII *Stavka* Directive No. 30041 to the Commander of the Briansk Front about the Sequence of the Destruction of the Enemy's Orel – Briansk Grouping

6 February, 01 40 min

With the aim of the most rapid encirclement and destruction of the enemy's Orel – Briansk grouping, the *Stavka* of the Supreme High Command orders:

1. With the arrival of the 48th and 13th Armies on the line Droskovo, Maloiaroangel'sk, Fatezh, the 48th Army is to attack toward Orel, enveloping it from the southwest. To link up with this thrust, prepare an offensive of the 61st Army from the Belev area with a general direction through Bolkhov toward Orel.
2. Simultaneously with the offensive of the 48th, 3rd and 61st Armies toward Orel, the 13th Army is to continue the offensive toward Karachev, Briansk with the task of creating a second ring of encirclement around the enemy and the seizure of Briansk and Karachev.

   Keep in view that the Western Front's 16th Army will attack from the Bryn', Zavod area in a general direction through Zhizdra to link up with the 13th Army's attack.
3. Complete the encirclement and destruction of the enemy's Orel grouping by the forces of the 43rd, 3rd and 61st Armies by 15-17 February 1943.

   The 13th Army in cooperation with the Western Front's 16th Army is to seize Briansk by 23-25 February 1943.
4. Keep in view that on the left, approximately from the line Fatezh, L'gov, the troops of Colonel General Rokossovsky will deploy and attack in the general direction of Sevsk, Unecha Station.
5. The boundary line with the Western Front from the morning of 8.02.1943 will be Kozel'sk, Khvostovichi, Zhurinichi (all for the Western Front). The boundary with Rokossovsky's forces will be indicated in another message.
6. Report your decision by code through the Baudot device by 24.00 6.02.1943.

Stavka of the Supreme High Command
I. Stalin
G. Zhukov

Source: TsAMO, F. 148a, Op. 3763, D. 103, L. 257-259.

XXXIII *Stavka* VGK Directive No. 30043 to the Commander of the Central Front for an Offensive with the Aim of Emerging in the Rear of the Enemy's Rzhev – Viaz'ma – Briansk Grouping

6 February 1943, 01 hr 40 min

With the goal of further developing the success of the Briansk and Voronezh Fronts and emerging in the rear of the enemy's Rzhev – Viaz'ma – Briansk grouping, the *Stavka* of the Supreme High Command orders:

1. By 12.02.1943, assemble:
   (a) the 2nd Tank Army – in the Dolgovo area;
   (b) the 2nd Cavalry Corps with three ski brigades and two tank regiments – in the Cheremisinovo area;
   (c) the 65th Army – in the area north of Dolgovo, south of Livny

   From the assembly areas, by the end of 14.02.1943 move the 2nd Tank Army, the 2nd Cavalry Corps and the 65th Army to a Fatezh, Kursk line of deployment. Assemble the remaining units of the 21st and 70th Armies, in pace with their arrival, in the Volovo, Dolgorukovo, Livny area, and send them behind the attacking forces of the Front's first echelon.
2. On the morning of 15.02.1943, the 2nd Tank Army, 65th Army and 16th Air Army will go on the offensive in the general direction of Sevsk, Uchena Station, with the nearest task to cut the Briansk – Gomel' railroad.

   Deploy Kriukov's mixed cavalry-rifle group on the left flank and send [it] through Novgorod-Severskii, Star[yi] Bykov and Mogilev, where it is to cross to the western bank of the Dnepr, and having secured its crossing point, it is to emerge in the Orsha area.

   Keep in view that the to the right of you, the Briansk Front's 13th Army will be attacking toward Briansk, and the Western Front's 16th Army will be attacking through Zhizdra toward Briansk.
3. Upon the arrival of the Front's armies on the Briansk, Gomel' line, launch the main attack through Klimovichi and Khislovichi toward Smolensk with the task of seizing the Smolensk area and cutting off the enemy's Viaz'ma – Rzhev grouping's path of retreat. With the emergence of the main grouping in the Uchena Station area, seize Gomel' with a force of two rifle divisions and establish a bridgehead on the western bank of the Dnepr in the Rechitsa, Zhlobin sector.

   Simultaneously as your forces go on the offensive from the Briansk, Gomel' line toward Smolensk, the Western Front will go on the attack toward Roslavl' and further on toward Smolensk, while the Briansk Front will attack toward Vitebsk, Orsha and with part of its strength toward Smolensk, to meet up with your main attack.
4.

5. The Front's boundary lines will be indicated in a following message. Have in view that to the left of the Front, Voronezh Front's 60th Army will be attacking in the general direction L'gov, Glukhov, Chernigov.

Stavka of the Supreme High Command
I. Stalin
G. Zhukov

Source: F. 148a, Op. 3763, D. 103, L. 263-265.

XXXIV *Stavka* VGK Order No. 0045 Regarding the Replacement of the Commander and Chief of Staff of the Western Front

27 February 1943

1. Relieve Colonel General I.S. Konev, who was unable to cope with the Front's leadership tasks, of his duties as commander of the Western Front, placing him at the disposal of the *Stavka* of the Supreme High Command.
2. Appoint Colonel General V.D. Sokolovsky as commander of the Western Front, freeing him from his duties as Front chief of staff.
3. Complete the acceptance and relinquishment of business by 02.00 28 February 1943, after which Comrade Sokolovsky is to assume command of the Front.
4. Appoint Lieutenant General A. P. Pokrovsky as chief of staff of the Western Front, freeing him from his duties as chief of the Front headquarters' operations department.

Stavka of the Supreme High Command
I. Stalin

Source: TsAMO, F. 148a, Op. 3763, D. 142, L. 36.

XXXV *Stavka* VGK Order No. 0046 Regarding the Replacement of Army Commanders of the Western Front

27 February 1943

1. Relieve Colonel General Ia.T. Cherevichenko from his post as commander of the 5th Army, since he has been unable to cope with the fulfillment of his combat assignments, and place him at the disposal of the *Stavka* of the Supreme High Command.
2. Appoint Lieutenant General V.S. Polenov as commander of the 5th Army, relieving him of command of the 31st Army.
3. Appoint Major General V.A. Gruzdovsky as commander of the 31st Army, freeing him from his post as chief of staff of the same army.

Stavka of the Supreme High Command
I. Stalin

Source: TsAMO, F. 148a, Op. 3763, D. 142, L. 40.

XXXVI *Stavka* VGK Directive No. 30062 to the Commanders of the Kalinin and Western Front on the Pursuit of the Retreating Enemy

CC: G.K. Zhukov

2 March 1943, 17 hr 15 min

The enemy in front of the left flank of the Kalinin Front and the right flank of the Western Front has begun to withdraw his troops to the south and southwest. The pursuit of the withdrawing foe is being conducted sluggishly and indecisively.

The *Stavka* of the Supreme High Command orders:

1. Immediately take measures for an energetic pursuit of the enemy's retreating forces.
2. Create mobile pursuit detachments from various types of troops, led by brave, ambitious commanders and send them into the enemy rear.
3. The general pursuit of the enemy must not follow along the routes of his withdrawal, but according to our offensive plan.
4. The *Stavka* is requiring the submission of a plan for an offensive by the forces of Kalinin Front's left wing and Western Front's right wing in connection with the enemy's retreat no later than 23.00 2.3.1943.

Stavka of the Supreme High Command
I. Stalin

Source: F. 148a, Op. 3763, D. 139, L. 171, 172.

Notes

Introduction

1 Examples of the literature from this time period include: *Istoriia Velikoi Otechestvennoi voiny Sovetskogo Soiuza 1941-1945* [History of the Great Patriotic War of the Soviet Union 1941-1945], in six volumes (Moscow: Volume 2, 1963; Volume 3, 1964); *Istoriia vtoroi mirovoi voiny 1939-1945* [History of the Second World War 1939-1945] in twelve volumes (Moscow: Volume 4, 1975; Volume 5, 1975; Volume 6, 1976; Volume 7, 1976); *Sovetskaia voennaia entsiklopediia* [*SVE*] [Soviet Military Encyclopedia] in eight volumes, Volume 7 (Moscow: 1979); *Voennyi entsiklopedicheskii slovar'* [Military Encyclopedic Dictionary] Moscow, 1983 and other years; K. N. Galitsky, *Gody surovykh ispytanii 1941-1944: Zapiski komandarma* [Years of severe trials 1941-1944: Notes of an army commander] (Moscow: Nauka, 1973), pp. 164-166, 170; M. E. Katukov, *Na ostrie glavnogo udara* [At the point of the main attack] (Moscow: 1985), pp. 174-200; *Velikaia Otechestvennaia voiny 1941-1945: Voenno-istoricheskie ocherki* [The Great Patriotic War 1941-1945: Military-historical essays] (Moscow: 1998) [hereafter referred to as *Velikaia otechestvennaia ... Ocherki*); Book 1, p. 303; Book 2, pp. 212-223, 239-242, 410; and others.

2 Response of the USSR Ministry of Defense's Institute of Military History to a query from the Rzhev Regional Museum, 1980; in the archives of the Rzhev Regional Museum.

3 See for example Krivosheev et. al., *Grif sekretnosti sniat* [The Seal of secrecy has been lifted] (Moscow, 1983); "Liudskie poteri Sovetskikh Vooruzhennykh Sil v 1941-1945: Novye aspekty" ["Human losses of the Soviet Armed Forces in 1941-1945: New aspects"], *Voenno-istoricheskii Zhurnal* (*VIZh*) No. 2 (February 1999); David M. Glantz, "Nedostatki istoriografii: zabytye bitvy germano-sovetskoi voiny (1941-1945)" ["Shortcomings of historiography: Forgotten battles of the German-Soviet war (1941-1945)"], in *Vtoraia mirovaia voina: Aktual'nye problemy* [The Second World War: Topical questions] (Moscow, 1985); David M. Glantz, "Operatsiia Mars" ["Operation Mars"], *Voprosy istorii*, No. 8 (August 1997); David M. Glantz, *Zhukov's Greatest Defeat: The Red Army's Epic Disaster in Operation Mars, 1942* (Lawrence, KS: University of Kansas Press, 2005) [Note: the author is actually using the Russian translation of this book, published in Moscow in 2006 by AST: Astrel'.]; V. V. Gurkin, "'Mars' v orbite 'Urana' i 'Saturna," [" 'Mars' in the orbit of 'Uranus' and 'Saturn'", *VIZh* No. 4 (April 2000); *Velikaia otechestvennaia ... Ocherki*, Book 2, pp. 212-221; *SVE* , Vol. 7 (Moscow: Voenizdat, 2003), pp. 231-235.

4 O. Kondrat'ev, "Rzhevskaia bitva: mif ili realnost'?" ["The battle of Rzhev: myth or reality?"], *Tverskaia zhizn'*, 21 March 1997; O. A. Kondrat'ev, "*Rzhevskaia bitva: polveka ulmolchaniia*" ["The battle of Rzhev: a half-century of silence"], Rzhev, 1998; S. A. Gerasimova, "Ne pora li pereosmyslit' rol' i znachenie boev pod Rzhevom?" ["Hasn't the time come to rethink the role and significance of the battles near Rzhev?"], *Voprosy istorii* No. 5 (May, 1998); S. A. Gerasimova, "Bitva za rzhevsko-viazemskii platsdarm" ["Battles for the Rzhev-Viaz'ma Bridgehead"], *VI* No. 4-5, 2000; E. Ozhegin, ed. *Istoriia Rzheva: ocherki po istorii rzhevskoi zemli*" [The History of Rzhev: essays on the history of the Rzhev land] (Rzhev, 2000).

5 Iu. N. Afanas'ev, "Drugaia voina: istoriia i pamiat'" ["A different war: history and memory"] in *Drugaia voina 1939-1945* [*A Different War 1939-1945*] (Moscow, 1996), p. 30.

6 The author gathered the materials for the book up until May 2007, when the files of a number of organizations had still not been declassified.

7 Editor's note: Alexander Matrosov is a famous Red Army infantryman, who according to Soviet sources blocked the embrasure of a German pillbox with his body, thereby obstructing the fire of its machine gun. For this action he was posthumously accorded the honor Hero of the Soviet Union. Soviet sources say this

deed took place on 22 February 1943, but some scholars today say the action occurred on 27 February, and was post-dated to 22 February to match the anniversary day of the Red Army's creation.

Chapter 1

1 Editor's note: *platsdarm* is also often translated as "bridgehead", when the staging area lies beyond a river. Depending on the specific context, I will use either translation: "staging area" or "bridgehead".

2 *Sovetskaia voennaia entsiklopediia.*

3 V. T. Eliseev, "Dokumenty Tsentral'nogo arkhiva MO RF o Viazemskom okruzhenii, poteriakh v Moskovskoi bitve I novoi kontseptsii po istorii vooruzhennoi bor'by na sovetskom-germanskom fronte v 1941-1945" ["Documents of the Central Archive of the Russian Federation's Ministry of Defense on the Viaz'ma encirclement, the losses in the Moscow battle, and a new conception of the history of the armed struggle on the Soviet-German front, 1941-1945"], *Voenno-istoricheskii arkhiv* [*VIA*], No. 12 (2006), p. 69.

4 B. Liddell Hart, *History of the Second World War* (Da Capo Press, 1999).

5 *SVE*, Volume 7, p. 119; K. von Tippelskirch, *Istoriia vtoroi mirovoi voiny* [History of the Second World War] Volume 1 (SPB, 1994), p. 205.

6 *Velikaia otechestvennaia ... Ocherki* [The Great Patriotic War. Essays] Book 2 (Moscow, 1998), p. 241.

7 *Istoriia vtoroi mirovoi voiny*, Volume 4 (Moscow: 1975), p. 305; Tippelskirch, *Istoriia vtoroi mirovoi voiny*, p. 204.

8 V. I. Dashichev, *Bankrotsvo strategii Germanskogo fashizma. Istoricheskie ocherki. Dokumenty i materialy* [Bankruptcy of German fascism's strategy. Historical essays. Documents and materials], Volume 2 (Moscow: 1973), pp. 322, 323; as cited by *Istoriia vtoroi mirovoi voiny*, Vol. 4, p. 304.

9 Liddell Hart, op. cit, p. 232.

10 L. M. Sandalov, *Pogorelo-gorodishchenskaia operatsiia* [The Pogoreloe Gorodishche operation] (Moscow: Voenizdat, 1960), pp. 20-21.

11 N. M. Afanas'ev, N. K. Glazunov, P. A. Kazansky, and N. A. Fironov, *Dorogami ispytanii i pobed: Boevoi put' 31-i armii* [Along the roads of trials and victories: The combat path of the 31st Army] (Moscow: 1986), pp. 56-57.

12 G. T. Riabkova (ed.), *Po dorogam boevoi slavy* [Along the paths of combat glory] (Smolensk: 1967), pp. 155, 160.

13 TsAMO [Central Archive of the Ministry of Defense], F. 354, Op. 5806, D. 118, L. 114; E. M. Rhein, *Das rheinisch-westfalische Infanterie/Grenadier-Regiment 18. 1921-1945* (Bergisch-Gladbach, 1993), pp. 167, 187, 189; *Recollections of M. K. Sushkov, veteran of the 215th Rifle Division, 1968*, p. 3, Rzhev Regional Museum of the Russian Federation; Materials of the 369th Rifle Division, Rzhev Regional Museum of the Russian Federation; *I. Ladygin and N. Smirnov, Na Rzhevskom rubezhe* [On the Rzhev line] (Rzhev, 1992), p. 183.

14 K. Ivanov, *Shla diviziia na zapad* [The division marched westward] (Perm: 1972), pp. 50-51.

15 S. Golikov, *Vydaiushchie pobedy Sovetskoi Armii v Velikoi Otechestvennoi voine* [Outstanding victories of the Soviet Army in the Great Patriotic War] (Moscow: Gospolitizdat, 1952), p. 74; *Velikaia Otechestvennaia. Ocherki*, Book 2, p. 65; TsAMO, F. 208, Op. 2511, D. 2606, L. 51 obr; TsAMO, F. 208, Op. 2511, D. 2337, L. 101.

16 TsAMO, F. 213, Op. 2002, D. 114, L. 48.

17 *Pravda*, 4 March 1943; Ladygin and Smirnov, *Na rzhevskom rubezhe*, p. 52; *Po dorogam boevoi slavy*, p. 159; F. Halder, *Voennyi dnevnik* [War Diary] Vol. 3, Book 2 (Moscow, 1969), p. 320; *Der Durchbruch, Soldatenzeitung an der Ostfront,* 23 August 1942, NVF No. 813, in materials of the Rzhev Regional Museum; E. M. Rzhevskaia, *Blizhnie podstupy* [Closest approaches] (Moscow, 1985), pp. 42, 110, 112; *Krasnaia zvezda* 1 December 1942; H. Grossmann, *Rzhev: Kraeugol'nyi kamen' Vostochnogo Fronta*

[Rzhev: The cornerstone of the Eastern Front] (Rzhev, 1996), p. 132; Halder, *Voennyi dnevnik*, pp. 359, 361.

Chapter 2

1 SVE, Vol. 7, p. 615 and Vol. 8, pp. 76-77; *Velikaia Otechestvennaia voina: Entsiklopediia* [The Great Patriotic War: Encyclopedia] (Moscow, 1985), pp. 197, 466, 699, 720; V. V. Gurkin, "Strategicheskie i frontovye operatsii Krasnoi Armii" ["Strategic and front operations of the Red Army"], *VIZh*, No. 2 (February 1998), p. 16; *Russkii arkhiv: Velikaia otechestvennaia voina 1941-1945. Seriia sbornikov dokumentov* [Russian archive: The Great Patriotic War 1941-1945. Series of document collections, Vol. 16 (5-2) The Stavka VGK: Documents and materials, 1943] (Moscow, 1996), p. 32; V. D. Sokolovsky (ed.), *Razgrom nemetsko-fashistskikh voisk pod Moskvoi* [The defeat of German-fascist forces at Moscow] (Moscow: 1964).

2 V. I. Dashichev, *Bankrotsvo strategii*, Vol. 2, p. 262.

3 *Istoriia vtoroi mirovoi voiny*, Vol. 4, p. 307; *SVE*, Vol. 7, p. 116.

4 *Voennaia entsiklopediia v 8 tomakh* [Military encyclopedia in 8 volumes], Vol. 7 (Moscow: Voenizdat, 2003), p. 230.

5 Sokolovsky, *Razgrom nemetsko-fashistskikh voisk*, p. 325.

6 Grossmann, *Rzhev: Kraeugol'nyi kamen'*, p. 32.

7 *Russkii arkhiv*, Vol. 16 (5-2) The *Stavka* VGK, p. 237

8 See Ladygin and Smirnov, *Na rzhevskom rubezhe*, p. 24.

9 Doroga na Smolensk: *Amerikanskie pisateli i zhurnalisty o Velikoi Otechestvennoi voine sovetskogo naroda, 1941 1945* [The Road to Smolensk: American writers and journalists on the Great Patriotic War of the Soviet people, 1941-1945] (Moscow, 1985), p. 74.

10 *Velikaia Otechestvennaia voina. Entsiklopediia*, p. 197; Belov, *Za nami Moskva*, pp. 188, 194; L. M. Sorochenko, "Proschety planirovaniya (Tylovoe obespechenie Viazemskoi vozdushno-desantnoi operatsii)" ["Miscalculations of planning (Logistic support of the Viaz'ma airborne operation), *VIZh*, No. 1 (1989), pp. 80-82.

11 T. P. Safronov, *Vozdushnye desanty vo 2-i mirovoi voine* [Airborne assaults in the 2nd World War] (Moscow, 1962); Belov, *Za nami Moskva*, p. 194; K. F. Vasil'chenko, "Tragicheskaia provalivshaia Viazemskaia nastupatel'naia operatsiia Zapadnogo fronta" ["The tragic failed Viaz'ma offensive operation of the Western Front", *VIA*, No. 1 (2007), p. 26; "K 110-letiiu so dnia rozhdeniia general-leitenanta M. G. Efremov" ["On the 110th anniversary of the birth of Lieutenant-General M. G. Efremov"], *VIA*, No. 3 (2007), p. 6; V. M. Mel'nikov, "Material'no-tekhnicheskoe obespechenie voisk v Moskovskoi nastupatel'noi strategicheskoi operatsii (6.12.1941-20.4. 1942) ["Logistical support of the forces in the Moscow offensive strategic operation (12/6/1941-4/20/1942), *VIA*, No. 4 (2006), p. 58.

12 TsAMO, F. 208, Op. 2511, D. 1025, L. 2.

13 Halder, *Voennyi dnevnik*, p. 161.

14 Tippelskirch, *Istoriia vtoroi mirovoi voiny*, p. 204

15 As cited by D. M. Proektor, *Agressiia i katastrofa* [Aggression and catastrophe] (Moscow, 1968), p. 316.

16 Ibid.

17 Grossmann, *Rzhev: Kraeugol'nyi kamen'*, p. 26

18 Proektor, *Agressiia i katastrofa*, pp. 314-315.

19 *Russkii arkhiv*, Vol. 16 (5-2), pp. 448, 458.

20 As calculated by P. P. Ionov in his article "Nastupaet Kalinskii Front" ["The Kalinin Front attacks"] *VIA*, No. 8 (2006), pp. 102, 106; and No. 10 (2006) pp. 91-92.

21 K. Reinhardt, *Povorot pod Moskvoi*, p. 306.

22 *Russkii arkhiv*, Vol. 16 (5-2), p. 79.

23 Halder, *Voennyi dnevnik*, p. 187.
24 Reinhardt, *Povorot pod Moskvoi*, p. 306.
25 Ionov, "Nastupaet Kalinskii Front", *VIA*, No. 9 (2006), p. 105.
26 See Ionov, "Nastupaet Kalinskii Front", pp. 105-106; I. I. Lisov, *Desantniki*, p. 92; TsAMO RF, F. 384, Op. 8529, D. 87, L. 17-18; Safronov, *Vozdushnye desanty*, p. 26; I. A. Vovchenko, *Tankisty* [Tankers] (Moscow: DOSAAF, 1976), pp. 73-80.
27 TsAMO RF, F. 384, Op. 8550, D. 12, L. 1-7; see Ladygin and Smirnov, *Na Rzhevskom rubezhe*, pp. 42-44.
28 See *Velikaia otechestvennaia ... Ocherki*. Book 1, pp. 295-296; Belov, *Za nami Moskva*, pp. 209, 212.
29 See *Velikaia otechestvennaia ... Ocherki*. Book 1, pp. 296-297; *Russkii arkhiv*, Vol. 16 (5-2), pp. 88-89; *VIA*, No. 3 (2007), p. 6.
30 See Belov, *Za nami Moskva*, pp. 216-230. The German general's quote is cited by Belov on p. 281.
31 *Russkii arkhiv*, Vol. 16 (5-2), pp. 98-99.
32 Istoriia vtoroi mirovoi voiny, Vol. 4, p. 311; Halder, Voennyi dnevnik, p. 191.
33 Ionov, "Nastupaet Kalinin Front", pp. 107-108.
34 *Velikaia otechestvennaia voina: Entsiklopediia*, p. 198; Belov, *Za nami Moskva*, pp. 227-229; A. Lukashenko, *Za frontom – front: Krylataia gvardiia* [Behind the front – a front: Winged Guard] (Moscow: DOSAAF, 1978), p. 27; Lisov, *Desantniki*, p. 115; see also S. D. Mitiagin, "Dokumenty i kommentariia k stat'e 'Boevye deistviia pod Viaz'moi v ianvare-aprele 1942': Operatsiia ili imitatsiia?" ["Documents and commentary to the article 'Combat operations at Viaz'ma in January-April 1942': Operation or imitation?"], *VIA*, No. 5 (2007), p. 45.
35 Mitiagin, "Dokumenty i komentarii", pp. 35, 45-46; "K 110-letiiu so dnya rozhdeniia general-leitenanta M. G. Efremov" ["On the 110th Anniversary of Lieutenant-General M. G. Efremov's birthday], *VIA,* No. 3 (2007), p. 6; Belov, *Za nami Moskva*, p. 223.
36 Tippelskirch, *Istoriia vtoroi mirovoi voiny*, p. 205.
37 *Russkii arkhiv*, Vol. 16 (5-2), pp. 137-138.
38 Ionov, "Nastupaet Kalinin Front", p. 97; *Velikaia Otechestvennaia Voina ... Ocherki ...* Book 1, pp. 300, 302.
39 *Soldaty Velikoi Otechestvennoi: Vospominaniia i ocherki* [Soldiers of the Great Patriotic: Recollections and essays] (Iaroslavl', 1987), p. 10.
40 *Sovetskaia kavaleriia* [Soviet cavalry] (Moscow, 1984), p. 202; Tippelskirch, *Istoriia vtoroi mirovoi voiny*, p. 205.
41 *Velikaia otechestvennaia ... Ocherki*. Book 1, pp. 300-301; see Iu. Kapusto, *Poslednimi dorogami generala Efremova* [Along General Efremov's last roads] (Moscow, 1992), p. 105; I. Zhorov, "V tylu pod Viaz'moi" ["In the rear at Viaz'ma"] *VIZh*, No. 6 (1965), p. 58; V. M. Safir, "Oborona Moskvy: Narofominskii proryv" ["The defense of Moscow: the Narofominsk breakthrough" *VIA*, 1st Ed. (Moscow, 1997), pp. 98-99; "K 110-letiiu so dnia rozhdeniia general-leitenanta M. G. Efremov", pp. 6-7.
42 "K 110-letiiu so dnia rozhdeniia general-leitnenta M. G. Efremov", pp. 7, 11, 16-18; Vasil'chenko, "Tragicheskaia provalivshaia Viazemskaia nastupatel'naia operatsiia", pp. 43-48; Mitiagin, "Dokumenty i kommentariia", pp. 17-18; Belov, *Za nami Moskva*, pp. 231-232.
43 *Istoriia Velikaia Otechestvennaia voiny*, Vol. 2 (Moscow, 1963), p. 332; *Istoriia Velikaia Otechestvennia voiny*, Vol. 4, pp. 312-313; Halder, *Voennyi dnevnik*, p. 234.
44 *Russkii arkhiv*, Vol. 16 (5-2), p. 303; Krivosheev et. al., *Grif sekretnosti sniat*, p. 176; S. N. Mikhalev, *Strategicheskie resheniia* [Strategic decisions], Book 2 (Krasnoiarsk, 1998), p. 49.
45 *Istoriia mirovoi voiny*, Vol. 4, p. 327; Belov, *Za nami Moskva*, pp. 170-171; B. N. Petrov, "Analiz prichin nezavershennosti nekotorykh nastupatel'nykh operatsii Velikoi otechestvennoi voiny" ["An analysis of causes of the non-completion of several offensive operations of the Great Patriotic War"] *VIZh*, No. 1

(January 1987), pp. 13-19; Zhukov, *Vospominaniia i razmyshleniia*, Vol. 2, pp. 243-245; M. A. Gareev, "O neudachnykh nastupatel'nykh operatsiiakh sovetskikh voisk v Velikoi otechestvennoi voine" ["On the unsuccessful offensive operations of Soviet forces in the Great Patriotic War"] *Novaia i noveishaia istoriia*, No. 1 (1994), pp. 3-4; V. A. Zolotarev, ed., *Strategicheskie resheniya i Vooruzhennye Sily* [Strategic decisions and the Armed Forces] (Moscow, 1995), as cited by Safir, Oborona Moskvy: Narofominskii proryv, p. 102; *Velikaia otechestvennaia ... Ocherki*. Book 1, pp. 302-303.

46 Zhukov, *Vospominaniia i razmyshleniia*, Vol. 2, p. 234; G. K. Zhukov, "Iz neopublikovannykh vospominanii" ["From the unpublished reminiscences"] *Kommunist*, No. 14 (1988), p. 96; N. G. Pavlenko, *Byla voina ... razmyshleniia voennogo istorika* [There was a war ... reflections of a military historian] (Moscow, 1994), p. 291.

47 For this school of thought, see B. V. Sokolov, *Tsena pobedy. Velikaia otechestvennaia: neizvestnom ob izvestnom* [The price of victory. The Great Patriotic War: the unknown about the known] (Moscow, 1991); Kapusto, *Poslednimi dorogami*; Safir, *Oborony Moskvy: Narofominskii proryv*; Mitiagin, "Boevye deistiia pod Viaz'moi v ianvare-aprele 1942: operatsiia ili imitatsiia?" *VIA*, No. 3 (1998), p. 67, 102; Mitiagin, "Dokumenty i kommentariia"; A. I. Biriukov and V. M. Safir, "Vo vsem li prav istorik general armii M. A. Gareev?" ["Is the historian General of the Army M. A. Gareev right in everything?"] *VIA*, Issue No. 3 (Moscow, 1998), p. 277; and A. N. Mertsalov and L. A. Mertsalov, *A. A. Zhomin, Osnovatel' nauchnoi voennoi teorii* [A. A. Jomini: founder of scientific military theory] (Moscow, 1998), p. 228.

48 Mitiagin, "Dokumenty i komentariia", p. 36.

49 Zhukov, "Iz neopublikovannykh vospominanii", p. 96.

50 Cited by Safir, "Oborona Moskvy: Narofominskii proryv", p. 102; Liddell Hart, *Istoriia Vtoroi mirovoi voiny*, p. 234.

51 *Velikaia otechestvennaia ... Ocherki*. Book 1, pp. 302-303.

52 Cited by Mitiagin, "Boevye deistviya pod Viaz'moi", p. 87; TsAMO RF, F. 213, Op. 2002, D. 326, L. 25.

53 *Velikaia otechestvennaia ... Ocherki*. Book 1, p. 303; V. D. Sokolovsky (ed.), *Razgrom nemetsko-fashistkikh voik pod Moskvoi* [Defeat of the German-fascist forces in front of Moscow] (Moscow, 1964), p. 361.

54 See Sokolovsky (ed.), *Razgrom nemetsko-fashistkikh voisk pod Moskvoi*.

55 Editor's note: As author Boris Gorbachevsky noted in his book *Generalissimo Stalin: The Myth of Stalin as a Great Military Strategist?* (Helion & Company, forthcoming), the term "unfinished operation" was coined by Joseph Stalin himself in 1944, as if the Red Army never suffered clear failures – it just failed to complete operations.

56 *Voennaia entsiklopediia* [Military Encyclopedia] Vol. 7 (Moscow: Voenizdat, 2003), p. 231; G. F. Krivosheev et. al., "Na podmoskovnykh rubezhakh: Sviashchennaia voina na Rosiiskikh zenliakh" ["On the lines before Moscow: Holy war on Russian lands"] *VIZh*, No. 12 (2006).

Chapter 3

1 Zhukov, *Vospominaniia i razmyshleniiai*, p. 251; S. M. Shtemenko, *General'nyi shtab v gody voiny* [The General Staff in the war years] Book 1 (Moscow, 1981), p. 57; A. Vasilevsky, "Nekotorye voprosy vooruzhennoi bor'by letom 1942" ["Certain questions of the armed struggle in the summer of 1942"] *VIZh*, No. 8 (August 1965), p. 9.

2 "Zapiski vracha "Skoroi pomoshchii"" ["Notes of an emergency doctor"] *Dokumenty russkoi istorii* No. 2 (1995), p. 65.

3 "Pitanie bylo kaloriinym: O prodovol'stvennom snabzhenii i chislennost' Krasnoi Armii v gody Velikoi otechestvennoi voiny" ["The nutrition was sustaining: On the food supply and manpower of the Red Army in the years of the Great Patriotic War"] *VIZh*, No.1 (1999), p. 96.

4 Zhukov, *Vospominaniia i razmyshleniia*, pp. 252-253; *Velikaia otechestvennaia ... Ocherki*. Book 1, p. 325;

Belov, *Za nami Moskva*, pp. 277-278; TsAMO RF, F. 213, Op. 2002, D. 219, L. 2-27.
5 Belov, *Za nami Moskva*, pp. 262, 283; *Russkii arkhiv*, Vol. 16 (5-2), pp. 194, 208.
6 TsAMO RF, F. 208, Op. 2511, D. 1522.
7 TsAMO RF, F. 354, Op. 5806, D. 67, L. 61; Halder, *Voennyi dnevnik*, pp. 254-255.
8 TsAMO RF, F. 208, Op. 2511, D. 1024, L. 98.
9 See Dashichev, *Bankrotsvo strategii*, Vol. 2, pp. 323-327.
10 Cited by Proektor, *Agressiia i katastrofa*, p. 350.
11 Ibid., p. 615; Grossmann, *Rzhev: Kraeugol'nyi kamen'*, p. 49.
12 Tippelskirch, *Istoriia vtoroi mirovoi voiny*, p. 241; Halder, *Voennyi dnevnik*, p. 249; *Istoriia vtoroi mirovoi voiny*, Vol. 5, p. 243; see also M. N. Mosiagin, "Reid gruppy voisk P. A. Belov v 1942" ["The raid of P. A. Belov's group of forces in 1942"] *VIA*, No. 6 (2007), pp. 56-58.
13 See Mosiagin, *"Reid gruppy voisk P. A. Belov"*, pp. 59-62; Belov, *Za nami Moskva*, pp. 298-299.
14 See Mosiagin, "Reid gruppy voisk P. A. Belov", p. 65; Belov, *Za nami Moskva*, pp. 302-303.
15 Belov, *Za nami Moskva*, p. 306, 307-320.
16 A. Lukashenko, *Dorogami vozdushnogo desanta* [Along the roads of an airborne landing] (Moscow, 1978), p. 140; K. K. Rokossovsky, *Soldatskii dolg* [A soldier's duty] (Moscow, 1988), pp. 118-122; Halder, *Voennyi dnevnik*, pp. 265-266; Belov, *Za nami Moskva*, pp. 312, 324.
17 For more details, see S. A. Gerasimova, "Oboronitel'naia operatsiia voisk Kalinin front v iiule 1942" ["The Kalinin Front's defensive operation in July 1942"] *VIA*, No. 8 (2001).
18 Grossmann, *Rzhev: Kraeugol'nyi kamen'*, pp. 48-62; Halder, *Voennyi dnevnik*, pp. 280-300.
19 H. Boucsein, *Halten oder Sterben: Die hessisch-thuringisch 129. Infanterie-Division im Russlandfelzug und Ostprussen 1941-1945* (Potsdam, 1999), p. 220; Grossmann, *Rzhev: Kraeugol'nyi Kamen'*, pp. 51-62.
20 Grossmann, *Rzhev: Kraeugol'nyi kamen'*, p. 48; *Formirovanie i perepodchinenie obshchevoiskovykh armii 1941-1945* [Formation and change of subordination of the combined arms armies 1941-1945] General Staff, 1954, p. 27 [In the collection of the Library of the TsAMO]; *Svedenie na kavalerskie korpusa s 1 po 19* [Data for the cavalry corps from 1 to 19] (Moscow: Archive of the USSR Ministry of Defense, 1954), p. 102 [In the collection of the Library of the TsAMO].
21 G. Krivosheev, Iu. Poliakov, and V. Andronikov, *Rossiia i SSSR v voinakh XX veka: Statisticheskoe issledovanie* [*Russia and the USSR in wars of the XX century: Statistical study*] (Moscow: OLMA-PRESS, 2001), p. 312.
22 TsAMO RF, F. 213, Op. 2002, D. 327, L. 71-75, 77, 81, 84, 85, 87, 90, 91.
23 TsAMO RF, F. 213, Op. 2002, D. 402, L. 2-4; F. 376, Op. 10803, D. 93, L. 5; F. 396, Op. 2908, D. 31, L. 2.
24 Grossmann, *Rzhev: Kraeugol'nyi kamen'*, p. 54.
25 Ibid. p. 57; Boucsein, *Halten oder Sterben*, p. 224; TsAMO RF, F. 396, Op. 9208, D. 31, L. 6.
26 M. Vorob'ev and V. Usov, *Za kazhdy klochok zemli* [For every little clump of earth] Part 2 (Moscow, 1990), p. 86; TsAMO RF, F. 213, Op. 2002, D. 402, L. 10; Boucsein, *Halten oder Sterben*, p. 224.
27 TsAMO RF, F. 213, Op. 2002, D. 402, L. 13 obr.; Halder, *Voennyi dnevnik*, p. 288.
28 A. S. Burakov, *Zapiski komissara* [Notes of a commissar], pp. 162-163. This is an unpublished manuscript typed in the 1980s in Krasnoiarsk which can be found in the archive of the Department of Soviet Social History of the Tver State Consolidated Museum.
29 L. Myl'nikov (ed.), *Eto bylo na Rzhevsko-Viazemskom platsdarme. Kniga pervaia.* [It was at the Rzhev-Viaz'ma bridgehead. Book One), (Rzhev, 1998), pp. 64-66.
30 TsAMO RF, F. 213, Op. 2002, D. 402, L. 15, 16 obr.
31 Boucsein, *Halten oder Sterben*, pp. 224, 225-228.
32 Vorob'ev and Usov, *Za kazhdyi klochok*, p. 89.

33 TsAMO RF, F. 213, Op. 2002, D. 402, L. 14-16, 18; D. 419.

34 TsAMO RF, F. 213, Op. 2002, D.419; *Der Ostfeldzug. Der 86. rhein.-wesf. Inf.-Division. 28.VI.1941-4. XI.1943*. Typed copy, 1962, p. 12, from the archive of the Department of Social History of the Tver State Consolidated Museum.

35 *Istoriia Velikoi otechestvennoi voiny Sovetskogo Soiuza 1941-1945*, Vol. 2, p. 475; Grossmann, *Rzhev: Kraeugol'nyi kamen'*, pp. 61-62.

36 *Pravda*, 14 July 1942.

37 *Izvestiia*, 20 July 1942.

38 TsAMO RF, F. 376, Op. 10803, D. 93, L. 93-94; F. 213, Op. 2002, D. 402, L. 23, 24, 25; *Eto bylo na Rzhevskom platsdarme*, Book 2, p. 117.

39 Boucsein, *Halten oder Sterben*, pp. 231, 232.

40 Vorob'ev and Usov, *Za kazhdyi klochok*, p. 91; Materials of the 3rd Air Army in the archive of Department of Social History of the Tver State Consolidated Museum; Boucsein, *Halten oder Sterben*, p. 232; N. I. Zhukov, "Polety na 'Trinadtsatom'" [Flights on a 'Thirteen'] in *Vremia i sud'ba: voenno-memorialnyi sbornik* [*Time and fate: a military-memorial collection* (Moscow, 1991), pp. 298-299.

41 Kapusto, *Poslednymi dorogami*, pp. 3-4.

42 TsAMO RF, F. 376, Op. 10803, D. 93, L. 129-129 obr.

43 TsAMO RF, F. 213, Op. 2002, D. 402, L. 25-28.

44 TsAMO RF, F. 376, Op. 10803, D. 87, L. 101-117; D. 93, L. 146.

45 TsAMO RF, F. 213, Op. 2002, D. 402, L. 29-30 obr.

46 Halder, *Voennyi dnevnik*, p. 300.

47 *Der Ostfeldzug. Der 86 rhein-westf. Inf.-Division*, p. 11; Boucsein, *Halten oder Sterben*, p. 233; G. Kippar, *Das kampfgeschehen der 161 (ostpr.) Infanterie-Division von der Aufstellung 1939 bis zum Ende* (Westerstede, 1990), p. 417; Ladygin and Smirnov, *Na rzhevskom rubezhe*, p. 91.

48 TsAMO RF, F. 213, Op. 2002, D. 402, L. 48, 49.

49 H. Grossmann, *Geschichte der rheinisch-westfalischen 6 Infanterie-Division, 1939-1945* (Bad Nauheim, 1958), p. 114; "Liudskie poteri Sovetskikh Vooruzhennykh Sil v 1941-1945: Novye aspekty" ["Human losses of the Soviet Armed Forces in 1941-1945: New aspects"] *VIZh*, No. 2 (February 1999), p. 5.

50 I. Senkevich, *Krasnoiarskaia gvardeiskaia* [The Kransoiarsk Guards Division] (Krasnoiarsk, 1973), p. 114; TsAMO RF, F. 3478, Op. 1; F. 394, Op. 9072, D. 1, L. 1; V. V. Gradosel'sky, "Natsional'nye voinskie formirovaniya v Velikoi Otechestvennoi voine" ["Ethnic military formations in the Great Patriotic war"] *VIZh*, No. 1 (2002), p. 21; V. I. Kozlov. V. E. Nazaretsky and V. V. Zamoluev, *Mirgorodskaia, trizhdy ordenonosnaia* [The Mirgorod, thrice Order-awarded Division] (Mirgorod, 1990), p. 6; *Russkii arkhiv*, Vol. 16 (5-2), p. 326.

51 I. S. Konev, "Vospominaniia" ["Reminiscences"], *Znamia*, No. 12 (December, 1987), p. 101; Senkevich, *Krasnoiarskaia gvardeiskaia*, pp. 113-114

52 TsAMO RF, F. 376, Op. 10803, D. 93, L. 146; Boucsein, *Halten oder Sterben*, p. 232; "*Pogibli za Rodinu*" ["They died for the Motherland"], *VIZh* No. 11 (November 1991), p. 27; No. 3 (March 1993), p. 3; No. 8 (September 1993), p. 17.

53 *Bel'skaia Pravda*, May 1992.

54 G. T. Riabkov (ed.), *Po dorogam boevoi slavy* [Along the roads of combat glory] (Smolensk, 1967), pp. 120, 150.

55 *Pravda*, 14 July 1942.

56 Boucsein, *Halten oder Sterben*, p. 233; Grossmann, *Rzhev: Kraeugol'nyi kamen'*, p. 60.

57 Proektor, *Agressiia i katastrofa*, pp. 350, 434, 615, 616.

58 Konev, *Vospominaniia*, p. 101.

Chapter 4

1 TsAMO RF, F. 213, Op. 2002, D. 402, L. 30.

2 *Istoriia Velikoi otechestvennoi voiny Sovetskogo Soiuza*, Vol. 2 (Moscow, 1963), pp. 475-476; *Istoriia Vtoroi mirovoi voiny 1939-1945*, Vol. 5 (Moscow, 1975), pp. 243-249; *Sovetskaya voennaia entsiklopediia*, Vol. 7 (Moscow, 1979), pp. 119-120; *Velikaia otechestvennaia ... Ocherki*. Book 1 (Moscow: Nauka, 1998); *Voennaia entsiklopediia*, Vol. 7 (Moscow: Voenizdat, 2003), pp. 232-234.

3 Elements of the analysis that I offer here can be found in S. A. Gerasimova, "Pervaia Rzhevsko-Sychevskaia nastupatel'naia operatsiia 1942: Novye vgliady" [The First Rzhev-Sychevka offensive operation of 1942: New views"], *Voprosy istorii*, No. 5 (May 2005), pp. 16-29.

4 TsAMO RF, F. 354, Op. 5806, D. 67, L. 61; F. 208, Op. 2511, D. 1495, 1522, 1525.

5 G. K. Zhukov, *Vospominaniia i razmyshleniia* [Reminiscences and recollections] 11th Ed., Vol. 2 (Moscow, 1992), p. 300.

6 TsAMO RF, F. 423, Op. 6631, D. 36, L. 170; F. 208, Op. 2511, D. 1494, 1539, 1541.

7 *Russkii arkhiv*, Vol 16 (5-2), pp. 311-312.

8 TsAMO RF, F. 208, Op. 2511, D. 1494, D. 1539, D. 1541; D. 1463, L. 128, 219, 244ob; Sandalov, *Pogoreloe-Gorodishchenskaia operatsiia*, p. 14; A. I. Radzievsky, *Proryv* (*Po opytu Velikoi otechestvennoi voiny*) [Breakthrough (According to the experience of the Great Patriotic War)] (Moscow: Voenizdat, 1979), p. 29; *Istoriia vtoroi mirovoi voiny*, Vol. 5, p. 245.

9 Radzievsky, *Proryv*, Map 6.

10 *Russkii arkhiv*, Vol. 16 (5-2), pp. 311-312; TsAMO RF, F. 213, Op. 2002, D. 402, L. 30; D. 65, L. 5; F. 384, Op. 8529, D. 130, L. 26 ob; F. 208, Op. 2511, D. 1463, L. 168; Sandalov, *Pogorelo-Gorodishchenskaia operatsiia*, p. 25.

11 *Obshchevoiskovye armii i ikh boevoi sostav za 1942 v Velikoi Otechestvennoi voine,* Part 1, p. 41; Part 2, pp. 51, 158, 172; Part 3, p. 12a, 36. TsAMO RF, F. 208, Op. 2511, D. 1463, L. 4ob, 45, 80, 162, 220, 221, 231; D. 1044, L. 187; D. 1464, L. 38; D. 2271, L. 4; D. 1466, L. 14; F. 384, Op. 8529, D. 152, L. 57; Sandalov, *Pogorelo-Gorodishchenskaia operatsiia*, pp. 14, 25, 38, 49; N. M. Afanas'ev, N. K. Glazunov, P. A. Kazansky and N. A. Fironov, *Dorogami ispytanii i pobed: Boevoi put' 31-i armii* [Along the roads of trials and victories: the combat path of the 31st Army] (Moscow: Voenizdat, 1986), p. 59.

12 N. M. Khlebnikov, *Pod grokhot soten battarei* [Under the thunder of hundreds of batteries] (Moscow: Voenizdat, 1974), p. 176; Krivosheev, et. al., *Rossiia i SSSR v voinakh XX veka*, p. 312.

13 *Voennaia entsiklopediia*, Vol. 7, p. 233.

14 TsAMO RF, F. 208, Op. 2511, D. 1449, L. 102; D. 1463, L. 165.

15 TsAMO RF, F. 208, Op. 2511, D. 1450, Appendix 5.

16 TsAMO RF, F. 208, Op. 2511, D. 1463, L. 4, 80, 162-164; D. 1044, L. 187; F. 384, Op. 8529, D. 130, L. 26.

17 See, for example, *Istoriia vtoroi mirovoi voiny*, Vol. 5, p. 249; Khlebnikov, *Pod grokhot soten battarei*, p. 173; Afanas'ev et. al., *Dorogami ispytanii i pobed*, p. 56.

18 Halder, *Voennyi dnevnik*, pp. 260, 261, 303. [Translator's note: The edited English translation of Halder's war diary doesn't contain all the material cited, and I have slightly adjusted the translation.]

19 L. Myl'nikov, *Bez grifa sekretnosti: Eto bylo na Rzhevsko-Viazemskom platsdarme* [Without the seal of secrecy: As it was at the Rzhev-Viaz'ma staging area], Book 2 (Rzhev, 2000), pp. 81-82; Grossmann, *Rzhev: Kraeugol'nyi kamen'*, p. 75.

20 Khlebnikov, *Pod grokhot soten battarei*, p. 180.

21 Ibid.

22 TsAMO RF, F. 384, Op. 8629, D. 130, L. 27.

23 *Istoriia vtoroi mirovoi voiny*, Vol. 5, p. 245.

24 TsAMO RF, F. 208, Op. 2511, D. 1024, L. 214, 158.
25 *Russkii arkhiv*, Vol. 16 (5-2), pp. 341-342.
26 Ibid., pp. 348, 352; L. M. Sandalov, "Avgustovskaia nastupatel'naia operatsiia armii pravogo kryla Zapadnogo fronta v 1942" ["The August offensive operations of the armies of Western Front's right-wing in 1942"] *VIZh*, No. 4 (April 1959), p. 30.
27 Halder, *Voennyi dnevnik*, pp. 316-318, 320; Tippelskirch, *Istoriia vtoroi mirovoi voiny*, p. 241.
28 Sandalov, *Pogorelo-Gorodishchenskaia operatsiia*, p. 90.
29 Belov, *Za nami Moskvy*, p. 179.
30 *Russkii arkhiv*, Vol. 16 (5-2), p. 321; TsAMO RF, F. 208, Op. 2511, D. 1466, L. 9-12.
31 As cited by Glantz, *Zhukov's Greatest Defeat*, pp. 11-12.
32 TsAMO RF, F. 208, Op. 2511, D. 1463, L. 247.
33 Ladygin and Smirnov, *Na Rzhevskom rubezhe*, p. 66.
34 Excerpts from the combat documents of the 139th Rifle Division. A brief historical account of the division compiled by A. Kopin in 1972, p. 4, in the possession of Tver State Consolidated Museum.
35 *Sovetskaia voennaia entsiklopediia*, Vol. 7, p. 12; Gurkin, "'Mars' v orbite 'Urana' i 'Saturna'", p. 16; TsAMO RF, F. 386 (31st Army), Op. 8583, D. 157, L. 1; F. 423 (20th Army), Op. 6632, D. 36, L. 170-174; F. 384 (29th Army), Op. 8529, D. 130, L. 26; F. 208 (Western Front), Op. 2511, D. 1044, L. 179; Grossmann, *Geschichte der rheinisch-westfalischen 6. Infanterie-Division*, p. 133.
36 TsAMO RF, F. 213, Op. 2002, D. 422, L. 47-48; F. 384, Op. 8529, D. 94, L. 139-140; Grossmann, *Rzhev – Kraeugol'nyi kamen'*, p. 70.
37 Gorbachevky, *Rzhevskaia miasorubka: Vremia otvagi, Zadacha – vyzhits'* [The Rzhev meat grinder: A time of courage, the Mission – to survive] (Moscow: Iauza, Eksmo, 2000), pp. 142-146; Gorbachevsky's memoirs have been expanded and translated into English as *Through the Maelstrom: A Red Army Soldier's War on the Eastern Front, 1942-1945*, published by the University Press of Kansas, 2008. The relevant passage can be found between pages 111 and 114.
38 P. Mikhin, "*Nastupali i umirali*: *Rzhevskaia bitva; Srazhenie za Polunino* (*30 July – 23 August 1942*). A collection of articles and materials. (Tver: Russkaia provintsiia, 2001), p. 152. Peter Mihin later produced a memoir based on these materials, which was published in Russia in 2006 by Iauza, Eksmo as *Artilleristy, Stalin otdal prikaz: My umirali, chtoby pobedit'* [Artillerymen, Stalin has given the order: We were dying, in order to be victorious]. This memoir was translated and published in English by Pen & Sword in 2010 under the title *Guns against the Reich: Memoirs of an Artillery Officer on the Eastern Front*. However, this particular passage didn't appear in his memoirs.
39 Petr Mikhin, *Guns Against the Reich*, pp. 27-31.
40 TsAMO RF, F. 386, Op. 8583, D. 136, L. 330, 344, 370; F. 208, Op. 2511, D. 1448, L. 830.
41 Halder, *Voennyi dnevnik*, p. 328. Halder is writing about an attack in the Belyi area, on the western side of the Rzhev-Viaz'ma salient. Apparently, certain forces of the Kalinin Front were also attacking here. [Editor's note: Though where possible I have been using the existing English translation of Halder's war diary, here the English translators erred and identified this part of the offensive as being on the *eastern* side of the salient. I have thus adjusted the translation.]
42 *Izvestiia*, 27 August 1942.
43 Grossmann, *Rzhev – Kraeugol'nyi kamen'*, p. 72
44 Halder, *Voennyi dnevnik*, p. 332.
45 TsAMO RF, F. 208, Op. 2511, D. 1112, L. 37; *Russkii arkhiv*, Vol. 16 (5-2), p. 376.
46 *Russkii arkhiv*, Vol. 16 (5-2), p. 542.
47 Ibid., p. 543.
48 TsAMO RF, F. 208, Op. 2511, D. 1463, L. 210, 247; D. 1448, L. 92, 95, 98; F. 326, Op. 5047, D. 101, L.

34, 40, 55.

49 G. F. Denisenko, "Zapiski pozhilogo soldata" ["Notes of an old soldier"] *VIA*, No. 1 (January 2005), p. 98.

50 TsAMO RF, F. 434, Op. 6631, D. 48, L. 28; D. 36, L. 139.

51 TsAMO RF, F. 213, Op. 2002, D. 429, L. 69-71; D. 422, L. 65-66.

52 TsAMO RF, F. 208, Op. 2511, D. 1045, L. 90; D. 1463, L. 26; D. 1473, L. 66, 236.

53 Luhter H., *Dunkle Jahre.Kriegsbriefe und Erinnerungen*, 1995, pp. 17-22. A typed manuscript in the possession of the Rzhev District Museum.

54 TsAMO RF, F. 208, Op. 2511, D. 1045, L. 90.

55 I. Maslennikov, *Eto bylo na Rzhevsko-Viazemskom platsdarme*, Book 2 (Rzhev, 2000), p. 42.

56 TsAMO RF, F. 208, Op. 2511, D. 1463, L. 26; D. 1473, L. 236; F. 386, Op. 8583, D. 147, L. 279-285.

57 TsAMO RF, F. 208, Op. 2511, D. 1045, L. 90, 94.

58 Rhein, *Das rheinisch-westfalisch Infanterie/Grenadier-Regiment 18*, pp. 193-194.

59 M. K. Sushkov, *Vospominaniia* [Recollections]; an unpublished manuscript in the files of the Rzhev District Museum.

60 *Istoricheskii arkhiv*, No. 4 (April 1998), p. 176; *Sotsialisticheskoe l'novodstvo*, 30 September 1942.

61 I. Erenburg, *Liudy, gody, zhizn'* [People, years, life] (Moscow, 1990), pp. 220-221.

62 Dunkle, *Jahre: Kriegsbriefe und Erinnerungen*, p. 21.

63 *VIA*, 6th Ed. (1999), p. 176.

64 Halder, *Voennyi dnevnik*, p. 351.

65 *Russkii arkhiv*, Vol. 16 (5-2), p. 394; TsAMO RF, F. 213, Op. 2002, D. 441, L. 31ob; I. Kranoshtanov, "114 osbr v boiakh po likvidatsii platsdarma severo-zapadnee Rzheva (sentiabr' 1942)" ["The 114th Separate Rifle Brigade in the battles to liquidate the bridgehead northwest of Rzhev (September 1942)," *VIZh*, No. 2 (February 1979).

66 TsAMO RF, F. 208, Op. 2511, D. 1044, L. 198; D. 1449, L. 100; D. 1450, L. 100; F. 384, Op. 8529, D. 130, L. 26.

67 *Istoriia vtoroi mirovoi voiny*, Vol. 5, p. 248; F. Halder, *Voennyi dnevnik*, p. 321; Ibid., p. 311; Rhein, *Das rheinisch-westfalisch Infanterie/Grenadier-Regiment 18*, pp. 184, 189, 201, 202; Grossmann, *Rzhev: Kraeugol'nyi kamen'*, p. 311; I. N. Sobolev, *Itogi vtoroi mirovoi voiny: Sbornik statei; perevod s nemetskogo* [Results of the Second World War: A collection of articles translated from German], (Moscow, 1957), p. 395.

68 *Istoriia vtoroi mirovoi voiny*, Vol. 5, p. 248.

69 TsAMO RF, F. 213, Op. 2002, D. 429, L. 69-71; F. 208, Op. 2511, D. 1450, L. 104, Appendix 6; D. 2277, L. 2; D. 1463, L. 248; D. 1464, L. 22; D. 2271, L. 39ob; D. 1044, L. 214, 215ob; D. 1466, L. 140; F. 386, Op. 8593, D. 17, L. 633; F. 243, Op. 6631, D. 48, L. 264, 294; Grossmann, *Rzhev – Kraeugol'nyi kamen'*, p. 91.

70 Cited by Ladygin and Smirnov, *Na Rzhevskom rubezhe*, pp. 70-71, 72, 74.

71 TsAMO RF, F. 208, Op. 2511, D. 1488, L. 107; D. 1044, L. 200.

72 TsAMO RF, F. 208, Op. 2511, D. 1449, L. 101.

73 Ibid, D. 1463, L. 213-213, 248; F. 384, Op. 8529, D. 130, L. 28ob.

74 TsAMO RF, F. 208, Op. 2511, D. 1463, L. 213-214, 248.

75 TsAMO RF, F. 208, Op. 2511, D. 1466, L. 9-12; *Voennaia entsiklopediia*, Vol. 7, p. 233; *Russkii arkhiv*, Vol. 16 (5-2), p. 321.

76 Reshin and Stepanov, "Sud'by genaral'skie... Spisok generalov Krasnoi Armii arestovannykh v nachale i v period Otechestvennoi voiny, podlezhashchikh sudu" ["Generals' fates ... List of the Red Army generals who were arrested and faced trial at the beginning and during the Patriotic War"] *VIZh*, No. 12 (December 1992), pp. 14, 18.

77 *Russkii arkhiv*, Vol. 16 (5-2), pp. 341-342; Sandalov, *Pogorelo-Gorodishchenskaia operatsiia*, p. 122.
78 Sandalov, *Pogorelo-Gorodischchenskaia operatsiia*, pp. 124-125.
79 TsAMO RF, F. 208, Op. 2511, D. 1448, L. 108; Khlebnikov, *Pod grokhot soten batarei*, pp. 183-184; Ladygin and Smirnov, *Na Rzhevskom rubezhe*, pp. 188-191.
80 *Eto bylo na Rzhevsko-Viazemskom platsdarme*, Book 1, p. 98.
81 Ibid., p. 49.
82 G. K. Zhukov, *Vopominaniia i razmyshleniia*, 9th Ed., p. 291.

Chapter 5

1 Tippelskirch, *Istoriia vtoroi mirovoi voiny*, p. 270.
2 *Istoriia Vtoroi mirovoi voiny*, Vol. 6, Appendix Map No. 2, p. 1430; Radzievsky, *Proryv*, pp. 49-51, Map 10; Katukov, *Na ostrie glavnogo udara*; Galitsky, *Gody surovykh ispytanii, 1941-1944*; Solomatin, *Krasnogradtsy* [Men of Krasnograd], (Moscow: Voenizdat, 1963), and others.
3 Glantz, "Operatsiia 'Mars'", *Voprosy istorii*, No. 8 (August 1997); Gurkin, "'Mars' v orbite 'Urana' i 'Saturna'" *VIZh*, No. 4 (April, 2000); *Voennaia entsiklopediia*, Vol. 7, pp. 234-235.
4 B. Nevzorov, "Operatsiia 'Mars': Pravda i domysli" ["Operation 'Mars": Truth and conjecture] *Krasnaia zvezda*, 1 April 2003; *Istoriia Vtoroi mirovoi voiny*, Vol. 6, Appendix Map No. 2, p. 1430; Radzievsky, Map 10, *Proryv*, p. 143.
5 Response to an abstract of S. A. Gerasimova's dissertation "Voennye deistviia v raione Rzhevsko-Viazemskogo vystupa v ianvare 1942-marte 1943: Rzhevskaya 'bitva'" ["Military operations in the area of the Rzhev-Viaz'ma salient in January 1942 – March 1943. The Rzhev 'battle'"] in pursuit of the Candidate of Science (History) academic degree, 07-00-2002, Institute of Military History of the Russian Federation Ministry of Defense, 2002; *Voennaia entsiklopediia*, Vol. 7, pp. 234-235.
6 *Perepiska Predsedatelia Soveta Ministrov SSSR s prezidentami SSHA i prem'er-ministrami Velikobritanii vo vremia Velikoi Otechestvennoi voiny 1941-1945* [Correspondence of the Chairman of the USSR Council of Ministers with the presidents of the USA and prime-ministers of Great Britain during the Great Patriotic War, 1941-1945] 2nd Ed., (Moscow 2000), Vol.1, p. 95 and Vol. 2, p. 37.
7 Glantz, "Operatsiia 'Mars'", p. 15; Glantz, *Krupneishee porazhenie Zhukova*, p. 350.
8 Grossmann, *Rzhev: Kraeugol'nyi kamen'*, p. 5.
9 *Istoriia Vtoroi mirovoi voiny*, Vol. 6, p. 35.
10 The figures are from Isaev's article "Poteriannoe zveno" ["Lost echelon"], as found in Glantz, *Krupneishee porazhenie Zhukova*, pp. 5, 6.
11 Gurkin, "'Mars' v orbite 'Urana' i 'Saturna'", p. 15; *Voennaia entsiklopediia*, Vol. 7, p. 234.
12 TsAMO RF, F. 208, Op. 2511, D. 1540; see Isaev, "Poteriannoe zveno", p. 15.
13 TsAMO RF, F. 208, Op. 2511, D. 1113, L. 2; F. 384, Op. 8529, D. 94, L. 218-220.
14 *Istoriia Velikoi Otechestvennoi voiny Sovetskogo Soiuza 1941-1945*, Vol. 3 (Moscow, 1964), p. 16.
15 *Voennaia entsiklopediia*, Vol. 7, p. 234; Gurkin, "'Mars' v orbite 'Urana' i 'Saturna'", pp. 15, 16.
16 TsAMO RF, F. 394, Op. 9072, D. 13, L. 45, 102ob.
17 *Voennaia entsiklopediia*, Vol. 7, p. 234.
18 Zhukov, *Razmyshleniia i vospominaniia*, pp. 348, 357.
19 S. I. Isaev, "Veki frontovogo puti" ["Milestones of a front path"] *VIZh*, No. 10 (October 1991), p. 24.
20 K. N. Galitsky, *Gody surovykh ispytanii*, p. 164.
21 Glantz, *Krupneishee porazhenie Zhukova*, p. 51.
22 TsAMO RF, F. 423, Op. 6631, D. 56, L. 2, 8, 9.
23 Ibid., D. 36, L. 275.
24 See Glantz, *Krupneishee porazhenie Zhukova*, p. 514.

25 P. A. Sudoplatov, *Razvedka i Kreml': Zapiski nezhelatel'nogo svidetel'ia* [Intelligence and the Kremlin: Notes of an undesired witness] (Mocow: Geia, 1996), pp. 188-189; Glantz, *Krupneishee porazhenie Zhukova*, pp. 71.

26 Halder, *Voennyi dnevnik*, pp. 347-348, 351.

27 Tippelskirch, *Istoriia Vtoroi mirovoi voiny*, p. 270.

28 V. Shimansky, "Vybor napravleniia glavnogo udara" ["Selection of the direction of the main attack"] *VIZh* No. 10 (October 1963), p. 10.

29 As cited by Glantz, *Krupneishee porazhenie Zhukova*, pp. 66-67.

30 G.-A. Jacobsen, "1939-1945 Vtoraia mirovaia voina" ["1939-1945 The Second World War"] in *Vtoraia mirovaia voina: dva vzgliada* [1939-1945 The Second World War: two views] (Moscow, 1995), p. 316; V. T. Eliseev, "Strategicheskie peregruppirovki sovetskikh voisk pri podgotovke zimnei kampanii 1942/1943" ["Strategic regroupings of Soviet forces during preparation of the winter campaign 1942/1943] *VIZh*, No. 11 (November 1987), p. 62.

31 Gurkin, "'Mars' v orbite 'Urana' i 'Saturna'", p. 17.

32 TsAMO RF, F. 208, Op. 2511, D. 1097, L. 272.

33 TsAMO RF, F. 208, Op. 2511, D. 1113, L. 244-245.

34 Rhein, *Das rheinisch-westfalische Infanterie/Grenadier-Regiment 18*, p. 214.

35 *Voennaia entsiklopediia*, Vol. 7, p. 234; Gurkin, "'Mars' v orbite 'Urana' i 'Saturna'", pp. 17-18.

36 A. Petrukhin, "Spetsdobrovol'tsy" ["Special volunteers"] *Rodina*, No. 5 (May 2000), p. 154; TsAMO RF, F. 860, Op. 1, D. 22, L. 3-5.

37 Solomatin, *Krasnogradtsy*, pp. 11-17.

38 *Voennaia entsiklopediia*, Vol. 7, p. 234; Gurkin, "'Mars' v orbite 'Urana' i 'Saturna'", pp. 17-18.

39 Rhein, *Das rheinisch-westfalische Infanterie/Grenadier-Regiment 18*, p. 220.

40 Ibid., p. 210.

41 Glantz, *Krupneishee porazhenie Zhukova,* p. 351.

42 Glantz, "Operation Mars", p. 22; Solomatin, *Krasnogradtsy*, pp. 28-31.

43 *Russkii arkhiv*, Vol. 16 (5-2), pp. 462-463.

44 Ibid., p. 460; Glantz, *Krupneishee porazhenie Zhukova*, pp. 314, 319-320, 343, 578.

45 *Russkii arkhiv*, Vol. 16 (5-2), p. 460; Glantz, *Krupneishee porazhenie Zhukova*, p. 291.

46 See Glantz, *Krupneishee porazhenie Zhukova*, pp. 368, 409, 412.

47 See the section *From the Archives* in Glantz, *Krupneishee porazhenie Zhukova*, p. 585. [Editor's note: The entry in the Russian version of the book is fuller and contains material not found in the original *Zhukov's Greatest Defeat*. I have translated the additional material for this book.]

48 Solomatin, *Krasnogradtsy*, pp. 33, 36.

49 Khlebnikov, *Pod grokhot soten batarei*, p. 197.

50 TsAMO RF, F. 396, Op. 9208, D. 179, L. 8.

51 Solomatin, *Krasnogradtsy*, pp. 37-38.

52 B. P. Boiko, *S dumoi o Rodine* [With a thought about the Motherland] (Moscow: Voenizdat, 1983), p. 48.

53 *Sovetskaia kavaleria*, pp. 216-217; P. N. Kudinov, *Za reidom reid* [The raid after a raid] (Kaliningrad 1983), pp. 63-88.

54 Katukov, *Na ostrie glavnogo udara*, pp. 182-183.

55 Grossmann, *Rzhev: Kraeugol'nyi kamen'*, p. 223; Glantz, *Krupneishee porazhenie Zhukova*, p. 594.

56 D. A. Dragunsky, *Gody v brone* [Years in armor] (Moscow: Voenzidat ,1973), p. 84. Krivosheev (ed). *Rossiia i SSSR v voinakh XX veka*, p. 312.

57 TsAMO RF, F. 3413, Op. 1, D. 5, L. 155, 161; F. 860, Op. 1, D. 22, L. 37; F. 213, Op. 2002, D. 180, L. 32; F. 3423, Op. 1, D. 1, L. 12-16; Krivosheev (ed.), *Rossiia i SSSR v voinakh XX veka*, p. 312; Gurkin, "'Mars'

v orbite 'Urana' i 'Saturna'", p. 18; *Russkii arkhiv*, Vol. 23 (12-2), p. 419.
58 See Glantz, *Krupneishee porazhenie Zhukova*, pp. 380, 382.
59 Grossmann, *Rzhev: Kraeugol'nyi kamen'*, p. 123.
60 *Velikaia Otechestvennaia: Ocherki*, Vol. 2 (Moscow 1998), p. 221.
61 Gurkin, "'Mars' v orbite 'Urana' i 'Saturna'", p. 19.
62 B. Liddell Hart, *Vtoraia mirovaia voina* [The Second World War] (Moscow 1976), p. 245. [Editor's note: This is the Russian translation of Liddell Hart's *History of the Second World War*.
63 Glantz, *Krupneishee porazhenie Zhukova*, p. 342.
64 Ibid., p. 352.
65 Ibid., pp. 342, 360, 361; Grossmann, *Rzhev: Kraeugolnyi kamen'*, p. 109.
66 Isaev, "Poteriannoe zveno", in Glantz, *Krupneishee porazhenie Zhukova*, pp. 25-26; Glantz, *Krupneishee porazhenie Zhukova*, pp. 389-390.
67 Including TsAMO RF, F. 208, Op. 2511, D. 1113, L. 245-246; F. 394, Op. 9702, D. 13, L. 61-68; F. 423, Op. 6631, D. 56, L. 64-66; *Sbornik materialov po izucheniiu opyta voiny*, No. 9, November-December 1942 (Moscow 1944), pp. 134-150; *Dopolneniia k prilozheniiam k knige* [Supplements to the appendices for the book] in Glantz, *Krupneishee porazhenie Zhukova*, pp. 511-539; Radzievsky, *Proryv* .
68 Zhukov, *Razmyshleniia i vospominaniia*, 11th Ed., p. 370.
69 M. Gareev, "Domysli i fakty ob istorii Velikoi Otechestvennoi: Operatsiia Mars kak primer neskonchaemoi polemicheskoi bitvy" ["Conjectures and facts about the history of the Great Patriotic [War]: Operation Mars as an example of an unending polemical fight"] *Nezavisimoe voennoe obozreni*, No. 14, 2006.
70 Zhukov, *Razmyshleniia i vospominaniia*, p. 370.
71 Radzievsky, *Proryv*, p. 50.
72 TsAMO RF, F. 423, Op. 6631, D. 56, L. 64; F. 394, Op. 9072, D. 13, L. 63.
73 TsAMO RF, F. 423, Op. 6631, D. 56, L. 64-65.
74 See *Dopolneniia k prilozheniiam* in Glantz, *Krupneishee porazhenie Zhukova*, pp. 597-598.
75 *Voennaia entsiklopediia*, Vol. 7, p. 234.
76 As cited by Glantz, *Krupneishee porazhenie Zhukova*, pp. 72-73.
77 Ibid., p. 374.
78 Ibid., pp. 376-378; E. Rzhevskaia, *Znaki prepinaniia* [Punctuation marks] (Moscow: 1983), p. 301.
79 Isaev, "Vekhi frontovogo puti", p. 25.

Chapter 6

1 *Istoriia vtoroi mirovoi voiny*, Vol. 6, p. 142; Ladygin and Smirnov, *Na rzhevskom rubezhe*, pp. 115-116.
2 Liddell Hart, *Istoriia vtoroi mirovoi*, p. 461.
3 TsAMO RF, F. 354, Op.5806, D. 256, L. 5ob.
4 Grossmann, *Rzhev: Kraeugol'nyi kamen'*, pp. 124-127.
5 Liddell Hart, *Istoriia vtoroi mirovoi*, p. 461.
6 Grossmann, *Rzhev: Kraeugol'nyi kamen'*, p. 127.
7 *Istoriia vtoroi mirovoi voiny*, Vol. 6, p. 141; *Velikaia Otechestvennaia ... ocherki*, Book 2, pp. 230-231
8 Rokossovsky, *Soldatskii dolg*, p. 186.
9 *Russkii arkhiv*, Vol. 16 (5-3), pp. 71-74.
10 Rokossovsky, *Soldatskii dolg*, p. 186.
11 See *Istoriia Velikoi Otechestvennoi voiny Sovetskogo Soiuza*, Vol. 3, pp. 140-142; *Istoriia vtoroi mirovoi voiny*, Vol. 6, pp. 141-143; *Velikaia Otechestvennaia ... ocherki*, Book 2, pp. 231-239.
12 Rokossovsky, *Soldatskii dolg*, pp. 186-187.
13 Ibid., p. 188.

14 Ibid., p. 190.
15 Ibid., pp. 190-191.
16 Shtemenko, *General'nyi shtab v gody voiny*, p. 168.
17 Rokossovsky, *Soldatskii dolg*, p. 191.
18 *Voennaia entsiklopediia*, Vol. 7, p. 231; Krivosheev, et. al., *Rossiia i SSSR v voinakh XX veka*, p. 313.
19 TsAMO RF, F. 354, Op. 5806, D. 220, L. 22, 29; F. 208, Op. 2511, D. 2605, L. 41, 76ob; D. 2606, L. 6, 177; *Russkii arkhiv*, Vol. 16 (5-3), p. 71.
20 TsAMO RF, F. 354, Op. 5806, D. 256, L. 5ob, 6; D. 220, L. 13.
21 TsAMO RF, F. 208, Op. 2511, D. 260, L. 40ob, 76; F. 354, Op. 5806, D. 220, L. 22.
22 E. Z. Vorob'ev, *Ognennaia metel'* [Fire storm] (Moscow 1977), pp. 205-206.
23 Grossmann, *Rzhev: Kraeugol'nyi kamen'*, p. 129.
24 TsAMO RF. F. 208, Op.2511, D. 2606, L. 1-2; D. 2605, L. 41; F. 213, Op. 2002, D. 961, L. 10-28, 29; D. 904, L. 101, 102, 104, 111.
25 TsAMO RF, F. 208, Op.2511, D. 2606, L. 2; F. 354, Op. 5806, D. 256, L. 5ob, 41.
26 TsAMO RF, F. 208, Op. 2511, D. 2605, L. 41.
27 TsAMO, F. 208, Op. 2511, D. 2606, L. 7; N. I. Krylov, N. I. Alekseev and I. G. Dragan, *Navstrechu Pobede: Boevoi put' 5-i armii, Oktiabr' 1941 – Avgust 1945* [Toward Victory: The Combat path of the 5th Army, October 1941 – August 1945] (Moscow: Nauka, 1970), pp. 135-136, 138.
28 Denisenko, "Zapiski pozhilogo soldata", pp. 106-107.
29 *Russkii arkhiv,* Vol. 16 (5-3), p. 81.
30 Grossmann, *Rzhev: Kraeugol'nyi kamen'*, pp. 129-132; G. Pabst, *Dnevnik nemetskogo soldata: Voennye budni na Vostochnom fronte, 1941-1945* [Diary of a German Soldier: Daily military life on the Eastern Front, 1941-1945] (Moscow: ZAO Tsentrpoligraf, 2005), p. 161. [Editor's note: Before the war, the city of Rzhev was a noted center of rope and cable production, involving a significant portion of the adult population.]
31 TsAMO RF, F. 208, Op. 2511, D. 2605, L. 42-43; F. 213, Op. 2002, D. 971, L. 5-7; D. 904, L. 122; F. 354, Op. 5806, L. 9.
32 *Russkii arkhiv*, Vol. 16 (5-3), p. 87.
33 *Eto bylo na Rzhevsko-Viazemskom platsdarme*, Book 1, p. 49.
34 *Rzhevskimi dorogami voiny*, p. 88.
35 E. Rzhevskaia, *Voroshennyi zhar: Blizhnie podstupy* [Raked embers: The nearest approaches] (Moscow 1985), pp. 115, 117.
36 *Materialy 30-i armii: vypiska iz zhurnala boevykh deistvii za mart 1943* [Materials of the 30th Army: extract from the journal of combat operations for March 1943]*; Materialy 274-i strelkovoi divizii: vypiska iz istoricheskogo formuliara 274 Iartsevskoi strelkovoi divizii* [Materials of the 274th Rifle Division: extract from the historical log-book of the 274 Iartsevo Rifle Division], both found in the Russian Federation's Rzhev District Museum.
37 *Pravda*, 4 March 1943.
38 TsAMO RF, F. 213, Op. 2002, D. 904, L. 125; D. 971, L. 7, 13, 22.
39 TsAMO RF, F. 208, Op. 2511, D. 2605, L. 44, 49, 116-117; D. 2606, L. 27, 37, 102.
40 D. E. Komarov, "Zdes' nam protivostoiala naibolee sil'naia iz gruppirovok protivnika ..." ["Here we were opposed by the strongest of the enemy groupings ..."] *VIZh*, No. 4 (April 2004), p. 7.
41 TsAMO RF, F. 208, Op. 2511, D. 2605, L. 43-44.
42 Ibid., L. 53-54.
43 *Denisenko*, "Zapiski pozhilogo soldata", p. 110. [Editor's note: Although the keeping of diaries was strictly prohibited in the Red Army during the war, more than a few men and women kept one anyway, risking

detection and harsh punishment.]

44 TsAMO RF, F. 208, Op. 2511, D. 2605, L. 51.

45 *Velikaia Otechestvennaia ... ocherki*. Book 2, p. 241.

46 TsAMO RF, F. 208, Op. 2511, D. 2605, L. 54.

47 TsAMO RF, F. 208, Op. 2511, D. 2605, L. 50 ob, 53 ob.; D. 2606, L. 158.

48 TsAMO RF, F. 208, Op. 2511, D. 2606, L. 191.

49 TsAMO RF, F. 213, Op. 2002, D. 971, L. 43, 44; D. 904, L. 175; F. 208, Op. 2511, D. 2605, L. 55 ob.; D. 2606, L. 128; F. 354, Op. 5806, D. 256, L. 15; *Voennaia entiklopediia*, Vol. 7, p. 231.

50 *Eto bylo na Rzhevsko-Viazemskom platsdarme*, Book 2, p. 46.

51 *Velikaia Otechestvennaia ... ocherki,* Book 2, p. 241. Other works state that the front had been reduced by 330 kilometers (*Voennaia entsiklopediia*, Vol. 7, p. 232) or by 300 kilometers (*Istoriia Velikoi Otechestvennoi voiny Sovetskogo Soiuza*, Vol 3, p. 142.

52 A. Werth, *Rossiia v voine 1941-1945* [Russia at war 1941-1945], translated from English (Moscow: Izdatel'stvo Progress, 1967), p. 454.

53 *Velikaia Otechestvennaia ... ocherki*, Book 2, p. 241; *Voennaia entsiklopediia*, Vol. 7, p. 232. Other works give different figures for the number of German divisions freed up and sent elsewhere – *Istoriia Velikoi Otechestvennoi voiny Sovetskogo Soiuza*, Vol. 3, p. 142 gives a figure of 16 divisions sent to the Orel and Kharkov sectors; *Istoriia Vtoroi miriovoi voiny*, Vol. 6, p. 145 gives a figure of 12 German divisions at Orel and Briansk.

54 Krivosheev et. al. *Rossiia i SSSR v voinakh XX veka*, p. 313.

55 TsAMO RF, F. 208, Op. 2511, D. 2605, L. 66-67, 135-137, D. 2606, L. 50-51, 155-160; F. 354, Op. 5806, D. 256, L. 16 ob-19.

56 TsAMO RF, F. 208, Op. 2511, D. 2605, L. 66-67, 135-137; D. 2606, L. 50-51, 155-160; F. 354, Op. 5806, D. 256, L. 16 ob-19; Komarov, "Zdes' nam protivostoiala naibolee sil'naia iz gruppirovok protivnika ...", p. 9.

57 I. Kh. Bagramian, *Tak my shli k pobede* [As we went on to victory] (Moscow: Voenizdat, 1977), p.173, as cited in *Velikaia Otechestvennaia ... ocherki*. Book 2, p. 242.

58 *Kto byl kto v Velikoi Otechestvennoi voine 1941-1945: Kratkii spravochnik* [Who was who in the Great Patriotic war 1941-1945: A short reference guide] (Moscow: Izdatel'stvo "Respublika", 1995), p. 350; *Velikaia Otechestvennaia ... ocherki*. Book 2, pp. 238-239.

59 *Istoriia Velikoi Otechestvennoi voiny Sovetskogo Soiuza 1941-1945*, Vol. 3, p. 146.

Chapter 7

1 See the *Voennaia entsiklopediia*, Vol. 8, pp. 670-671; and the *Voennyi entiklopedicheskii slovar'* [Military encyclopedic dictionary] (Moscow: Voenizdat, 2007), p. 698.

2 N. K. Glazunov, B. I. Pavlov and V. S. Shlomin, "K voprosu o strategicheskikh operatsiiakh Velikoi Otechestvennoi voiny" ["On the question of strategic operations of the Great Patriotic War"] *VIZh*, No. 4 (April 1986), pp. 48-52; Kh. M. Dzhelaukhov and B. I. Petrov, "K voprosu o strategicheskikh operatsiiakh Velikoi Otechestvennoi voiny 1941-1945" ["On the question of strategic operations of the Great Patriotic War 1941-1945"] *VIZh*, No. 7 (July 1986), pp. 46-48; "Itogi diskussii o strategicheskikh operatsiiakh Velikoi Otechestvennoi voiny 1941-1945" ["Results of the discussion about the strategic operations of the Great Patriotic War 1941-1945"] *VIZh*, No. 10 (October 1986).

3 Reponse from the Russian Federation's Ministry of Defense's Institute of Military History to an abstract of S. A. Gerasimova's thesis "Voennye deistviia v raione Rzhevsko-Viazemskogo vystupa v ianvare 1942 – marte 1943: Rzhevskaia bitva" ["Military operations in the area of the Rzhev-Viaz'ma salient in January 1942 – March 1943: The Battle of Rzhev"], presented in candidacy for the Candidate of Historical

Science degree.

4 *Russkii arkhiv*, Vol. 16 (5-2), pp. 32, 98-99, 137-138, 311-312, 462-463; Vol. 16 (5-3), pp. 73-74.

5 *Voennyi entsiklopedicheskii slovar'*, p. 621.

6 *Perepiska Predsedatel'ia Sovmina SSSR s presidentami SSHA i prim'er-ministrami Velikobritanii vo vremia Velikoi Otechestvennoi voiny 1941-1945* [Correspondence of the Chairman of the USSR Council of Ministers with the presidents of the USA and the prime ministers of Great Britain during the Great Patriotic War 1941-1945] 2nd Ed., Vol. 1 (Moscow: Politizdat, 1989), pp. 116, 122; Vol. 2, p. 37.

7 Ibid., Vol. 1, p. 95.

8 I. G. Ehrenburg, "7 October 1942", in *Letopis' muzhestva, 1941-1945* [A Chronicle of Courage, 1941-1945] (Moscow 1983), pp. 170-171.

9 *Pravda*, 23 February 1943.

10 Correspondence of German veterans with the Tver' State Consolidated Museum, in the Museum's archives of the Department of Contemporary History; Grossmann, *Rzhev: Kraeugol'nyi kamen'*.

11 B. Iampol'sky, "Osen'" ["Autumn"], in A. S. Dushenkov and S. M. Fligel'man (ed.), *Eto bylo na Kalininskom fronte* [It was on the Kalinin Front] (Moscow: Moskovskii rabochii, 1985), pp. 67-68; cited by D. Proektor, *Agressiia i katastrofa* [Aggression and Catastrophe], 2nd Ed. (Moscow 1972), p. 427.

12 Cited by Proektor, *Agressiia i katastrofa*, p. 430.

13 Grossmann, *Geschichte der reinisch-westfalischen 6. Infanterie-Division*, p. 133.

14 A. M. Samsonov, *Stalingradskaia bitva* [The Battle of Stalingrad], 3rd Ed., (Moscow 1982), p. 282.

15 E. Rzhevskaia, *Voroshennyi zhar*, p. 54.

16 Krivosheev (et. al.), *Rossiia i SSSR v voinakh XX veka*, pp. 277, 279, 281, 312, 313.

17 S. N. Mikhalev, *Strategicheskie resheniia* [Strategic Decisions] (Krasnoiarsk 1998), p. 49; Grossmann, *Rzhev: Kraeugol'nyi kamen'*, p. 91; Gerasimova, "Pervaia Rzhevsko-Sychevskaia nastupatel'naia operatsiia 1942 goda: Novye vzgliady" ["The First Rzhev-Sychevka offensive operation of 1942: New views"] *Voprosy Istorii*, No. 5 (May 2005), p. 23; Glantz, *Krupneishee porazhenie Zhukova*, pp. 380, 382.

18 A. M. Kharchenko, "Neoplatnyi dolg pered pamiat'iu" ["An Unpaid Debt before Memory"] *Tveskaia zhizn'*, 3 March 1998; *Rzhevskaia bitva i ee znachenie istorii Velikoi Otechestvennoi voiny. Materialy nauchno-prakticheskoi konferentsii, April 1999* [The Battle of Rzhev and its Significance to the History of the Great Patriotic War. Materials of the Scientific-practical Conference, April 1999] (Rzhev 2001), p. 6; *Tverskaia zhizn'*, 8 May 1999.

19 *Rzhevskaia bitva i ee znachenie v istorii Velikoi Otechestvennoi voiny*, p. 66.

20 TsAMO RF, F. 213, Op. 2002, D. 402, L. 48.

21 Response of the Tver' Oblast Military Commissariat No. 4/107 from 14 February 2002 to a query from the Tver' State Consolidated Museum; Response of the Smolensk Oblast Military Commissariat No. 4/40 from 28 March 2002 to a query from the Tver' State Consolidated Museum; both in the archive of the Department of Contemporary History of the Tver' State Consolidated Museum.

22 Booklet of the Scientific-Historic Military-Patriotic Center 'Deed', (Tver' 2003).

23 *Izvestiia*, 20 June 1998.

24 A. P. Khorev, "Poklonimsia ikh pamiati" ["We will honor their memory"] *VIZh*, No. 1 (January 1989), p. 94.

25 Response of the Tver' Oblast Military Commissariat No. 4/138 from 13 April 2007 to a query from the Tver' State Consolidated Museum; Response of the Smolensk Oblast Military Commissariat No. 4/1071 from 27 April 2007 to a query from the Tver' State Consolidated Museum; Response from the Military Commissariat of Kalinin Oblast's Iukhnov district No. 268 from 17 April 2007 to a query from the Tver' State Consolidated Museum.

26 R. E. Kantor and D. Glantz, "Spotknuvshis' koloss: Krasnaia Armiia nakanune mirovoi voiny"

["Stumbling Colossus: The Red Army on the eve of the world war"] *Voprosy istorii*, No. 6 (June 1999), p. 169.

27 Rhein, *Das rheinisch-westfälische Infanterie/Grenadier-Regiment 18*, p. 190; Grossmann, *Geschichte der rheinisch-westfälischen 6. Infanterie-Division*, p. 311; Exposition in the German Hall of the Rzhev Memorial Complex museum; E. S. Fedorov, *Pravda o voennom Rzheve* [The Truth about Military Rzhev] (Rzhev 1995), p. 217; E. Rzhevskaia, *Voroshennyi zhar*, p. 54; see *Deutschland Grosser Atlas und Lexikon* (RV Verlag, 1992), the articles "Cottbus" and "Ingolstadt".

28 P. Mikhin, "Nastupali i umirali" ["We Attacked and Died"], in *Rzhevskaia bitva: Srazhenie za Polunino*, p. 150. [Editor's note: Petr Mikhin's memoirs were translated into English and published in 2010 by the English publisher Pen & Sword under the title *Guns against the Reich: Memoirs of an Artillery Officer on the Eastern Front.*]

29 Exposition in the German Hall of the Rzhev Memorial Complex museum.

30 A. Mertsalov, "Tsena Pobedy" ["The Price of Victory"] in A. I. Sakhorov (ed), *Kniga istoricheskikh sensatsii* [Book of Historical Sensations] (Moscow 1993), p. 57.

31 Mikhin, "Nastupali i umirali", pp. 150, 151.

32 *Der Durchbruch. Soldatenzeitung an der Ostfront*, 23 August 1942; E. Rzhevskaia, *Voroshennyi zhar*, pp. 42, 110, 112; *Krasnaia zvezda*, 1 December 1942;

33 Letter from H. Boucsein to the author from 25 January 2001 (author's personal files).

34 *Istoriia vtoroi mirovoi voiny*, Vol. 4, pp. 311, 313; Vol. 5, p. 248; *Voennaia entsiklopediia*, Vol. 7, pp. 231, 233, 234;

35 Proektor, *Agressiia i katastrofa*, p. 350.

36 Tippelskirch, *Istoriia vtoroi mirovoi voiny,* Vol. 1, p. 241.

37 Halder, *Voennyi dnevnik*, p. 249.

38 Proektor, *Agressiia i katatrofa*, pp. 434-436, 439.

39 Ibid., pp. 615-616.

40 Gurkin, "'Mars' v orbite 'Urana' i Saturna'", pp. 15-16.

41 Liddell Hart, *Vtoraia mirovaia voina*, p. 245.

42 Isaev, "Poteriannoe zveno" in Glantz, *Krupneishee porazhenie Zhukova*, pp.25-26; Glantz, *Krupneishee porazhenie Zhukova*, pp. 389-390.

43 I. S. Konev, "Vospominaniia" ["Recollections"] *Znamia*, No. 12 (December 1987), pp. 92-93.

44 D. D Leliushenko, *Moskva-Stalingrad-Berlin-Praga: Zapiski komandarma* [Moscow-Stalingrad-Berlin-Prague: Notes of an Army Commander], 3rd. Ed. (Moscow 1975), pp. 132-134.

45 N. N. Voronov, *Na sluzhbe voennoi* [At the service of the military] (Moscow 1973), pp. 384-385.

46 *Istoriia vtoroi mirovoi voiny*, Vol. 7, p. 241; *Perepiska Predsedatelia Sovmina SSSR s prezidentami SSHA i prem'er-ministrami Velikobritanii vo vremia Velikoi Otechestvennoi voiny*, Vol. 2, pp.77-78; Vol. 2, p. 167; S. M. Shtemenko, *General'nyi shtab v gody voiny* [The General Staff in the War Years], Book 2 (Moscow 1973), p. 314; A. Eremenko, *Gody vozmezdiia* [The Years of Retribution] (Moscow 1986), pp. 36-38; D. Volkogonov, *Triumf i tragediia* [Triumph and Tragedy] Book 2 (Moscow 1989), pp. 367-368; D. Boffa, *Istoriia Sovetskogo Soiuza* [History of the Soviet Union] Vol. 2 (Moscow 1990), p. 93; "Byl li Stalin na fronte?" ["Was Stalin at the front?"] *Den'* No. 6 (March 1991); E. Khrutsky, "Khrustalev, mashinu!" ["Khrustalev, to the vehicle!"] *Sovershenno sekretno*, No. 10 (October 2005).

47 "Reshenie Kalininskogo oblispolkoma ot 23 Avgusta 1945" ["Resolution of the Kalinin Oblast executive committee from 23 August 1945"] NVF 747/12 in the Rzhev Museum of Regional History.

48 V. M. Kulish, "O nekotorykh aktual'nykh problemakh istoriografii Velikoi Otechestvennoi voiny" ["On several topical problem of the historiography of the Great Patriotic War"] in A. N. Mertsalov (ed.) *Istoriia i stalinizm* [History and Stalinism] (Moscow 1991), p. 309.

49 A. N. Mertsalov and L. A. Mertsalov, *A. A. Zhomini – osnovatel' nauchnoi voennoi teorii (1779-1869)* [A. A. Jomini – the founder of scientific military theory (1779-1869-1999] (Moscow 1999), p. 367.

50 As cited by O. A. Kondrat'ev, *Rzhevskaia bitva: polveka umolchaniia* [The Battle of Rzhev: A Half-century of Silence] (Rzhev 1998), p. 46.

51 See A. Tvardovky, "Ia ubit podo Rzhevom" in I. A. Vasil'ev (ed.), *V boiakh za Rzhev* [In the Fighting for Rzhev] (Kalinin, 1973), pp. 312-317; M. Nozhkin, "Pod Rzhevom" ["Near Rzhev"] in *Rzhevskimi dorogami voiny*, p. 4; N. Ignat'ev, "Nezakhorennym ostalsia ..." ["Remained unburied ..."] in *Rzhevskaia bitva: Srazhenie za Polunino* [The Battle of Rzhev: The struggle for Polunino] (Tver': Izdatel'stvo "Russkaia Provintsiia"), back cover.

52 *Rzhevskaia bitva v kamne i metalle: Pamiatniki voiny Rzhevskogo raiona* [The Battle of Rzhev in Stone and Metal: Monuments of the War of the Rzhev Region] (Rzhev 2006), pp. 9-10.

53 K. B. Pal'mina, *Istoriia sozdaniia Memorialy Slavy vsem voinam-sibiriakam, pogibshim v Velikuiu Otechestvennuiu voinu* [History of the creation of the Memorial of Honor to all the Siberian soldiers, who died in the Great Patriotic War] (Novosibirsk, 2002).

54 "Kollektsiia materialov po istorii sozdaniia Rzhevskogo memoriala" ["Collection of materials on the history of the creation of the Rzhev Memorial"], KVF No. 11898, pp. 31-32 in the Tver' State Consolidated Museum; O. A. Kondrat'ev (ed.), *Slovar'-spravochnik* [Glossary] (Rzhev 2005), pp. 104-105.

55 *Tverskie Gubernskie Izvestiia*, No. 1 (2007); *Rzhevskaia Pravda*, 15 November 2007.

56 B. I. Nevzorov, "O znachenii Bitvy pod Moskvoi v khode Vtoroi mirovoi voiny" ["On the significance of the Battle of Moscow in the course of the Second World War."] *VIZh*, No. 2 (February 2007), p. 22.

Bibliography

A) Unpublished

Central Archive of the Ministry of Defense (TsAMO)

F. 208 (operations department of the field command [Russian acronym OO PU] of Western Front headquarters), Op. 2511, D. 1024, 1025, 1044, 1045, 1085, 1097, 1112, 1113, 1447, 1448, 1449, 1450, 1463, 1464, 1466, 1473, 1522, 2271, 2276, 2277, 2278, 2281, 2337, 2605, 2606.
F. 213 (OO PU of the Kalinin Front), Op. 2002, D. 65, 69/8, 114, 180, 187, 219, 326, 327, 402, 411, 419, 422, 441, 961, 971.
F. 326 (OO PU 5th Army), Op. 5047, D. 101, 132, 285.
F. 423 (formerly F. 373 – OO PU 20th Army), Op. 6631, D. 36, 48, 56.
F. 376 (OO PU 22nd Army), Op. 10803, D. 87, 93, 100, 101.
F. 384 (OO PU 29th Army), Op. 8529, D. 94, 130, 152; Op. 8550, D. 12, 87.
F. 354 (OO PU 10th Guards/30th Army), Op. 5806, D. 67, 99, 120, 220, 256.
F. 386 (OO PU 31st Army), Op. 8583, D. 6, 134, 136, 147, 151, 157.
F. 388 (OO PU 33rd Army), Op. 8712, D. 54, 135, 181.
F. 394 (OO PU 39th Army), Op. 9072, D. 1, 7, 13, 87.
F. 396 (OO PU 41st Army), Op. 9208, D. 31, 35, 88, 90, 91, 179.
F. 860 (6/19th Guards Rifle Corps), Op. 1, D. 22, 205.
F. 3413 (6/11th Guards Tank Corps), Op. 1, D. 5.
F. 3423 (1st Mechanized Corps), Op. 1, D.1.
F. 3478 (11th Cavalry Corps), Op. 1.

TsAMO Library

Formirovanie i perepodchinenie obshchevoiskovykh armii 1941-1945 [Formation and reassignment of the combined-arms armies, 1941-1945]. General Staff, 1954.

Obshchevoiskovye armii i ikh boevoi sostav za 1942 v Velikoi Otechestvennoi voine [Combined-arms armies and their operational strength for 1942 in the Great Patriotic War]. Military-historical Directorate of the General Staff of the USSR Armed Forces, 1949.

Obshchevoiskovye armii i ikh boevoi sostav za 1943 v Velikoi Otechestvennoi voine [Combined-arms armies and their operational strength for 1943 in the Great Patriotic War]. Military-historical Directorate of the General Staff of the USSR Armed Forces, 1949.

Operativnoe ispol'zovanie armii [Operational use of the armies], Part 3. Military-historical Directorate of the General Staff of the USSR Armed Forces.

Svedeniia na kavaleriiskie korpusa s 1 po 19 [Information on the 1st-19th Cavalry Corps]. Archive of the USSR Ministry of Defense, 1954.

Tver' State Consolidated Museum

Responses to queries to the Tver' and Smolensk Oblast military commissariats and the Iukhnov District military commissariat in the archive of the Museum's Department of Contemporary History.

Correspondence with German participants in the fighting in the Rzhev area, 1998-1999.

A. S. Burakov, *Zapiski kommisara* [Notes of a commissar], (Krasnoiarsk, 1980s). Typewritten copy in the archive of the Museum's Department of Contemporary History.

Materialy o 3-ei vozdushnoi armii Kalininskogo fronta [Materials on Kalinin Front's 3rd Air Army] in the archive of the Museum's Department of Contemporary History.

Kratkaia istoricheskaia spravka 139-i strelkovoi divizii [Short historical reference guide of the 139th Rifle Division], compiled by A. Kopin, in the Tver' State Consolidated Museum, Great Patriotic War, 5.

G. Kippar, *Das Kampfgeschen der 161 (ostpr.) Infanterie-Division von der Aufstellung 1939 bis zum Ende.* (Westerstede, 1990?). Typewritten copy in the archive of the Museum's Department of Soviet Social History.

Der Ostfeldzug. Der 86. rhein-westf. Inf.-Division. 28.XI.1941-4.XI.1943. Typewritten copy, 1962, in the archive of the Museum's Department of Soviet Social History.

Rzhev Museum of Local History. Manuscript Collection.

Materials of the 30th Army and of the 215th, 274th, 359th, 369th and 375th Rifle Divisions.

M. K. Sushkov, veteran of the 215th Rifle Division, *Vospominaniia* [Recollections], 1968.

Correspondence of the Rzhev Museum of Local History

H. Luhter, *Dunkle Jahre. Kriegsbriefe und Erinnerungen*, 1995. Typewritten copy.

Museum of the Rzhev Memorial Complex

Exhibition materials in the German Hall.

B) Published

Printed Documents

Bitva pod Moskvoi. Khronika, fakty, liudi [Battle of Moscow: Chronicle, facts, people] in two volumes (Moscow: OLMA-PRESS, 2001), Book 2.

Voenno-istoricheskii arkhiv [Military-historical archive], 3rd Ed. (Moscow, 1998), 6th Ed. (Moscow, 1999).

Vasil'chenko, K. F. "Tragicheskaia provalivshaiasia Viazemskaia nastupatel'naia operatsiia Zapadnogo fronta" [Tragic failed Viaz'ma offensive operation of the Western Front], *Voenno-istoricheskii arkhiv* [*VIA*] No. 1 (January 2007).

Dashichev, V. I. *Bankrotstvo strategii germanskogo fashizma. Istoricheskie ocherki: Dokumenty i materialy* [Bankruptcy of the strategy of German fascism. Historical essays: Documents and materials], Vol. 2 (Moscow: Nauka, 1973)

"Zapiski vracha 'Skoroi pomoshchi'" ["Notes of an Emergency Doctor"], *Istochnik*, No. 2 (February 1995)

Perepiska Predsedatelia Soveta Ministrov SSSR s prezidentami SSHA i prem'er-ministrami Velikobritanii vo vremia Velikoi Otechestvennoi voiny 1941-1945 [Correspondence of the Chairman of the USSR Council of Ministers with the presidents of the USA and prime-ministers of Great Britain during the Great Patriotic War 1941-1945], Vols. 1 and 2, 2nd Ed. (Moscow: Politizdat, 1989).

Russkii arkhiv. Velikaia Otechestvennaia voina 1941-1945. Collection of documents under the general editorship of V. A. Zolotarev (Moscow, Tsentr "Terra") in multiple volumes. For this book, specifically Vol. 16 (5-2) 1999: *Stavka* VGK, *Dokumenty i materialy 1942* [The *Stavka* VGK: Documents and materials 1942]; Vol. 16 (5-3) 1999: *Stavka* VGK, *Dokumenty i materialy 1943* [The *Stavka* VGK: Documents and materials 1943]; Vol. 23 (12-2) 1999: *General'nyi shtab v gody Velikoi Otechestvennoi voiny: 1942* [The General Staff in the years of the Great Patriotic War: 1942]; Vol. 23 (12-3) 1999: *General'nyi shtab v gody Velikoi Otechestvennoi voiny: 1943* [The General Staff in the years of the Great Patriotic War: 1943]

Stalin, I. V. *O Velikoi Otechestvennoi voine Sovetskogo Soiuza* [On the Great Patriotic War of the Soviet Union], 3rd Ed. (Moscow: Gosudarstvennoe izdatel'stvo politicheskoi literatury, 1953).

Wartime Periodical Literature

Vpered na vraga [Forward toward the enemy] (newspaper of the Kalinin Front), various army issues for the years 1942 and 1943.

Izvestiia, various issues in July and August 1942; 3 April 1943.

Krasnaia zvezda, 1 December 1942

Pravda 14 July 1942; 23 February, 4 March 1943.

Sotsialisticheskoe l'novodstvo, 30 September 1942.

Der Durchbruch. Soldatenzeitung an der Ostfront, 23 August 1942.

Memoirs of Soviet Participants in the War

Bagramian, I. Kh. *Tak shli my k pobede* [As we went on to victory] (Moscow: Voenizdat, 1977)

Belov, P. A. *Za nami Moskva* [Moscow is behind us] (Moscow: Voenizdat, 1963)

Beloborodov, A. P. *Vsegda v stroiu* [Always in formation] (Moscow: Ekonomika, 1984)

Bitva za Moskvu [Battle for Moscow], 2nd Ed. (Moscow: Moskovskii rabochii, 1968)

Boiko, V. P. *S dumoi o Rodine* [With a thought about the Motherland] (Moscow:Voenizdat, 1983)

Denisenko, G. F. "Zapiski pozhilogo soldata" ["Notes of an elderly soldier"] *Voenno-istoricheskii arkhiv* No. 1 (January 2005).

Dragunsky, D. A. *Gody v brone* [Years in armor] (Moscow: Voenizdat, 1973).

Eremenko, A. *Gody vozmezdiia* [Years of retribution] (Moscow, 1986).

Eto bylo na rzhevsko-viazemskom platsdarme [It was at the Rzhev-Viaz'ma staging area] Book 1 (Rzhev 1998), Book 2 (2000).

Getman, A. L. *Tanki idut na Berlin (1941-1945)* [Tanks advance on Berlin (1941-1945)] (Moscow: Voenizdat, 1982).

Galitsky, K. N. *Gody surovykh ispytanii 1941-1945: Zapiski komandarma* [Years of severe trials 1941-1945: Notes of an army commander] (Moscow: Nauka, 1973).

Gorbachevsky, B. N. *Rzhevskaia miasorubka: Vremia otvagi, Zadacha – vyzhit'!* [Rzhev meat grinder: A time of courage, Task – survive!] (Moscow: Iauza, Eksmo, 2007).

Ivanov, K. *Shla diviziia na zapad* [The division headed west] (Perm 1972).

Kaliagin, A. Ia. "Na dal'nikh podstupakh k Moskve" ["On the distant approaches to Moscow"] *VIZh*, No. 11 (November 1970).

Katukov, M. E. *Na ostrie glavnovo udara* [At the point of the main attack], 3rd Ed. (Moscow: Voenizdat, 1985).

Khlebnikov, N. M. *Pod grokhot soten batarei* [Under the thunder of hundreds of batteries] (Moscow: Voenizdat, 1974)

Kondrat'ev, O. and Myl'nikov, L. *Rzhevskimi dorogami voiny* [Along the Rzhev roads of war] (Rzhev 1992).

Konev, I. S. *Zapiski komandueshchego frontom, 1943-1944* [Notes of a *front* commander, 1943-1944] (Moscow: Nauka, 1972)

_________. "Vospominaniia" ["Recollections"] *Znamia*, No. 12 (December 1987).

Kozlov, V. I., Nazaretsky, V. E., and Zamoluev, V. V. *Mirgorodskaia, trizhdy ordenonosnaia* [The Mirgorod, thrice Order-awarded division] (Mirgorod, 1990).

Krasnoshtanov, I. K. "114 os br v boiakh po likvidatskii platsdarm severo-zapadnee Rzheva (sentiabr' 1942)" ["114th Special Brigade in the fighting to liquidate the bridgehead northwest of Rzhev (September 1942)] *VIZh*, No. 2 (February 1979).

Kudinov, P. I. *Za reidom reid* [Raid after raid] (Kaliningrad: Knizhnoe izdatel'stvo, 1983).

Leliushenko, D. D. *Zaria pobedy* [Dawn of victory] (Moscow: Voenizdat, 1966).

_______________, *Moskva-Stalingrad-Berlin-Praga* [Moscow-Stalingrad-Berlin-Prague] 4th Ed. (Moscow: Nauka, 1987).

Leont'iev, N. "Byl li Stalin na fronte. Beseda s A. Rybin" ["Was Stalin at the front? A conversation with A. Rybin"] *Den'* No. 6 (June 1991).

Malygin, K. A. *V tsentre boevogo poriadka* [In the center of the combat formation] (Moscow, Voenizdat, 1986).

Mikhin, P. "Nastupali i umirali" ["We attacked and died"] in *Rzhevskaia bitva:Srazhenie za Polunino* [Battle of Rzhev: Struggle for Polunino] (Tver': Russkaia provintsiia, 2001).

Nasha 252-ia:Veterany divizii vspominaiut [Our 252nd Rifle Division: Veterans of the division recollect] (Perm, 1983).

Rokossovsky, K. K. *Soldatskii dolg* [Soldier's duty] (Moscow: Voenizdat, 1988).

Senkevich, I. *Krasnoiarskaia gvardeiskaia* [Krasnoiarsk Guards Division] (Krasnoiarsk, 1973).

Shtemenko, S. M. *General'nyi shtab v gody voiny* [General Staff in the war years] (Moscow: Voenizdat, 1981)

Soldaty Velikoi Otechestvennoi voiny: Vospominaniia i ocherki [Soldiers of the Great Patriotic War: Recollections and essays] (Iaroslavl', 1987).

Solomatin, M. D. *Krasnogradtsy* [Krasnograd men] (Moscow: Voenizdat, 1963).

Soshnev, V. G. *S veroi v pobedu* [With faith in victory] (Moscow: Voenizdat, 1982).

Vasilevsky, A. M. *Delo vsei zhizni* [A lifelong cause]. (Moscow: Politizdat, 1983).

Vasilev, I. A., ed. *V boiakh za Rzhev* [In the fighting for Rzhev]. (Kalinin: Moskovskii rabochii Kalinin branch 1973).

Vovchenko, I. A. *Tankisty* [Tankers] (Moscow: DOSAAF, 1976).

Voronov, N. N. *Na sluzhbe voennoi* [At the service of the military] (Moscow: Voenizdat, 1973).

Zhukov, G. K. "Iz neopublikovannykh vospominanii" ["From the unpublished memoirs"] *Kommunist*, No.14 (1988).

___________. *Vospominaniia i razmyshleniia* [Reminiscences and recollections] 9th Ed., Vol. 2 (Moscow: Izdatel'stvo Agetnstva pechati Novosti, 1988); 11th Ed., Vol. 2 (Moscow: Izdatel'stvo Novosti, 1992).

Zhukov, N. I. "Polety na 'Trinadtsatom'" ["Flights on a 'Thirteen'"] in *Vremia i sud'ba: Voenno-memorial'nyi sbornik* [Time and fate: Military-memorial collection] (Moscow 1991).

Diaries and Memoirs of German Veterans of the War

Alte Kameraden. Unabhangige Zeitschrift deutscher Soldaten. Heft 517. February 1997.

Haape, H. *Endstation Moskau, 1941-1942.* 2 Auflage (Stuttgart: Motorbuch Verlagspezial, 1980)

Halder, F. *Voennyi dnevnik* [War Diary] Vol.3, Book 2 (Moscow: Voenizdat, 1969).

Pabst, G. *Dnevnik nemetskogo soldata: Voennyi budni na Vostochnom fronte 1941-1943* [Diaryof a German soldier: the realities of war on the Eastern Front, 1941-1943; translated from the English by L. A. Igorevsky] (Moscow: ZAO Tsentropoligraf, 2005).

Reference books and encyclopedias

Deutschland. Grosser Atlas und Lexicon. RV Verlag, 1992.

Kondrat'ev, O. A. *Rzhev: Slovar'-spravochnik* [Rzhev: Dictionary-reference] (Rzhev 2005).

Krivosheev, G. F.; Andronikov, V. M.; Burikov, P. D.; and Gurkin, V. V. *Velikaia Otechestvennaia voina bez grifa setkretnosti: Kniga poter'* [Great Patriotic War without a seal of secrecy: Book of losses] (Moscow: Veche, 2009).

Kto byl kto v Velikoi Otechestvennoi voine 1941-1945: Kratkii spravochnik [Who was who in the Great Patriotic War 1941-1945: Short handbook] (Moscow: Izdatel'stvo Respublika, 1995).

Rzheshevsky O. A., ed. *Velikaia Otechestvennaia voina 1941-1945: Sobytiia, Liudi, Dokumenty.* [Great Patriotic War 1941-1945: Events, People, Documents] (Moscow 1990).

Rzhevskaia bitva v kamne i metalle: Pamiatniki voiny Rzhevskogo raiona [The Battle of Rzhev in stone and metal: War monuments of the Rzhev area] (Rzhev 2006).

Sovetskaia voennaia entsiklopediia: V vos'mi tomakh [Soviet military encyclopedia: in eight volumes] (Moscow: Voenizdat, Vol. 2, 1976; Vol. 7, 1979; Vol. 8, 1980).

Velikaia Otechestvennaia voina 1941-1945. Entsiklopediia [Great Patriotic War 1941-1945. Encyclopedia] (Moscow: Sovetskaia entsiklopediia, 1985).

Voennaia entsiklopediia [Military encyclopedia], (Moscow: Voenizdat, Vol. 1, 1997; Vol. 2, 1998; Vol. 7, 2003).

Voennaia entsiklopedicheskii slovar' [Military encyclopedic dictionary] (Moscow: Voenizdat, 2007).

Scholarly Works

Afanas'ev A., Badanin, B. "O nekotorykh voprosakh inzhenernogo obespecheniia bitvy pod Moskvoi letom i osen'iu 1941" ["On certain questions of the engineering support of the Battle of Moscow in the summer and autumn of 1941"] *VIZh*, No. 12 (December 1966).

Afanas'ev, Iu. N. "Drugaia voina: istoriia i pamiat'" ["The other war: history and remembrance"] in *Drugaia voina 1939-1945* [The other war 1939-1945] (Moscow: BI, 1996).

Afanas'ev, N. M., Glazunov, N. K., Kazansky, P. A., and Fironov, N. A. *Dorogami ispytanii i pobed: Boevoi put' 31-u armii* [Along the roads of ordeals and victories: Combat path of the 31st Army] (Moscow: Voenizdat, 1986).

Anishchenko, P. and Shurinov, B. *Tret'ia vozdushnaia: Voenno-istoricheskii ocherk o boevom puti VVS Kalininskogo fronta i 3-i vozdushnoi armii v gody Velikoi Otechestvennoi voiny* [3rd Air Army: Military-historical study of the combat path of the Kalinin Front air force and the 3rd Air Army in the years of the Great Patriotic War] (Moscow: Voenizdat, 1984).

Anfilov, V. A. *Krushenie pokhoda Gitlera na Moskvu* [The failure of Hitler's campaign onMoscow] (Moscow: Nauka, 1989).

Biriukov, A. I. and Safir, V. M. "Vo vsem li prav istorik general armii M. A. Gareev?" ["Is the historian General of the Army M. A. Gareev right in everything?"] *VIA*, Issue 3 (Moscow 1998).

Dzhelaukhov, Kh. M. and Petrov, B. I. "K voprosu o strategicheskikh operatsiiakh Velikoi Otechestvennoi voiny 1941-1945" ["On the question of strategic operations of the Great Patriotic War 1941-1945"] *VIZh*, No. 7 (July 1987).

Eliseev, V. T. "Dokumenty Tsentral'nogo arkhiva MO RF o Viazemskom okruzhenii, poteriakh v Moskovskoi bitve i novoi kontseptsii po istorii vooruzhennoi bor'by na sovetskom-germanskom fronte v 1941-1945" ["Documents of the Central Archive of the Russian Federation's Ministry of Defense about the Viaz'ma encirclement, loss in the Moscow battle and a new conception on the history of the military struggle on the Soviet-German front in 1941-1945"] *VIA*, No. 12 (December 2006).

__________. "Strategicheskie peregruppirovka sovetskikh voisk pri podgotovke zimnei kampanii 1942/1943" ["Strategic regroupings of Soviet forces during preparation of the winter campaign 1942/1943"] *VIZh*, No. 11 (November 1987).

Fedorov, E. S. *Pravda o voennom Rzheve* [Truth about wartime Rzhev] (Rzhev 1995).

Gareev, M. A. "O neudachnykh nastupatel'nykh operatsiiakh sovetskikh voisk v Velikoi Otechestvennoi voine" ["On the unsuccessful offensive operations of Soviet forces in the Great Patriotic War"] *Novaia i noveishaia istoriia*, No. 1 (January 1994).

___________. "Uroki ne vprok" ["Lessons not for future use"] *VIZh*, No. 5 (May 2001).

___________. "Domysli i fakty ob istorii Velikoi Otechestvennoi: Operatsiia Mars kak primer neskonchaemoi polemicheskoi bitvy" ["Conjectures and facts about the history of the Great Patriotic War: Operation Mars as an example of an unending polemical struggle"] *Nezavisimoe voennoe obozrenie*, No. 14 (2006).

Gerasimova, S. A. "Ne pora li pereosmyslit' rol' i znachenie boev pod Rzhevom?" ["Isn't it time to re-think the role and significance of the fighting at Rzhev?"] *Voprosy istorii*, No. 5 (May 1998).

______________. "Bitva za rzhevsko-viazemskii platsdarm" ["Battle for the Rzhev-Viaz'ma staging area"] *Voprosy istoriia*, No. 4-5 (April-May 2000).

______________. "Oboronitel'naia operatsiia voisk Kalininskogo fronta v iule 1942" ["Defensive operation of the Kalinin Front in July 1942"] *VIA*, No. 8 (August 2001).

______________. "Rzhevskaia bitva: tsena neudach" ["The battle of Rzhev: the price of failures"], in *Rzhevskaia bitva: Srazhenie za Polunino.* A collection of articles and materials. (Tver': Russkaia provintsiia, 2001).

______________, and Gareev, M. A., "O nashikh poteriakh podo Rzhevom i Viaz'moi" ["About our losses at Rzhev and Viaz'ma"] *VIZh*, No.3 (March 2002).

______________. "Rzhev – Stalingrad: paralleli voennoi istorii" ["Rzhev – Stalingrad: the parallels of military history"] in *My pobedu priblizhali, kak mogli* (*Materialy Mezhdunarodnoi nauchnoi konferentsii*) [We were approaching victory, as far as we could (Materials of an international academic conference] (Smolensk: Smiadyn', 2003).

______________. "Pervaia Rzhevsko- Sychevskaia nastupatel'naia operatsiia 1942 (Novyi vzgliad)" ["First Rzhev-Sychevka offensive operation 1942 (New view)"] *Voprosy istorii* No. 5 (May 2005).

Glazunov, H. K., Pavlov, B. I. and Shlomin, V. S. "K voprosu o strategicheskikh operatsiiakh Velikoi Otechestvennoi voiny" ["On the question of strategic operations of the Great Patriotic War"] *VIZh*, No. 4 (April 1986).

Golikov, S. *Vydaiushchiesia pobedy Sovetskoi Armii v Velikoi Otechestvennoi voin* [Outstanding victories of the Soviet Army in the Great Patriotic War] (Moscow: Gospolitizdat, 1952).

Gradosel'sky, V. V. "Natsional'nye voinskie formirovaniia v Velikoi Otechestvennoi voine" ["Ethnic military formations in the Great Patriotic War"] *VIZh*, No. 1 (January 2002).

Gurkin, V. V. "'Mars' v orbite 'Urana' i 'Saturna': O vtoroi Rzhevsko-Sychevskoi nastupatel'noi operatsii 1942 g." ["'Mars' in the orbit of 'Uranus' and 'Saturn': On the second Rzhev-Sychevka offensive operation of 1942"] *VIZh*, No. 4 (April 2000).

__________. "Strategicheskie i frontovye operatsii Krasnoi armii" ["Strategic and *front* operations of the Red Army"] *VIZh*, No. 2 (February 1998).

Iakovlev, N. N. *Sud'ba polkovodtsa: Zhukov, Makartur, Rommel'; kniga dlya uchashchikhsia starykh klassov* [The Commander's Fate: Zhukov, MacArthur, Rommel; book for students of upper classes] (Moscow: Prosveshchenie, 1995).

Ionov, P. P. "Nastupaet Kalininskii front" ["The Kalinin Front attacks"] *VIA*, Nos. 6-11 (June- November 2006).

Isaev, A. V. "Poteriannoe zveno" ["Lost echelon"] in the Foreword to D. Glantz, *Krupneishee porazhenie Zhukova: Krupneishee porazhenie Krasnoi Armii v operatsii "Mars"* [Zhukov's Greatest Defeat: The Red Army's Epic Disaster in Operation Mars] (Moscow: AST/Astrel', 2006).

Isaev, S. I. "Vekhi frontovogo puti" ["Milestones of a front path"] *VIZh*, No. 10 (October 1991).

Istoriia Velikoi Otechestvennoi voiny Sovetskogo Soiuza 1941-1945 [History of the Great Patriotic War of the Soviet Union 1941-1945] in six volumes (Moscow: Voenizdat; Volume 2, 1963; Volume 3, 1964).

Istoriia vtoroi mirovoi voiny 1939-1945 [History of the Second World War 1939-1945] in twelve volumes (Moscow: Voenizdat; Vol. 4, 1975; Vol. 5, 1975; Vol. 6, 1976; Vol. 7, 1976).

"Itogi diskussii o strategicheskikh operatsiiakh Velikoi Otechestvennoi voiny 1941-1945" ["Results of the discussion of the strategic operations of the Great Patriotic War 1941-1945"] *VIZh* (1987).

"K 110-letiiu so dnia rozhdeniia general-leitenanta M. G. Efremov" ["On the 110th anniversary since Lieutenant-General M. G. Efremov's date of birth"] *VIA*, No. 3 (March 2007).

Kantor, R. E. and Glantz, D. M. "Spotknuvshiishsia' koloss: Krasnaia armiia nakanune mirovoi voiny" ["Stumbling colossus: the Red Army on the eve of the world war"] *Voprosy istorii*, No. 6 (June 1999).

Kapusto, Iu. *Poslenimi dorogami generala Efremova* [Along the last roads of General Efremov] (Moscow: Izdatel'stvo politicheskoi literatury, 1992).

Khorev, A. P. "Poklonimsiia ikh pamiati" ["We will honor their memory"] *VIZh*, No. 1 (January 1989).

Kochetkov, A. D. *Dvinskii tankovyi: boevoi put'5-go tankogo dvinskogo korpusa* [Dvina tank corps: combat path of the 5th Dvina Tank Corps] (Moscow: Voenizdat, 1989).

Komarov, D. E. "'Zdes' nam protivostoiala naibolee sil'naia iz gruppirovok protivnika ...':Nekotorye osobennosti likvidatsii rzhevsko-viazemskogo platsdarma v Marte 1943" ["'Here we were opposed by the strongest of the enemy groupings ...': Certain details of the liquidation of the Rzhev-Viaz'ma staging area in March 1943"] *VIZh*, No. 4 (April 2004).

Kondrat'ev, O. A., *Rzhevskaia bitva: polveka molchaniia* [The Battle of Rzhev: a half-century of silence] (Rzhev, 1998).

Krivosheev, G. K., *Grif sekretnosti sniat: poteri Vooruzhennykh Sil SSSR v voinakh, boevykh deistviiakh, i voennykh konfliktakh XX veka* [The seal of secrecy has been removed: losses of the USSR Armed Forces in the wars, combat operations and military conflicts of the XX century] (Moscow: Voennoe Izdatel'stvo, 1993).

______________, (ed). *Rossiia i SSSR v voinakh XX veka: Statisticheskoe issledovanie* [Russia and the USSR in the wars of the XX century: Statistical study] (Moscow: OLMA- PRESS, 2001).

Krylov, N. I., Alekseev, N. I. and Dragan, I. G. *Navstrechu pobede: Boevoi put' 5-ia armiia, oktiabr' 1941 – avgust 1945* [Toward victory: Combat path of the 5th Army, October 1941 – August 1945] (Moscow: Nauka, 1970).

Kulish, V. M. "O nekotorykh aktual'nykh problemakh istoriographii Velikoi Otechestvennoi voiny" [On certain topical problems of the historiography of Great Patriotic War], in Mertsalov, A. N., ed. *Istoriia i Stalinizm* [History and Stalinism] (Moscow: Izdatel'stvo politicheskoi literatury, 1991).

___________. "Sovetskaia istoriografiia Velikoi Otechestvennoi voiny" [Soviet historiography of the Great Patriotic War], in Afanas'ev, Iu. N. ed. *Sovetskaia istoriografiia* [Soviet historiography] (Moscow: BI, 1996).

Ladygin, I. Z. and Smirnov, N. I. *Na rzhevskom rubezhe* [On the Rzhev line] (Rzhev, 1992).

Lisov, I. I. *Desantniki* [Paratroopers] (Moscow: Voennoe izdatel'stvo Ministerstva Oborony SSSR 1968).

Lukashenko, A. I. *Dorogami vozdushnogo desanta* [Along the roads of an airborne landing] (Moscow: Moskovskii rabochii, 1978).

______________. *Za frontom – front* [Behind the front – a front] in *Krylataia gvardiia* [Winged Guard] (Moscow: DOSAAF, 1978).

"Liudskie poteri Sovetskikh Vooruzhennykh Sil v 1941-1945: Novye aspekty" ["Human losses of the Soviet Armed Forces in 1941-1945: New aspects"] *VIZh*, No. 2 (February 1999).

Mel'nikov, V. M. "Material'no-tekhnicheskoe obespechenie voisk v Moskovskoi nastupatel'noi strategicheskoi operatsii (6.12.1941 – 20.04.1942)" ["Logistical support of the forces in the Moscow offensive strategic operation (12/6/1941 – 04/20/1942)" *VIA*, No. 4 (April 2006).

Mertsalov, A. "Tsena Pobedy" [The Price of Victory] in Sakharov, A. I. *Kniga istoricheskikh sensatsii* [Book of historical sensations] (Moscow: Raritet, 1993).

Mertsalov, A. N. and Mertsalov, L. A. *G. K. Zhukov – Novoe prochtenie ili staryi mif?* [G. K Zhukov – New reading or an old myth?] (Moscow: Prometei, 1994).

Mertsalov, A. N. and Mertsalov, L. A. *A.-A Zhomini: osnovatel' nauchnoi voennoi teorii (1779- 1869-1999)* [A. A. Jomini: The founder of scientific military theory] (Moscow: self- published, 1999).

Mikhalev, S. N. *Strategicheskie reshenie* [Strategic decisions], Book 2 (Krasnoiarsk, 1998).

Mitiagin, S. D., "Boevye deistviia pod Viaz'moi v ianvare-aprele 1942: operatsiia ili imitatsiia" ["Combat operations at Viaz'ma in January-April 1942: operation or imitation?] *VIA*, Issue No. 3 (Moscow, 1998).

Mosiagin, M. N. "Reid gruppy voisk P. A. Belov v 1942 g." ["The raid of P. A. Belov's group of forces in 1942"] *VIA*, No. 6 (June 2007).

Muriev, D. "Nekotorye voprosy sovetskoi voennoi strategii v Moskovskoi bitve" ["Certain questions of Soviet military strategy in the battle of Moscow"] *VIZh*, No. 12 (December 1971).

Muriev, D. Z. *Proval operatsiia "Taifun"* [Failure of Operation "Typhoon"] (Moscow: Voenizdat, 1972).

Nevzorov, B. I. "O znachenii Bitvy pod Moskvoi v khode Vtoroi mirovoi voiny" ["On the significance of the Battle of Moscow in the course of the Second World War"] *VIZh*, No. 2 (February 2007).

Nevzorov, B. "Operatsiia 'Mars': pravda i domysli" ["Operation 'Mars': truth and conjectures"] *Krasnaia zvezda*, 1 April 2003.

Ozhogin, E., ed. *Istoriia Rzheva: Ocherki po istorii Rzhevskoi zemli* [The History of Rzhev: Essays on the history of the Rzhev land] (Rzhev, 2000).

Pal'mina, K. B. *Istoriia sozdaniia Memoriala Slavy vsem voinam-sibiriakam, pogibshim v Velikuiu Otechestvennuiu voiny* [History of the creation of the Memorial of Honor to all the Siberian soldiers, who died in the Great Patriotic War] (Novosibirsk, 2002).

Pavlenko, N. G. *Byla voina ... razmyshleniia voennogo istorika* [There was a war ... reflections of a military historian] (Moscow: IK 'Rodnik', 1994).

Petrov, B. N. "Analiz prichin nezavershennosti nekotorykh nastupatel'nykh operatsiia Velikoi Otechestvennoi voiny"["An analysis of causes of the non-completion of several offensive operations of the Great Patriotic War"] *VIZh*, No. 1 (January 1987).

Petrushin, A. "Spetsdobrovol'tsy" ["Special volunteers"] *Rodina*, No. 5 (May 2000).

"Pitanie bylo kaloriinym. O prodovol'stvennom snabzhenii i chislennosti Krasnoi Armii v gody Velikoi Otechestvennoi voiny" ["The nutrition was sustaining: on the food supply and manpower of the Red Army in the years of the Great Patriotic War"] *VIZh*, No. 1 (January 1999).

Pobeda pod Moskvoi: po materialam voenno-nauchnoi konferentsii [Victory at Moscow: according to materials of a military-scientific conference] (Moscow: Voenizdat, 1982).

Proektor, D. M. *Agressiia i katastrofa* [Aggression and catastrophe] (Moscow: Nauka, 1968).

Radzievsky, A. I. *Proryv (po opytu Velikoi Otechestvennoi voiny 1941-1945)* [Breakthrough (according to the experience of the Great Patriotic War 1941-1945] (Moscow: Voenizdat, 1979).

Reshin, L. E. and Stepanov, V. S. "Sud'by general'skie ... Spisok generalov Krasnoi Armii, arestovannykh v nachale i v period Otechestvennoi voiny, podlezhashchikh sudu" [Generals' fates ... List of the Red Army generals who were arrested and faced trial at the beginning and during the Patriotic War] *VIZh*, No. 12 (December 1992).

Riabkov, G. T., ed. *Po dorogam boevoi slavy* [Along the roads of combat glory] (Smolensk, 1967).

Rzhevskaia bitva i ee znachenie v istorii Velikoi Otechestvennoi voiny: materialy nauchno-prakticheskoi konferentsii [The battle of Rzhev and its significance in the history of the Great Patriotic War: materials of a scientific-practical conference] (Rzhev, 2001).

Safir, V. M. "Oborona Moskvy: Narofominskii proryv 1-5 dekabria 1941 g." ["Defense of Moscow: the Naro-fominsk breakthrough of 1-5 December 1941"] *VIA*, Issue No. 1 (Moscow 1997).

__________. "General armii M. A. Gareev ne priemlet fakty i prodolzhaet tirazhovat' mify o Velikoi Otechestvennoi voine" ["General of the Army M. A. Gareev doesn't accept facts and continues to propogate myths about the Great Patriotic War"] *VIA*, Issue No. 10 (Moscow, 2000).

Samsonov, A. M. *Porazhenie vermakhta pod Moskvoi* [*Wehrmacht's* defeat in front of Moscow] (Moscow: Moskovskii rabochii, 1981).

_____________. *Stalingradskaia bitva* [Battle of Stalingrad], 3rd. Ed. (Moscow: Nauka, 1982).

Sandalov, L. M. "Avgustovskaia nastupatel'naia operatsiia armii pravogo kryla Zapadnogo fronta v 1942" ["August offensive operation of the armies of the right wing of the Western Front in 1942"] *VIZh*, No. 4 (April 1959).

____________. *Pogorelo-gorodishchenskaia operatsiia* [Pogoreloe-Gorodishche operation] (Moscow: Voenizdat, 1960).

Shekhovtsev, N. I. "Nekotorye voprosy dostizheniia vnezapnosti v nastupatel'nykh operatsiiakh Velikoi Otechestvennoi voiny" ["Certain questions of achieving surprise in offensive operations of the Great Patriotic War"], in A. A. Grechko, ed., *Vsemirno-istoricheskaia pobeda sovetskogo naroda. 1941-1945* [Epochal victory of the Soviet people. 1941- 1945] (Moscow, 1971).

Shilovsky, E. A. *Razgrom nemetsko-fashistskikh voisk pod Moskvoi* [Smashing of the German- fascist forces in front of Moscow] (Moscw, 1944).

Shimansky, A. "Vybor napravleniia glavnogo udara" ["Selection of the axis of the main attack"] *VIZh*, No. 10 (October 1963).

Sidorov, A. D. "Pogibli za Rodinu" ["They died for the Motherland"] *VIZh*, No. 11 (November 1991), No. 6-7 (June, July 1992), No. 3, 8 (March, September 1993).

Sofronov, T. P. *Vozdushnye desanty vo vtoroi mirovoi voine* [Airborne landings in the Second World War] (Moscow, 1962).

Sokolov, B. V. *Tsena pobedy. Velikaia Otechestvennaia: neizvestnoe ob izvestnom* [Price of victory. The Great Patriotic War: the unknown about the known] (Moscow: Moskovskii rabochii, 1991).

Sokolovsky, V. D., ed. *Razgrom nemetsko-fashistskikh voisk pod Moskvoi* [Defeat of the German-fascist forces in front of Moscow] (Moscow, 1964).

Sorochenko, L. M. "Proschety planirovaniia (Tylovoe obespechenie Viazemskoi vozdushno- desantnoi operatsii" ["Miscalculations of planning (Logistic support of the Viaz'ma airborne landing operation"] *VIZh*, No. 1 (January 1989).

Sovetskaia kavaleriia [Soviet cavalry] (Moscow, 1964).

Strategicheskie operatsii Sovetskikh Vooruzhennykh Sil v Velikoi Otechestvennoi voine [Strategic operations of the Soviet Armed Forces in the Great Patriotic War] *VIZh*, No. 10 (October 1987).

Sudoplatov, P. A. *Razvedka i Kreml': Zapiski nezhelatel'nogo svidetelia* [Intelligence and the Kremlin: Notes of an unwilling witness] (Moscow: Geia, 1996).

Tel'pukhovsky, B. S. *Velikaia Otechestvennaia voina Sovetskogo Soiuza 1941-1945: Kratkii ocherk* [Great Patriotic War of the Soviet Union 1941-1945: A brief history] (Moscow: Gosudarstvenno izdatel'stvo politicheskoi literatury, 1952).

Vasil'ev, A. *Velikaia pobeda pod Moskvoi* [Great victory in front of Moscow] (Moscow, 1953).

Vasilevsky, A. M. "Nekotorye voprosy vooruzhennoi bor'by letom 1942 g." ["Certain questions of the armed struggle in the summer of 1942"] *VIZh*, No. 8 (August 1965).

______________. *Nachalo korennogo povorota v khode voiny: Bitva za Moskvu* [Start of the fundamental turn in the course of the war: the Battle for Moscow] (Moscow: Moskovskii rabochii, 1968).

Velikaia bitva pod Moskvoi: Kratkii istoricheskii ocherk [Great Battle of Moscow: A brief history] (Moscow, 1961).

Velikaia Otechestvennaia voina 1941-1945: Voenno-istoricheskie ocherki [Great Patriotic War 1941-1945: Military-historical essays], in four volumes. Books 1 and 2 (Moscow: Nauka, 1988).

Volkogonov, D. *Triumf i tragediia* [Triumph and tragedy] Book 2, Part 1 (Moscow: Izdatel'stvo Agentstva pechati Novosti , 1989).

Vorob'ev, F. D. and Kravtsov, V. M. *Pobedy Sovetskikh Vooruzhennykh Sil v Velikoi Otechestvennoi voine 1941-1945: Kratkii ocherk* [Victory of the Soviet Armed Forces in the Great Patriotic War 1941-1945: A brief history] (Moscow, 1953).

Vorob'ev, M. V. and Usov, V. V. *Za kazhdyi kliuchok zemli* [For every little clump of earth] (Smolensk: Moskovskii rabochii Smolensk branch, 1990).

"Zagadka gibeli general-leitenanta M. G. Efremova" ["Enigma of Lieutenant-General M. G. Efremov's death" *VIZh*, No. 1 (January 1990).

Zhilin, P. A., ed. *Vazhneishie operatsii Velikoi Otechestvennoi voiny 1941-1945 gg.* [Most important operations of the Great Patriotic War 1941-1945] (Moscow, 1956).

__________ ed. *Velikaia Otechestvenna Narodnaia 1941-1945: Kratkii istoricheskii ocherk* [Great Patriotic People's War 1941-1945: A brief history] (Moscow, 1985).

Zhorov, I. "V tylu pod Viaz'moi" ["In the rear near Viaz'ma"] *VIZh*, No. 6 (June 1965).

Soviet publicists

Ehrenburg, I. "Za iug!" ["For the south!"] *Krasnaia zvezda*, 9 August 1942.

__________. *Letopis' muzhestva, 1941-1945* [Chronicle of courage, 1941-1945] (Moscow: Sovetskii pisatel', 1983).

__________. *Liudy, gody, zhizn'* [People, years, life] (Moscow: Sovetskii pisatel', 1990).

Iampol'sky, B. "Osen'" ["Autumn"] in A. S. Dushenkov and S. M. Fligel'man, *Eto bylo na Kalininskom fronte* [It was on the Kalinin Front] (Moscow: Moskovskii rabochii, 1985).

Khrutsky, E. "Khrustalev, mashinu!" ["Khrustalev, to the vehicle!"] *Sovershenno sekretno*, No. 10 (October 2005).

Rzhevskaia, E. M. *Byla voina* ...[There was a war ...] (Moscow: Sovetskii pisatel', 1979).

_______________. *Blizhnie podstupy* [Nearest approaches] (Moscow: Sovetskii pisatel', 1985).

_______________. *Znaki prepinaniia* [Punctuation marks] (Moscow: Sovetskii pisatel', 1989).

Vorob'ev, E. Z. *Ognennaia metel'* [Fire storm] (Moscow: Moskovskii rabochii, 1977).

Works by Foreign Scholars

Bleier, W. et. al., *Germaniia vo vtoroi mirovoi voine (1939-1945)* [Germany in the Second World War (1939-1945)] (Moscow: Voenizdat, 1971).

Boucsein, H. *Halten oder Sterben. Die hessisch-thuringisch 129. Infanterie-Division im Russlandfeldzug und Ostpreussen 1941-1945.* (Potsdam: Kurt-Vowinckel Verlag, 1999).

Boffa, D. *Istoriia Sovetskogo Soiuza* [History of the Soviet Union; translated from Italian] Vol. 2 (Moscow: Mezhdunarodnye otnosheniia, 1990).

Conrady, Alexander. *Rshew 1942/43/ Aus der Geschichte der 36. Inf.-Div. (mot).1.1.1942-25.3.1943.* (Neckardemünd, 1976).

Doroga na Smolensk: Amerikanskie pisateli i zhurnalisty o Velikoi Otechestvennoi Voine sovetskogo naroda 1941-1945 gg. [The Road to Smolensk: American writers and journalists on the Great Patriotic War of the Soviet people 1941-1945] (Moscow: Progress, 1985).

Forster, G. *Der zweite Weltkrieg. Militarhistorischer Abriss* (Berlin, 1981).

Fuller, J. F. C. *Vtoraia mirovaia voina, 1939-1945 gg.: Strategicheskii i takticheskii obzor* [The Second World War, 1939-1945: A Strategical and Tactical History] (Moscow: Izdatel'stvo inostrannoi literatury, 1956).

Glantz, D. M. "Nedostatki istoriographii: zabytye bitvy germano-sovetskoi voiny (1941-1945)" ["Shortcomings of historiography: forgotten battles of the German-Soviet War (1941- 1945)] in *Vtoraia mirovaia voina: Aktual'nye problemy* [The Second World War: Topical problems] (Moscow: Nauka, 1995).

___________. "Operatsiia 'Mars'" [Operation 'Mars'] *Voprosy istorii*, No. 8 (August 1997).

___________. *Krupneishee porazhenie Zhukova: Katastrofa Krasnoi Armii v operatsii 'Mars', 1942* [Zhukov's Greatest Defeat: The Red Army's Epic Disaster in Operation Mars 1942] (Moscow: ACT/Astrel', 2006).

Grossmann, H. *Geschichte der rheinisch-westfalischen 6. Infanterie-Division 1941-1945.* (Bad Nauheim: Verlag Hans-Henning Podzun, 1958).

_________. *Rzhev-Kraeugol'nyi kamen' Vostochnogo fronta* [Rzhev: The Cornerstone of the Eastern Front] (Rzhev, 1996).

Haupt, Werner. *Moskau – Rshew – Orel – Minsk. Bildbericht der Heeresgruppe Mitte 1941-1944* Podzum-Pallas-Verlag. Friedberg, 1978.

Jacobsen, G. -A. "1939-1945. Vtoraia mirovaia voina" ["1939-1945: The Second World War"], in *Vtoraia mirovaia voina: dva vgliada* [The Second World War: Two views] (Moscow: "Mysl'", 1995).

Kondratjew O.A. *Die Schlacht von Rshew: Ein halbes Jahrhundert Schweigen*. (München: Arethousa Verlag, 2000).

Liddell Hart, B. *Vtoraia mirovaia voina* [The Second World War] (Moscow: Voenizdat, 1976).

Mirovaia voina, 1939-1945: Sbornik statei. [The World War, 1939-1945 – a collection of articles translated from German] (Moscow: Izdatel'stvo inostrannoi literatury, 1957).

Reinhardt, K. *Povorot pod Moskvoi: Krakh gitlerovskoi strategii zimoi 1941/42 goda* [Moscow: The Turning Point? The Failure of Hitler's Strategy in the Winter of 1941-1942] (Moscow: Voenizdat, 1980).

Rhein, E. -M. *Das rheinisch-westfalische Infanterie/Grenadier-Regiment 18, 1921-1945.* (Bergisch-Gladbach: Merker Druck, 1993).

Stowe, L. "S Krasnoi Armiei na Rzhevskom fronte" ["With the Red Army on the Rzhev front"] *Znamia*, No. 1 (January 1943).

Tippelskirch, K. von *Istoriia vtoroi mirovoi voiny* [History of the Second World War] (Moscow: Izdatel'stvo inostrannoi literatury, 1956; SPb Poligon, 1994).

Werth, A. *Rossiia v voine 1941-1945* [Russia at War, 1941-1945] (Moscow: Izdatel'stvo Progress, 1967).

Weidinger, Otto *Division Das Reich. Der Weg der 2. SS-Panzer-Division "Das Reich". Die Geschichte der Stamm-division der Waffen-SS. Band III: 1941-1943.* (Osnabrück: Munin Verlag, 1977.

Dissertation

Gerasimova, S. A. "Voennye deistviia v raion rzhevsko-viazemskogo vystupa v ianvare 1942 – marte 1943 gg.: Rzhevskaia bitva" ["Combat operations in the area of the Rzhev- Viaz'ma salient in January 1942 – March 1943: The Rzhev 'battle'"] in pursuit of the Candidate of Science (History) degree, Tver' State University, 2002.

Response to an abstract of S. A. Gerasimova's dissertation "Voennye deistviia v raione Rzhevsko-Viazemskogo vystupa v ianvare 1942-marte 1943: Rzhevskaya 'bitva'" ["Military operations in the area of the Rzhev-Viaz'ma salient in January 1942 – March 1943: The Rzhev 'battle'"] in pursuit of the Candidate of Science (History) degree, 07-00-2002, Institute of Military History of the Russian Federation Ministry of Defense, 2002.

Periodical literature

Bel'skaia pravda, May 1992.

Veche Tveri segodnia, March-August 2001.

Izvestiia, 20 June 1998.

Istoricheskii arkhiv, No. 4, 1998.

Rzhevskaia pravda, 29 March 2001; 15 November 2007.

Tverskaia zhizn', 21 March 1997; 3 March, 5 June 1998; 8 May 1999; 4 March, 23-25 August 2000.
Tverskie vedmosti, 7-13 May 1999.

Index